LONDON RECORD SOCIETY
PUBLICATIONS

VOLUME XXX
FOR THE YEAR 1993

LONDON DEBATING SOCIETIES, 1776–1799

COMPILED AND INTRODUCED BY
DONNA T. ANDREW

LONDON RECORD SOCIETY
1994

PN 4191
.G7
L66x

Phototypeset by
Wyvern Typesetting Ltd., Bristol
Printed and bound in Great Britain
by Antony Rowe Ltd., Chippenham

CONTENTS

INTRODUCTION

London in the first decades of the eighteenth century was already rich in a variety of public entertainments. In addition to the theatres and shows, to the coffee houses and inns, there was a series of forums in which people came together to listen to and participate in conversation. By the 1770s, these private or semi-private clubs or societies increased in size and number in the metropolis, as gripping political and religious issues seized the interests and imaginations of Londoners. In 1780 these now enlarged clubs were transformed into large-scale, commercial events, whose managers used the publicity that the burgeoning press sold to advertise their topics of debate, to rouse and create a paying public for such debates, and to combine an expanding interest in public speaking with the respectable pursuit of profit.

This volume contains almost a quarter-century's worth of such advertisements, taken from eleven of the most popular of London's daily newspapers.[1] Though the commercial, large-scale, inexpensive debating societies which are the chief focus of this book only began in 1780, the debates from the outbreak of the American Revolution in 1776 to 1780 are also included, to illustrate both the earlier societies, and to highlight the changes in structure and question which such expansion brought. The volume ends with the disappearance, in June 1799, of such advertisement in the popular press, due to government repression of most public assembly and free speech.

The immediate progenitors of the debating societies of the 1780s were the smaller disputing clubs like the Robin Hood Society, which met at a pub of the same name in Butcher Lane, and the Society which met at the Queen's Arms, Newgate Street. In an anonymous *History of the Robin Hood Society*, published in 1764, the author claimed that the Robin Hood began in 1613, as a small gentlemen's club of only fifteen members. Though this account seems unlikely, it is clear that by the 1730s the Robin Hood was a flourishing concern,[2] and that by the late 1740s, the Queen's Arms society joined it. The early topics of debate of both these groups were questions of religion, politics and culture.

1 *Daily Advertiser, Gazetteer, General Advertiser, London Courant, Morning Chronicle, Morning Herald, Morning Post, Parker's General Advertiser, St. James Chronicle, The Times, The World;* also *A short history of the Westminster Forum* by the President (London, T. Cadell, 1781), which is a pamphlet, not a newspaper.
2 *The History of the Robin Hood Society,* (London, James Fletcher and Company, 1764). See also John Brewer, *The Common People and Politics 1750–1790* (Cambridge, 1986) and John Timbs, *Club Life of London* (2 vols., London, 1866) 1, pp. 196–198 and Robert J. Allen, *The Clubs of Augustan London* (Cambridge, Mass., 1933) pp. 129–136.

However, other groups also contributed to and helped form the societies of the 1780s. Among these were the informal clubs that lawyers and actors formed to train novices. Thus, in writing to a young man studying the law, Sir William Weller Pepys noted that:

> It is high time [he] established a Mooting Club, for it is by talking constantly upon Law Subjects, by Whetting his own understanding against that of his contemporaries, and trying the truth and clearness of his own Ideas in conversation, that a Man becomes a Lawyer.[3]

Fanny Burney's shocked rejection of the suggestion that she might have taken lessons in a 'spouting club' for aspiring actors informs us that these too remained active, even after the formation of their more generally accessible and popular offspring.[4] There is some evidence, as well, that schools for the teaching of elocution set up debating societies as arenas in which their pupils could gain practice while publicly displaying their facility. These societies mirrored in some ways the contemporary creation of circuses as showcases for riding academy students.[5]

Another possible source for such public debating was the eccentric Oratory set up by William Henley as an adjunct to his sermonizing activities. Although the questions raise there could be very bizarre, like 'Whether Scotland be anywhere in the world?' this popular entertainment, which mixed religion and politics in a potent and sometimes explosive brew, must have exposed many ordinary Londoners to the possibilities, and pleasures, of public discussion.[6]

Finally, we must note the appearance of mixed-mode entertainment in the 1750s, one element of which was debate. The 'Temple of Taste', the 'Female Inquisition' and the 'Female Lyceum' all attempted both to combine music, poetry, acrobatics with female participation in debate. Unlike their later descendants, however, these earlier societies were expensive and relatively short-lived.[7]

The number and location of London's debating societies altered from year to year. Because of the frequent change of venue and even of name, it is often difficult to be sure of the identities of some of these

3 *A Later Pepys: The Correspondence of Sir William Weller Pepys*, ed. Alice C. C. Gaussen (2 vols, London, 1904), 1, pp. 231–2.
4 For Fanny Burney, see *Diary and Letters of Madame D'Arblay*, ed. Charlotte Barret (6 vols., London, 1904), 1, p. 103.
5 Spouting clubs were also satirized in Arthur Murphy's 'Apprentice' of 1756; on the development of circus, Marius Quint, unpublished paper delivered at the Eighteenth Century Material Culture Seminar, Victoria and Albert Museum, 1989.
6 For Henley see Graham Midgeley, *The Life of Orator Henley* (Oxford, 1973). The *Fifteen Orations on Various Topics* (John Wetherall, 1756) of the Queen's Arms Society also suggests that this society began in order to discuss religious and theological issues. The role of public religious debate has not received much attention from historians. The Amico Collatio of 1783, run by the Rev. Pennington from Margaret's Chapel, Barbican, was probably similar to Henley's Oratory, of half a century before.
7 The advertisement of the Temple of Taste of February 19, 1752 (*Daily Advertiser*) noted that they hoped to provide 'For the Entertainment of the Ladies, as well as Gentlemen'. The Female Lyceum noted that only ladies were allowed actually to debate. The former cost half a crown (2s. 6d.) admittance, and the later ranged from 3s. to 1s.

societies. For example, was the Select Society, whose debates were held at the Old Theatre, Portugal Street, Lincoln's Inns Fields, in 1779 the same as the Religious Society that met in these rooms in 1780? We know of a number of societies that changed names: the Debating Society at the Crown Tavern, Bow Street, became the Coachmakers' Hall Debating Society when it moved quarters in 1777, the Oratorical Academy became the Mitre Tavern Society after a similar move in 1780 and then changed names to become the Original London Debating Society on its move to Capel Court, Bartholomew lane, in 1787, thereafter changing its name yet again to become City Debates in 1789. Was there any connection or identity between the 1779 Select Society of Portugal Street and the 1792 Select Society which met at the Globe Tavern, Fleet Street? Was the Ciceronian Society, which in 1784 and 1785 met in Margaret Street, Oxford Market, any relation to the society of the same name which met in 1797 at the Haymarket? We do not yet know.[8] Despite these serious difficulties of identification, a number of generalizations about the chronology, geography and number of debating societies can be hazarded.

Until 1779 the number and sorts of debating societies stayed about constant; in each of those years about five forums advertised, either regularly or intermittently. In the spring of 1779, the number started to rise, and by 1780 hit an amazing peak of 35 differently named societies advertising debating subjects. Several of these societies were specialized ventures run in the rooms of, and probably by the proprietors of, the parent institution. Such, for example, were the three separate debating societies which met at the Casino, Great Marlborough Street, under the general title of the University for Rational Amusements. This 'University' sponsored separate general debates, debates on theological subjects, and was the home to the Female Parliament, at which only women could speak. Similarly, the Oratorical Society had a theological session and a general one and the Carlisle House Society's School of Eloquence shared its venue with a debating society for ladies only. After 1780, but even more markedly after 1781, the number of societies fell precipitously, with the crackdown on Sunday debating societies launched by Bishop Porteus. In the next few years only two or three societies bothered to advertise, but by 1785 enthusiasm for this form of entertainment seemed to return, and to remain at a steady level until 1792. Though the societies continued to function thereafter, their numbers diminished, as political discussion was outlawed by Parliamentary Act.

---

8 Little has yet been written about these groups. Recent historians who have written about debating societies are: John Money, 'Taverns, Coffee Houses and Clubs: Local Politics and Popular Articulacy in the Birmingham area in the Age of the American Revolution', *Historical Journal* 14 (1971), Iain McCalman, 'Ultra Radicalism and Convivial Debating Clubs in London 1795–1838', *English Historical Review* 102 (1987); John Brewer, *Party Ideology and Popular Politics at the Accession of George III* (Cambridge, 1976); J. Ann Hone, *For the Cause of Truth* (Oxford, 1982); T. Fawcett, 'Eighteenth-Century Debating Societies', *British Journal for Eighteenth Century Studies* 3 (1980); and Mary Thale, 'London Debating Societies in the 1790s', *Historical Journal* 31 (1989).

Only in 1797 were there more than three societies advertising their discussions.[9]

As the advertisements show, the societies met in several different sorts of rooms. Many societies met in large rooms, purpose-built for various entertainments, in pubs and taverns. Others met in assembly rooms, display rooms or auction rooms. Many shared their facilities with other attractions: the Coachmakers' Hall, for example, was the site of a dancing academy when not occupied by its debating society, the Lyceum on the Strand featured animal exhibits as well as debate, and the Oratorical Hall met in the former Cox's Museum.[10] A number of societies also shared rooms; at one time or another at least eight societies of different names used Greenwood's Rooms, Haymarket, for their meetings. The number and size of such rooms through the greater London area in this period is surprising. I have located at least 48 such rooms throughout the metropolis. Thus the School of Oratory met at China Hall, Rotherhithe, in the extreme east, the Theological Debating Society in the Surrey Bridewell, St. George's Fields, in the south, the Summer Lyceum at Smith's Tea Rooms, Islington, in the north, and the Lyceum for the Investigation of Historical, Political, Literary and Theological Subjects at the Black Horse Tavern, New Bond Street, in the west. Although, after the 1770s, most of the newer societies met in Westminster, a significant number originated and remained in the City, the most important of these being the Coachmakers' Hall Debating Society, which, in terms of advertisements, is the best-represented group in this volume.

We know little of the proprietors of these institutions. Some were consortiums who invested large sums, others, especially theologically-interested societies, were set up by small groups of believers, while others still, like Mr. Smeathman's Lyceum, were practical arenas for a display of the oratorical skills of the proprietor's students in eloquence. By the late century, some of the societies became the vehicles for, if not the properties of, radical voices; both Thomas Holcroft and John Gale Jones were involved in the management of these groups. Though there is no evidence that radicals had earlier acted as debating society owners, Peter Annet of the Robin Hood, and Richard Price, the 'fiery oratory of the Haymarket Forum', were well-known debating personalities.[11]

In addition to the proliferation in the number of societies, the size of the audiences increased dramatically. While the Robin Hood Society,

---

9 Number of Debating Societies Advertising by Year: 1776, 6; 1777, 5; 1778, 5; 1779, 9; 1780, 35; 1781, 13; 1782, 2; 1784, 3; 1785, 10; 1786, 5; 1787, 8; 1788, 7; 1789, 5; 1790, 5; 1791, 5; 1792, 1; 1793, 2; 1794, 2; 1795, 3; 1796, 2; 1797, 6; 1798, 2; 1799, 3.
10 For more on the venues of popular entertainments, see Richard Altick, *The Shows of London* (Cambridge, Mass., 1978).
11 For Holcroft see R.M. Baine, *Thomas Holcroft and the Revolutionary Novel* (Athens, Georgia, 1965). John Gale Jones spoke at the Westminster in the 1790s and became proprietor of his own 'British Forum' in 1806 (see *Encyclopedia of British Radicals*). For Annet, see John Timbs, *Club Life of London* and Price, *The Morning Chronicle*, January 29, 1780.

for instance, is said to have had between forty and one hundred spectators, the size of the audiences at meetings after 1779 ranged from 400 to 1200.[12] Even with miscellaneous expenses (i.e. rent, heat and light, advertisement, decor), with an average audience of 800, the proprietors' net profit must have been a few hundred pounds.

But what sorts of people came to these debates, and what sorts of questions did they discuss? Again, the evidence is slender, and often comes either from detractors and satirical accounts, or from puffs of the societies themselves. Thus, for example, a review for a mocking theatrical piece, *The School for Eloquence*, noted 'the present rage for Debate, which seems to inflame all ranks of people'.[13] Many critics lamented their 'level[ling of] all distinctions [of rank]' which led to the indiscriminate jostling together of 'wits, lawyers, politicians and mechanics'.[14] In contrast, *The History of the Westminster Forum*, by their President, claimed that speakers regularly included a 'noble Lord' (an earl in fact), a young gentleman just come from Eton, the son of an eminent Irish patriot, a City Alderman, clergymen both Anglican and dissenting, and a Scottish clergyman who was preceptor to the children of an English earl.

As surprising as attendance of this medley of high and low was the presence and involvement of women. Again we get different accounts of who such women were. Though we read of a fair Quaker and an alderman's wife in the audiences,[15] more often female participants were merely described as 'fair orators' by their proponents, and as 'hired Reciters of a studied Lesson', bar-maids or Strand girls (i.e. prostitutes), or even men in women's clothes, by their detractors.[16] That they attended these vast public meetings, and spoke at all, whoever they were, deserves to be noted, for both the press and public critics were harsh in their condemnation, *The Times* of 1788 opining that '. . .the debating ladies would be much better employed at their needle and thread, a good sempstress being a more amiable character than a female orator.'[17]

The sorts of questions discussed by the societies were as heterogeneous as the makeup of their audiences. While the societies of the 1770s had discussed mainly political and theological questions, with a

---

12 Five hundred, it was said, were turned away from the Westminster Forum debate of October 9, 1786, and 600 from the same society on November 3 of that year (*The Times*). Hundreds were reported turned away from the Mitre Tavern Society for Free Debate on March 8, 1787 and many ladies had to stand for lack of seats at the Ancient Debating Society meeting of April 9, 1787 (*Morning Herald*). Between 800 and 1000 people attended the Carlisle House School of Eloquence on February 10, 1780 (*St. James Chronicle*); two weeks later, 1,100 people are reported to have been present (*Morning Chronicle*).
13 *Morning Chronicle*, April 5, 1780.
14 Harum Scarum, *Account of a Debate in Coachmakers Hall* (London, G. Kearsley, 1780), pp. 1–2.
15 *Morning Post*, April 12, 1780, October 27, 1780.
16 *Morning Chronicle*, May 17, 1780; *The Times*, November 29, 1788; *Morning Chronicle*, March 17, 1780.
17 *The Times*, October 29, 1788.

sprinkling of topics of wider concern, as the century went on, it was these last sorts of topics that were to grow in number. While never neglecting to discuss national or international issues, or perennially interesting questions of salvation and the afterlife, the proportion of questions about the nature of courtship, marriage, and morals grew. These types of question not only satisfied the new female audiences, but allowed men and women together to consider both the political and social shape they wished for their society. In many ways these social/ moral questions raised problems involving as much fundamental reform and reorganization of the civic polity as did the political questions of suffrage and Parliamentary representation.

It is the very range of the questions and topics debated that makes these societies so full of interest for students of the period. We not only can get an insight into which political issues excited the public, but also what forms such excitement took. In the debates we can also observe the broad spectrum of cultural concerns in which a large, literate public evinced interest. The debates both illustrate the growth of a potent and novel 'public opinion' and the authority it came to claim, but simultaneously display the self-creation of a new type of citizenry, and its interactions with a complex commercial culture of objects and ideas.[18] Thus the debates form an important part of a unique cultural enterprise: the creation of a public culture both 'learned, sensible and judicious' and amusing, whose object was 'to delight while they reform; eradicate pernicious errors and warm the heart with benevolence'.[19] In contrast to the unenlightened, who wasted their lives and 'dissipate their Time in Gaming, brutal Diversions, and Frivolity', the audience of the societies was 'a Multitude of both Sexes assembled for the Purposes of rational Entertainment and mental Improvement'.[20]

Note on editorial method
These advertisements have been culled from a close reading of eleven of the most popular of London's daily newspapers.[21] I have arranged

18 For a most useful and innovative elaboration of this point, see Jurgen Habermas, *The Structural Transformation of the Public Sphere*, translated by Thomas Burger (Cambridge, Mass., 1989).
19 *Gazetteer*, April 25, 1780; *Morning Post*, October 5, 1788.
20 *The Times*, September 18, 1788; *Daily Advertiser*, March 18, 1790; *The Times*, March 26, 1789.
21 The papers consulted, and the years in which they actually appear in this volume, are as follows:
   Morning Chronicle: 1776–82, 1788, 1794–9
   Gazetteer: 1776–88, 1790, 1792
   London Courant: 1780, 1781
   St. James Chronicle: 1780
   Morning Post: 1780, 1782, 1783, 1787–9
   Morning Herald: 1780–7, 1792–9
   Daily Advertiser: 1780, 1784–6, 1788–94
   Parker's General Advertiser: 1782, 1783
   General Advertiser: 1785, 1786
   The Times: 1785, 1786, 1788–93
   The World: 1787–91

them in a uniform format, quite unlike their layout in the newspapers. In the papers, they might have appeared on page 1 or 4 as ordinary advertisements, or been interspersed with other news on pages 2 or 3. I have standardised their presentation, consecutively numbering each notice, then using the following as a template for all information:

Number Date of the debate Name of the debating Society
Topic of the debate
Lecture or other entertainment [if given]
Outcome of debate [if known]
Any other interesting or pertinent information
Newspaper in which advertisement placed, and date of advertisement
if different from date of debate

The outcome of the debate was usually found in the following week's advertisement. However, if the vote came from another source, the paper and date of that source is indicated by a / followed by the necessary information. The only exceptions to the above format are in those cases where what is being presented is not a notice of debate, but a newspaper comment or letter to the editor about debating societies. These have been included in their proper chronological place, and are identified by having their date of publication followed by the name of the newspaper in which the column appeared.

The index, which refers to the number of the relevant item, assembles debating topics under general and specific headings (such as 'Religion' or 'Fox, Charles James', with cross-references as appropriate. Strictly logical grouping and alphabetisation proved impossible, but the reader will not find it difficult to locate debates on any particular topic of discussion.

I would like to thank the Social Sciences and Humanities Research Council of Canada for a variety of grants which made this research possible, Nicholas Rogers for supporting the project and encouraging me to publish the complete manuscript, and the wonderfully helpful staff of the Microtext Room, University of Toronto, who provided assistance of all sorts for the often tedious process of culling eighteenth century newspapers.

LONDON DEBATING SOCIETIES

1. January 4, 1776 Morning Chronicle
'As a proof that the Society for the Recovery of Drowned Persons is well received by the publick, the Debating Society at the Crown Tavern in Bow lane where every subject is fully discussed, have given 5 guineas as a token of their approbation.'

2. January 5, 1776 Queen's Arms, Newgate Street
'Which are the most loyal subjects, and the best friends to liberty, those who in their Addresses to the King approve or those who in their Petitions condemn, the present proceedings against America?'
Lecture on pleasure.
'Notwithstanding the exhausted state of the American debate, the question was very ingeniously handled, and some new matter thrown out on both sides. Determined by a very small majority in favour of the petitions.'
Gazetteer January 4

3. January 12, 1776 Society for Free Debate, Queen's Arms, Newgate Street
'Is not the doctrine of justification, as held by the Church of Rome, a damnable doctrine? – Would it not be advisable for the legislative body to treat with the Congress upon terms of reconciliation, without considering it as derogatory to their dignity?'
Philosophical Lecture on Reason.
Gazetteer January 11

4. January 12, 1776 Gazetteer
'A correspondent hopes that the *dissolution* (which will, it is said, shortly be) of a certain disputing society in Bow-lane, will be the cause of a great *revolution* in another society in Newgate-street; that instead of the tedious speeches of an O—ll and a C—n, the auditory will be entertained with the flowery language of a D—n, and the patriotic declamations of a F—r, those two ornaments of elocution. Our correspondent does not mean to insinuate, that there is a total want of pleasing oratory in the latter society; that will never be the case so long as a P—d and a D—s favour it with their sanction and the exercise of their abilities; to hear them our correspondent has often been induced to devote some of his leisure time; and whenever it has then happened that the little *unmeaning, consequential* President, and the flaming Catholic (wou'd-be President) have trespassed upon the patience of the audi-

1

ence, by the insignificant cant of the one, and the unbounded assurance of the other, our correspondent has not wondered at his disappointment, but rather considered it as a matter of surprize, that the society has so long continued its establishment.'

5. January 15, 1776 Robin Hood
'The comparative excellence of a Monarchial and Republican Government' was argued a third time, and at last determined in favour of a Monarchical form; so this side of the question has had two verdicts out of three trials. The company was very respectable and the speakers very ingenious.'
Morning Chronicle January 22

6. January 20, 1776 Queen's Arms, Newgate Street
'Would it not be advisable for the legislature of Great-Britain to treat with the American Congress on terms of reconciliation, without derogation to their dignity?'
Lecture on Oratory.
Gazetteer January 18

7. January 22, 1776 Robin Hood
'Whether a surrender of all claims to Canada, on the part of Great Britain, unto the Crown of France, would not be an eligible measure at this time?
The question concerning the propriety of surrendering all claim to Canada unto the French Government &c. was carried almost nem. con. in the negative; some, not unplausible arguments, however, were offered on the contrary side, as, that removing all ground of dispute about the local limits or boundaries, by totally expelling the French, was the original cause of the bounds of British authority over the rest of America being disputed.'
Morning Chronicle

8. January 26, 1776 Queen's-Arms, Newgate-street
'Which of the two Governments is more likely to preserve the liberties of the people, the English or a Republican?
Which, after many ingenious arguments, was almost unanimously determined in favour of the English.'
Lecture on lines from Thomson's *Winter*.
Gazetteer January 25

9. January 29, 1776 Robin Hood
'Whether Administration, or the Opposition at this juncture, proceed more upon the true principles of the British Constitution? Another question likely to come on, is, Whether Coercive or Conciliatory Measures, respecting the Colonies, are *now* most eligible?'
Debated 'with candour and ingenuity' and adjourned.
Morning Chronicle January 27

10. February 2, 1776 Society for Free Debate, Queen's Arms, Newgate Street
'Can a Roman Catholic Prince govern a free People, consistent with Religion and their Liberties?'
Lecture on Friendship.
'Debated and determined in the negative.'
Gazetteer February 1

11. February 4, 1776 Theological Society, One Tun, near Hungerford, Strand
The President will deliver 'a Discourse introductory to the establishment of Lectures at this place, and a Lecture on the succeeding lines:
How is our reason to the future blind,
When vice enervates, and enslaves the mind;
What sense suggests how fondly we believe,
And with what subtilty ourselves deceive.
The Theme, relating to the discovery of Anti-Christ, debated here . . . after hearing many ingenious arguments, was adjourned; in consequence of which will be reheard subsequent to the foregoing Discourse and Lecture: And if time will permit, the following text will be investigated: "Know this first, that no prophecy of scripture is of any private interpretation." 2 Peter, chap. 2, ver. 20.'
Gazetteer February 3

12. February 5, 1776 Robin Hood
'Whether Administration, or the Opposition at this juncture, proceed more upon the true principles of the English constitution? Whether coercive or lenient measures, respecting the Colonies, at *this time* are more eligible?'
On the first question 'it was extremely difficult, or rather impossible, to know which side had most hands: the room being crowded, some persons on the floor and others mounted on the benches; it was left doubtful.'
Morning Chronicle

13. February 9, 1776 Society for Free Debate, Queen's-arms, Newgate Street
'Would an Act of Perpetual Insolvency be of general advantage?'
Lecture on the Advantages resulting from Society.
'Owing to the unfavourableness of the weather, the company was rather thin, and of course a dearth of speakers; but notwithstanding, many sensible arguments were advanced on both sides.' Determined almost unanimously 'that the proposed act would be of no public utility'.
Gazetteer February 8

14. February 12, 1776 Robin Hood
'Is the breach between England and the Colonies reparable – And is it manifest that the Americans affect independency? Another question put, viz. Whether coercive or lenient measures are more eligible, &c.

3

was manifestly included in the first, as administration are for one and opposition for the other.'
The first question 'was carried almost *nem. con.* in the affirmative; but the mode thereof may afford a question of more difficulty.'
Morning Chronicle

15. February 16, 1776 Society for Free Debate, Queen's Arms, New-gate Street
'Would it be prudent in the Livery of London to entrust a person with the care of the city cash, who has already been accused of robbing a public charity, without refuting a charge?
Determined in favour of Mr. Wilkes.'
Gazetteer February 15

16. February 19, 1776 Gazetteer
'In consequence of the very extraordinary question advertised to be debated at the Queen's Arms tavern in Newgate-street, on Friday evening last, the croud was so great, that many persons could not get into the room; the friends of the respective candidates for the office of Chamberlain had occupied all the seats early in the evening, and those who came afterwards time enough to gain admittance remained upon their legs. At length the Chairman ascended the rostrum, and with the utmost gravity acquainted the assembly, that the author of the question had been informed, that it was couched in such terms as would render a free discussion of it liable to legal notice; that several members of the society had expressed their disapprobation of it, and for those reasons the author, who declined to avow himself, had authorised him to beg permission to withdraw it. Mr. Saffory, the surgeon, then arose, and animadverted on the baseness of the author to bring a question so evidently levelled to prejudice one of the candidates for the office of Chamberlain at this critical period. He said, that the author's reasons, as assigned by the Chairman, did not operate with him as the most striking objection against a discussion of the question. Justice and equity should have prevailed with the author more forcibly than any disagreeable apprehensions of the consequence; those were motives that actuated him (Mr. Saffory) to move 'that the question be expunged out of the book.' This was seconded by Mr. Denham, who supported his ingenious leader by remarking, that when public societies descended to personal disputes, and stepped out of the path of general discussion, they were no longer worthy the countenance of the public. The Chairman, with evident reluctance, complied with the almost unanimous cry of "expunge the question"; of which (our correspondent avers) *himself* was the author, without attempting to answer the just reflections cast upon him for his *uncandid, ungenerous* design.'

17. February 19, 1776 Robin Hood
'Is it manifest that the Colonies affect independency?'
Morning Chronicle

18. February 23, 1776 Society for Free Debate, Queen's-arms, Newgate Street
'Are those magistrates, commonly called Trading Justices, hurtful or beneficial to this country? And, if time permits, Do those Constables who are remarkable for their vigilance, in apprehending the unfortunate women of the town, deserve censure or applause?
The two Questions relating to TRADING Justices and REFORMING Constable . . . being by their principal speakers reduced to one, produced many ingenious and sensible arguments, both for and against those officers. In the conclusion, however, a great majority appeared in their favour.'
Gazetteer February 22

19. March 1, 1776 Society for Free Debate, Queen's-arms, Newgate Street
'Does the Scotch Militia Bill, now depending in the House of Commons, tend to the good of this country? And Would not a reformation of the abuses of the press redound to the honour of this kingdom?
The Question relating to the Scotch Militia Bill was . . . unanimously decided in favour of that measure: the other subject proposed for discussion in reference to a Reformation of the Abuses of the Press, was postponed by the unanimous desire of the company . . .'
Gazetteer February 29

20. March 3, 1776 Theological Society
'The following theme will be investigated, "For he saith to Moses, I will have mercy on whom I will have mercy, and I will have compassion on whom I will have compassion." – "So that it is not of him that willeth, nor of him that runneth, but of God that sheweth mercy." Romans, chap. ix, ver. 15 and 16 – And, if there remains sufficient time, this also, "By which likewise he went and preached unto the spirits in prison" together with the succeeding verse, taken from the third chapter of the first of Peter.'
Preceded by a lecture on Sincerity.
Gazetteer March 2

21. March 4, 1776 Robin Hood
'Whether endeavouring to carry the measures of Administration, respecting America, by force, will not ultimately tend to the destruction of the liberties of the whole empire?
Debated in a spirited manner: the decision was declared in the affirmative, though many of the opposite side thought the majority in their favour.'
Morning Chronicle March 11

22. March 8, 1776 Society for Free Debate. Queen's Arms, Newgate Street

5

'Is it consistent with the dignity and impartiality of a Chief Magistrate in this City, to interfere in any depending election of officers of the Corporation?'
The Question 'was warmly debated by the principal speakers, and carried in the negative by a great majority'.
Gazetteer March 7

23. March 11, 1776 Robin Hood
'Have philosophy and the abstruse sciences been advantageous to mankind in general?'
Question 'was carried in the affirmative. – It was expected that a proposer of such a question would have taken (Mons. Rousseau's, or) the uphill side; but it happened otherwise, and a speaker, who wondered such a question could be put, very ingeniously supported the difficult side of it.'
Morning Chronicle

24. March 15, 1776 Society for Free Debate. Queen's Arms, Newgate Street
'Would not correcting the present abuses of the press be a proof of the good sense of the nation?'
The Question was 'almost unanimously determined in the negative'.
Gazetteer March 14

25. March 18, 1776 Robin Hood
'Whether Dr. Price's assertion, that the Americans have half a million of *determined fighting men* is supportable?'
Question 'was carried in the negative. It was allowed that the number of capable men might exceed the Doctor's numbers: but a doubt of their unanimity or concurrence in the same cause, when the English should appear, put the negative to the position. One orator was very conspicuous both as to elegance of language, and a knowledge of the American country, as well as to the controversy respecting the same.'
Morning Chronicle

26. March 22, 1776 Society for Free Debate, Queen's Arms, Newgate Street
'Whether the Legislature differ from what is called the Constitution? If so, in what?'
Lecture on the Poem *Delia to Strephon* 'published some time since in Every Man's Magazine'.
Gazetteer March 21

27. March 25, 1776 Robin Hood
'Whether triennial Parliaments are not preferable to any other mode?'
The Question 'was carried in favour of triennial: some ironical arguments were thrown out in favour of annual, as that the constituents and representatives would become better acquainted by feasting together annually, &c. but the serious part of the debate was between the

favourers of the other two modes [triennial or septennial], and passed as above by a considerable majority.'
Morning Chronicle

28. April 1, 1776 Robin Hood
'Whether a late publication on the subject of *Civil Liberty,* &c. is likely to do more good or hurt to the community?'
The Question 'was very candidly and ingeniously discussed before a very numerous and respectable audience, and the decision (by a small majority) was, "that the said Pamphlet was likely to be more prejudicial than beneficial". Possibly upon the idea, that as truth may not be spoken at all times there might be some political truths which should not be divulged to the whole world at any time, or at least at this time.'
Morning Chronicle

29. April 5, 1776 Society for Free Debate
'Whether Vice or Virtue affords superior pleasures?
Those who contended for vice observed, that virtue restrains its votaries from partaking of various enjoyments grateful to human nature. Those who supported virtue insisted that vice cannot produce pleasure, every sin being attended by pain. The latter of these arguments prevailed.'
Gazetteer April 11

30. April 8, 1776 Robin Hood
'Whether a liberal and learned Education is proper for a Person intended for Commerce?'
The Question 'was very agreeably and ingeniously discussed. Two avowed classical gentlemen were opponents, which gave the question consequence; and it was determined in the affirmative, i.e. that a classical education was proper for a merchant.'
Morning Chronicle

31. April 12, 1776 Society for Free Debate
'Can a Roman Catholic, consistent with his religious principles, be a good subject to a Protestant Prince? and Are all the works of creation alike beautiful, or can there be a general criterion attained, to distinguish real beauty?'
Gazetteer April 11

32. April 15, 1776 Robin Hood
'Whether Study or Conversation tend most to the advancement of useful knowledge?'
Morning Chronicle

33. April 19, 1776 Society for Free Debate
'Whether the Principles advanced in Dr. Price's pamphlet on Civil Liberty are consistent with the Principles of the English Constitution?
Those gentlemen who supported the affirmative, built their arguments on the ground of their being taxed without representation; those who

7

maintained the negative, observed, that the reasoning contained in that celebrated performance was merely ideal; that it tended to confusion and anarchy; and the plan of government there laid down such as never had, or can have any existence, and therefore totally inapplicable to the general principle of legislation, and to those of the British constitution in particular; the latter opinion was confirmed by a considerable majority of the company.'
Gazetteer April 18

34. April 22, 1776 Robin Hood
'Which of the Passions is most prevalent and most destructive in its effects?
It was determined by hands, that *pride* was the most prevalent and pernicious.'
Morning Chronicle April 29

35. April 26, 1776 Society for Free Debate
'Can Mr. Wilkes and his friends be justified in their present opposition to the Chamberlain?
On behalf of Mr. Wilkes and his supporters it was urged, that as friends to free elections, they were consistent in endeavouring to destroy the effect of one, wherein freedom had been grossly violated. On the other hand it was argued, that a scrutiny would have been much better, as by it every one who affirmed a privilege to which by law or equity they had no claim, would have been detected; and, that declining this, shewed an attachment to private interest more than to public justice. These arguments met with the approbation of a majority of the company.'
Gazetteer April 25

36. April 29, 1776 Robin Hood
'Whether Doctor Price, by his late publication, hath not done more to promote Civil and Religious Liberty, than those Bishops who voted for establishing Popery in Canada? Another question was read, viz. Whether impressing of Sailors is justifiable in any case whatsoever?'
Morning Chronicle

37. May 3, 1776 Society for Free Debate
'Which is the more honourable profession, that of law, or that of arms' and 'Are all the works of the creation alike beautiful, or can there be a general criterion ascertained, to distinguish real beauty?'
Gazetteer May 2

38. May 6, 1776 Robin Hood
'Whether impressing sailors to serve on board his Majesty's ships, is defensible in any emergency, &c.?'
Question 'was very ingeniously debated, and, on the division, carried in the negative'.
Morning Chronicle May 13

39. May 10, 1776 Society For Free Debate
'Which is the more honourable profession, law or arms?'
The question was 'determined in favour of arms'.
Gazetteer May 16

40. May 13, 1776 Robin Hood
'Whether appealing from the Ecclesiastical to a Superior Court, will be more beneficial or injurious to the community?'
Question 'was carried for its being more beneficial. Some people were for supporting the definitive power of the Ecclesiastical Courts, to prevent endless litigation and expence; others were for totally abolishing the same as a remnant of papal authority; others (who indeed carried the question) were for allowing the usual proceedings of superogative courts under the controul, like other law courts, of the supreme legislative body.'
Morning Chronicle

41. May 17, 1776 Society for Free Debate
'Is a certain Apothecary justifiable in the liberties he has taken with the Rev. Mr. Wesley, in a recent publication, called An Examination of Primitive Physic?
Determined almost unanimously in favour of the Apothecary, though Mr. W. had some sensible arguments adduced in favour of his pamphlet.'
Gazetteer May 16

42. May 20, 1776 Robin Hood
'Is it now compatible with the dignity, interest, and duty of Great Britain, to treat with America on terms of accommodation?'
Morning Chronicle

43. August 9, 1776 Society for Free Debate
'Would it tend to the security of the liberties of Great Britain, to increase the number of Representatives in the House of Commons? Is it reasonable to suppose that any person, otherwise than in a state of insanity, can commit the act of suicide?
The arguments on [the first] subject tended rather to prove the necessity of a more equal representation, than an increase of number, and consequently was determined in the negative. In the discussion of [the second] question, the causes of madness were explained; and the delicate situation of jurymen in cases of suicide, with respect to their oath on the one hand, and tenderness to the friends of the deceased on the other (as a verdict of Felo de se works a forfeiture of personal estate) were fully and ingeniously investigated. It passed in the negative.'
Gazetteer August 15

44. August 16, 1776 Society for Free Debate
'Is a true Patriot less able to serve his country when called to the House of Peers, than when a Member of the House of Commons?'
Gazetteer August 15

45. September 1, 1776 Theological Society
' "What think ye of Christ? Whose son is he?" Matt. chap. xxii, ver.
42. The investigation of the text leads to an examination of the divinity
of Christ.
Preceded by lecture on the following lines:
  "By gentle methods Truth we'll still pursue,
  And prove by candour, till alone our view".'
Gazetteer August 31

46. September 13, 1776 Society for Free Debate, Queen's-Arms,
Newgate Street
'Which is the happier period of human life, Youth or Old Age? and, if
time will permit, the succeeding: Would electing our Representatives
in Parliament by ballot, be an additional security of our liberties?'
Lecture on lines from the Fourth Epistle of Mr. Pope's Essay on Man.
The Question, 'which, after an ingenious and spirited investigation, was
determined in favour of Youth'.
Admittance four-pence each person.
Gazetteer September 12

47. September 20, 1776 Society for Free Debate, Queen's-Arms,
Newgate Street
'Would electing our Representatives in Parliament, by ballot, be an
additional security to our liberties? and, if time will permit, the suc-
ceeding one also: Are Critics in general serviceable to Literature?'
Lecture on Trade and Commerce.
Gazetteer September 19

48. September 24, 1776 Society for free Debate, at the Hand and
Racket, Blue Cross Street, Leicester fields
'Whether a state of nature is as capable of happiness as a state of civil
society?'
Was determined in favour of civil society.
Gazetteer September 30

49. October 1, 1776 Society for free Debate, at the Hand and Racket,
Blue Cross Street, Leicester fields
'If the Americans (in consequence of the present contest) become inde-
pendent, who ought to be censured for the event, the members of
administration, or those of opposition?'
Gazetteer September 30

50. October 7, 1776 Theological Society
' "All that ever came before me are thieves and robbers, but the sheep
did not hear them." John chap x, ver. 8 And, if time will allow, a
comparative examination "Therefore we conclude, that a man is justified by faith without the deeds of law." Romans chap iii, ver. 28. "Ye
see that by works a man is justified, and not by faith alone".'
Gazetteer October 6

51. October 21, 1776 Robin Hood Society
'Whether Mr. Molesworth's Calculations upon Lotteries were of advantage to adventurers, or an imposition on the credulity of the public?
Last Monday night, at the Robin Hood Society, there was the most numerous and respectable meeting known for many years, upwards of 400 persons being present, and as many obliged to return for want of room . . . It was almost unanimously resolved (not above six hands being held up against the motion) that Mr. Molesworth's Calculations were beneficial to the public.'
Gazetteer October 23

52. October 29, 1776 Society at the Hand and Racquet, Blue Cross Street, Leicester Fields
'Did not Administration (by rejecting the Remonstrance sent by Mr. Penn) put a stop to a reconciliation of the differences subsisting between Great Britain and her colonies?'
Gentleman will deliver a lecture on lines from *The Grave.*
Gazetteer October 28

53. November 4, 1776 Robin Hood
'Whether the public as well as private evils, which disgrace this country, do not originate from gaming rather than luxury?'
Question 'was passed in the negative, *i.e.* that luxury was the cause, &c. Much excellent argumentation and declamation were displayed against the vice of Gaming; but Luxury appearing the motive to Gaming, might determine the division.'
Morning Chronicle November 11

54. November 8, 1776 Society for Free Debate, Queen's-Arms, Newgate Street
'Does the Lord-Mayor of London act as a good citizen, in refusing to back press-warrants at this alarming crisis?'
Lecture on evils of human life.
Gazetteer November 7

55. November 11, 1776 Robin Hood
'Is not the cohabitation of an unmarried man and woman, though attended with harmony and fidelity till death, an immoral connection? and Would it be consistent with Whig principles to adhere to the cause of the Americans, if the French government should openly declare in their favour?'
Morning Chronicle

56. November 22, 1776 'The Society for Free Debate lately held at the Queen's Arms, Newgate Street, is . . . removed to the Horn, in Doctors Commons, at which place the Society will be conducted on the same liberal plan which has hitherto given general satisfaction to the lovers of rational amusement.'

11

'Would not a plan to regulate the price of labour be beneficial to the community?'
Gazetteer November 21

57. November 22, 1776 Society for Free Debate, Queen's Arms
'Would not balloting be the most eligible mode of electing Members of Parliament?'
Gazetteer

58. November 25, 1776 Robin Hood
'Whether the acceptance of a place under the Crown, as it vacates a seat in Parliament, ought not to be an exclusion of such member during his holding said place?'
Question was 'very ingeniously debated and carried in the affirmative. The arguments are at times equally clear on both sides [of] this question; for gentlemen in opposition, whether Whigs or Tories, see the desperate consequences of ministerial dependants sitting in the senate; and gentlemen in favour of the government in being, whether Tories or Whigs, can see the necessity of a little influence arising from places, pensions, riding behind, &c. so all parties in power practice, what all out of power reprobate.'
Morning Chronicle December 2

59. November 29, 1776 Queen's Arms, Newgate Street, Society for Free Debate continued as usual.
'1. Are predestination and punishment of human actions consistent with our ideas of wisdom and justice? 2. Will not the increase of national debt, in consequence of the American war, greatly over-balance any possible advantage from the reduction of that country?
The disappointment which took place . . . could not have been avoided, but it is now remedied.'
Gazetteer

60. November 29, Society for Free Debate, Horn Tavern
'Are high duties and the prohibition of foreign commodities beneficial to a commercial state? and Can the Athanasian creed be defended on the principles of reason and reflection?'
Gazetteer November 28

61. December 2, 1776 Robin Hood
'Whether the Lord Mayor of London restraining press warrants is any benefit to that city? and Whether a man will sooner arrive at the character of an orator by getting sense by heart, or speaking nonsense extempore?'
First question was 'altered to Whether the Lord Mayor was justifiable in refusing to back press warrants? and it was carried in the affirmative by a great majority.'
Morning Chronicle

62. December 7, 1776 Queen's Arms, Newgate Street. Society for Free Debate
'1. Is it possible, consistent with the nature of British Government, that it can be conducted without Bribery and Corruption?
2. What influence have Lotteries on the Morals of the People?'
Gazetteer

63. December 7, 1776 The Society for Free Debate, Horn, Doctors Commons
'1. Can the Athanasian creed be defended on the Principles of Reason and Revelation? 2. Would it be consistent with the Duty the Corporation of London owe to their Constituents, to pay the Debts contracted by Mr. Wilkes during his Mayoralty, out of the City Cash?'
Gazetteer December 6

64. December 9, 1776 Robin Hood
'Whether facilitating the means of *divorce* by application of both the married parties, would not promote the happiness of individuals and prosperity of the community? and, Whether a person will sooner arrive at the character of an orator by speaking sense by heart, or nonsense extempore?'
Morning Chronicle

65. December 14, 1776 Society for Free Debate held at the Queen's Arms, Newgate Street
'First, Can press warrants be justified, consistent with the liberty and privileges of Englishmen?
Second, Whether, or in what cases, is one man obliged to accuse another?
Third, Whether, or in what cases, monopolies may be lawful?'
Gazetteer December 13

66. December 21, 1776 Debating Society, Queen's-arms Tavern, Newgate Street
'First, Whether a judge may lawfully condemn a man found guilty by the jury, while he himself knows him to be innocent?
Second, Whether it is possible to establish one form of government so perfect, as to suit every different state in the universe?
N.B. On the part of the managers no attention will be spared to render the entertainment such an agreeable relish of literary amusement, as not to fail suiting the palate of the scholar and the gentleman. The members presume to rely upon the generosity of the public, not to suffer the private views of a few self important beings to overturn, by a hasty vote, a society which for these thirty years has preserved its establishment.
The utility of an acquaintance with history being universally acknowledged, Lectures on that important science will be delivered every evening, previous to the commencement of the debate. A Discourse intro-

ductory to the establishment of the above Lecture, will be delivered
from the Chair this evening.'
Gazetteer

67. December 21, 1776 Society for Free Debate, Horn, Doctors-
Commons (Removed from the Queen's-Arms, Newgate Street)
'Whether the Athanasian Creed can be defended on principles of reason
and revelation? Is it consistent with the duty the Common Council owe
to their constituents, to apply the city cash in discharge of the debts
contracted by Mr. Wilkes during his mayoralty?'
Determined in the negative.
Gazetteer

68. December 25, 1776 Debating Society. Queen's Arms, Newgate
Street
'1. Is it possible to constitute any one form of Government which will
suit all states in the world? And 2. Is the doctrine lately urged by an
eminent and noble lawyer, to wit, that Judges may not qualify their
verdicts, founded on reason and equity?
In order to place this Society on a footing equally respectable with other
assemblies of the like nature, the price of admission is raised to 6d each
person, to compensate for which all possible attention will be paid to
the improvement of the entertainments and accommodations.'
Lecture concerning the Antediluvian World and the Heathen
Mythology.
Gazetteer

69. December 27, 1776 Society for Free Debate, Horn, Doctors
Commons
'1. Is it consistent with the duty the Common-council owe their constituents, to apply the City cash in discharge of the debts contracted by Mr.
Wilkes during his Mayoralty? 2. Would not an equal Poor Rate be a
national advantage?'
Gazetteer

70. January 1, 1777 Debating Society, Queen's-Arms, Newgate Street
'1. Which tends more to improve the morals of mankind, Tragedy or
Comedy? 2. Which is the best school of oratory, the Pulpit, the Bar or
the Stage?
To relieve the author of the Historical Lectures, a Discourse will be
delivered this evening on lines from *The Grave*.'
Gazetteer

71. January 3, 1777 Society for Free Debate, Horn
'Whether the Common Council would act consistent with the duty they
owe their constituents, in discharging the debts contracted by Mr.
Wilkes during his Mayoralty, out of the city cash? and

14

Do not those preachers, who teach doctrines founded on Fatality, prejudice the interests of morality?'
Gazetteer

72. January 10, 1777 Society for Free Debate, Horn, Doctors-Commons
'Do not those preachers, who teach doctrines founded on Fatality, prejudice the interests of morality? And, if time permits, the subsequent: Has not the conduct of the Americans, in the last campaign, justified the censure Lord Sandwich passed on them in the House of Lords?'
Lecture on fame.
'After ample discussion of the doctrines of predestination, free-will, &c. determined in the affirmative.'
Gazetteer

73. January 17, 1777 Society for Free Debate, Horn, Doctors-Commons
'Has not the conduct of the Americans, in the last campaign, justified the censure Lord Sandwich passed on them in the House of Lords? And, if time permits, the following: Upon what grounds doth the Church of England reject some ceremonies commanded in Scripture and comply with others?'
The Question was 'very ingeniously and ably debated. Those who maintained the negative observed, that retreating was not always a proof of cowardice, but frequently of wisdom; that discipline was superior to courage, and that though this country, aided by foreign mercenaries, had exerted a great part of its strength against America, they had done little towards effecting a conquest thereof. Those who maintained the affirmative, compared the state of the two countries, that every advantage was on the side of America, as provisions, recruits, situation, &c. aided by the most masterly intrenchments, which yet they had not defended in a single instance. The latter opinion was confirmed by the company.'
Gazetteer

74. January 22, 1777 Debating Society. Queen's-Arms, Newgate Street
'1. Which is of more service to a State, a wise Minister, or a great General? 2. Can Love subsist without Lust?
N.B. A President and Speakers now regularly attend on which account these disappointment that have lately taken place, will in future be avoided.'
Historical lectures on 'the characters of Semiramis, Cyrus, and other celebrated Personages amongst the Ancients'.
Gazetteer

75. January 24, 1777 Society for Free Debate, Horn, Doctors-Commons
'Upon what ground doth the Church of England retain some Ceremonies commanded in Scripture and reject others?'

Question debated and 'most of the ceremonies alluded to as rejected by the church, proved to be of a slight or temporary nature, and consequently that she was justified in such omission on the ground both of reason and scripture; which opinion was confirmed by the company.'
Gazetteer

76. January 31, 1777 Society for Free Debate, Horn, Doctors-Commons
'Are Truth and Justice eternal and independent Principles? and, if time permit, the following: Is not the Church of Rome guilty of idolatry in their worship of the Virgin Mary and Saints?'
Gazetteer

77. February 3, 1777 Robin Hood
'Whether people of high life, are generally more serious than their inferiors?'
Question 'was carried in the affirmative'.
Morning Chronicle February 10

78. February 5, 1777 Debating Society, Queen's-Arms, Newgate Street
'Which tends more to establish female power, wit or beauty?'
Lectures on the Canaanites being the 4th of a Course on the study of History.
Gazetteer

79. February 7, 1777 Society for Free Debate, Horn, Doctors-Commons
'Whether the Church of Rome is not guilty of Idolatry in their Worship of the Virgin Mary and Saints?
Farther discussed, and determined in the affirmative.'
Gazetteer

80. February 10, 1777 Robin Hood
'If a man hath a father, a wife, and a son, in equal and imminent danger, (of drowning &c.) and has the possibility of saving only one of them, which ought he to preserve? And after that, Whether the stage is, or can be made, the school of virtue?'
The vote in the first Question 'went for saving the wife'.
Morning Chronicle

81. February 14, 1777 Society for Free Debate, Horn, Doctors-Commons
'1. What single Qualification is preferable in a Wife? – 2. Which is more agreeable to the Tenor of Scripture, Infant or Adult Baptism?'
Lecture on Inconsistency.
Determined in favour of Good Sense.
Gazetteer

82. February 17, 1777 Robin Hood

'Whether the stage is or can be made a school of virtue? Would not suspending the Habeas Corpus Act, be a proper measure at this juncture?'
Second Question 'was carried in the negative by a great majority'.
Morning Chronicle

83. February 19, 1777 Society for Free Debate, Queen's Arms, Newgate Street
'The Argument at this place . . . concerning the treason Bill, was carried on with spirit and ingenuity on both sides. The company was numerous and respectable; and the decision against the measure. But as it was urged by the advocates for the bill, that it had been misrepresented, the President was desired not to enter the determination, but leave it open for further discussion. With this request he complied.'
Gazetteer February 26

84. February 21, 1777 Society for Free Debate, Horn, Doctors-Commons
'Would it be a proper measure at this time, to vest the Crown with a power to suspend the Habeas Corpus Act, in certain cases, for a limited time?'
Lecture on peace.
'After a variety of sensible and ingenious arguments, determined in favour of the bill depending in Parliament for that purpose.'
Gazetteer February 28

85. February 24, 1777 Robin Hood
'Whether the stage is, or can be made, a school of virtue?'
Question 'was debated with ingenuity, candour, and humour; the division was in favour of the stage being the school of virtue'.
Morning Chronicle

86. February 26, 1777 Society for Free Debate, Queen's Arms, Newgate Street
'Is a particular attention to the cultivation of commerce, beneficial to a community?'
Gazetteer

87. February 28, 1777 Society for Free Debate, Horn, Doctors Commons
'Which is more agreeable to the Tenor of Scripture, Infant or Adult Baptism?'
Gazetteer

88. March 3, 1777 Robin Hood
'Whether an eloquent writer, or an eloquent speaker, is the more desirable character?'
Morning Chronicle

89. March 5, 1777 Society for Free Debate, Queen's-Arms, Newgate Street
'Is the Constitution of a Land to be supposed capable of any Alterations at the Will of the Legislature? And, Can shameful Punishments tend to the Prevention of Crimes?
As every question which relates to the constitution and laws, of a country is of the highest importance, the Managers of the above Society cannot doubt, but that those before mentioned will excite public attention; and have the satisfaction to say, that several ingenious speakers have promised to honour them with their sentiments on the above subjects.'
Gazetteer

90. March 7, 1777 Society for Free Debate, Horn, Doctors-Commons
'Whether Baron Montesquieu's Observation, That Virtue is not the Principle of Monarchical Government, is founded in truth? And, if time permit, the following: Which ought a man to relieve preferable to the other, his father or his son, supposing both to be in an equal state of poverty or distress?'
Lecture will be delivered on Conjugal Happiness.
Gazetteer

91. March 12, 1777 Society for Free Debate, Queen's-Arms, Newgate Street
'1. Can shameful punishments tend to the prevention of crimes? 2. Is it indispensably necessary, in a moral sense, for a man to marry the woman he has debauched? 3. Can a man be strictly moral, without professing any particular religious principles whatsoever?
The Directors of this Society return their grateful thanks to the public for the general support afforded to their undertaking at the three last meetings, and beg leave to assure the lovers of rational entertainment, that nothing shall be omitted which can render the above assembly worthy of further countenance and favour.'
Lecture on Happiness.
Gazetteer

92. March 14, 1777 Society for Free Debate, Horn, Doctors-Commons
'Is that man a friend to his country, who, in a time of national danger, exposes the weakness and distress of the State?'
Question was 'very ably and ingeniously debated, and determined in the negative'.
Gazetteer

93. March 19, 1777 Society for Free Debate, Queen's Arms, Newgate Street
'1. Is not the practice of purchasing at a low rate annuities on the lives of young men of fortune, a species of usury, and consequently criminal? – 2. Can a man who does not profess some religious principles, be strictly moral?'
Gazetteer

94. March 21, 1777 Society for Free Debate, Horn, Doctors-Commons
'1. Which ought a man to relieve, (supposing it in his power to relieve but one) his father or his son, both being in an equal state of poverty or danger? 2. Is not Mr. Grenville's act deciding controverted elections, likely to be productive of more harm than good?'
On the Question 'a debate equally ingenious and entertaining, in which the speakers were no less distinguished by their knowledge and eloquence, than by their feelings as men, and their moral rectitude as Christians; upon these principles the parent had the universal preference; but from political considerations, as affecting the interests of society at large, that preference was adjudged to the son by the majority of a single hand.'
Gazetteer

95. March 26, 1777 Society for Free Debate, Queen's Arms, Newgate Street
'Were all the methods taken to convict John the Painter justifiable? 2. Is it possible, by arguments deduced from the nature of matter, to prove the existence of an immaterial soul in man?'
Lecture on death.
Gazetteer

96. March 28, 1777 Society for Free Debate, Horn, Doctors-Commons
'Is Mr. Grenville's act for determining controverted elections likely to be productive of more harm or good?'
Lecture on Honour and Shame.
Question 'received a very ample discussion . . . and its utility [was] universally acknowledged, although it admitted some improvements were still wanting to render its operation as extensively beneficial as the intention of its author, and equal to the warmest wishes of the friends to the constitution.'
Gazetteer

97. April 4, 1777 Society for Free Debate, Horn, Doctors-Commons
'Is Oratory in the Courts of Law of any real use to the cause of Justice? The majority of the speakers argued in favour of the affirmative, and strengthened their opinions with many examples of its utility; while those for the negative alleged that justice, as being founded in truth, stood in no need of any adventitious aid; that oratory, in such cases, was more likely to mislead than inform a jury; and that from the confessions of their opponents, a judge was not to be biassed by the opinion of council, however eloquent, if not founded in laws; which is the only rule by which the judge and jury are bound to determine all causes, and further consideration of this important subject was adjourned.'
Gazetteer

98. April 7, 1777 Robin Hood
'Whether a certain City Officer was so far reprehensible as to deserve an opposition at Midsummer next?'

The Question 'was very warmly, candidly and ingeniously debated; and, on the division, carried in the negative by a majority of four or five hands'.
Morning Chronicle April 14

99. April 9, 1777 Society for Free Debate, Queen's Arms, Newgate Street
'Does eloquence in the Senate tend to the advantage of the community? And also the subsequent: Are the practices with which the present Chamberlain is charged such as render him an improper person to hold that office?'
Gazetteer

100. April 11, 1777 Society for Free Debate, Horn, Doctors-Commons
'Whether the Oratory of the Bar is of any real Use in promoting Justice?'
Question 'determined in the affirmative'.
Gazetteer

101. April 14, 1777 Robin Hood
'Is it honourable to follow the profession of arms for hire (this question relates to auxiliary, or mercenary troops, fighting the battles of Aliens, &c.) And whether making a mere *conclave* of the House of Commons is not an insult to the British nation?'
Morning Chronicle

102. April 18, 1777 Society for Free Debate, Horn, Doctors-Commons
'1. Can it be proved from the New Testament, that the first day of the week ought to be observed as the Sabbath Day? Which is preferable, an hereditary or elective monarchy?'
Gazetteer

103. April 21, 1777 Robin Hood
'The Question relative to the order for the exclusion of strangers from the galleries of St. Stephen's chapel, was carried by a small majority of hands against that measure, tho' the weight of oratory was in favour thereof.'
Morning Chronicle April 28

104. April 25, 1777 Society for Free Debate, Horn, Doctors-Commons
'Whether an Elective or Hereditary Monarchy is preferable?'
Adjourned.
Gazetteer May 2

105. April 28, 1777 Robin Hood
'Whether a certain unfortunate personage, under conviction of a capital crime, is not a proper object of Royal Mercy? And Whether doth any real utility arise either to individuals or the community from a thorough knowledge of the dead languages?

When the Question was agitated at the Robin Hood concerning an unfortunate Divine, many persons evidently came prepossessed for the rigour of the law, but the humanity of Englishmen soon yielded at the remembrance of the many thousands who have been relieved in various ways by his benevolent exertion; and it was voted unanimously, with an anxious zeal that did honour to their feelings, that he is a proper object of Royal mercy.'
Morning Chronicle/Gazetteer May 2

106. May 2, 1777 Society for Free Debate, Horn, Doctors-Commons
'Whether an Elective or Hereditary Monarchy is preferable? The following subject also, if time permit, will be investigated: Whether the conduct of the present Chamberlain merits his re-election without opposition the ensuing Midsummer?'
Lecture on the Infelicities of Human Life.
Question 'was further debated . . . and determined in favour of' hereditary monarchy.
Gazetteer

107. May 9, 1777 Society for Free Debate, Horn, Doctors-Commons
'Is the general tendency of Lord Chesterfield's Letters to his Son, more likely to promote the cause of Virtue or Vice?
The President and Committee will continue to exert their best endeavours in conducting it upon the same liberal plan which has hitherto received the countenance and esteem of the ingenious and candid of every party and denomination.'
Gazetteer

108. June 13, 1777 Society for Free Debate, Horn, Doctors-Commons
'Upon what ground can the Court of Common Council be justified in their application to the throne, in behalf of Dr. Dodd?'
Gazetteer

109. July 28, 1777 Robin Hood
'Whether an honest lawyer, or an honest physician, is the most valuable member of the community?
After a variety of arguments (numerous, serious, ironical, &c.) the shew of hands was in favour of the physician.'
Morning Chronicle August 4

110. August 4, 1777 Robin Hood
'Whether a standing army, in regal pay, or a well-established militia, is the more eligible defence for this country?'
Question 'was very ingeniously debated, and at last adjourned . . . .. The Militia seemed to have the advantage when the contest ended.'
Morning Chronicle

111. August 11, 1777 Robin Hood

21

'Whether a standing army under regal pay, or a well regulated Militia, is the more eligible defence for this country? Are not the penal laws of this country disproportionate to the crimes they are adapted to?'
The first Question 'went in favour of the army. Perhaps this determination was owing to the militia gentlemen being absent; as they seemed most formidable the prior evening.' The second 'went in the affirmative'.
Morning Chronicle

112. August 18, 1777 Robin Hood
'Whether the love of fame may be truly said to be a universal passion?'
Question 'was carried in the affirmative'.
Morning Chronicle

113. August 25, 1777 Robin Hood
'Whether there is not more true courage in refusing a challenge (from conscientious motives) than in complying with the prevailing custom of modern honour?'
Question 'was answered in the affirmative'.
Morning Chronicle

114. September 1, 1777 Robin Hood
'Whether is the prodigal or the miser the worse member of society?'
It 'was determined that the miser was so. In this debate the elder persons repudiated the miser, and most of the younger ones took against the prodigal.'
Morning Chronicle

115. September 6, 1777 Theological Society, One Tun, near Hungerford, Strand
'Ye have heard that it hath been said, "thou shalt love thy neighbour and hate thine enemy." But I say unto you, love your enemies, bless them that curse you, do good to them that hate you, and pray for them which despitefully use you and persecute you.' Matt. chap v. verse 43 and 44.
Opening discourse by the late President on lines from Pope.
Gazetteer

116. September 8, 1777 Robin Hood
'Whether sudden joy or sudden grief hath the greater effect on the human mind? and Is it possible that the people of an extensive empire (like Great Britain) can be equally represented?'
Morning Chronicle

117. September 14, 1777 Theological Society
A passage from the Scripture 'taken from the 38th verse of the 2nd chapter of Acts . . . concerning the necessity, time, form and effects of baptism'.
Preceded by a lecture on lines from *The Grave*.
Gazetteer September 13

118. September 15, 1777 Robin Hood
'Whether bishops are of any real utility in church or state?
Some exceptions were taken to the general face of the question, as the word church, in this country, implies the episcopal office. Then an emphasis was laid on the word *are* Bishops, as if the present ones were meant, and the Canada bill was introduced. However, when hands came to be laid on the question, the Bishops were confirmed in their consequence, &c.'
Morning Chronicle September 22

119. September 22, 1777 Robin Hood
'Whether a son's extravagance is a justification of a father's disinheriting him? And after that, Whether the Lord Mayor was commendable respecting the Newgate rioters?'
Adjourned.
Morning Chronicle

120. September 30, 1777 Robin Hood
'Whether the Lord Mayor was commendable respecting the Newgate rioters? Whether love or money is the greatest inducement to matrimony?'
The first Question 'was dropped without debate. The warm regard of a young Gentleman for the Magistrate, cast cold water on the question. The second question . . . went for love nem. con. Then the question about Lord Abingdon's pamphlet [which must have been added on the spot] was debated and adjourned to this evening.'
Morning Chronicle, September 29

121. October 4, 1777 Society at the Crown in Bow-lane
'Whether Great Britain, in case of the North American Colonies being lost, might not be in as a flourishing a state as before they were discovered?
The speaker, who opened the question, wished it to be considered under the heads of the state of England before the settlement of the Colonies; the advantages reaped from trading with them; and consequences likely to ensue from the trade of this empire being diverted into a different channel. Under these heads it was accordingly considered; and after many ingenious debates, in the course of which the *affirmative* side of the question seemed to prevail, it was adjourned.'
Gazetteer

122. October 6, 1777 Robin Hood
'Whether Ladies ought to wear their hats in the Theatres during the performance? Whether Lord Abingdon's late production deserves the favour or censure of the public?'
The Question about Lord Abingdon's publication 'was carried, that said [the] production deserved the favour and applause of the public'.
Morning Chronicle

123. October 10, 1777 Society for Free Debate, Horn, Doctors-Commons
'Whether dramatic representations have not a tendency to injure the cause of Virtue and Religion?
This Society was opened last Friday, pursuant to adjournment, and honoured with a genteel company.'
Lecture on Friendship.
The Question was debated 'with spirit and ingenuity, and adjourned for further consideration'.
Gazetteer

124. October 13, 1777 Robin Hood
'Whether the female part of a theatrical audience should be allowed to wear hats during the performance? and Whether it can be shewn that the present age is worse as to morals than the preceding one?
The question about wearing hats in the Theatres was superseded . . . and [of] the second question . . . much was said, and very ingeniously on both sides; perhaps proof positive in the premises, cannot possibly be adduced, so from certain conspicuous instances of humanity and other virtues, it was at last determined, that if the present was no better than the last age, it could not be proved to be worse.'
Morning Chronicle

125. October 17, 1777 Society for Free Debate, Horn, Doctors-Commons
'Whether Theatrical Entertainments have a tendency to promote the cause of virtue and religion? The next subject for consideration (which if time permit will also be investigated . . .) Is an appeal to the sword properly called an appeal to Heaven?'
Lecture on Wisdom.
The first Question 'after a variety of learned, interesting and ingenious arguments, determined in the affirmative.'
Gazetteer

126. October 20, 1777 Robin Hood
'Would not an accommodation with the Colonies, be more eligible than prosecuting the war, notwithstanding the present prospect of success? And, Is the character of a rigid patriot consistent with that of a good Christian?'
The first Question 'was carried nearly *nem. con.* in the affirmative. As was also the second question.'
Morning Chronicle

127. October 23, 1777 Society at Crown Tavern, Bow lane
'Hath the suppression of the grave-diggers scene in Hamlet by Mr. Garrick contributed to the advantage or disadvantage of that Tragedy?'
Gazetteer October 22

24

128. October 24, 1777 Society for Free Debate, Horn, Doctors-Commons
'Mr. Locke's celebrated position, Whether an appeal to the sword can properly be called appeal to Heaven?'
The Question 'was considered in three views; first, in reference to duelling; secondly, in respect of war between foreign nations; and lastly, as relative to civil war; and determined in the negative in each particular'.
Gazetteer

129. October 27, 1777 Robin Hood
'Whether encreasing the number of play-houses in this kingdom would be expedient? And Whether an egregious aggressor (in any matter) is justifiable in accepting a challenge from the person he has injured?
Both these questions dropt, as neither the proposer, nor any other person, owned or opened them. – The next question on course came on, and was very briefly debated, viz. "Whether America subjugated, or America being independent would tend more to the preservation of English liberty?" '
Morning Chronicle

130. October 31, 1777 Society for Free Debate, Horn, Doctors-Commons
'Would it not be for the interest of Great Britain, to end the present contest with America, by declaring the Colonies independent of the Mother Country?'
Adjourned.
Gazetteer

131. November 1, 1777 Society for Free Debate, Horn, Doctors-Commons
'Whether it would not be for the Advantage of Great Britain to end the present Contest with America, by declaring the Colonies independent of the Mother Country?
Determined in the negative.'
Gazetteer November 7

132. November 3, 1777 Robin Hood
'Whether beauty in women is in general more conducive or detrimental to their happiness? and To which are we more indebted for our safety, our courage or our fear?'
The first Question 'was determined in favour of beauty – i.e. [as] conducive to happiness'. The second 'went that fear is so'.
Morning Chronicle

133. November 6, 1777 The Debating Society, which formerly assembled at the Crown Tavern, Bow-Lane, will in future meet at Coachmakers Hall, Foster Lane, Cheapside

'Is it not become a duty incumbent on the people, at this critical and alarming period, to petition the throne, to put a stop to the war in America?'
Morning Chronicle

134. November 7, 1777 Society for Free Debate, Horn, Doctors-Commons
'1. Is it good Policy in the Church of England to admit the validity of ordination by Bishops of the Greek and Romish Churches, and reject that of Protestant Dissenters? – 2. What are the Characteristics of a real Patriot?'
Second question adjourned.
Gazetteer

135. November 10, 1777 Robin Hood
'Whether the freedom taken in speaking and writing, concerning exalted personages, is more deserving censure or commendation? and, Whether is hope of reward or fear of punishment the greater inducement to virtue?'
The decision of the second question was in favour of hope.
Morning Chronicle

136. November 14, 1777 Society for Free Debate, Horn, Doctors-Commons
'What are the Characteristics of a Real Patriot? Would not an equal assessment of the land tax be a measure of expediency and justice?
After a thorough investigation of the subject, in which was displayed an extensive knowledge of the landed and commercial interests of this country, determined unanimously in the affirmative.'
Gazetteer

137. November 17, 1777 Robin Hood
'Whether hope of reward, or fear of punishment, is the greater inducement to virtue?'
The question was answered 'in favour of Hope'.
Morning Chronicle November 24

138. November 21, 1777 Society for Free Debate, Horn, Doctors-Commons
'May not many of the virtues of the ancients be more properly denominated splendid vices?'
Question 'determined in the affirmative'.
Gazetteer

139. November 24, 1777 Robin Hood
'Is it consistent with the honour of Great Britain, to be a pacific spectator of the assistance which the French give to the Americans? and, Whether maidens or widows have the greater propensity to matrimony?'

26

The first Question 'was carried in the affirmative'.
Morning Chronicle

140. November 27, 1777 Society removed from the Crown-tavern, Bow-lane to Coachmakers-hall, Foster-lane
'Would it be wise in a state to give rewards to virtue, as well as to punish vice?'
Gazetteer

141. November 28, 1777 Society for Free Debate, Horn, Doctors-Commons
'Is not the love of Woman one of the greatest incitements to Military Valour?'
The Question, 'after a critical investigation of the passions, and an appeal to the concurrent testimony of history, determined in the negative'.
Gazetteer

142. December 1, 1777 Robin Hood
'Whether maids or widows have the greatest propensity to matrimony? and, Which situation is more favourable to female chastity, a nun or maid of honour? and, Is employing savages in a military capacity against the Americans justifiable?'
On the first question, it was decided that 'widows have the greater propensity.' The second question was dropped. The last question 'went in the affirmative'.
Morning Chronicle

143. December 4, 1777 Coachmakers' Hall
'Is it probable the amendment proposed by the Earl of Chatham, to the address on the subject of the King's speech, would have produced any beneficial consequences to Great Britain?'
Gazetteer

144. December 5, 1777 Society for Free Debate, Horn, Doctors-Commons
'Is it true that man acts as the tyrant as well as the lord of creation? And, if time permit, the following – Has curiosity been productive of more harm or good?'
Question 'determined in the negative'.
Gazetteer

145. December 8, 1777 Robin Hood
'Whether talents for the stage are so rare as is generally imagined? and Whether the rejection of Lord Chatham's motion for a cessation of hostilities in America was prudent?'
The first question 'went in the negative', the other 'was very spiritedly debated till the usual hours of debate were elapsed, as was, by a vote, adjourned'.
Morning Chronicle

146. December 11, 1777 Coach-makers-hall
'Is the Practice of impressing Seamen, as a Prerogative of the Crown, consistent with natural Justice, or the Rights and Privileges of Englishmen?'
Adjourned.
Gazetteer

147. December 12, 1777 Society for Free Debate, Horn, Doctors-Commons
'Whether a cessation of hostilities against America would now be politic?'
Question 'debated upon the ideas adopted by some persons of distinguished rank in opposition, of withdrawing the British troops from America, as a ground work of conciliation; and, after a variety of interesting and ingenious arguments (in which it was proved that it would be dishonourable and injurious to the interests of this country, and by no means likely to answer so desirable an end) determined in the negative.'
Gazetteer

148. December 15, 1777 Robin Hood
'Whether the rejection of Lord Chatham's motion for cessation of hostilities in America was a prudent method? and Whether the liberty of free speaking and writing, allowed in this country, doth not carry off political ill-humours, and tend more to preserve the state than subvert it?'
Morning Chronicle

149. December 18, 1777 Coachmakers-hall
'Is the practice of impressing seamen, as a prerogative of the Crown, consistent with natural justice, or the rights and privileges of Englishmen?'
Gazetteer

150. December 19, 1777 Society for Free Debate, Horn, Doctors-Commons
'Would not the allowing the Independency of America, expose us to the insults of foreign Nations?'
Question 'determined in the affirmative.'
Gazetteer

151. December 22, 1777 Robin Hood
'Whether the freedom in speaking and writing, used in this country, doth not, by carrying off the people's ill humours, tend to support rather than to subvert the government? and Whether courage is natural or acquired?'
The first question 'went in the affirmative'. The second Question 'went for natural'.
Morning Chronicle December 29

152. December 26, 1777 Society for Free Debate, Horn, Doctors-Commons
'Can any but a defensive war be justified upon principles of morality and religion?'
Gazetteer

153. December 29, 1777 Robin Hood
'Whether a public or a private education is the more useful? and Whether an agrarian law, limiting the possession of landed property to a certain prescribed value, would not be beneficial to the public?'
The first Question 'went in favour of private education'.
Morning Chronicle

154. January 5, 1778 Robin Hood
'Whether an Agrarian law, limiting the possession of landed property to certain bounds, would not be useful in this country? and Which is the more dangerous doctrine to the liberties of Great Britain, the omnipotence of Parliament, or the powers of the Royal Prerogative?'
The first Question 'went in the negative; – and the question 'Whether the professed reviewers of books and pamphlets are of more benefit or detriment to literature?' went that they were detrimental.'
Morning Chronicle

155. January 7, 1778 EXTRA meeting of the Society at Coachmakers-Hall
'Will there not greater glory redound to this nation from relieving the distresses of the American prisoners, than was derived from the humanity shewn to the French prisoners in the late war?
The whole income of which, for that night, with any other benefaction that may be received on the occasion, will be appropriated to the relief of the American prisoners.'
Gazetteer January 5

156. January 8, 1778 Coachmakers-Hall
'Which is most to be feared in the decline of a free state, anarchy or despotism?'
Gazetteer

157. January 12, 1778 Robin Hood
'Whether all laws enacted by the legislature of this country are not ultimately obligatory? and Whether an error proceeding from a zeal in the service of one's country is not venial?'
First Question 'went in the negative'.
Morning Chronicle

158. January 15, 1778 Coach-makers-hall

29

'Can a friendship subsist between the different sexes without the passion of love?'
Gazetteer

159. January 19, 1778 Robin Hood
'Whether an error produced by zeal for the good of one's country is not venial? and Whether abridging the law proceedings and reducing the number of practitioners in that profession, would not be beneficial to the community?'
First Question 'went in the affirmative. – Then the question, "Whether gaming, or excess in drinking, is more prejudicial to society?" went that drinking was so.'
Morning Chronicle

160. January 22, 1778 Coach-makers-hall
'Supposing the Americans to possess the right of taxing themselves, in its fullest latitude and extent, would it not be more to their advantage to be dependent on the Crown of Great Britain, than to exist as an independent state?'
Gazetteer

161. January 25, 1778 Theological Society, One Tun, near Hungerford, Strand
' "What think ye of Christ, whose son is he." 22 chap. St. Matthew, 42nd ver. As this text leads to an enquiry into the true character of a personage whom some have esteemed as the very and eternal God, others looked on as a superior, though not Supreme Being, and a third class deemed a mere mortal, doubtless the argument upon it will be spirited and ingenious.'
Gazetteer January 24

162. January 26, 1778 Robin Hood
'Is not long imprisonment of delinquents more likely to harden than reclaim them? And, Whether our vices proceed more from error in judgment or depravity of the will? and also, Whether the City of London acted properly or improperly, in refusing to raise troops to prosecute the war in America?'
Last Question 'went, that such conduct in the City was improper'.
Morning Chronicle

163. January 29, 1778 Coachmakers Hall
'Supposing the Americans to possess the right of taxing themselves in its fullest extent and latitude, would it not be more to their advantage to be dependent on the Crown of Great Britain, than to exist as an independent state?'
Gazetteer

164. February 2, 1778 Robin Hood

'Whether Mr. Soame Jenning's assertion, that patriotism is a false virtue, is founded in truth? And Whether stealing human bodies after interment, and exposing them to sale, ought not to be made a capital offence?'
The first Question 'was begun and adjourned'; the second, 'went in the negative'.
Morning Chronicle

165. February 5, 1778 Coach-makers-hall
'Is it better to aim at a general but imperfect knowledge of things, or at a complete knowledge of some particular art or science?'
Gazetteer

166. February 9, 1778 Robin Hood
'Whether Mr. Jenning's assertion be true, that patriotism is a false virtue? and Whether promulgating vague reports of the success of their land or sea forces is not highly detrimental to a commercial nation?'
The first Question 'went in the negative! The speakers did not forget to maintain patriotism to be a christian, as well as a political virtue.'
Morning Chronicle

167. February 12, 1778 Coach-makers-hall
'Does peace or war afford greater opportunities to a King for the display of virtue and abilities?'
Gazetteer

168. February 16, 1778 Robin Hood
'Whether it be not highly injurious to a commercial nation to spread vague reports respecting the success of their naval and land forces? and Would not repealing the late acts relative to the colonies, be a certain degradation, without a probable advantage to Great Britain?'
The first Question 'went in the affirmative'. The second was adjourned.
Morning Chronicle

169. February 19, 1778 Coach-makers-hall
'Which is most to be condemned, Avarice or Prodigality?'
Gazetteer

170. February 23, 1778 Robin Hood
'Would not repealing the late acts relative to the colonies, be a certain degradation, without a probable advantage to Great Britain? and Whether it is not of as much consequence to a nation to preserve its dignity, as for a man to preserve his honour, or a woman her virtue?'
First Question 'was again debated, and in a spirited manner, on both sides of the argument. An idea was thrown out, that some circumstances, not yet divulged, had produced the measure in question; but that time would justify the same, &c.' therefore this question adjourned. 'The author of the last question professed his intention of treating the same in a general, rather than a particular manner.'
Morning Chronicle

171. February 26, 1778 Coachmakers-Hall
'Ought not the proposals of Lord North, for reconciliation with America, to be considered as a proof of the ignorance or wickedness of those, who have been the advisors and conductors of the present war?'
Gazetteer

172. March 2, 1778 Robin Hood
'Would not repealing the late acts relative to the colonies, be a certain degradation, without a probable advantage to Great Britain?'
Morning Chronicle

173. March 5, 1778 Coach-makers-hall
'Does not the perilous situation of public affairs require an immediate change of men and measures?'
Gazetteer

174. March 12, 1778 Coach-makers-hall
'Does Comedy or Tragedy require the greater exertion of genius and abilities?'
Gazetteer

175. March 16, 1778 Robin Hood
'Whether political controversies were of any use to the community? Whether the married or single life was more happy?'
The first question 'went in the affirmative. Then, as if to avoid political discussion' the second question 'was selected from others' and adjourned.
Morning Chronicle March 23

176. March 19, 1778 Coach-makers-hall
'Is not the present Plan for Reconciliation with America, considering the present state of affairs, as of any of the former schemes of Administration, as unlikely to have effect?'
Gazetteer

177. March 23, 1778 Robin Hood
'Whether a married or a single life is in general more happy? Hath not a patriotic Peer as great opportunities of serving the public, as an equally patriotic Commoner? and Whether allowing the Americans their claim of independence, or entering into a French war on their account, is the more eligible measure for Great Britain?'
The first Question 'went, almost nem. con. in favour of the married state'. The last question 'was began and very warmly debated 'till past the usual hour, and then . . . adjourned'.
Morning Chronicle

178. March 26, 1778 Coachmakers-Hall

'Is not the glaring depravity of the times owing to a bad system in the education of youth?'
Gazetteer

179. March 30, 1778 Robin Hood
'Whether acceding to American Independency, or engaging in a war with France, is the more eligible measure for Great Britain? Hath not a patriotic Peer as great opportunities of serving his country as an equally patriotic Commoner? and Whether it is proper that a Peer of France should sit and vote in the English senate?'
The first Question 'went (after a scrutiny) in favour of the war with France; – some speakers said that American Independency was a point absolutely fixed, certain, and unfructable, and wondered at the idea of a new war in our present situations; others insisted, that a possibility existed of punishing the perfidy of France, in nursing the American revolt. – And also to prevent future assistance, so that the Colonies should, when left to themselves, be obliged to return to their allegiance, &c.'
Morning Chronicle

180. April 1, 1778 Society for Free Debate, Half Moon Tavern, Aldersgate Street
'A Society will be held at the above Tavern on Wednesday the 8th instant . . . and every Wednesday throughout the year.'
Gazetteer

181. April 2, 1778 Coachmakers-Hall
'Is not continuation of present Ministry more to be dreaded than the united powers of France and Spain?'
Adjourned.
Gazetteer

182. April 6, 1778 Robin Hood
'Whether it be proper that a French Peer, should have a voice in the English Senate?'
The Question 'was warmly debated. The question was general, yet the parliamentary conduct of his Grace of Aubigny, became the matter of conversation: the question was at last adjourned, to give the proposer a week's time to bring his proofs, that the oath of fealty, taken by the Duke in question, to the French monarch, was so express an obligation, as to constitute the impropriety of his seat among the British Lords.'
Morning Chronicle

183. April 9, 1778 Coachmakers-Hall
'Is not continuation of present Ministry more to be dreaded than the united powers of France and Spain?'
Gazetteer

184. April 13, 1778 Robin Hood

'Whether it be proper that a French Peer, should have a voice in the English Senate? Would it be politically wise in the present situation of affairs, to wage war with France, without first declaring the Americans independent? And is it consistent with the honour, dignity, and interest of Great Britain to pass an act for the independency of the colonies?' The first Question 'went in the negative; as well it might, for no such circumstance is or can be. The Dukedom of Aubigny, as was clearly evinced by authentic quotations, is not among the Peerages of France, but is a mere honourary title. Much of the debate related to the Duke of R−d, who, some said, acted as a French, others as an English patriot. Certainly his Grace of Richmond and Aubigny, may act on the same motives as his compeers in opposition.' Of the second question 'it was insinuated [that] England should pocket the present affront from France, and resent it thereafter &c. Query, will policy and Christianity agree in this bearing malice in mind?'; question adjourned.
Morning Chronicle

185. April 16, 1778 Coach-makers-hall
'Is not the extreme refinement of nations more destructive of happiness, than the rude state in which nations existed previous to civilization?'
Gazetteer

186. April 20, 1778 Robin Hood
'Whether it would be politically wise to declare war against France, without first declaring America independent?'
Question 'went in the affirmative'.
Morning Chronicle

187. April 23, 1778 Coach-makers-hall
'Would it not be politic, in the present crisis, for Great Britain to acknowledge the independence of America?'
Adjourned.
Gazetteer

188. April 27, 1778 Robin Hood
'Whether repealing the penal statute against Catholics in Ireland, would not assimilate the affections of that people to the British Government, and tend to prevent an invasion of that country? and, Have not the measures of opposition since the year 1763, principally contributed to bring this nation into the present crisis? and, Is a Satyrist a promoter of virtue?'
The debate 'went *nem. con.* in favour' of a repeal of the laws against Catholics. The second question 'was begun, but not concluded; the gentlemen who entered on the subject coincided, though on different grounds, in the affirmative, and had the question been then put, the patriots would have been condemned as the cause of our calamities &c.' The question was adjourned.
Morning Chronicle

189. April 30, 1778 Coachmakers-hall
'Would it not be politic, in the present crisis, for Great Britain to acknowledge the independence of America?'
Gazetteer

190. May 3, 1778 Robin Hood
'Whether the conduct of the opposition since the year 1763, hath not principally contributed to bring this nation into the present alarming crisis? Whether it is consistent with the honour, interest and dignity of Britain to accede to American Independence in any case whatsoever?' The first Question 'went in the negative. The question was in a manner lost through the absence of the author of it, as only one Speaker rose to reply to what was urged in the affirmative the preceding night before. Then the question concerning the frequency of capital punishments was begun, and adjourned.'
Morning Chronicle

191. May 7, 1778 Coachmakers-hall
'Do female deviations from chastity in general originate in the artifice of the men, or the levity of the women?'
Gazetteer

192. May 11, 1778 Robin Hood
'Whether capital punishments are not too frequently inflicted in this country? Is it political after the loss of the American trade, to take off the restrictions upon that between England and Ireland?'
The first Question 'was not spoke to at all, owing to the absence of the proposer, and the gentlemen who argued it the preceding evening and moved for its adjournment.' The second Question 'went in favour of passing said Bills without one dissenting voice or hand'.
Morning Chronicle

193. May 14, 1778 Coachmakers-hall
'Which of the two evils is the least, that a nation should be governed by Minister of good moral character, but destitute of due knowledge and capacity; or one of eminent abilities, with bad heart?'
Gazetteer

194. May 18, 1778 Robin Hood
'Whether capital punishments are not too frequently inflicted in this country?'
Morning Chronicle

195. May 21, 1778 Coachmakers-hall
'Whether the Bills at present under consideration, for taking off certain restrictions on the trade of Ireland, ought to receive the sanction of the British Legislature?'
Gazetteer

196. May 25, 1778 Robin Hood
'Whether a satyrist is a promoter of virtue? and Is universal benevolence possessed by any human being?'
The first Question 'went in the affirmative'; the second 'went in the negative'.
Morning Chronicle June 1

197. May 28, 1778 Coachmakers-hall
'Ought not the father, who would oblige his daughter to marry a person greatly different from herself in age, and for whom she has no affection or esteem, to be considered by the Legislature as a flagrant violator of nature and justice, against whose arbitrary power provision should be made?'
Gazetteer

198. June 1, 1778 Robin Hood
'Would it be good policy at this time to relax the rigour of the laws against Roman Catholics, in favour of such of them, as are willing to give a clear and explicit test of their civil subjection? and Whether the negative put upon the enquiry into a certain general's conduct, doth not prove that his ill success proceeded more from ministerial blunders than any misconduct of that officer?'
The second Question 'went in the negative. – It was allowed a strong presumption obtained, – but not proof positive of the affirmative.'
Morning Chronicle

199. June 4, 1778 Coachmakers hall
'Whether the present situation of this country does not require that an immediate and exemplary punishment should be inflicted on the advisors and promoters of those measures, which have produced our national misfortunes?'
Gazetteer

200. June 8, 1778 Robin Hood
'Whether the present crisis doth not demand an immediate change of men and measures in the Administration of affairs in this country? and Which would be the most proper place for the interment of a lately deceased Earl, – St. Paul's Cathedral, or Westminster Abbey?'
On the first Question 'the speaking was all on the affirmative, except indeed some ironical compliments on Lord N—'s vivacity, S—'s piety, W—th's temperance, G—n's valour, &c. &c. might be called taking the other side; but being no controversy on the question, it stands adjourned.'
Morning Chronicle

201. June 15, 1778 Robin Hood
'Whether the present crisis doth not demand an immediate change of men and measures, in the administration of public affairs in this country? Are not those men who have rejoiced at and abetted the defection

of the subjects of Great Britain, and excited insults from our enemies, chargeable with all the calamities experienced by this country at this juncture?'

First Question 'went in the negative by a considerable majority'.

Morning Chronicle

202. June 22, 1778 Robin Hood

'Whether marriages in youth, or more advanced years, are more likely to produce connubial happiness? The age of 26 is proposed, as the medium for the husband, and in proportion for the bride; and, Whether a union with Ireland, similar to that of Scotland, would not be injurious to the commercial interests of England?'

The first Question 'went in favour of youth'.

Morning Chronicle

203. June 29, 1778 Robin Hood

'Whether a union with Ireland, similar to that with Scotland, would not be injurious to the commercial interests of Great Britain?'

The Question 'was very ingeniously discussed, and passed, that such a union would not be injurious to both countries'.

Morning Chronicle

204. July 6, 1778 Robin Hood

'Would it not be proper at this time to withdraw the British forces from America, and in order to act with greater vigour against France?'

Question 'went in the affirmative'.

Morning Chronicle

205. July 13, 1778 Robin Hood

'Whether the restrictions upon the interest of money, discover in their inventors just commercial notions, and enlightened attention to the welfare of mankind?'

The Question, 'Whether virtue is productive of temporal happiness?' went in the affirmative.

Morning Chronicle

206. July 20, 1778 Robin Hood

'Whether the restrictions upon the interest of money discover in their inventors just commercial notions, and an enlightened attention to the welfare of mankind? And also, Whether the observation of the general rule of appealing to arms upon particular affronts or personal insults, deserves greater censure than a deviation therefrom?'

First Question 'went in the affirmative. – The question on Duelling was very ingeniously debated, and adjourned.'

Morning Chronicle

207. July 27, 1778 Robin Hood

'Whether the observation of the general rule of appealing to arms upon particular affronts or personal insults, deserves greater censure than a

deviation therefrom? Would it not be impolitic in Great Britain to take an active part in the disputes which subsist on the continent of Europe?' First Question 'determined that giving in to the practice of duelling on any account deserved greater censure than avoiding the same upon any provocation'.
Morning Chronicle

208. August 3, 1778 Robin Hood
'Would it not be very impolitic in Great Britain to take any part in the disputes on the continent of Europe? and Whether in strict friendship (between individuals) any secret may be concealed without censure?' The second Question 'went in the affirmative: – The debate was very entertaining, and produced many curious sentiments upon the nature and obligations of friendship.'
Morning Chronicle

209. August 10, 1778 Robin Hood
'Whether it would not be proper immediately to recall the Commissioners from America? and Whether Admiral Keppel's rencounter with the Duke of Chartres, is more like a victory or a defeat?' The first Question 'went in the negative. Some speakers were for the *immediate* recall, as well to save expence, as to resent the indignity thrown upon them: others were for postponing such recall, as well to have the sense of Parliament on the case, as to see what effect any prosperous event in the French war might have on the colonists: others were for changing them for another suit of Commissioners, &c. and others for keeping them there as a memorial of the infamy of administration, in bringing England into so humiliating a predicament. Those various opinions were all well supported, though the heads decided as above.'
Morning Chronicle

210. August 17, 1778 Robin Hood
'Whether Admiral Keppel's rencontre with the Brest fleet appears more like a victory or a defeat?' The Question 'was very warmly debated. The proposer did not appear, so the question was pushed and chased around the room for some time; at length the gentlemen made a *handsome* set too, and Admiral Keppel had the *victory*; or, his combat was rather a victory over the French, than a defeat by them.'
Morning Chronicle

211. August 24, 1778 Robin Hood
'Whether all real Antigallicans ought not now (if consistent) to be Anti-Americans? The Question 'Whether in the present situation of affairs in this country, an immediate change of men (and administration) and a direct acknowledgement of America's Independence, would not be advisable, &c.' was ingeniously debated, and adjourned.
Morning Chronicle

212. August 31, 1778 Robin Hood
'Whether in the present situation of affairs in this country, an immediate change of men (and administration) and a direct acknowledgement of America's Independence, would not be advisable? and, Doth not a contempt of fame, beget a contempt of virtue?'
The first Question 'was determined in the negative'.
Morning Chronicle

213. September 3, 1778 Society at Coach-makers-hall
'Has the discovery of America been more beneficial or detrimental to mankind in general?'
Gazetteer

214. September 4, 1778 Society for Free and Candid Debate, for many years held at the Queen's Arms Tavern, Newgate street, but late at the Horn Tavern, Doctor's-Commons, returned to the Queen's arms
'Are the indulgences lately granted to the Roman Catholics of this kingdom consistent with the safety thereof, as a Protestant Church and State?
N.B. The Society is continued upon its ancient disinterested liberal plan, which has so many years recommended it to the approbation of those who have attended it.'
Carried in the affirmative.
Gazetteer September 11

215. September 6, 1778 Theological Society, One Tun, near Hungerford, Strand
'So then, it is not of him that willeth, nor or him that runneth, but of God that sheweth mercy'. Romans, 9th chap.
Gazetteer September 3

216. September 7, 1778 Robin Hood
'Doth not a contempt of fame, on the part of reputation, &c. beget a contempt of virtue? And Ought not all real Antigallicans, if constant, to be now Anti-Americans?'
The first Question 'was very ingeniously discussed by a respectable company, and was carried in the affirmative'; second question adjourned.
Morning Chronicle

217. September 8, 1778 Gazetteer
'To the President of the Disputing Society at Coachmakers-Hall
Sir,
I was present last Thursday, when the question respecting the utility of the discovery of America to mankind in general was debated by this Society; and I must acknowledge the discourse to have been entertaining and instructive. However, I think, was the committee to make it a rule not to admit of too many scripture quotations, the debates would

be rendered far more agreeable; for many of the speakers, thinking to give their arguments greater weight, have recourse to the New or Old Testament for passages, to enforce what they have advanced; and are, by this means, often so much taken up with the sublimity of their authors, that they leave the matter in debate at a great distance, and make what would otherwise be good reasoning, appear the bombastic nonsense of a Moorfields Enthusiast. – My noticing this was owing to the unnecessary and frequent bringing in the names of Shem, Ham, and Japhet, by a gentleman on the right hand side of the Hall, and who likewise made often mention of the resting of the Ark on Mount Ararat, which had as little relation to the matter in debate as the times of Shem, Ham or Japhet had to do with America. There is also a young gentleman, who I believe spoke last Thursday for the first time, and who gave evident signs of a promising genius; but he must excuse me, if I tell him he seemed to favour too much of the Methodist in his discourse; I therefore hope he will pardon me, in reminding him of this imperfection, which, if he can break himself of, he may no doubt in time be a great acquisition to the Society. In short, as to religious quotations, I think they are highly prejudicial to this Society, as it affords an opportunity to Administration, and their emissaries (who often meet with deserved and severe censure) to ridicule the same as an assembly of religious madmen and fanatics. I therefore hope what I have said will be taken in good part; and if respect is paid to the hint, it will oblige

AMICUS SOCIETATIS

218. September 10, 1778 Coach-Makers Hall Society
'Does not the awful situation of public affairs require that the people should form themselves into associations for the preservation of their rights and privileges?'
Gazetteer

219. September 11, 1778 Society for Free and Candid Debate, Queen's Arms
'Are the indulgences lately granted to the Roman Catholics of these kingdoms consistent with the safety thereof, as a Protestant Church and State?
After a very able and full discussion, was carried in the affirmative.'
Gazetteer

220. September 11, 1778 Gazetteer
'To the Editor of the Gazetteer
Give me leave, through the channel of your useful paper, to congratulate the lovers of rational entertainment, on the revival of the debating society, at the Queens Arms, in Newgate Street. I was present on Friday evening last, and much pleased was I to observe so numerous an audience assembled, for the laudable purpose of edifying each other, by a search after truth. The question (which related to the indulgence lately granted by Parliament to the Roman Catholics of this kingdom) was

40

discussed with the greatest candour and ingenuity by several gentlemen, long and well known in the society for their eminent abilities as to sound knowledge and real argument. Some new and juvenile speakers made their first essay, and were received with all that warmth of applause which is so fostering to the budding genius, and for which the society has always been remarkable, from its early institution to the present time.

Societies of this kind, Sir, I need not inform you, are certainly beneficial to mankind, if managed upon candid and liberal principles; but when the original intent of them becomes perverted, when, instead of solid and rational argument, detraction and scandal against our superiors takes place, they not only become hurtful to individuals, but prove dangerous enemies to the state. I am by no means, Sir, averse to *freedom* of debate, when confined within the proper limits of decorum; nor should I have been led to the preceding reflection, but that I have my eye on a certain society of the same nature, not a mile from Foster-lane, where the most abandoned political doctrines are frequently broached, which cannot fail (particularly at the present crisis) to have a bad effect on the minds of the weaker part of the audience. This too is done without any sort of restraint; for if a person happens to differ in opinion from these high and mighty advocates for *liberty*, he is treated with a degree of illiberality unbecoming an assembly of sensible beings . . .

MODERATOR

221. September 14, 1778 Robin Hood
'Whether all real Antigallicans (if consistent) ought not now to be Anti-Americans? and, Whether the delaying a declaration of war against France has been prudent and political conduct on the part of Great Britain?'
The room and lights much improved.
Both Questions went in the affirmative.
Morning Chronicle

222. September 17, 1778 Coach-Makers-Hall Society
'Does a servile compliance with the reigning fashions of the times, or an obstinate singularity in opposition to them, constitute the more contemptible character?'
Gazetteer

223. September 18, 1778 Debating Society, Queen's Arms Tavern, Newgate Street
'Can the propositions made on this part of Great Britain, by her Commissioners, to the American Congress, be deemed a reasonable ground for reconciliation?'
Gazetteer

224. September 21, 1778 Robin Hood
'Would not America enjoy more civil and religious liberty under French government, than under that of the dominion of a Congress, or any

41

other form of government of their own people? And Whether granting a pension to the heirs of Lord Chatham, doth not reflect an honour on the present House of Commons? and Whether laws, enjoining some positive duties, and forbidding things not morally bad, are binding in conscience?'
The first Question 'went (after a strong and ingenious debate) in the negative'.
Morning Chronicle

225. September 24, 1778 Coachmakers-Hall Society
'Can any Act of united Legislature of this Country be denominated unconstitutional?'
Gazetteer

226. September 28, 1778 Robin Hood
'Whether granting a pension to the heirs of the late Lord Chatham, doth not redound of the British Parliament?'
Question 'went in the affirmative. Several speakers offered arguments on the negative side, but the hands were nearly unanimous as above.'
Morning Chronicle

227. October 1, 1778 Coachmakers-Hall Society
'Which is the best adapted to the Culture of the Arts and Sciences, a Monarchy or a Republick?'
Gazetteer September 30

228. October 5, 1778 Robin Hood
'Whether monopolizing or underselling of the necessaries of life is more blameable in a tradesman? And, Whether such laws as enjoy certain duties (game laws, &c.) and prohibit actions not really evil, are binding on conscience?'
The second question 'went in the affirmative'; the first 'went against the monopolizers. Then was debated the question, Whether the agreement betwixt the managers of the winter theatres, reciprocally to employ each other's performers, will promote the interests of the drama in general? was began and adjourned.'
Morning Chronicle

229. October 8, 1778 Coachmakers-Hall Society
'Has France, by entering into a treaty with the Americans, violated the law of nations?'
Gazetteer

230. October 9, 1778 Society for Free Debate, Queen's Arms, Newgate Street
'Which are the most excellent, those talents that are the effect of study and application; or those which result from nature alone? And, Can the American insurgency be justified upon Christian principles?'
Admittance 4d. each person.
Gazetteer

231. October 12, 1778 Robin Hood
'Whether the agreement betwixt the managers of the winter theatres, reciprocally to employ each other's performers, will promote the interests of the drama in general?
The Question, Whether the Love of the Fair Sex, hath not been one of the greatest inducements to heroic actions? went in the affirmative.'
The other question went in the negative.
Morning Chronicle

232. October 15, 1778 Coachmakers-Hall Society
'Does the force of Love excite more to noble or ignoble actions?'
Gazetteer

233. October 16, 1778 Society for Free Debate, Queen's Arm Tavern
'Are not the arbitrary laws by which the soldiery of England are governed, dangerous to British liberties? and, Can the American insurgency be justified on Christian principles?'
Gazetteer

234. October 19, 1778 Robin Hood
'Whether referring a political controversy between states, to a decision by the sword, is properly called an appeal to Heaven? And, Whether insuring the ships of an open enemy, is not a nefarious and impolitic practice?'
The first Question 'went in the negative. The other question . . . was began, and after some spirited debated, adjourned.'
Morning Chronicle

235. October 22, 1778 Coachmakers-Hall Society
'Is it Policy in a State to suffer its Subjects to insure the Property of an Enemy in a Time of War?'
Gazetteer

236. October 23, 1778 Society for Free Debate, Queen's arms, Newgate Street
'Are not the severe laws by which the soldiery of England are governed, dangerous to British Liberty? and, Ought Great Britain to give up the dependency of America, or declare war with France?'
Gazetteer

237. October 26, 1778 Robin Hood
'Whether insuring the ships of an open enemy, is not a nefarious and impolitic practice? and, Whether a dissolution of the present Parliament, immediately after their next meeting, would not be a salutary measure?'
The first Question 'went in the affirmative; though many ingenious sentiments were offered on the contrary side of the argument'. The second

question 'was debated in a candid, though spirited manner, and went in the negative'.
Morning Chronicle

238. October 29, 1778 Coachmakers-Hall Society
'Which is the more excellent form of government, a Monarchy or a Republic?'
Gazetteer

239. November 2, 1778 Robin Hood
'Whether the commercial returns into the ports of Great Britain do not compensate for the late extraordinary and expensive armaments? and, Whether a steady or a flexible temper is productive of more happiness to the possessor? and, Whether a lately deceased Earl did not treat with a certain person for an appointment in administration?'
Morning Chronicle

240. November 5, 1778 Coachmakers-Hall Society
'Is not Beauty, in general, a greater source of misfortune than advantage to the female sex?'
Gazetteer

241. November 9, 1778 Robin Hood
'Whether virtue is more conspicuous in prosperity or adversity? and, Whether any degree of ill-treatment from a husband to a wife, can justify the latter in defiling the marriage-bed?'
The first Question 'was determined, that it was more conspicuous in adversity'. The second question 'was debated for some time, when the speakers being undetermined on the point, desired an adjournment'.
Morning Chronicle November 16

242. November 12, 1778 Coachmakers-Hall Society
'Would it not be more conducive to the happiness of mankind, that one form of government should universally prevail, rather than different nations should be governed by different forms?'
Gazetteer

243. November 16, 1778 Robin Hood
'Whether Lord C—m did court a negotiation with Lord B—e for an appointment in administration &c.? and, Whether it is not now become necessary to declare war against France?'
The first Question 'went in the negative. The most elaborate speaking was on the Wright side of the question, but the division was on the Addington side.'
Morning Chronicle

244. November 23, 1778 Robin Hood
'Whether the punishment for treason, which forfeit from children the estates of their ancestors, is not too severe?'
Morning Chronicle

245. November 26, 1778 Coachmakers Hall
'Is the opinion of Soame Jenyns, founded in truth, that patriotism and friendship are not of the nature of true virtues?'
Gazetteer November 23

246. November 30, 1778 Robin Hood
'Whether punishing of treason, by forfeiture of estates from posterity, is in a political light too severe?'
Question 'went in the affirmative'.
Morning Chronicle December 7

247. December 3, 1778 Coach-makers Hall
'Is not the refusal of Congress to treat with his Majesty's Commissioners a demonstration that they would rather sacrifice the real happiness of America, than give up hope of aggrandizing themselves?'
Gazetteer December 1

248. December 7, 1778 Robin Hood
'Which tends more to improvement of the head and heart, a public or private education? and, Whether an extreme rigorous war of short duration, is not more humane on the whole, than a lenient long one?'
Second Question 'went in the affirmative by a great majority'.
Morning Chronicle

249. December 10, 1778 Coach-makers Hall
'Is not the refusal of Congress to treat with his Majesty's Commissioners a demonstration that they would rather sacrifice the real happiness of America, than give up hope of aggrandizing themselves?'
Gazetteer December 8

250. December 11, 1778 Society for Free Debate, Queens Arms, Newgate Street
'Can any man be a friend to Great Britain who wishes the Independency of her American Colonies?'
Gazetteer

251. December 14, 1778 Robin Hood
'Whether it is proper in this country that a judge should sit in a legislative capacity in the House of Peers? and, Whether the common rights of war are not due to even (supposed) rebels?'
The first Question 'went in the affirmative'; the other, 'debated with spirit, candour, and ingenuity till past ten' was adjourned.
Morning Chronicle

252. December 17, 1778 Coach-makers Hall

'Is not the refusal of Congress to treat with his Majesty's Commissioners a demonstration that they would rather sacrifice the real happiness of America, than give up hope of aggrandizing themselves?'
Gazetteer December 15

253. December 21, 1778 Robin Hood
'Whether the common rights of war are not due to even (supposed) rebels? and, Whether the freedom with which public characters and measures are treated and investigated in this country, is a proof of the vigour, or of the decline of our constitution?'
First Question 'went in the affirmative'; second question 'was very warmly debated, and by vote adjourned'.
Morning Chronicle

254. December 24, 1778 Coach-makers Hall
'Is not the neglect to punish duelling in the most exemplary manner a severe reflection on the humanity and justice of civilized states?'
Gazetteer December 22

255. December 28, 1778 Robin Hood
'Whether the freedom with which public characters and measures are treated and investigated in this country, is a proof of the vigour, or of the decline of our constitution?'
Question resolved that this freedom was a proof of vigour.
Morning Chronicle

256. December 31, 1778 Coach-makers Hall
'Would it be consistent with good policy, in the present crisis, to promote a public enquiry into the state of the nation?'
Gazetteer December 29

257. January 2, 1779 Morning Chronicle
'To the Directors of the Society at Coachmakers Hall
Gentlemen,
Being a frequenter of your respectable body, and ever willing to promote an institution from which I have received so much entertainment and improvement, I shall beg leave to propose a question for your discussion, which I doubt not, will be argued in that society in that able manner for which the society is so famous!
Q. Which causes the greatest commotion in the intestines, a purge or a vomit?
I am, Gentlemen,
Your very obedient servant,
W. BEAVER'

258. January 4, 1779 Robin Hood
'Whether the warrant issued by the Lords of the Treasury, respecting the Principality of Wales, will not *unconstitutionally* affect the landed property of that country? and, Whether abundant modesty or abundant

46

assurance is the most likely to promote a man's interest in the world?' The first Question 'went in the negative. The question lingered some time, as if thought not worthy attention; however somewhat late in the even it was debated with spirit, and carried as above by one vote.' Morning Chronicle

259. January 7, 1779 Coach-Makers-Hall
'Is not taste founded in certain and fixed principles?'
Gazetteer January 5

260. January 11, 1779 Robin Hood
'Whether a Member of the House of Commons publishing in a common newspaper, a charge of embezzlement, against the officers of the state, doth not act in an unparliamentary and improper manner? and, Would not a critical enquiry into the political state of this nation, be a very proper measure immediately on the meeting of Parliament?'
The Question 'was very warmly debated, and at last passed in the negative'.
Morning Chronicle

261. January 14, 1779 Coachmakers Hall
'Is not the continuation of the present Ministry, in this dangerous crisis, a proof that they would rather sacrifice the true happiness of this country, than give up the power of aggrandizing themselves?'
Gazetteer January 12

262. January 15, 1779 Society for Free Debate, Queen's Arms, Newgate Street
'Were the Passions given to govern Reason, or Reason to govern the Passions? and, Which was the greater Blessing to this Nation, the Restoration or the Revolution?
In consequence of an unanimous resolution of the company last Friday, the price of admittance in future will be Six-pence, the former sum being found inadequate to the expence.'
Gazetteer

263. January 18, 1779 Robin Hood
'Whether a critical enquiry into the political state of the nation ought not to be one of the first objects of Parliamentary business on their return from their late recess? and, Whether that *Judge* who requires a witness to give an opinion, after giving his evidence in a cause, acts with official propriety?'
The debate on the second Question 'went in the negative almost *nem. con.* The next question "Whether a desire (or affectation) of popularity, hath been more favourable or prejudicial to liberty in this country?" was began and adjourned.'
Morning Chronicle

264. January 21, 1779 Coach-maker's Hall

'Is not the continuation of the present Ministry, in this dangerous crisis, a proof that they would rather sacrifice the real happiness of their country, than give up the power of aggrandizing themselves?'
Gazetteer January 19

265. January 22, 1779 Society for Free Debate, Queen's-arms, Newgate Street
'From whence arises the fearful apprehensions of Death? and, Are not those who make Sunday a day of pleasure, enemies to civil society?'
Gazetteer

266. January 25, 1779 Robin Hood
'Whether the desire of popularity has been more favourable or unfavourable to the cause of Liberty? and, Whether those Martial Judges, who publickly disavow a respect to established law, are not objects of publick censure?'
The first Question 'went that it had been unfavourable'; the second question 'was entered on, and adjourned'.
Morning Chronicle

267. January 28, 1779 Coachmakers Hall
'Are theatrical Representations more favourable or unfavourable to the Cause of Virtue?'
Gazetteer January 26

268. January 29, 1779 Society for Free Debate, Queen's-arms
(The First Institution of the Kind)
'Is Parliament constitutionally authorized to pass acts to compel men into his Majesty's service?
The greatest attention will be paid to the accommodation of those gentlemen with refreshments who honour the Society with their company, and the strictest impartiality observed in conducting the debates.'
Gazetteer

269. February 1, 1779 Robin Hood
'Whether a late celebrated actor was more eminent in Tragedy or Comedy?
The questions on course were dropped, the company was exceedingly respectable; but not inclined to debate. . . A question was introduced "Whether the great honours and applause paid to a deceased player was proof of an increase or decline of publick virtue?" was started and argued, and went in favour of the character in question.'
Morning Chronicle

270. February 4, 1779 Coachmaker's Hall
'Has a British King more to fear from the flattery of his courtiers, or the opposition of parties?'
Gazetteer February 2

271. February 5, 1779 Society for Free Debate, Queen's-Arms
'Whether the Libertine or the Enthusiast is most hurtful to religion?'
Gazetteer

272. February 8, 1779 Robin Hood
'Whether that Martial Judge who avows a disregard to established law, is not an object of public censure? and, Whether a late celebrated actor was more eminent in Tragedy or Comedy?'
Second Question 'went for tragedy. The other question "Whether it is for the interest of this nation that placemen and pensioners should sit in the House of Commons?" went in the negative.'
Morning Chronicle

273. February 11, 1779 Coachmakers Hall
'Whether does hereditary or elective monarchies conduce most to the happiness of a state?'
Gazetteer February 9

274. February 12, 1779 Society for Free Debate, Queen's-Arms
'What are the differences between Wit, Humour and Ridicule?'
Gazetteer

275. February 15, 1779 Robin Hood
'Whether a state of extreme rusticity, or extreme refinement, is the most advantageous to human beings? and, Whether the appointments of general fasts, or general illuminations, are attended with the most evil consequences?'
Question 'respecting rusticity and refinement, was superceded by the question "Whether a certain Vice Admiral, after bringing a false and malicious charge, &c. &c. ought not himself to be tried for disobedience of orders"; which question went, (saving one hand) *nem. con.* in the affirmative.' The first Question was resumed, and 'went in favour of refinement'.
Morning Chronicle

276. February 18, 1779 Coachmakers Hall
'Does not so malicious and ill-grounded an accusation as that against Admiral Keppel demand the strictest investigation, that the accuser and his abettors may, if possible, be brought to justice?'
Gazetteer February 16

277. February 19, 1779 Society for Free Debate, Queen's-Arms
'Is Parliament constitutionally authorized to pass an act to compel men into his Majesty's service?'
Gazetteer

278. February 22, 1779 Robin Hood
'Whether general fasts, or general illuminations, are attended with the most evil consequences? and, Whether from the similar conduct of dif-

49

ferent parties when in power, we have any reason to suppose their principles are essentially different?'
Morning Chronicle

279. February 25, 1779 Coachmakers Hall
'Does not so malicious and ill-founded an accusation as that against Admiral Keppel, demand the strictest investigation, that the accuser and his abettors may if possible be brought to justice?'
Gazetteer February 23

280. February 26, 1779 Society for Free Debate, Queen's-Arms
'Does it not appear that the Minority are at present making use of a private quarrel to inflame the public?'
Gazetteer

281. March 2, 1779 Literary Society For Free Debate, Three Kings in the Minories
'Have we any reason to suppose, from the similar conduct of opposition parties, (when in power) that their principles are essentially different?'
Admission 6d.
Morning Chronicle

282. March 4, 1779 Coachmakers Hall
'Which of the two principles of human action is the most forcible: the dread of evil, or the prospect of good?'
Gazetteer March 2

283. March 5, 1779 Society for Free Debate, Queen's-Arms
'Did the conduct of the Courtmartial lately held on Admiral Keppel, deserve the thanks of the people of England?'
Gazetteer

284. March 11, 1779 Coachmakers Hall
'Is the supreme magistrate of a free country justifiable in continuing in office any set of men contrary to the general sense and known wishes of the nation?'
Gazetteer March 9

285. March 12, 1779 Society for Free Debate, Queen's-Arms
'Whether does moderation in prosperity, or magnanimity in adversity, discover most greatness of soul?'
Gazetteer

286. March 15, 1779 Robin Hood
'Whether Whigs in Opposition do not become Tories, and *visa versa?*'
The Question 'was argued, but not determined' and is adjourned.
Morning Chronicle March 22

287. March 18, 1779 Coachmakers Hall

'If the present Ministers were dismissed from the conduct of affairs, is it probable the nation would be benefited by the change?'
Gazetteer March 16

288. March 19, 1779 Society for Free Debate, Queen's-Arms
'Is the taking away a citizen's vote, upon his receiving alms under casual necessities, consistent with a free constitution? and, There being some vacancies upon Temple Bar; whose heads are most proper to fill them?'
Gazetteer

289. March 22, 1779 Robin Hood
'Whether Whigs in Opposition do not become Tories, and *visa versa?* and, Whether popular tumults, are not necessary in a popular state, in order to reduce it to its first principles? and, Whether civil and religious liberty, are more secure under the American Congress, than the British Government?
The questions on course lingered, on account of the absence of the proposers; then a question was offered in, accepted, and warmly debated, viz. "Whether the conduct of a certain Admiral in declining to serve against the common enemy, unless the Sovereign dismissed the first Lord of the Admiralty, is not dangerous and presumptuous?" which question went almost *nem. con.* in the affirmative.'
Morning Chronicle

290. March 25, 1779 Coachmakers Hall
'If the present Ministers were dismissed from the conduct of affairs, is it probable the nation would be benefited by the change?'
Gazetteer March 23

291. March 26, 1779 Society for Free Debate, Queen's-Arms
'Does a free investigation of the constitution of this country, tend to weaken the executive power?'
Gazetteer

292. March 29, 1779 Robin Hood
'Whether the Americans have now any right to the terms tendered to them last year by the English Commissioners? and, Whether popular tumults are not necessary in a popular state to reduce the constitution thereof to its first principles?'
The first Question 'went hollow in the negative'.
Morning Chronicle

293. March 30, 1779 Lyceum for the Investigation of Historical, Political, Literary and Theological Subjects, Black Horse, New Bond Street
'Are Theological matters proper subjects for the investigation in Societies of this kind? And, if time permit . . . Are the Laws of Scotland against Roman Catholicks, consistent with Civil and Religious Liberty?'
Admittance 6d.
Morning Chronicle

294. April 1, 1779 Coachmakers Hall
'Is the system of education generally practiced in this nation, more favourable or unfavourable to liberty?'
Gazetteer March 30

295. April 3, 1779 Morning Chronicle
'Mr. Macklin, the stage veteran, was unmercifully abused on Thursday night at Coach-maker's-hall, by a young prig, who fell upon the old man *pell mell*, to the disgrace of the Chairman, who should have checked such a flow of abuse without a shadow of argument. Mr. Macklin, in speaking to the question told a humourous story of a voter between a lawyer and his parson, and in his reply said the young gentleman had laughed at his lawyer and a parson, but he would not laught at *him*. The force of the retort was felt by every part of the audience.'

296. April 5, 1779 Robin Hood
'Whether popular tumults are not necessary in a popular state to reduce the constitution thereof to its first principles? and, Would not a law to *compel* convicted adulterers to marry each other (after divorce from former ties being obtained) tend, upon the whole, to prevent *crim. con.* more than a law to hinder such marriages?'
The first Question 'went in the affirmative'.
Morning Chronicle

297. April 6, 1779 The Lyceum, Black Horse, New Bond Street
'Are the Laws of Scotland against the Roman Catholics, consistent with Civil Liberty? and, Is Great Britain obliged, at this time, to abide by the terms offered by the Commissioners on her part to the Americans last year, as they have rejected the same?'
Morning Chronicle

298. April 8, 1779 Coachmakers Hall
'Was the conduct of Admiral Keppel justifiable in not accepting the command of the fleet?'
Gazetteer April 6

299. April 10, 1779 Morning Chronicle
'At Coachmakers Hall, on Thursday evening, a gentleman moved the previous question before the debate commenced, 'Whether Admiral Keppel *was* justifiable in not *accepting* the command of the fleet'. The gentleman who made the objection said, that until there was evidence of an *offer* to the Admiral, he could not perceive how in point of reason or propriety, he could be charged with *refusing* the command, as the reports so confidently believed, that Administration had requested him to head the navy, were contradicted with an authority that seemed to come from the Admiralty, or his friends, and no reply had been made, therefore the question ought not to be put. A gentleman who opposed the objection, rested himself on a single observation, which rather strengthened than weakened the force of the motion for the previous

question; he relied on the declaration of the Admiral in Parliament, that he never would serve whilst the present ministry held the reins of government, which was the best reason to suppose, that after such an avowal of his sentiments administration would not make him an *offer* to meet with a contemptuous refusal. But the Chairman, without answering a tittle of the objection, or the reasons adduced in support of it, told the mover he was too late, and that the question must be discussed according to the rules of the society. The gentleman attempted to reply, but was interrupted, and the question was proceeded on under the idea of a *refusal* to serve on the part of Admiral Keppel, without even a bare assertion in the whole course of the debate to support the fact alledged in the question, which was carried in the affirmative by an almost unanimous shew of hands.'

300. April 12, 1779 Robin Hood
'Whether a law to *compel* the parties in adultery, &c. to marry each other would not tend more to prevent *crim. con.* in the *beau monde* than a certain Bishop's proposed law to hinder such marriages? And, Is the bringing a man to trial upon matter arising in a previous trial, and without a particular prosecutor, a *judicious* proceeding?'
Both Questions 'waved through want of proposers presence, but will be resumed'.
Morning Chronicle

301. April 13, 1779 Lyceum, Black Horse, New Bond Street
'Is Great Britain obliged, at all future times to abide by the terms offered by the Commissioners on her part to the Americans last year? and, Were the Lords of the Admiralty justifiable in granting a Court-Martial on Admiral Keppel, on the charge of Sir Hugh Palliser?'
Morning Chronicle

302. April 15, 1779 Coachmakers Hall
'Which is most likely to produce happiness, the nice feelings of extreme sensibility, or the apathy of cold indifference?'
Gazetteer April 13

303. April 19, 1779 Robin Hood
'Whether a law to compel persons convicted of Adultery, to marry each other, &c. would not tend more to prevent that crime, than the depending bill to hinder such marriages? and Whether the trial of a certain Vice Admiral, without a particular prosecutor, is not an injudicious proceeding &c.?'
Questions superseded by 'Whether the conduct of a noble *Lord in high office*, respecting a late Lieutenant-Governor of a certain Hospital, is defensible?' 'The question was introduced by a gentleman rather a stranger to the society, who, to prevent silence, &c. desired the President to take one side, and he would take the other; so the President, to promote debate, adopted the cause of Capt. B. and the gentleman very

ably defended Lord S.; after which, at ten o'clock, the question was, by vote, adjourned.'
Morning Chronicle

304. April 22, 1779 Coachmakers Hall
'Does not the power vested in the Sovereign of this country to pardon criminals after they are convicted, shew a deficiency in our laws? [Hackman case]'
Gazetteer April 21

305. April 26, 1779 Robin Hood
'Whether the conduct of a noble *Lord in high office*, respecting a late Lieutenant-Governor of a certain Hospital, is defensible?'
The Question 'was debated some time, but a decision waved till the noble Lord should make his defence, so that question remains postponed'.
Morning Chronicle

306. April 29, 1779 Coachmakers Hall
'Is eloquence more favourable or unfavourable to the cause of truth?'
Gazetteer April 27

307. May 3, 1779 Robin Hood
'Whether a strict Parliamentary enquiry into the conduct of a late Commander in Chief in America is not necessary at this juncture?'
Question 'went in the affirmative'.
Morning Chronicle

308. May 6, 1779 Coachmakers Hall
'Are the Americans, having refused the terms offered them in the late commission, now entitled to the same?'
Gazetteer May 4

309. May 10, 1779 Robin Hood
'Whether the vote of the House, &c., to address the Crown to direct a prosecution against Mr. S—n, and others, respecting the death of Ld. Pigot, was constitutionally justifiable?'
Morning Chronicle

310. May 13, 1779 Coachmakers Hall
'Is it probable that the leniency shewn to the Roman Catholics will be advantageous to this kingdom?'
Gazetteer May 11

311. May 17, 1779 Robin Hood
'Whether a certain Admiral was strictly justifiable, in deviating from his destination, to go to the relief of a distressed island?'
The Question was 'very freely, ingeniously, and candidly debated for some time' and then adjourned.
Morning Chronicle May 24

312. May 20, 1779 Coachmakers Hall
'Has not that custom which precludes a virtuous woman from making the first overtures for a matrimonial union to the man she loves, originated in false delicacy?'
Gazetteer May 18

313. May 24, 1779 Robin Hood
'Can the relaxations in the laws respecting Roman Catholics, be of any advantage to the community at large in this Protestant country?'
Morning Chronicle

314. May 27, 1779 Coachmakers Hall
'Is it consistent with public freedom, that the power of making peace and war should be vested in the Crown?'
Gazetteer May 25

315. June 3, 1779 Coachmakers Hall
'Has the House of Lords acted constitutionally in committing the printer of the General Advertiser to prison for an unlimited time, on the charge alleged against him?'
Gazetteer June 1

316. June 10, 1779 Coachmakers Hall
'Whether the various public charities in and about London, yield greater hope to desponding virtue or encouragement to profligacy of manners?'
Gazetteer June 8

317. June 10, 1779 Morning Chronicle
'The following question is proposed for this evening, at Coachmakers Hall, viz. Whether Sir Alexander Leith, in his capacity as one of the legislative body, can be justified, either to his constituents or the public at large, in perverting the course of justice against a most attrocious violator of private peace, by accepting any private compensation as a satisfaction for the injury he sustained in being arraigned and tried for his life, at the Old Bailey, on a charge which the Judges declared groundless and malicious, and how far a jury, in their award of damages, ought to distinguish between a private and a public character.'

318. June 17, 1779 Coachmakers Hall
'Is it not become the duty of the Minority to secede from Parliament, and form associations for the public good?'
Gazetteer June 15

319. September 2, 1779 Coachmakers Hall
'Ought not every Englishmen, especially in these alarming times, to learn the use of arms?'
Gazetteer August 31

320. September 2, 1779 Gazetteer
To the Gentlemen of the Society for free Debate, Coachmaker's-Hall
Gentlemen,
As all societies of the nature of yours, are, when properly conducted, of advantage to society, so, when improperly conducted, they are a detriment to it. It is for this reason, gentlemen, that I trouble you with this letter. I cannot sufficiently admire your plan of excluding all questions concerning religion; and I think there is but one objection to be made to your present mode of chusing your questions, which is, that there are more questions on politics than on all other subjects together; which I object to for these reasons: 1st. That the time thus spent might be employed to better advantage, by debating on historical and moral subjects, by which the minds of young men would be improved, instead of being distracted with politics. 2nd. Because when men talk about politics, they seldom argue so reasonably and coolly as upon other subjects: most men talk as their interest leads them, very few as they think. And supposing this was not the case, what improvement can be derived from it? or what good to the nation? For a Ministry who has disregarded every argument that has been used in the Senate, will never submit to your resolves. In hopes you will pay some attention to this, I subscribe myself,
Gentlemen, your humble servant
W.R.

321. September 5, 1779 Theological Society, One Tun, near Hungerford, Strand
'A Text of Scripture, taken from the 5th chapter of St. Matthew, verses 10, 11 [will be investigated] which will lead to an enquiry relative to the propriety of Religious Persecution.'
Admittance 6d. each person.
Gazetteer September 3

322. September 9, 1779 Coachmakers Hall
'Whether it is the interest of the maritime powers of Europe to assist America in her present contest for independence?'
Gazetteer September 7

323. September 16, 1779 Coachmakers Hall
'Does the City of London, in withholding their assistance in the present alarming crisis, act upon principles of true patriotism?'
Gazetteer September 14

324. September 20, 1779 Westminster Forum, Greenwood's Great Room, Haymarket
'Whether the charge against the Members of Opposition of endeavouring to foment the rebellion in America, to answer the personal views of power, emolument, and ambition, can be supported upon principles of truth and justice?

Whereas, a Society for the purpose of discussing such questions as may afford both instruction and entertainment, upon genteel and liberal principles, has long been desired and requested by many gentlemen of distinction and character, who reside at the west-end of the town.'
Morning Chronicle

325. September 27, 1779 Westminster Forum
'Whether it is not the duty of every good subject, in the present critical state of the empire, to unite for the defence of the empire at large, by a dutiful and loyal representation humbly to implore his Majesty to withdraw his troops from America, in order to regain the valuable commerce of that country?
As many gentlemen who attended the meeting on Monday night last made objections to the regulations which then took place, this is to inform the public, that for the future it will be conducted on the same plan as the society at Coach-maker's-hall.'
Morning Chronicle September 25

326. September 30, 1779 Coachmakers Hall
'Would not a tax on Jews be a very proper measure in the present urgency of affairs?'
Gazetteer September 28

327. October 1, 1779 Gazetteer
'On Thursday last, when the grand question was debated at Coachmaker's-hall, whether the City of London acted properly or improperly in refusing, at the present juncture of public affairs, to strengthen the hands of the present Ministry, a Common-Councilman who happened to be present rose in great warmth, and observed, "that the City of London was the most respectable body of men in the universe. That gentlemen were very impertinent in talking of London following the example of such petty boroughs as Glasgow and Manchester. London was born not to follow, but to give examples". . . .'

328. October 4, 1779 Westminster Forum
'Whether the present mode adopted by the Ministry, of carrying on the war, by burning and destroying towns, &c. in America, is not more likely to create eternal enmity, than a reconciliation with the Colonies?'
Short History of the Westminster Forum

329. October 7, 1779 Coachmakers Hall
'Will it not be more to the advantage of this country in the present to make peace with the Americans on the terms of independence, than to risk the consequences of continuing the war?'
Gazetteer October 5

330. October 9, 1779 Revived (Robin Hood) Society
'At the King's Arms tavern, and Gentlemen's Hotel, next door to the Hummums, Convent-Garden . . . will be opened a society for free

debate, exactly on the plan of the late Robin Hood, Butcher-row, viz. Admittance 6d. liquours included. – The total banishment of beverage has been much complained of by many respectable attendants on these kind of societies; and the situation of the King's Arms being so convenient to gentlemen disappointed on the theatres being crouded, &c. &c. it is presumed will apologize for the above institution, and procure it respectable countenance and support.'
Morning Chronicle

331. October 11, 1779 Westminster Forum
'Whether publick or private education is the best calculated to form a man for society?'
Public education won by four votes.
Morning Chronicle October 7/Short History of the Westminster Forum

332. October 11, 1779 King's-arms society
'Whether it would be more eligible, at this crisis, for Great Britain to acknowledge the independence of the Colonies, or carry on the war to recover the sovereignty thereof?'
The Question 'was very ingeniously debated, and went by a great majority for war'.
Morning Chronicle

333. October 14, 1779 Coachmakers Hall
'Whether would an union between Ireland and Great Britain be for the general advantage?'
Gazetteer October 12

334. October 18, 1779 Westminster Forum
'Is refinement of manners to be considered as being most conducive to virtue or vice?'
Majority said most conducive to virtue.
Morning Chronicle October 14/Short History of the Westminster

335. October 18, 1779 King's Arms society
'Whether augmenting the requisite pecuniary qualifications of representatives in Parliament, and of constituents also, would not procure a more independent House of Commons?
A question is this evening expected (from a gentleman's promise) relating to the theatre. – N.B. Questions on the Drama, will be frequently and regularly admitted.'
Morning Chronicle

336. October 21, 1779 Coachmakers Hall
'To whom are we to attribute the true cause of our national calamities, Ministry or Opposition?'
Gazetteer October 19

337. October 22, 1779 Apollo Society, for the determination of all Questions in History, Literature, Policy and Theology, Kings Arms Tavern, Grafton Street, Soho
'Should not the Freeholders of the County of Middlesex, consistent with their political conduct, support the pretensions of Mr. Wood, in opposition to Colonel Tufnell? and, To which ought we to attribute the present alarming crisis; want of spirit and capacity in our ministers, or military officers? and, Is the charge of idolatry, against the Roman church, founded in justice, charity, and equity?'
Admittance six-pence.
Morning Chronicle

338. October 23, 1779 Select Society, Old Theatre, Portugal Street
'Whether the conduct of the Minister, in withholding from one Gentleman, and granting to another, the opportunity of vacating his seat in Parliament, they both having declared to him their intention of standing Candidates for another place, is or is not injurious to the right of free Representation?
The early attendance of the Friends of Freedom, Literature and Virtue, will be esteemed a favour.'
Morning Chronicle

339. October 25, 1779 Westminster Forum
'Can the conduct of a Minister, in preventing a gentleman from vacating his seat, with intention of becoming a candidate for another place, be warranted by the constitution, when he assigns as the reason that he hath given an absolute promise to another?'
Against Minister by a great majority.
Morning Chronicle October 21/Short History of the Westminster

340. October 25, 1779 King's Arms Society
'What will be the consequences of the unnatural union of winter theatres?'
The first Question was postponed, 'for want of some person to own, explain and introduce it . . . Then the question, Whether it is not apparent that France aims at erecting a Gallic Empire in America? went in the negative.'
Morning Chronicle November 1

341. October 28, 1779 Coachmakers Hall
'Is the slave trade justifiable?'
Gazetteer October 26

342. October 29, 1779 Apollo Society, King's Arms Tavern, Graftonstreet, Soho, for the *discussion* of all questions in History, Literature, Policy and Theology
'To which ought we to attribute the present alarming crisis, want of spirit and capacity in our Ministers, or military Officers?

59

Lemonade and Porter for those who chuse to refresh themselves in an adjacent room.'
Morning Chronicle October 27

343. November 1, 1779 Westminster Forum
'Can a member of a Commonwealth, alienate himself therefrom, and regain the liberty of the state of nature, upon the laws of natural justice? or Is a union with Ireland, somewhat similar to that with Scotland, to be wished; and, as things are now situated, would it be for the mutual interest of Great Britain and Ireland?'
Adjourned.
Morning Chronicle October 28/A Short History of the Westminster

344. November 1, 1779 King's Arms Society
'Whether it is politically necessary, that an opposition should always exist in a Government like that of Great Britain?'
Question 'was very ingeniously argued, and went in the negative'.
Morning Chronicle

345. November 2, 1779 The Lyceum for the Investigation of all Questions in HISTORY, POLICY and LITERATURE, Black Horse Tavern, New Bond Street
'Is not the conduct of the Irish Parliament, at this time, ungenerous and unjust? and, Is the present method of carrying on the American war, in a depredatory manner, likely to bring that people back to their allegiance?'
Gazetteer

346. November 3, 1779 Select Society, Old Theatre, Portugal-street, Lincoln's-inn Fields
'Whether the conduct of the City of London with respect to Mr. Wilkes, is, or is not reprehensible?'
Admission Six-pence.
Morning Chronicle

347. November 4, 1779 Coachmakers Hall
'Whether, considering the manners of the present age, a single or a married life is most likely to produce happiness?'
Gazetteer November 2

348. November 5, 1779 Apollo Society
'Whether not a union between Great Britain and Ireland be the best mode of redressing the grievances of that country, and securing this?'
Morning Chronicle November 4

349. November 8, 17779 Westminster Forum
'Is a closer union with Ireland, somewhat similar to that with Scotland, to be wished, and as things are now situate[d], would it be for the mutual interest of Great Britain and Ireland?'

Carried in favour of free trade and against union.
Morning Chronicle November 4/A Short History of the Westminster

350. November 8, 1779 King's Arms (or new Robin Hood) Society
'Whether smuggling is not as great an evil as robbery, when considered in its effects upon commerce and the community?
There are now no less [than] six advertising disputing societies in this metropolis, besides some smaller ones who do not advertise; – 'tis remarkable that those of them which admit ladies, allow no liquour; and those who allow liquour, admit no ladies; there is one indeed, in the Strand, which admits both ladies and liquour, all for four pence; but that is for religion – the cheapest of all subjects.'
The first Question 'passed in the negative, – as did also, Whether the passion of love can exist for more than one object at the same time?'
Morning Chronicle

351. November 9, 1779 Lyceum, Black Horse
'Is the present mode of carrying on the war in America likely to bring that people back to their allegiance?'
Gazetteer

352. November 10, 1779 Morning Chronicle
'A correspondent, under the signature of Dubious, desires that some of our readers would propose the following question at Coach-maker's Hall: – In which did Mr. Garrick display the *greatest* excellence – in tragedy or comedy?'

353. November 11, 1779 Morning Chronicle
'As the disputing societies are within a few months much encreased, they are intended the next session to constitute part of the Premier's budget; a license must be taken out by every person letting a room for the discussion of political, moral, or religious questions, and for which they are to pay 500l. to the Government.
A person who was present a few nights since at the Westminster Forum, in the Haymarket, was asked by his friend what he thought of it, "a little snug hot house for sedition", replied the other.'

354. November 11, 1779 Coachmakers Hall
'Would a free trade in Ireland be a prejudice to this country?'
Gazetteer November 9

355. November 15, 1779 Westminster Forum
'Whether the Administration in abandoning the Island of Jamaica, have not, so far, abdicated the Government of Britain, and acknowledged their incapacity of holding the reins?'
Vote went against Administration.
Morning Chronicle/Short History of the Westminster

356. November 15, 1779 (new Robinhood or) King's Arms

'Whether is a love of *glory*, or a propensity to cultivate the fine arts, the more desirable quality in a sovereign? and, Whether are the theatres (on the whole) schools of virtue or of vice?'
The first Question went in favour of the fine arts; the second question went in favour of virtue. 'Then a question, "Whether the acquisition of knowledge, or the communication thereof, affords the highest satisfaction to the human mind?" went for the latter.'
Morning Chronicle

357. November 18, 1779 Coachmakers Hall
'Would a free trade in Ireland be a prejudice to this country?'
Gazetteer November 16

358. November 22, 1779 Westminster Forum
'Whether the Livery of the city of London, ought, or ought not to reward Mr. Wilkes's conduct as a Magistrate and Member of Parliament with the lucrative office of Chamberlain?'
Only two spoke against him, 'there being none hardy enough to oppose so popular a hero'. Vote in favour of Wilkes.
Morning Chronicle/A Short History of the Westminster

359. November 22, 1779 (New Robin Hood or) King' Arms
'Whether State Lotteries are, on the whole, more beneficial or injurious to the public at large?'
Morning Chronicle

360. November 25, 1779 Coachmakers Hall
'Is extensive commerce necessary to the well-being of this country?'
Gazetteer November 23

361. November 29, 1779 Westminster Forum
'Is Government in honour bound to support American Refugees?'
Great majority determined government not so bound.
Morning Chronicle/Short History of the Westminster

362. December 2, 1779 Coachmakers hall
'Is fortitude in adversity, or temperance in prosperity, the greater virtue?'
Gazetteer November 30

363. December 3, 1779 Apollo Society
'To which ought we attribute the present language in the Irish Parliament, Constitutional Freedom or Factious discontent?'
Morning Chronicle

364. December 6, 1779 Westminster Forum
'Whether the encouragement given by this country to our inveterate enemies, the French and Spaniards, is not at all times impolitic, and in the present crisis dangerous?'

Decision that we ought not to encourage them.
Morning Chronicle/Short History of the Westminster

365. December 7, 1779 The Lyceum for the investigation of all questions in history, policy and literature, Black Horse, New Bond Street
'Is the conduct of Holland justifiable in refusing to deliver Paul Jones, and the vessels captured by him, and belonging to his Britannic Majesty, after having been required by the Ambassador from Great Britain to do so?'
Gazetteer

366. December 9, 1779 Coachmakers Hall
'Is not the restoration of annual parliaments, and of an equal representation, indispensably necessary to preserve this country from its present dangers, secure the Constitution and perpetuate the glory and freedom of Englishmen?'
Gazetteer December 7

367. December 13, 1779 Westminster Forum
'Have or have not the noble Lords who have withdrawn from Administration shewn themselves friends to their King and Country in so doing?'
Decision was that these Lords had shown themselves to be friends.
Morning Chronicle/Short History of the Westminster

368. December 14, 1779 The Lyceum
'Are the Irish Constitutionally or Politically entitled to be Independent of the British Legislature?'
Gazetteer

369. December 16, 1779 Coachmakers Hall
'Ought not the delay of the Ministry respecting Ireland to be considered as a criminal neglect that merits the public censure of the whole nation?'
Gazetteer December 14

370. December 20, 1779 Westminster Forum
'Which of the two is the most hurtful to civil society, the Spendthrift or the Miser?'
Carried against Spendthrift.
Morning Chronicle/Short History of the Westminster

371. December 23, 1779 Coachmakers Hall
'Is it not impolitic and illiberal to speak of the French nation as our natural enemies?'
Gazetteer December 21

372. December 27, 1779 Westminster Forum
'Whether the Calamities of the Empire are to be attributed more to the intrigues of the Cabinet, the venality of Parliament, or the profligacy and servility of the people?'

Seven hundred men and women attended this debate. Adjourned.
Short History of the Westminster

373. December 28, 1779 The Lyceum
'Is the conduct of that part of the Opposition who left the House of
Commons when Lord North moved his propositions respecting Ireland
proper or improper?'
Gazetteer

374. December 30, 1779 Coachmakers Hall
'Whether the Livery of London ought to petition Parliament for leave
to elect a new Member, since one of their Representatives is now in
the Grenadas, where he has by oath transferred his allegiance to the
French king?'
Gazetteer December 28

375. January 3, 1780 Westminster Forum
'Whether the calamities of the empire are to be attributed more to the
intrigues of the cabinet, the venality of parliament, or the profusion
and servility of the people?'
Decision against Cabinet intrigues.
London Courant/Short History of the Westminster

376. January 4, 1780 The Oratorical Academy, Old Theatre, Portugal
Street
'Ought the bold or the timid lover to succeed best with the Ladies?'
Mr. Dodd, President.
London Courant

377. January 4, 1780 Lyceum, Black Horse, New Bond Street
'Was the conduct of that part of the Opposition who left the House of
Commons, when Lord North moved his propositions respecting Ireland,
proper or improper?'
Gazetteer

378. January 5, 1780 Coachmakers Hall
'Would it not be a just and equitable law, that every man who had
seduced a woman should be obliged to marry her?'
Gazetteer January 4

379. January 10, 1780 Westminster Forum
'Which is most apt to procure general estimation, the reality of virtue
or the appearance of it?'
Audience in favour of the reality of virtue.
London Courant January 6/Short History of the Westminster

380. January 11, 1780 Oratorical Academy, Old Theatre, Portugal
Street

'Whether a public, a private, or a mixt mode of education, is likely to be more advantageous? N.B. The president begs leave to inform the public, that having, in consequence of the unanimous opinion of the society, renounced his design of giving an honorary medal, he has now no pretension to having the price of admission greater than in similar societies, and that in future, Admission six-pence only.'
London Courant

381. January 12, 1780 Lyceum, Black Horse
'Was it a politic step to bring the Dutch vessels into the British harbour?'
Gazetteer

382. January 14, 1780 Coachmakers Hall
'Is not imprisonment for debt in civil cases contrary to law, humanity and sound policy?'
Gazetteer January 12

383. January 17, 1780 Westminster Forum
'Which is more detrimental to the constitution, prerogative as it stood before the Revolution, or the influence of the crown, as it hath arisen since?'
London Courant January 13

384. January 18, 1780 Oratorical Academy
'Is female beauty more often of advantage or detriment to the possessor?'
London Courant January 17

385. January 18, 1780 Lyceum, Black Horse
'Was the seizing the Dutch vessels by Commodore Fielding a measure consistent with policy and the law of nations?'
Gazetteer

386. January 20, 1780 Coachmakers Hall
'Is it not a criminal indifference to be of no party in the present alarming and divided state of the nation?'
Gazetteer January 18

387. January 24, 1780 Westminster Forum
'Which is more detrimental to the constitution, prerogative as it stood before the Revolution, or the influence of the crown, as it hath arisen since?'
The vote went against the influence of the crown.
London Courant January 20/Short History of the Westminster

388. January 25, 1780 Oratorical Academy

'Whether the seizure of the Dutch vessels, in the present critical situation of affairs was prudent or impolitic?'
London Courant January 24

389. January 27, 1780 Coachmakers Hall
'Whether the virtues and qualifications of men, or those of women, are most conducive to the good and happiness of society?'
Gazetteer January 25

390. January 31, 1780 Westminster Forum
'Are the present Country Meetings likely to produce any salutary effects?'
London Courant January 27

391. February 1, 1780 Oratorical Academy
'Is not a king of Great Britain bound by his Coronation Oath, to redress the grievances of his subjects when they appeal to him?
N.B. The Colonel, Officers and Commander of the Ancient and Honourable Lumber Troop (meeting at New-Street-Square) intend to honour the Academy with a visit, in their Formalities, and with their Regalia.'
London Courant

392. February 2, 1780 London Courant
CARLISLE HOUSE
'Agreeable to a former advertisement, and to a plan delivered to the public, a large and elegant Room will be opened this present evening at Carlisle House, for the purpose of Debate and Public Speaking; where gentlemen and ladies will not be separated, but may continue in their respective parties, as at other places of public entertainment: and to accommodate those, who, from diffidence, or any other objection, may be discouraged from appearing as public speakers, masques and dominos will be provided and be permitted to be used, under the following restrictions; first, That every person shall put on his domino in a room appointed for that purpose, as no masques will be admitted at the doors. 2dly. That if any improper behaviour or expression shall be used under the concealment of a masque, the person offending shall submit, at the injunction of the President, to unmask or retire.
The question for the evening is, "Whether the art of oratory be of any real utility and importance?" A coffee room will be opened for the reception of company at seven, and the President will take the chair precisely at eight. The debate will be closed at ten.
Admittance two shillings and six pence.'

393. February 3, 1780 Coachmakers Hall
'Is it not to be wished that the county associations now forming might extend their views to effect a reform in the representation of the people, as well as the public oeconomy of the nation?'
Gazetteer February 1

394. February 3, 1780 St. James Chronicle
'This celebrated Place was opened, on Wednesday Evening, on a Plan of Literature entirely new . . .

During the whimsical, though brilliant Reign of Mrs. Cornelys, this very extensive and elegant Building wore alternatively the Appearance of Desolation, and of wild Extravagance and Enchantment. The Proprietors have therefore turned their Thoughts to more useful and permanent Views; and have induced Men of Letters to enter on a Plan of an *Academy of Sciences and Belles Lettres*, different, in several Circumstances, from any other in Europe. As they mean to make it the Theatre of Merit in all Branches of Learning, and to open their Doors to every Man who has Merit to recommend him, they have not sought Patronage, which is seldom procured but at the Expense of Independence.

The Whole is said to be under the Direction of the Gentleman who furnished them with the Plan; and he is to regulate every Department of it as Rector Academiae, or Principal of the Academy. It is to be his Business to draw together all the scattered Lecturers of this Place, or to appoint others in the several Branches of Philosophy, and to regulate an academick and dramatick Society, from which very beneficial Consequences are expected to arise.

But the more immediate Object of the Academy seems to be that of assisting young Gentlemen in their Preparation for the Senate, the Bar, and the Pulpit. First, by private Lessons, and then by publick Exercises, in a Room open to all the Town.

This Room, called *The School of Eloquence*, has a Moderator, and it was opened on Wednesday Evening, with a Speech from the Chair, which did Honour to the Institution. The Debate was conducted with very promising Abilities, in several young Speakers. But the mechanical Managers, not having had the Experience of such Undertakings, had disposed the great Room very injudiciously.

We would advise the Chair to be raised higher, and removed to the Centre, and that the Sophas may be disposed of in the Form of a Parallelogram. The Place is so beautiful, the Ornaments so elegant, and the Plan is so good, that it would be Faulty not to give every Circumstance of it the utmost Effect.

The Company on Wednesday Evening was very elegant, and the Ladies not being separated from their Parties, seemed highly delighted with the Contentions of the Orators.'

395. February 4, 1780 London Courant
CARLISLE HOUSE
'One branch of the institution, to be established at Carlisle-House, under the appellation of *Academy of Sciences and Belles Letters*, was entered upon last night. The plan itself is simple, comprehensive, and noble; and there seems to be little doubt of its being executed with ability and integrity. The design seems to concentrate, in the *Academy*, all that scattered learning and merit, which is with some trouble to be found in the various lectures of this metropolis. The school of Eloquence is to be truly a *Palaestra* for pupils, as well as a place of amuse-

ment for strangers. The whole is under the direction of a *Principal*, who is the author of the plan, and the school of Eloquence under the direction of a *President*, of whose abilities the public may judge, by the following speech, taken down verbatim.

It may be expected, at the opening of a society professedly instituted in favour of eloquence, that the praises of oratory should be celebrated, by the chair, in the flowery pomp of declamation. The subject would animate, and in any other situation impel me to appear with the most zealous of its advocates. But the properties of oratory being here submitted to investigation, it is not my opinion, but yours, that must determine whether it be an accomplishment to be desired or not. I shall therefore preface the question with a short explanation of the institution, as well for my own credit, as for your satisfaction and information.

It is incumbent on the projectors of every undertaking, which depends on public support, to demonstrate their pretensions to public favour. The entertainment for which you are now assembled, though similar in appearance, to many others, which the prevailing passion of the times hath produced, is peculiar in its nature, and is recommended by an object to which no other society or institution can pretend; it constitutes an essential part of a large, useful and comprehensive plan, which will be faithfully, and I trust ably, executed, in the Academy of Sciences and Belles Lettres, to be established in this house. If debate were proposed with no other view than the employment of an idle hour, or the discussion of questions uninteresting to an audience, and above the comprehension of the declaimers, it would require more courage and greater abilities than I possess to stand here in its defence.

The objects of oratory are as various as the circumstances of men; its exertions as manifold as the incidents of human life, for, though the powers of eloquence are peculiarly essential in the pursuit of fame, fortune, or honour, in any public or professional capacity; yet there is an oratory which belongs, and is adapted to every station, rank, and character, from the monarch who harangues his senate from the throne, to the beggar who supplicates an alms at your gate. – The institutors of this society have therefore considered oratory, not merely as a professional study, but a branch of general education; and this place is the scene of exercise for the pupils of their academy.

The brightest talents, the most brilliant abilities, are rendered, by inexertion, useless to their possessor; and, like the treasure of a miser, unprofitable to the community. In this practical application of the documents of theory, a spirit of emulation will be rouzed; the capacity of every pupil be measured; his daily improvement be manifested; and the habit acquired in this early exertion of abilities will render the delivery of his sentiments, on any future subject or occasion, easy and graceful.

The questions to be agitated in this society will be carefully directed to the discovery of truth, or to the establishment of just opinions, on such temporary subjects of importance, as must daily arise in a country so critically circumstanced as this, in times so replete with danger as these.

In this view we presume to hope that the institution of debate, considered either as an object of utility, a branch of education, or a source of entertainment, will be honoured with your unanimous approbation, and find a friend in every member of this assembly.

We presume likewise to hope, that the expedient adopted to induce modest merit, or gentlemen in particular situations, to engage in the exercise of debate, will remove every obstacle of delicacy or diffidence, and, by calling forth latent abilities, bring credit to the society, honour to the speakers, and benefit to the public. – To what cause will you impute the scarcity of orators in the senate, the want of characters of eminence of the bar, or the almost universal drowsiness of religious assemblies?

If depravation of morals be the cause; if national corruption of manners be the bane of oratory – the cultivation of eloquence may contribute to national reformation – and if this conclusion be admitted, your love of virtue, your love of your country, your love of yourselves, and of your children, will secure your patronage and encouragement to an institution which hath the boldness to cherish science, to explore the recesses of truth, and to meditate the restoration of virtuous times.'

396. February 7, 1780 Westminster Forum
'Are the present County Meetings likely to produce any salutary effects?
As some inconveniences have arisen from servants keeping places for Ladies at the Forum, the Proprietor, anxious to accommodate the generous Public, has converted a gallery into a range of boxes, which may be taken, or places had, by applying as above, at One Shilling each person.'
Vote was in the affirmative.
London Courant January 3/Short History of the Westminster

397. February 8, 1780 The Oratorical Academy is removed to the Mitre Tavern, Fleet Street
'Is the Prude or the Coquette, the most odious character?'
London Courant February 5

398. February 10, 1780 Coachmakers Hall
'Whether the penal laws of this country would not be more efficacious if they were rendered milder in their denunciations, and more certain in their execution?'
Gazetteer February 8

399. February 10, 1780 Carlisle House, that Branch of Sciences and Belle Lettres which relate to the practice of Eloquence
'An enquiry into the reasons, causes, propriety and probable effects of the present County Associations, by which will be decided that very important question, "Whether they are efforts of a disappointed faction

in opposition to government, or the noble exertion of true patriotism in favour of an oppressed people?"

The Nobility and Gentry are requested to observed, that the Exercises of Debate and public Speaking will be for the future on THURSDAY EVENINGS; that the situation of the chair, the disposition of the sophas, &c. are now so contrived, that no confusion can arise from the fullest company. Dominos and Masques are provided for those who chuse them.

When the time alloted for the Debate had elapsed, the Question was decided in Favour of the Minority; but we must own the Decision was obtained by the disposition of the Audience rather than by the Arguments of the Speakers, for though the Opposition had many Advocates, and Administration had but one, the Weight of Eloquence was in Favour of Administration. The Moderator held the Scale with the utmost impartiality, and kept an Audience of 800 or 1000 People, in a Degree of Order and Decency which we have not often been a Witness to.'

Gazetteer/St. James Chronicle

400. February 14, 1780 Westminster Forum
'Which is more eligible, a State of Liberty without Property, or a State of Property without Liberty?'
London Courant February 10

401. February 15, 1780 Oratorical Academy removed from Lincoln's Inn fields to the Mitre Tavern, Fleet Street
'Did King Charles the First, or Oliver Cromwell, make the greatest Encroachments on the Liberties of the Subject?'
London Courant February 14

402. February 17, 1780 Coachmakers Hall
'Does not the present state of affairs respecting this nation require that all parties should unite, to give the utmost energy to the plans of Administration?'
Gazetteer February 15

403. February 17, 1780 Westminster Forum
'Which is more eligible, a state of Liberty without Property, or a state of Property without Liberty?' This question was dismissed, and replaced by 'Whether, in the present state of the Empire, a dissolution of Parliament would be of national advantage?'
Carried by a great majority in the affirmative.
Short History of the Westminster

404. February 17, 1780 Carlisle House, the Department of the Academy of Sciences and Belle Lettres, called the SCHOOL OF ELOQUENCE
'Whether parties, in a free state, are beneficial to it or not?

The Moderator, not presuming to expect such a numerous and brilliant company as honoured the debate on Thursday last, did not think it necessary to take any precautions to favour the introduction of modest speakers, or diffident pupils, into convenient situations to be heard; on receiving the slightest intimation from any Gentleman who intends to speak, he will endeavour to accommodate him.

The Tea-Rooms will be opened at six. A magnificent Suite of Rooms, intended for the Library, will be opened at seven, for the Inspection of the company.

The Principal of the Academy will attend to explain all the circumstances of the Plan; and books will be ready for subscriptions.

The Dramatic, as well as other branches of Academic business, are under consideration; but they will require more time than some of the warm friends of the Institution seem to imagine. Gentlemen are instructed in the Principles and Practice of Eloquence, either by private lessons, or by exercises, in small parties, at a Room at the Academy.'
Gazetteer

405. February 19, 1780 Carlisle House
'Thursday last there was a great Overflow of Company at the debating Department of the Academy instituted there. The Efforts of the Moderator and of the other Gentlemen concerned, to suppress the Irregularities and Rudenesses which are connived at in other Places, are commendable; but will require some Time in accomplishing, as they are against the Privileges of the Mob, some of whom find Means to creep into the genteelest Assemblies. The Company on the Whole was very respectable. And we would advise the Proprietors to be very sparing of their Tickets of Admission to those whose Wishes are to see the House; but who, on being admitted into better Company than they are used to, behave with indecent Insolence. The Debate (on Parties) was carried on with great Ability on each side of the Question; and we prognosticate, by the Specimens given of Eloquence on Thursday Evening, and by the resolute Determinations of the Society, that the Debates here will be the Means of considerable Amusement and Improvement.

Mr. B—, the well-known friend of the notorious Jack R— took upon him the *heroick* Business of disturbing the Entertainment, and frightening two or three Ladies; but at last submitted quietly to be carried out of the Room under the Arm of a Gentleman who took him up like a Monkey.'
St. James Chronicle

406. February 21, 1780 Westminster Forum
'Are not the Bishops and others of the clergy who have denied their support and assistance to the Protestant Association, highly culpable in so doing?'
Decided that Bishops were highly culpable.
London Courant February 17/Short History of the Westminster

407. February 22, 1780 Oratorical Academy, Mitre Tavern

'Is it prudent for the Lord Mayor of London to call a Common Hall, for the declared purpose of Petitioning and Associating in like manner with the County of Middlesex?'
London Courant February 21

408. February 22, 1780 London Courant
'The passion for public speaking is become epidemical, not content with Forums, Apollo's, Lyceum, and Schools of Eloquence, we have now on the tapis *La Belle Assemblee*, which is to be opened this week at the Hay-market. This plan, we are informed, is set on foot by several ladies of distinguished abilities in the literary world, where public and free debate will be agitated by ladies only.'

409. February 22, 1780 Old Theatre, Portugal Street, Lincolns Inn Fields
'Which has been the more prejudicial to Great Britain, the influence of the crown or the spirit of party?'
London Chronicle

410. February 23, 1780 Oratorical Hall, Spring Gardens
'Whether the reasons assigned by the Minority Lords in their last Protest, had fully justified their Position to the present Ministry?'
The Question 'was carried by a very respectable majority'.
Admittance One Shilling.
London Courant February 22

411. February 24, 1780 Coachmakers Hall
'Are there motives sufficient, independent of the prospect of a future existence, to influence mankind to the practice of virtue?'
Gazetteer February 22

412. February 24, 1780 Carlisle House School of Eloquence
'Whether genius be the gift of nature, or the effect of education?
The Nobility and Gentry are requested to observe, that the short interruption in the Debate on Thursday last, was suspected by the Moderator to be occasioned by persons who came with that design; that being apprised of such intention, he did not in the first moment of resentment distinguish between the company and the persons he suspected to be the offenders; but being convinced of his mistake, he made an apology, which was received with applause, and restored peace and harmony to the assembly. In such circumstances it would be an insult to the judgment and candour of the assembly, to suppose that any spark of resentment against the Moderator should remain, as his very error arose from his zeal to accommodate and entertain the company. The Nobility and Gentry will therefore have the justice to refer all hints and paragraphs on this subject . . . to their true sources, envy and interested views.'
Gazetteer February 23

413. February 25, 1780 Morning Chronicle

'Last night there was a very numerous meeting of Ladies and Gentlemen, at the School of Eloquence, opened at Carlisle House; above 1,100 persons being present. The harmony of the assembly was disturbed about nine o'clock, by some persons not deporting themselves in a becoming manner, but interrupting the Speakers repeatedly with hisses and coughing. The Moderator was so provoked, that he lost his temper, and said, there were *constables* at the door, and that such Gentlemen that made any more interruptions, ought to be *kicked* out. This threw the meeting into a flame, and it was a very considerable time before the tumult was quelled, and order restored. The Moderator was called on repeatedly, for his apology for his having talked in so unbecoming a manner in so respectable an assembly, but for a long time he persisted in refusing, declaring that he was not conscious of having said any thing that ought to be construed as an offence. At last he said, he meant not to offend, and if any Gentlemen felt themselves hurt at his expressions, he was sorry for it. This quieted the meeting, and the debate proceeded and continued till ten o'clock.'

414. February 26, 1780 Morning Chronicle
'Carlisle-House, Thursday Night, on the Question, "Whether Genius be the Gift of Nature, or the acquirement of art."

Nature, Genius, and Art, were a-dancing the hays,
Cutting capers, and winding a *mystical maze!*
Attention, tho' puzzled, encouraged the ball,
As the vent'rous dancers, by turns, got a fall! –
Pretty women betray'd, by their eloquent smiles,
By the *look* that inflames, and the *look* that beguiles.
Beauty's *look* was the *Music* that set them a-going –
And they danced, 'till they knew not what either was doing.
Frolic came to the door, and he set up a laugh,
Thought the dance was too *dull*, and too *tedious* by half.
This rude interruption soon altered the tune,
Debate took a the dumps, and gave way to *wild* Fun;
Fun called up a *Fury* in masculine shape,
But the *Fury* was led int'a devilish scrape!
Hell seem'd to break loose – yet some *Angels* were there,
Who pitied the *Fury*, thus cast to despair;
Their Mercy entreated *Good Humour* to save him.
The *Fury* ask'd pardon, and *Frolic* forgave him.'

415. February 26, 1780 La Belle Assemblee
'Whether Oratory is, or should be, confined to any sex?
The chair will be taken by Rev. Mr. Phillips . . .. Admittance Two Shillings each.'
London Courant February 24

416. February 28, 1780 Westminster Forum
'Which are the true Friends of the King, the Supporters or Opposers of the present Measures?'

It was decided, by a very small majority, that the Opposers were the true friends.
London Courant February 24/Short History of the Westminster

417. February 28, 1780 Morning Chronicle
'There were 700 persons at Mr. Greenwood's Room on Saturday evening to pay their compliments to *La Belle Assemblee*; some of the ladies spoke well, but the Moderator appeared to be but very moderately qualified for his office. After quitting a post, he gave no proof of his being fit to hold, a sprightly female seized it, and entertained the audience highly by an excellent recital of a well known poetical tale.

Various are the opinions formed by the public, of the entertainments to be presented on Wednesday evening at the Haymarket; some think the fabricators are suborned by the Majority, to ridicule the associations, others, that the protests are their subject of satire, and others, that the Lord-Mayor of London, and Court of Aldermen, are to be virulently abused.

A Correspondent informs us that a most exact representation of the House of Commons, is to be exhibited at the Haymarket next Wednesday evening, and a mock budget to be opened in the manner, and in imitation of the peculiarities of the noble Lord, to whose share this important part of the national business generally falls.'

418. February 28, 1780 London Courant
'Thursday evening the business, at Carlisle House, of that part of the Academy there, called *The School of Eloquence*, drew an astonishing number of the genteelest company, but whether from the machinations of envy, or interest against so promising an institution, or from accidental causes, several attempts were made to disturb the debate. These attempts were resented by the assembly, and by the moderator, in warm and pointed terms, which were thought to require an apology, and which he handsomely made. The question, however, had not justice done it, for the speakers were heard only on one side. It will require time and prudence in accomplishing the designs of the Academy; for the assembly is too formidable for their pupils, and the number of candidates for fame in speaking will fully occupy them. The passions for oratory are now like the jarring winds in chaos; we hope some spirit will direct them to regular and beneficent purposes.'

419. February 29, 1780 Oratorical Academy, Mitre Tavern
'Have political publications in newspapers been of more good or hurt to the nation?'
London Courant February 26

420. February 29, 1780 Old Theatre, Portugal Street, Lincoln's-inn-fields
'Was the sentence of the Court of Kings-Bench on the Members of the Council of Madras, for unlawfully deposing and confining Lord Pigot, adequate to their offence?'
Gazetteer

421. March 1, 1780 Oratorical Hall, Spring Gardens
'Whether Arrests for Debts upon Mesne Process, be Political and Constitutional?'
London Courant February 28

422. March 2, 1780 Coachmakers Hall
'Are there motives sufficient, independent of the prospect of a future existence, to influence mankind to the practice of virtue?'
Gazetteer February 29

423. March 2, 1780 Carlisle House, The School of Eloquence
'1. Whether a man should act with his friends and benefactors, though they do not, in his opinion, peruse right measures for the public interest?
As this Question may not admit of debate, it will be enquired
2. Whether a bad Administration, or a corrupt Parliament, be the juster object of popular indignation?
The Nobility and Gentry are requested to observe, that the short Interruption in the Debate on Thursday last, was suspected by the Moderator to be occasioned by persons who came with that design; that being apprised of such intention, he did not in the first moment of resentment distinguish between the company and the persons he suspected to be the offenders; but being convinced of his mistake, he made an apology, which was received with applause, and restored peace and harmony to the assembly. In such circumstances it would be an insult to the judgment and candour of the assembly, to suppose that any spark of resentment against the Moderator should remain, as his very error arose from his zeal to accommodate and entertain the company. The Nobility and Gentry will therefore have the justice to refer all hints and paragraphs on this subject (not countenanced or authorized by the advertisement of the Academy) to their true sources, envy and interested views.'
Gazetteer

424. March 4, 1780 'A Society for debating Cases and Questions in Law and Equity is held weekly at Staples Inn Coffee-house, Southampton Buildings, Chancery lane.'
Morning Chronicle

425. March 4, 1780 La Belle Assemblee
'Would it be sound Policy to make the Salique Law general?
The Debate to be wholly maintained by Ladies, but, for the sake of preventing tumult, a Gentleman will be in the Chair.'
London Courant

426. March 4, 1780 Religious Society, Old Theatre, Portugal Street, Lincoln's inn fields

'Is the Bill now depending in Parliament for the relief of Insolvents, consonant to policy and justice?

Order, decency, and liberality will be sedulously observed; which it is hoped, together with the central situation and elegance of the room, and other requisites, will amply recommend this institution to the public patronage and esteem.'

Morning Chronicle

427. March 6, 1780 London Courant

'The meeting at La Belle Assemblee on Saturday night was exceedingly crowded, many gentlemen being obliged to go away for want of room. Among the female part of the Assembly were many ladies, who, while they *struck the sight* with the elegance of their persons, displayed in the debate such superior accomplishments and refined understandings, as may truly be said *to win the soul* – The subject for that evening's discussion was *Whether it would be sound Policy to make the Salique Law general?*

There were several speakers who took different sides of the question, which, nevertheless, was disputed with the utmost candour and moderation, and with real ability. Those ladies, who were for abolishing a law so tyrannical to the softer sex, instanced the glorious reigns of our Elizabeth, of Margaret of Denmark, and Christina of Sweden, while others, who, with humble modesty, were for declining all female pretensions to imperial sway, urged that from the natural softness and sensibility of their minds, women were too liable to be seduced from their attention to the public weal by the smooth and silken parasites who constantly infest a court, and who leave no artifice unemployed to captivate and ensnare the weaker sex. One of the fair orators asserted in a charming tone, that "there was one ingredient in the cup of sovereignty, which ought peculiarly to discourage females from tasting its flattering contents. It is, said she, when the rigid voice of inexorable justice demands the execution of the guilty delinquent; how shall woman, with all the trembling tenderness and sympathetic pity of her sex, sign the dreadful warrant denouncing death!" – This sentiment, delivered in a most graceful and expressive manner, was received with universal, and repeated tokens of deserved applause. – A most elegant, and beautiful figure in one of the galleries, with a black masque on the upper part of her face, spoke with uncommon propriety, elegance and dignity. – At ten o'clock the lady who opened the debate, rose up to speak some lines in conclusion, which however could not be heard, some persons among the audience, being shamefully noisy and tumultuous, but who on her sitting down called to her to proceed; the lady seemed confused, but replied, with great politeness to the gentlemen, that she should be very happy *to entertain them all night*, but that she had already finished what she had to say. The unguarded innocence of this expression produced a general laugh, which increasing her confusion, a very general acclamation of applause from the company made amends for the temporary distress which they occasioned.'

428. March 6, 1780 Westminster Forum

'Whether the Bill now depending in Parliament for extending the Privileges of Debtors, has not the strongest tendency to encourage Fraud and Dishonesty, and in consequence to produce effects highly injurious and destructive to the Commercial Interest of this Kingdom?'
Question carried in the affirmative.
London Courant March 2/Short History of the Westminster

429. March 6, 1780 London Courant
SOCIÉTÉ DISPUTATOIRE
'On Friday the 10th instant will be opened, at Mr. Greenwood's Rooms, in the Hay-market, a Society for free and liberal Debate, to be wholly conducted in French. It has been universally agreed upon that we cannot in this country acquire the proper pronunciation of, and a fluency in speaking that language, for want of such an opportunity as is now offered. Gentlemen by study and application in their closets may gain such a proficiency as to be able to read it with ease, and write it with elegance, but it is only by conversation that they can perfect themselves in the idiom, pronunciation, and delivery. The beauties of familiar conversation in any language, are lost to a foreigner; the fitness of peculiar allusions; the elegance of bon mots; the turn of well pointed periods are concealed from the man whose ear is not familiar with the articulation and modes of speaking practiced in the Country. Thus do we find that the big swelling passions of a Corneille are perfectly understood and highly relished by men who are unacquainted with the point, wit, and raillery of a Moliere; the reason is obvious, the passions are common to all countries, while the turn, wit, and humour of conversation are local, and peculiar to each. It is hoped that this institution will be productive of the most salutary advantage in facilitating Gentlemen in the acquisition of the language.

It will be conducted with the utmost regularity, and that the diffident may be invited to overcome their scruples, Masks and Dominos will be provided in an adjourning room. The Institution does not interfere with any other of the Debating Societies. Their principle is to cherish the growth of Eloquence, as it maybe useful to Gentlemen in their profession; this is calculated to perfect them in a language which in every situation of life is necessary as an accomplishment.

The Question for discussion on Friday evening will be "Quelle est l'étude la plus utile, et la plus necessaire – Celle des Langues mortes, ou celle des Langues vivantes?"
Admittance One Shilling.'

430. March 7, 1780 Oratorical Academy, Mitre Tavern
'Has the Union with Scotland been of more Benefit or Detriment to England?'
London Courant March 6

431. March 9, 1780 Coach Makers Society
'Is the Bill to prevent Imprisonment for Debt, now under consideration of Parliament, more likely to produce advantage or prejudice to the trading interest of this country?

Mr. Hopkins respectfully informs the public, that finding his gallery for the Ladies is not sufficient to accommodate the numbers that have generally applied, and being desirous of making every improvement to merit the public approbation, he has erected a convenient department in the Hall for the use of the Ladies. And for the future, to prevent the trouble of applying for Tickets, Ladies will be admitted on the same terms as the Gentlemen.'
London Courant

432. March 9, 1780 Carlisle House, School of Eloquence
'Whether it be practicable, in a Free State, to admit Colonies to a full participation of the rights of the Mother Country?
The sophas will be gradually raised, so that all the company will be seen at one view. Seats near the centre will be appropriated for those speakers who cannot command the room from every part of it; and some regulations will be proposed to this company to preserve that order and decent attention, without which no modest and ingenious men will be at the trouble of speaking.'
London Courant March 6

433. March 11, 1780 La Belle Assemblee
'Whether is connubial felicity more likely to arise from similarity or contrast of temper?'
London Courant

434. March 13, 1780 Westminster Forum
'Is it agreeable to the Constitution that the Commissioners of the Excise should determine Causes without a Jury, when their own Servants or Excise Officers, are always Plaintiffs, and that the said Commissioners' determination is final? and Is not a Reformation of the Representative Body necessary to prevent undue influence?'
It was decided that the actions of the Commissioners was not agreeable to the Constitution; second question adjourned.
London Courant March 9/Short History of the Westminster

435. March 13, 1780 London Courant
LYCÉE FRANCOIS
'On Friday evening there was opened at Mr. Greenwood's Rooms in the Hay-market, a society under the title of Lycée Francois, for conversation and debate, to be wholly conducted in the French language. A very genteel and numerous company were present, and the debate was supported mostly by English Gentlemen, with great spirit, argument and humour . . . It was exceedingly pleasant to mark with how much personal respect and polite attention the Gentlemen who took up the opposite sides of the question treated each other, as it shewed how well and how successfully argument might be maintained without connecting it with illiberality. The President in a very genteel address, ushered in the debate with some just recommendations of the plan and nature of the institution, and he said, that so long as the society forbore the

introduction of religious and political questions, they would not be interrupted in the discussion of such as were moral and philosophical. Science, he said, was of no country, it entered into none of the jealousies and enmities of nations, but even in the midst of war it busied itself in cultivating the acts of peace. The name of the Society was changed from that of *Sociétie Disputoire* to *Lycée Francois.*'

436. March 14, 1780 Oratorical Academy, Mitre Tavern
'Does an uncorrupted Senator, or an able General, render the greater Services to the State?'
London Courant March 13

437. March 14, 1780 Oratorical Society, Portugal Street
'Is there a possible situation of human nature in which suicide is justifiable? and, Which is the more common character, the female or male coquet?'
Morning Chronicle

438. March 14, 1780 Morning Chronicle
'A correspondent says, he is happy to see the School of Eloquence at Carlisle House (in consequence of some judicious regulations, which took place on Thursday night) assume such a degree of good order and decorum, as might be expected from an institution so useful in its plan, and elegant in its institution. – The Question was important, and debated with great ability by several ingenious partisans of opposition; they were replied to by a person in a mask, who with equal ingenuity, and in a train of pleasing irony, professed to support the same side of the question, whilst he proved by arguments drawn from Montesquieu, and other authors, *that it is impracticable to communicate to infant colonies, a full participation of the rights of the parent state.* – It was whispered, that the mask was a young Gentleman who has upon several occasions contributed to the entertainment of this polite assembly; but we are at a loss to assigning a reason for the disguise of his person and voice.'

439. March 15, 1780 Lycee Francois
'L'Education publique est elle plus propre a former l'homme et le Citoyen que l'Education particulière?'
London Courant March 13

440. March 16, 1780 Coachmakers Hall Society
'Doth the present mode of educating the Fair Sex in Boarding Schools, contribute more to corrupt or to reform the Manners of the Rising Generation?'
London Courant

441. March 16, 1780 Carlisle House School of Eloquence
'Would a repeal of the Marriage Act be consistent with the principles of sound policy?'
Gazetteer March 13

442. March 16, 1780 London Courant
'Omne tulit punctum qui miscuit utile dulci.
The public are respectfully informed, that the suite of rooms, No. 53, Great Marlborough street, known heretofore by the name of the Casino, will be opened on Saturday the 18th instant, under the title of The University for Rational Amusements, one part of which will be appropriated for Elocution, Oratory, and Exercise, not only for those that are proficient in matters of disputation, but where young pupils may improve in that useful science; and although this plan may be supposed to resemble many other institutions, yet upon the whole, it will be found to be new and agreeable, as it is intended to consist in variety, calculated to amuse and instruct, adhering to the motto.

With respect to the rooms, the Proprietors have exerted themselves to render them elegantly commodious, and the strictest attention will be paid to preserve that regularity so essentially necessary to the good order, accommodation, and pleasure of the company.

The Proprietors are bold to say, that this edifice possesses an evident superiority over every other place of the kind; being so well adopted for Public Oratory, that the most timid speaker, or weak voice, need not apprehend being led into embarrassment, from the Company not distinctly hearing; as the ordinary utterance of conversation, may with ease be heard at any part of the room.

The Proprietors of this University, not only mean it as a place for the improvement of Elocution, and the Science of Debate, but likewise as an agreeable substitute for the want of a winter Ranelagh. There is an elegant tea room, situated near the gallery, for the conveniency of the company, and a coffee room, equally desirable, adjoining the debating room.

The Question for that evening, Which deserves most admiration, a good orator or a good writer?'
Admittance 2s. 6d.
London Courant

443. March 17, 1780 Morning Chronicle
'A correspondent informs us, that the next question of debate at the Ladies Assembly is, "Whether such public publications as the pamphlet called the *Picture Gallery*, tend to improve or injure the morals of the sex." As there are near two hundred of the most distinguished women in this kingdom taken notice of in the above pamphlet, and very few of them pleased in an advantageous point of view, it is expected there will be a crouded room and warm debates; it is also said the author of the pamphlet intends to open the business, disguised in women's cloaths, which he has borrowed of Lady L—, who is to accompany him.'

444. March 18, 1780 La Belle Assemblee
'Whether variety is more predominant in the male or female breast?'
London Courant

445. March 19, 1780 Oratorical Society [on Sunday]
Exodus ch. xx, verse 5, & ch. xxii, verse 16.
Morning Chronicle March 14

446. March 20, 1780 Westminster Forum
'Is not a Reformation in the Representative Body necessary to prevent undue influence?'
Carried in the affirmative.
London Courant March 16/Short History of the Westminster

447. March 21, 1780 Oratorical Academy, Mitre Tavern
'Did the conduct of Adminstration toward the Speaker of the House of Commons, justify his late pointed Censure on the ostensible Minister?'
London Courant March 18

448. March 22, 1780 Free Mason Hall, The Palladium, or Liberal Academy of Eloquence
'What reason can be assigned for precluding the Fair from the privilege of Civil Society, or from a liberal participation in their discussions?'
Admittance Two Shillings and Six-pence.
Gazetteer

449. March 23, 1780 Coachmakers Hall Society
'Which is the most to be dreaded in this country, the influence of the Crown, or the spirit of party?'
London Courant

450. March 23, 1780 Carlisle House School of Eloquence
'Whether it will be most conducive to the general good of the Community that the East India Company should be dissolved, or their Charter renewed?'
Audience voted for renewal by a considerable majority. 'Carlisle House is now become as much the place of fashionable resort on a Thursday, as it was in the zenith of Mrs. Cornely's popularity. The Company last night amounted to nearly 1,200, among which number, were many persons of rank.'
London Courant March 20

451. March 24, 1780 Lycee Francois
'La poligamie est-elle d'aucun advantage dans un Gouvernment & son utile l'emporte t-elle sur ses abus?'
London Courant March 18

452. March 25, 1780 La Belle Assemblee, Greenwood's Rooms in the Haymarket
'Whether do the innocent gaieties of youth, or the mature wisdom of age, afford the greatest happiness?

81

N.B. It has been thought necessary to make some arrangements: For the future the galleries will be appropriated to Ladies only; and in the other part of the house the Ladies and Gentlemen may sit together.
Tea and coffee. Masks and Dominos provided.
Admittance Two shillings.'
'Such is the great propensity, as well as the propensity of the great, to frequent *La Belle Assemblee*, that on Saturday last soon after seven, Mr. Greenwood's room was crowded with persons of the first distinction, and the street rendered impassable by the great number of coaches of nobility, gentry, &c. who had left their homes to hear the ladies argue.'
Gazetteer March 22

453. March 25, 1780 Spring Garden's Oratory
'What is the propriety of this country permitting the sister kingdom [Ireland] to have a constitution similar to that of Great Britain?
There was scarcely an Irish Student in town, who did not attend, and pour forth his eloquence in support of the affirmative. It is but justice to say that the *Amor Patriae* was not more conspicuous in all of these orators, than the power of argument in many. A little closer attention to the real drift of the question will, however, do no harm to the young gentlemen who stood up for the honour of Ireland on Saturday evening; it will, at least, assist them in their endeavours to convince their hearers, which to men who wish to support truth, is surely a better object than barely attempting to amuse.'
Morning Chronicle March 27

454. March 25, 1780 The University for Rational Amusements
'Are we more indebted to Courage or Fear for our Protection? and Is Sincerity more frequently a Male or Female Virtue?'
London Courant March 21

455. March 25, 1780 The University for Rational Amusements
'Is challenging a Member of Parliament for any freedom he may take in debate, contrary to any principles of the Constitution?'
Masks and dominos permitted.
London Courant March 24

456. March 27, 1780 Morning Chronicle
'The rage for publick debate now shews itself in all quarters of the metropolis. Exclusive of the oratorical assemblies at Carlisle House, Free-mason's Hall, the Forum, Spring Gardens, the Cassino, the Mitre Tavern and other polite places of debating *rendezvous*, we hear that new Schools of Eloquence are preparing to be opened in St. Giles, Clare-Market, Hockley in the Hole, Whitechapel, Rag-Fair, Duke's Place, Billingsgate, and the Back of the Borough.'

457. March 27, 1780 Morning Chronicle

'An admirer of every institution which has ever a probability of enlightening the understanding and polishing manners, was much pleased to see the first meeting at the Palladium at Free-Masons Hall, attended by so brilliant and respectable an audience. This institution most undoubtedly completes a system of Oratory, upon a pleasing and rational plan; at the Belle Assemblee, Ladies will accustom themselves to lay aside all mauvaise honte, and gentlemen become familiarized to their pleasing stile: Ladies by attending Carlisle-house, will learn to adopt the eligible part of gentlemen's stile of reasoning: and at Free Masons Hall both will have it in their power to display their talents, and give their unconstrained opinions.'

458. March 27, 1780 Westminster Forum
'Would or would not the depriving the petty boroughs of the liberty of sending Members to Parliament, and adding their quota to the counties and cities, be likely to remove the evils attending an influenced election?'
Question carried in the affirmative.
London Courant March 23/Short History of the Westminster

459. March 28, 1780 Oratorical Academy, Mitre Tavern
'Does the British stage, in its present state, tend more to improve or corrupt morals?'
London Courant March 27

460. March 29, 1780 Lycee Francois
'Laqueele des trois professions savantes, est la plus utile, la jurisprudence, la medecine, ou la theologie?'
London Courant March 27

461. March 29, 1780 Carlisle House School of Eloquence
'Whether any remedy can be applied to the present licentiousness of the press, by which its liberty will not be materially affected?'
London Courant March 28

462. March 29, 1780 University of Rational Amusement
'Have the People of England a right to demand a Restoration of annual Parliaments?'
Horns and Clarinets will assist to fill up the vacancy of time previous to the commencement of the debate.
London Courant March 28

463. March 30, 1780 Coachmakers Hall Society
'Would not the study of Mathematics be preferable to that of the Classics, in the general idea of educating Youth in this Commercial Country?'
London Courant

464. April 1, 1780 La Belle Assemblee

'Is the spirit of duelling esteemed by the Ladies, to proceed from a true or a false sense of honour?

The new arrangements that were made in the mode of sitting last evening, produced some inconveniencies that will be provided against in future. Several applications to this purpose have been made by Ladies who came with an intention to deliver their sentiments on the question, but who were intimidated by the Company's sitting promiscuously. For the future, therefore, the lower part of the house and the galleries will be appropriated to the Ladies only – the Ladies and Gentlemen may sit promiscuously in the other part of the room.'
Gazetteer

465. April 1, 1780 Oratorical Hall, Spring Garden
To the Nobility and Gentry
'Does Great Britain enjoy an inherent and constitutional right to subjugate and coerce the American Colonies? and, Is the promotion of Men from the Bar, the Desk or the Plough to Military Rank, injurious to the Soldier, or beneficial to the Country?
It was determined . . . almost unanimously, by a respectable assembly of the Nobility and Gentry, that Great Britain had a right to coerce America, and that the promotion of the lawyer, the clerk, or the farmer, to rank in the army, was not injurious to the old soldier, but beneficial to him and his country.'
London Courant

466. April 1, 1780 University for Rational Amusement
'Do the Reviews, as they are now conducted, tend to the prejudice or advantage of literature? and, Are the claims of the Irish for repeal of Poynings Law, and of the English Statues enacted to bind Ireland and declaring her dependent founded in right, and on the principles of the English Constitution?
The Rooms are so commodious, that any Lady or Gentleman may, with the greatest ease, retire from the debating room to the coffee-rooms, or to an elegant tea room, situated near the gallery. . .. The Proprietors are bold to say, that this edifice possesses an evident superiority to every other place of the kind; being so well adapted to public oratory, that the most [ ] speaker or weak voice, need not apprehend being left in embarrassment from the company not distinctly hearing . . . the ordinary utterance of conversation may with ease be heard at any part of the room.'
London Courant/Morning Post

467. April 1, 1780 London Courant
'Notwithstanding the prevailing depravity of manners, and the too great neglect of Religion, yet we have happily a number of well-disposed persons, who would wish to dedicate a few hours to serious disquisitions into the texts of Holy Writ, propose their doubts, receive explanations, and display their eloquence, *on the noblest of all subjects.* – For the entertainment and improvement of such persons, a Society of Gentle-

men propose to open an assembly, under the name of *the Religious Association*, to be held every Sunday evening at Mr. Greenwood's Room in the Hay-Market. – The chair to be taken at half-past seven, and conclude at half past nine. The text to be explained on next Sunday evening [April 2] is, Romans xvi 17. *Mark them which cause divisions, and offences contrary to the doctrine which ye have learned, and avoid them.* Admittance 6d.
N.B. As religion is equally important to both sexes, Ladies will be admitted.'

468. April 2, 1780 Theological Society, Portugal Street
'Charity suffereth long, and is kind; Charity envieth not; Charity vaunteth not itself, is not puffed up.' Paul to Cor. ch. viii. v.4. From whence the proposer of the theme adduces the following question:
'Are not the late indulgencies granted to Roman Catholics, consistent with religious liberties of this country?'
Morning Post April 1

469. April 2, 1780 University for Rational Amusement
Theological Question
'Whether we are authorized by Scripture to believe that the honest and virtuous Heathen will be accepted by the Maker?'
London Courant April 1

470. April 2, 1780 Free Masons Hall, The Palladium or Liberal Academy of Eloquence
'Whether is fortitude superior in the male or female breast?'
Thirteen speakers; decided that 'fortitude was more superior in the female than in the male breast.'
Admittance Two-Shillings and Six-pence.
Morning Chronicle April 3

471. April 2, 1780 Religious Association
Romans xvi, 17 'Mark them which cause divisions and offences contrary to the doctrine which ye have learned, and avoid them.'
Morning Chronicle March 27

472. April 3, 1780 The Oratorical Hall, Spring Gardens
'Are not Masquerades more beneficial to the Commerce, than injurious to the Morals of a Nation?
Is it not detrimental to the world to restrain the female sex from the pursuit of classical and mathematical learning?'
The hall 'will be open for the reception of the Nobility and Gentry, mask'd and unmask'd, as was usual on Masquerade Nights in the time of Mr. Cox's Museum. – Admittance, Two Shillings.
The Hall will be grandly illuminated, and the Company entertained with Music until the Debate commences.
N.B. Ladies and Gentlemen accommodated with Tea and Coffee.

It is particularly hoped that Ladies will avail themselves of their masks and join in the debate.'
Morning Chronicle

473. April 3, 1780 Westminster Forum
'Is it agreeable to the maxims of sound policy for any Protestant Government to tolerate Popery?'
Decision that it is not agreeable to tolerate Popery.
London Courant April 1/Short History of the Westminster

474. April 4, 1780 La Belle Assemblee
'In acts of real humanity, whether does the generous giver or the grateful receiver, feel the greater pleasure?
The Ladies have taken into their consideration the uncommon distresses of the sufferers at the late fire near Cavendish-square, intend assembling for their benefit.'
London Courant

475. April 4, 1780 Oratorical Academy, Mitre Tavern
'Is it probable that the American Colonies will be ever reunited to the British Empire?'
London Courant April 3

476. April 4, 1780 Oratorical Society, Old Theatre
'Is there a greater prospect of happiness in a married or single state?'
Debate 'to be opened by a lady'.
London Courant

477. April 4, 1780 Morning Post
'The interlude advertised this evening at Drury lane, under the title of the *School of Eloquence*, threatens the disputing clubs, which have so suddenly filled every large room in the metropolis with a severe check, which will probably be more useful than pleasing to the numerous frequenters who employ their time and attention in pursuits far beyond their knowledge or abilities. The quarter from which it originates, and the great comic strength of the representation, we hope the check will be effectual. Several of the disputing club members have reason to apprehend that the ridicule will be heightened by a *personal caricature* of the speakers; a liberty, which tho' highly reprehensible when exercised against private characters, is perfectly justifiable when directed against those who place *themselves* in so absurd a point of view.'

478. April 5, 1780 Lycee Francois
'A-t-on besoin, pour devenir orateur, de l'etude des Maitres de l'art, ou les talents naturel suffisent-ils?'
London Courant April 3

479. April 5, 1780 University for Rational Amusements

'Is the effeminate Man, or the Masculine Woman the more contemptible character? and, Are newspapers of use or prejudice to Society?'
London Courant

480. April 6, 1780 Carlisle House School of Eloquence
'Whether any restraints can be applied, to the licentiousness of the
press, by which its liberty will not be materially affected? and, Is it
consistent with the necessary freedom of Parliamentary debate, that the
gentlemen should not be accountable in a private capacity, for any
expression they may use as members of the Senate?'
London Courant April 3

481. April 6, 1780 The Religious Association
Deut. 24, 16 'Every man shall be put to death for his own sins.'
London Courant April 3

482. April 6, 1780 Coachmakers Hall
'Is the practice of public oratory a fit accomplishment for the ladies?
On the decision of the question . . . respecting the propriety of the
ladies speaking in public, a numerous company were almost unanimously against it; so that, as our correspondent remarks, that species of
female departure from a reserved and modest character is not chargeable on the ladies in general, nor on the public but only on some particular characters.'
Gazetteer April 4

483. April 6, 1780 Oratorical Hall, Spring Garden
'Has not the conduct of opposition been uniformly consistent with
public utility these ten years past? and, Is it true, that the people of
Ireland have grounded their claims upon the example and conduct of
America?'
Decided that it was not consistent with public utility.
'It is particularly hoped that Ladies will join in the debate.'
London Courant

484. April 6, 1780 London Courant
'A correspondent recommends it to the Proprietors of the several
Debating Societies, who have so closely imitated the plans of the rooms
in the Haymarket, to persist in their laudable endeavours, and follow
the example of generosity, as well as interest, by bestowing the profits
of one night at least on the unhappy sufferers by fire.

La Belle Assemblee – The unhappy sufferers by the late fire in
Princes-street, Cavendish square, return their grateful thanks to the
Ladies of *La Belle Assemblee* for the sum of Twenty Pounds, which
they have this day received from them.'

485. April 7, 1780 Free Masons Hall, The Palladium, or Liberal Academy of Eloquence

'Is the character of a Patriot adorned or sullied by coinciding in the views and exertions of the Minority?
Whether is lenity or severity in the Sovereign most likely to prove conducive to the happiness of his subjects?'
Gazetteer April 5

486. April 7, 1780 Apollo Society, King's Arms Tavern
'Whether is the acquisition or communication of knowledge, productive of the greater pleasure to the human kind? And, Is it consistent with honour for a man to refuse a challenge?'
Gazetteer April 6

487. April 8, 1780 University for Rational Amusements
'Should the Execution of Charles I be considered as a Martyrdom? and, Would it be prudent in England to go to war with the Dutch?'
London Courant

488. April 8, 1780 La Belle Assemblee
'Whether is the reality or appearance of merit more likely to gain general estimation?'
Morning Chronicle April 6

489. April 8, 1780 Oratorical Hall, Spring Garden
'Is it true that the people of Ireland have grounded their claims upon the example and conduct of America?'
Morning Chronicle

490. April 9, 1780 Religious Association
Deut. 24, 16 'Every man shall be put to death for his own sin.'
Morning Chronicle April 6

491. April 9, 1780 University for Rational Amusements, Theological Question
'Behold, all Souls are mine, as the Soul of the Father, so also the Soul of the Son is mine; the Soul that sinneth, it shall die.
To begin with an Anthem by a Lady, . . .accompanied on the organ by Mr. Clark and others.'
London Courant April 8

492. April 10, 1780 Westminster Forum
'Whether it would be more consistent with the interest of the people of Great Britain, to immediately acknowledge the American Independence, upon the terms of a general peace, and a free trade with them in common with the rest of Europe, rather than to continue the war against the allied powers under our present circumstances?'
The question was decided in the affirmative, almost unanimously.
London Courant April 6/Short History of the Westminster

493. April 10, 1780 Oratorical Academy, Mitre Tavern

'Would it be prudent in Administration to employ Sir Hugh Palliser in any naval command? and, Would a total abolition of confinement for debt be of more good or hurt to a commercial country?'
London Courant April 8

494. April 11, 1780 Oratorical Society, Old Theatre
'Have not the Ladies as good a right to a classical education as the men?
The Lady who opened the question on Tuesday last being greatly confused by the repeated testimonies of applause given her by the society, it is earnestly requested in future of the Ladies and Gentlemen present to reserve their plaudits to the conclusion of the speech, when they will be more competent judges of the merits of the speakers; which will at the same time prevent the confusion that must obviously occur from the natural timidity of those who have but lately assumed their rights and privileges, by bursting those chains, with which through custom and illiberality, they have hitherto been fettered.'
Morning Post

495. April 12, 1780 Lycee Francois
'D'apres les preuves d'eloquence donnies depuis peu, par les deux sexes, doit on conclure, que les femmes l'importent sur les hommes dans les science de oratoire?'
London Courant

496. April 12, 1780 University for Rational Amusements
'Should a Minister resign when the Petitions of the People have created a Majority against him?'
Debate preceded by a public breakfast.
London Courant

497. April 12, 1780 Morning Post
'Mr. Adam, the famous combatant of Charles Fox, in a speech last Thursday night, at the Oratorical Academy, held at Coachmakers Hall, took an occasion to animadvert, with great severity, upon the Quakers. He was attacked, in reply, with very considerable acrimony, as well as great strength of argument, for the absurdity of pronouncing such vague unproved imputations against general characters and large bodies of men. A little struck with the impropriety of what he had said, Mr. Adam rose again to apologize for his rashness, when a neat, genteel, well dressed, female Quaker, got up and said, "Thou mayst hold thy peace; thou hast already spoken to very little purpose, and thou wilt hardly improve by saying more." This brief rebuke, coming from so engaging a character, was received with the loudest applause, and Mr. Adam was stunned into silence.'

498. April 13, 1780 Coachmakers Hall

'Ought the right to electing Representatives to serve in Parliament to depend on the property, or to be considered as the personal privilege of every Englishman?'
Gazetteer April 11

499. April 13, 1780 Carlisle House School of Eloquence
'Is it consistent with the necessary freedom of Parliamentary debate, that Gentlemen should be answerable in a private capacity, for any expressions they may use as members of the Senate? and, If a Senator should differ in opinion from those whom he represents, is he to act on his own sentiments, or those of his constituents?'
London Courant April 11

500. April 14, 1780 Female Parliament, for Rational Amusements
'Is that assertion of Mr. Pope's founded in Justice, which says "Every Woman is at Heart a Rake"?'
London Courant

501. April 14, 1780 Apollo Society, King's Arms Tavern, Grafton Street, Soho
'Can a man, consistent with honour refuse a challenge?'
N.B. The room lighted with wax, and a separate gallery for the Ladies.
Gazetteer

502. April 14, 1780 Free Masons hall, The Palladium, or Liberal Academy of Eloquence
'Does the late Minority, now turned Majority, forbode good or evil to the subjects of Great Britain?
Will it be a general good to the subjects of Great Britain, if the East-India debt is discharged by Government, and the trade thrown open?'
Gazetteer

503. April 15, 1780 Morning Post
'Many of the common speakers, as shopkeepers, etc. at the modern oratorical assemblies, begin to see what coxcombs they have been, to exert their faculties, and exhaust their breath and brains for the mere emolument of other people, who make their fortunes of these affairs; and many of the above orators have begun to form plans of partnership, to occupy large sets of rooms, and divide the spoil all alike. This is said to be carried into execution already at one place, in the western circuit of the town, and will soon be so in the city.
Religion exposed in an auction room, and on a Sunday night too, (says a Lady coming down the Haymarket) – well it is a going! a going! a going! sure enough.'

504. April 15, 1780 La Belle Assemblee
'To which is the world more indebted for their protection, their courage or their fear?'
London Courant April 12

505. April 15, 1780 University for Rational Amusements
'Should a Minister resign when the Petitions of the People have created a Majority against him?'
Begun by duet by two ladies, concluded with lady singing an Italian song.
London Courant April 14

506. April 15, 1780 Assembly Rooms, Crown and Rolls Tavern, Chancery Lane, for the Discussion of Liberal Opinions
'Has not the conduct of our patriotic opposition been consistent with the public utility these 13 years? and, Is the omnipotence of Parliament a doctrine consistent with reason and the principles of the Constitution? and, Is not a triennial Parliament more conducive to the security of our liberties, than any other?'
A society composed of students of the Inns of Court.
Clarinets and french horns, 2s. 6d. tea & coffee included.
Morning Chronicle April 15

507. April 16, 1780 Religious Association, Greenwoods Rooms
Genesis i. – 27 'God created man in his own image, in the image of God created he him'. – ii. 16 'And the Lord God commanded the man, saying, of every tree of the garden thou may freely eat.' – 17. 'But of the tree of knowledge of and evil thou eatest thereof thou shalt surely die.'
London Courant April 12

508. April 16, 1780 University for Rational Amusements, Theological Question
'I say therefore to the unmarried and widows, it is good for them, if they abide even as I.' I Cor. ch. vii vers 8
London Courant April 15

509. April 16, 1780 Theological Society, One Tun, Strand
20th verse of first chapter of the second epistle of Peter, 'Knowing this first, that no prophecy of the scripture is of any private interpretation.' Intended as a candid inquiry into whether or no scripture is the only rule of faith.
Includes original lecture.
Morning Chronicle April 15

510. April 17, 1780 Westminster Forum
'Is it not a general duty to associate for the restoring of annual Parliaments, and equal representation, as being immediately necessary in order to effectual oeconomy, and constitutional independence, the safety and happiness of the people?'
Carried almost unanimously.
London Courant April 13/Short History of the Westminster

511. April 18, 1780 Oratorical Academy, Mitre Tavern

'Would a total abolition of confinement for debt be of more good or hurt to a commercial country?'
London Courant April 15

512. April 18, 1780 Oratorical Society, Portugal Street
'Has the Art of Printing been more advantageous or detrimental to Mankind?'
Morning Post

513. April 19, 1780 Assembly Room, Crown and Rolls Tavern, Chancery Lane
'First, Has not the conduct of opposition been consistent with public interest since the year 1767?
Second, Is the omnipotence of parliament a doctrine consonant to reason and the principles of the constitution?
Third, Is not a triennial parliament more conducive to the security of our liberties, than any other of longer or shorter duration?'
Admission one shilling.
Morning Post

514. April 19, 1780 University for Rational Amusements
'Should a Minister resign when the petitions of the people have created a majority against him?
Previous to the debate a favorite DUET will be sung by two Ladies, and after the debate a Lady will sing the much admired Italian Song, "Tortsrella adandonato".'
Morning Post

515. April 20, 1780 Carlisle House, the School of Eloquence
'If a British Senator differs in opinion from his Constituents, is it his duty to vote in Parliament from his own judgement, or from their instructions?
2d. Whether anonymous criticisms, in periodical publications, and particularly in Reviews, be of real benefit or injury to Literature?
No persons will be admitted but subscribers, and none allowed to subscribe who are not perfectly agreeable to the Society.'
Gazetteer April 17

516. April 20, 1780 Coachmakers-hall
'Would it not greatly conduce to connubial happiness, if the means of total separation were less difficult than at present, and within the abilities of all ranks and situations?
After a learned, sensible, and judicious debate, it was unanimously carried in the negative.'
Gazetteer April 18

517. April 21, 1780 Female Parliament, University for Rational Amusements

'Is that assertion of Mr. Pope's founded in justice which says, 'Every Woman is at Heart a Rake'?'
It was decided this was unjust.
London Courant

518. April 21, 1780 Palladium or Liberal Academy of Eloquence
'Is there not cruelty in the law, that punishes a woman with burning, for the same crime which a man is only hanged for? and, Would not permitting Papists to realize property, and enjoy every other immunity in common with Protestant Dissenters, be the best means to secure their allegiance to a Protestant Prince?'
Gazetteer April 19

519. April 22, 1780 University for Rational Amusement
'Which is more to be dreaded in future in this country, the Influence of the Crown or the spirit of party?'
Morning Post

520. April 22, 1780 La Belle Assemblee
'Whether is jealousy the result of extreme love, or the effect of mental depravity?
The Rooms are altered for the better accommodation of the Ladies.
Determined that jealousy was the result of extreme love. An Italian lady, who was supposed to have given the question, spoke to it herself.'
Gazetteer

521. April 23, 1780 University for Rational Amusements, Theological Question
'For I the Lord thy God am a Jealous God, visiting the sins of the Fathers upon the Children, unto the third and fourth generations of them that hate me.' Exod. ch. xx. v. 5.
London Courant April 21

522. April 23, 1780 Religious Association
Hebrews vi. vers. 4, 5, 6 'For it is impossible for those who were once enlightened, and have tasted of the Heavenly gift, and were made partakers of the Holy Ghost. And have tasted the word of God, and the powers of the world to come. If they fall away, to renew them again unto repentance; seeing they crucify to themselves the Son of God afresh, and put him to open shame.'
London Courant April 20

523. April 24, 1780 Westminster Forum
'Are there sufficient reasons to justify Englishmen in continuing the Slave Trade?'
Decided against the slave trade.
London Courant April 20/Short History of the Westminster

524. April 25, 1780 Oratorical Academy, Mitre Tavern

'Is that maxim of the poet true, which affects, that
  Women born to be controll'd
  Stoop to the forward and the bold.
This question was sent by some Ladies who promised *to join in the debate.*'
London Courant April 20

525. April 25, 1780 Oratorical Society, Portugal Street
'Is lenity or severity in a Sovereign most conducive to the happiness of the subjects?'
Morning Post

526. April 26, 1780 University for Rational Amusements
'Is Love or Hatred the most powerful passion? and, Was Cato justifiable in killing himself?
Previous to the debate, a Lady will sing the favourite Scotch air of 'Johnny and Mary,' introduced by Miss Catley, in Love in a Village: and after the debate, a Gentleman and Lady will sing the favourite duet of 'Dalmon and Clara.'
London Courant

527. April 27, 1780 St. James Chronicle
CARLISLE-HOUSE
'That Department of the Academy, called *The School of Eloquence*, like a young but robust Child, is subject to some violent Indispositions. The Audience last Thursday Evening not finding the usual Entertainment, owing to an Alteration in the Disposition of the Room, called upon the Moderator for Redress. He lamented, that from some unfortunate Perverseness in the Tenants, who depended on the Society for the very Payment of their Rent, he was prevented from doing what by his Contract he had a proper Power to do, and what he sincerely wished to do for the perfect Accommodation of the Company. The Proprietors were called for, and an elderly Man appeared. He faultered, and hesitated, and spoke bad English amidst the Hisses of the Audience; but at last, to complete his Disgrace, said "that every Thing should be put in Order, at the Request of the Audience, but not by Desire of the Moderator, who was only a Servant." The coarse Illiberality and Falsehood of the Insult was resented by the severest Expressions of Detestation. The Moderator was desired to quit the Chair, and a young Gentleman, glowing with a large Portion of the generous fire which animate the whole Assembly, took his Place. The Audience then with cordial Unanimity voted the Moderator Thanks for his impartial, candid, and judicious Conduct, ever since he had presided over that Society; pledged themselves to take him under their Protection, and to see him supported. The Moderator expressed his Gratitude, as well as the Fullness of his Heart would admit him. The Assembly broke up with the most generous good Humour; and we suppose, that having adopted the Moderator as their own, they will in future enforce their own Regulations, and redress their own Grievances.

The Company was very brilliant; and some Personages of the most distinguished Rank were active in the generous Parts of this Business.'

528. April 27, 1780 Carlisle House The School of Eloquence
'1. Whether anonymous criticisms, in periodical publications, particularly in Reviews, be of real benefit or injury to Literature?
2. Is the British House of Commons sufficient, without the concurrence of the other branches of the Legislature, to determine any character or description of men to be a disqualification for a seat in that House?'
Gazetteer

529. April 27, 1780 Coachmakers Hall
'Are not the Representatives of the Commons in Parliament, bound to obey the instructions of their particular constituents?'
Gazetteer April 25

530. April 28, 1780 Free Masons Hall, The Palladium, or Liberal Academy of Eloquence
'Was it politic in England, to assist Russia to become a Maritime Power? And, if the time permit, the second Question, Which is most in danger from flattery, a woman of singular beauty, or ample fortune?'
Gazetteer April 27

531. April 28, 1760 University for Rational Amusements, Female Parliament
'Are not Male Encroachments on Female Occupations, an hardship on the Sex, which ought to be remedied by a restrictive Law?'
London Courant April 26

532. April 29, 1780 La Belle Assemblee
'Which is the most amiable accomplishment in Woman, Fine Natural Sense or Extensive Learning?
The debate was spirited, and the language pointed and chaste. The question was carried in favour of fine natural sense.'
London Courant

533. April 29, 1780 University for Rational Amusement
'Is that circumstance of managers of Theatres, being authors themselves, of detriment to Dramatic Literature? and, Was Cato justifiable in killing himself?'
London Courant April 28

534. April 29, 1780 Gazetteer
CARLISLE HOUSE
'On Thursday evening the business of the School of Eloquence at that place was interrupted, in consequence of an alteration in the disposition of the room, and the situation of the chair. The company were seated inconveniently, and the speakers were so discouraged, that all the usual entertainment was lost: they therefore called on the Moderator, to

account for their ill treatment. He candidly told them, that his situation was such with a troublesome person who was a tenant in the house, that he could get nothing done as he wished to accommodate an audience by whom he was so much honoured, and by whom the tenants were maintained. The tenants were called for, and one of them appeared, who made many excuses; concluding the whole with saying, that thing should be put in their former situation, in compliance with the request of the audience, but not at the desire of the Moderator, who was his *servant*! This, from a man who was considered as deriving his subsistence from a society in which the Moderator presided, under a contract with the tenants, threw the whole room into a tumult; and he was forced to engage, and promise a punctual compliance. The Moderator then received an unanimous vote of thanks from the assembly, attended with acclamations, and assurances of support, which may be improved very favourably to the institution. There were some of the *very first* personages in the kingdom, who did themselves, as well as the Moderator, great honour, by the part they took in the business.'

535. April 30, 1780 University for Rational Amusement, Theological Question
'For I say unto you, that unto every one which hath shall be given, and from him that hath not, even that he hath shall be taken away.' Luke, ch. xix. v. 26.
London Courant April 28

536. April 30, 1780 Religious Association
1 Corinthians, chap. xiii, vers. 3 'And though I bestow all my goods to feed the poor, though I give my body to be burned, and have not charity, it profiteth me nothing.'
London Courant April 29

537. May 1, 1780 School for Oratory, China-Hall, Rotherhithe
'1st If a Member of the House of Commons should think differently from a majority of his Constituents in parliamentary matters, ought he to follow their instructions, or the dictates of his own judgment?
2nd. In most instances, where the affections of the female sex are improperly attached, who is most blameable, the man or the woman?'
Gazetteer

538. May 1, 1780 Carlisle House
'The opening of Carlisle House on tomorrow Evening, for the discussion of a question by LADIES only, being advertised, and the Advertisement concluding in the form with which the subjects to be debated in the School of Eloquence have usually been announced, viz. that "The Moderator will take the Chair at Eight;" I beg leave to inform the Public that neither the Principal of the Academy or myself have any concern in that undertaking; and though I am evidently alluded to in the advertisement, that I received my first information upon the subject from a news paper.

I think it necessary to declare this, not only to prevent a seeming deception upon the public, but to protect myself and the institution from that ridicule which must deservedly follow the introduction of an entertainment so inconsistent with the Academic Plan, which the Public have been assured will be faithfully executed at Carlisle House.

I cannot omit this opportunity of repeating my warmest thanks, for the very flattering and unanimous vote of approbation with which I was honoured on Thursday last by the Nobility and Gentry, assembled at the School for Eloquence; and of assuring them, that I retain the most grateful sense of their favour, and will pay the most respectful attention to their future accommodation and entertainment.'

T. Martyn, Moderator

Morning Post

539. May 1, 1780 Westminster Forum
'Whether the candidates for seats in parliament refusing to sign a *test*, obliging themselves to exert their endeavours to obtain a reformation in the expenditure of the public money, the more equal representation, and shortening the duration of parliaments, ought to be depended upon as sincere friends of the people?'
It was decided that the candidates ought to sign a test.
London Courant April 27/Short History of the Westminster

540. May 2, 1780 Gazetteer
'A *male* correspondent, who was on Saturday evening last at *La Belle Assemblee* at the Haymarket, was filled with chagrin and admiration; admiration at the very able manner the question then discussed [was] treated; and chagrin to perceive, that with all the disadvantages of education which the fair sex labour under, how infinitely superior those who are formed by nature *to excite* the *tender* passions, are to excite *every other*. In short, not only to lead captive by all the graces of colloquial harmony, of pure diction, of varied and expressive emphasis, of language cloathed in the diversity of the several passions which were felt or wished to be personified, but likewise by sterling sentiments, founded in truth, forcibly directed to ultimate persuasion, and presenting in the whole to the attentive auditor, the *unmixed result* of well supported facts, or well-presumed premises, sufficient to bring home indubitable conviction to every mind capable of determining upon the only test of all human knowledge, logical conclusion, deduced from facts not denied, or premises not controverted.'

541. May 2, 1780 Carlisle House, Ladies Only
'Is the study of Politics and the affairs of state compatible with the station and character of the Fair Sex?'
London Courant April 29

542. May 2, 1780 Oratorical Society, Portugal Street
'Which is more to be desired by a female, beauty or good sense?'
Morning Chronicle

543. May 2, 1780 Oratorical Academy, Mitre Tavern
'Can the measure of arming the Third Regiment of Foot, and doubling the Horse Guards, on the day when the fate of the Petitions of the People was to be decided in the House of Commons, be vindicated?'
London Courant April 29

544. May 2, 1780 St. James Chronicle

CARLISLE HOUSE

'Tuesday Evening a Room was opened for Debate by *Ladies only*, at this House. The Inconsistency of this Measure with the academical Plan delivered to the Publick, and the Advertisement of the Moderator, that neither he nor the Principal of the Academy had any Concern in the Business, gave the Publick a disadvantageous Impression of it, as a desperate Expedient of the Tenants to get Money.

The Chair was not taken till Half after Eight; and we were sorry to see that a Gentleman of Character should be the Person engaged in such unworthy and dishonourable Business. He proposed the Question, to which some Women spoke; or rather read Speeches out of Papers; but the chief Dependence of the Evening was on a Mr. McNally in Woman's Clothes. He squeaked several Speeches to eke out the Time, but the Offence taken at such an indecent Artifice, and the Impatience of the Audience from Want of Entertainment, induced them to precipitate poor Marriott from the Chair, and to place an old discarded Actress in his Stead. She acquitted herself to the Satisfaction of those who surrounded the Chair, and who seemed to wish, like the Praetorian Band, to be occupied in placing and displacing Presidents. Whether the Freedom of her Behaviour, and the Luxuriance of her Language, aided by the Appearance of Men in Women's Clothes, may have any Effect in rendering this Assembly popular, and profitable to the Tenants, we leave to the Determination of the Publick.'

545. May 3, 1780 Morning Post
Letter, to the President of School for Eloquence, Freemasons Hall
[Schoolboy tells story of how his father took him, and two younger brothers to debate. Remarks on how expensive entry was.] Then says he 'thought, from the shabbiness of the dress of the speakers, they were very extravagant and foolish, to give away that money which would have been better laid out for shoes and stockings.' Says question, *which* is most liable to flattery, men or women should be *who* is most liable. Father 'lamented much the temerity of men who expose an ignorance of the simplest rules of language, and the plainest principles of reasoning, and exhibit to the public, for imitation, and a model of eloquence, aukward actions, vulgar idioms, and discordant ideas'.

546. May 4, 1780 Carlisle House, The School of Eloquence
'Is the British House of Commons, without the concurrence of the other branches of the Legislature, competent to determine any character or description of men to a disqualification for a seat in that House?

2d Is an Address from Parliament immediately to his Majesty, or a proceeding by an Act of the Legislature, the most proper mode to obtain the abridgement of the Civil List, and the economy requested by the present Petitions?'
Gazetteer

547. May 4, 1780 Coachmakers Hall
'Are not the Representatives of the Commons in Parliament bound to obey the instructions of their particular constituents?'
Gazetteer May 2

548. May 6, 1780 La Belle Assemblee, Mr. Greenwood's Rooms in the Haymarket
'Do the manners of the Ladies, in the present day, tend more to invite the Gentlemen to, or to deter them from matrimony?'
London Courant May 6

549. May 7, 1780 University for Rational Amusements, Female Parliament
'Was Adam or Eve more culpable in Paradise?'
London Courant

550. May 7, 1780 Religious Association
5th chapter St. Matthew, verses the 11th and 12th. 'Blessed are ye when men shall revile *you*, and persecute you, and shall say all manner of evil against you for my sake. Rejoyce, and be exceedingly glad; for great *is* your reward in Heaven; for so persecuted they the Prophets which were before you.'
London Courant May 6

551. May 7, 1780 University for Rational Amusements, Theological Question
'And she took of the fruit, and did eat thereof, and gave also unto her husband with her, and he did eat.'
London Courant May 5

552. May 8, 1780 Carlisle House School of Eloquence
'lst. Is an Address from Parliament immediately to his Majesty, or a proceeding by act of the Legislature, the most proper mode to obtain the abridgement of the Civil List, and the oeconomy requested by the present Petitions?
2d. Whether it is consistent with the principles of the constitution, that the Legislature of Great Britain should control the Legislature of Ireland?'
Gazetteer

553. May 8, 1780 The School of Oratory, China Hall, Rotherhithe
'In most Instances, when the affections of the female sex are improperly attached, who is most blameable, the man or the woman? Are the

people, by the English Constitution, intitled to short or frequent Parliaments? And, Are women in general, most in danger, from men of strong, or weak intellectual faculties?'
Admission One Shilling.
Gazetteer

554. May 8, 1780 Westminster Forum
'What interest is the most susceptible of corruption, and consequently demands the most rigid and immediate reform – the ecclesiastical, civil or military?'
It was decided that the ecclesiastical interest was most in need of reform.
London Courant/Short History of the Westminster

555. May 9, 1780 Carlisle House, Ladies Only
'Is the Diffident or Resolute, the most persuasive Lover?'
London Courant May 8

556. May 9, 1780 Oratorical Academy, Mitre Tavern
'Can friendship subsist between the two sexes, without the passion of love?'
London Courant May 8

557. May 11, 1780 Coachmakers Hall
'Is the observation founded in truth, that the manners of the present age are more depraved than in former times?'
Gazetteer May 9

558. May 11, 1780 Carlisle House School of Eloquence
'1st. Is an Address from Parliament immediately to his Majesty, or a proceeding by an act of Legislature, the most proper mode to obtain the abridgement of the Civil List, and the oeconomy requested in the present Petitions?
2nd. Whether it is consistent with the principles of the constitution, that the Legislature of Great-Britain should controul the Legislature of Ireland?'
Gazetteer May 8

559. May 11, 1780 St. James Chronicle
'SIR,
The English are said to be *Lions* in War, so I believe they are; but in common Life they are *Sheep*. There is always a *Bellwether* in our Politicks, Morals, Fashions, and Diversions, who is followed by the Crowd as eagerly as the Bellwether of a Common; the Ton once given, the whole Nation appears running made the same Way. Who had the Merit of giving the present Rage for the Schools of Eloquence I know not, but certainly the Disorder is become so epidemical, that we are in Danger of dying a Nation of Orators.

I have attended several of these Schools, Mr. Baldwin, and have now and then heard a sensible Speaker: but more generally Weak Reasoning, false Conclusions, and illiterate Language. As I write Short-Hand I have taken down a few Orations from the scientific lips of Tailors, Shoemakers, Haberdashers, etc. with which I may hereafter amuse that Part of the World who are unfortunately at too great a Distance from these Seminaries of Learning, to have their Minds elucidated by their Labours.

At present I shall confine myself to that one Head of the Hydra, called *La Belle Assemblee*. I am really, Sir, ashamed. I blush at seeing the lovely, tender, timid Sex, appear in a Light so very disadvantageous; and I am sorry for the Countenance given to their Excentricity by the Men, who, by insidious Applause, encourage the Folly they laugh at.

Were it really a Fact that these female Orators were any Thing more than the *hired* Reciters of a studied Lesson, it would be very little to their Honour: for what Women of the slightest Pretensions to Modesty, or common Decency could stand up in an Assembly of a thousand Persons, and hazard their Thoughts and Language on Subjects which they are supposed never to have studied till the Moment they begin to hold forth? Would not such Assurance and Effrontery render them absolutely disgustful? Is there a Man on Earth who from such a Set of Women would choose a Wife? or a Husband, Father, or Brother, who would not be shocked to find his Sister, Daughter or Wife in this garrulous Society?

But the Truth is (and it is a Fact in Favour of the Women who speak) their Lessons are all composed for them; so that they have no more to do with the Arguments they utter, than my Pen has with the Characters I force it to trace. But this though in Favour of the *Speakers*, is no Sort of Recommendation of the *Society*, for our Newspapers and Magazines present us infinitely better Essays on the same Subjects, and these we may enjoy in our Parlours, without the Disadvantages of hearing them from Mouths where they seem unnatural (for not the least Trace of *feminine Thinking* is to be found in these female Orations), or having them clipped and murthered by a vulgar pronunciation.

INDIGNUS'

560. May 12, 1780 Oratorical Academy, Mitre Tavern
'If the people receive no redress in consequence of their petitions, can any legal and constitutional method be adopted to procure it?'
London Courant May 11

561. May 12, 1780 University For Rational Amusements, Female Parliament
'Is publick Abuse, or private Scandal, the most injurious to society?'
London Courant

562. May 13, 1780 Religious Association
Revel. chap. xiv. vers 11 'And the smoke of their torments ascendeth up for ever and ever.'
London Courant

563. May 13, 1780 La Belle Assemblee
'Do the exhibitions of the Stage tend more to the promotion of Vice or Virtue?
The arguments adduced by the fair orators were genteel and sprightly, free from that censure and invective which so ample a field might have afforded, and the question was unanimously carried, that stage exhibitions, well regulated, tend more to the promotion of *virtue*.
Tea-rooms open at six. Ice creams, &c.'
Gazetteer

564. May 13, 1780 Westminster Forum
'Is not a federal Union with America the most desirable at present of all political events, next to the Reformation of our internal Policy?'
London Courant

565. May 13, 1780 University for Rational Amusements
'Was Cato justifiable in killing himself? and, Are the tedious Law Proceedings of England, or the summary Law Proceedings of the Eastern Countries, to be preferred?'
London Courant

566. May 14, 1780 University for Rational Amusements, Theological Question
'But to him that worketh not, but believeth on him that justifieth the ungodly, his faith is counted for righteousness.' Romans, c. iv. v. 5.
London Courant May 13

567. May 15, 1780 China Hall, Rotherhithe
'1. Are women most in danger from men of strong, or weak intellectual faculties?
2. Which is the happiest state, weakness or wisdom?
3. What parliamentary term would be most advantageous to the people at large, Annual, Duennial, or Triennial?'
Adjourned.
Gazetteer

568. May 15, 1780 Westminster Forum
'Is not a federal union with America, the most desirable, at present, of all political events, next to the reformation of our internal policy?'
Question decided in the affirmative.
Short History of the Westminster

569. May 16, 1780 Carlisle House, Ladies Only
'Is not a liberal acquiescence with the prevalence of fashion, in the improvements of the person, as necessary as an attention to the cultivation of the understanding?'
Gazetteer

570. May 16, 1780 Oratorical Academy, Mitre Tavern
'If the people receive no redress in consequence of their petitions, can any legal and constitutional means be adopted to procure it?'
London Courant

571. May 17, 1780 University for Rational Amusement
'Are the tedious law Proceedings of England or the summary Law proceedings of the Eastern countries, to be preferred?'
London Courant

572. May 18, 1780 Carlisle House, School of Eloquence
'Is Pride in the class of the Virtues or the Vices?'
Gazetteer

573. May 19, 1780 Lyceum
'Whether the Discovery of America has been productive of Benefit or Injury to Europe? – If, of Benefit; what are the best means to preserve and encrease it? – if, of Injury; What are the best means to remedy it? In order to associate Genius, and give every Encouragement to an Institution founded on the most liberal Principles, that ever gave rise to any Society in this Country, the Select Committee have resolved, that those who may wish to subscribe for the remaining Nights of this Season, shall not be obliged to pay the full subscription, as if they had been Members from the Beginning: – But to preserve a proper Degree of Respect in the Company, the Subscription will never be lower than HALF A GUINEA.'
Morning Herald

574. May 19, 1780 University for Rational Amusement, The Female Parliament
'Is an old woman marrying a young man, or a young woman marrying an old man, the more blameable?
As the decorations of the Rooms gave such universal satisfaction on the night of the Carnival Masquerade, they will be illuminated this evening in the same style of elegance.'
Admittance 2s. 6d. refreshments of tea, coffee, capillaire, orgeat &c. included.
Gazetteer

575. May 20, 1780 La Belle Assemblee
'Which is the more censurable, an obstinate adherence to old fashions or the servile compliance with new?'
Gazetteer May 18

576. May 21, 1780 Religious Association
Rev. xiv. ver 11 'And the smoke of their torment ascendeth up for ever and ever.'
London Courant May 20

577. May 21, 1780 University for Rational Amusement, Theological Question
'Whosoever speaketh against the Holy Ghost, it shall not be forgiven him, neither in this world, neither in the world to come.' Matt. ch. xii, v. 32.
London Courant May 20

578. May 22, 1780 Tusculanum or Rural Assembly
'Whether platonic love can exist between man and Woman?
Question was carried, that Platonic love cannot exist between the sexes. At the present period, when eloquence is become the favourite object of public attention, little need be said to recommend an establishment of this kind, as to its general nature or tendency; but it is proper to observe, that no Oratorical Society whatever has hitherto opened up with so fair a prospect of entertainment as the RURAL ASSEMBLY may challenge. The season is now arrived, when the confinement of the town must be irksome enough to depreciate its most favoured amusements: that the moments of relaxation should then be allotted to Rural Entertainment, seems to be the suggestion of true taste, and will be found to be most conducive to health and pleasure, which this institution is well calculated to promote. . . those who chuse to attend this institution, previous to their visiting Vauxhall Gardens, will not be precluded, by reason of the early hour at which the debates conclude, and may find thereby an agreeable variety in their evening's entertainment. NB the introduction of Masks in societies of this kind have been attended with several inconveniences, none will be admitted.'
Morning Post

579. May 22, 1780 China Hall, Rotherhithe
'1. Are women most in danger from men of strong or weak intellectual faculties?
2. Which is the happiest state, weakness or wisdom?
3. What parliamentary term would be most advantageous to the people at large, ANNUAL, DUENNIAL or TRIENNIAL?'
Gazetteer

580. May 22, 1780 Westminster Forum
'Is not giving a Military Command to a man who has never seen service, a discouragement to the army?'
Question decided in the affirmative.
Morning Chronicle/Short History of the Westminster

581. May 22, 1780 Morning Post
Lines on Hearing the Debates of the FEMALE PARLIAMENT at the Casino, May 19, 1780

'Lo! Now the mandate of despotic fate
Is fled – and women mingle in debate!
Op'd are those lips which bashful prudence clos'd,

And bar'd that breast where modesty repos'd.
Anxious in every course to win the bays,
They start, undaunted, candidates for praise!
But this ambition asks not for redress,
If human acts are measured by success!
Not *Fletcher* fills the Senatorial Chair
With more applause, than when a B—'s there.
Even in this infancy of female fame,
A Fox already lisps, and Burkes declaim!
An embryo minister the sex shall yield,
And young Minorities dispute the shield.
Ah! long victorious in the realms of Wit,
In all to thee must humbled man submit?
Content not *Phoebus*' envied heights to reach,
Ye claim the dormant privilege of *speech!* –
Ierned-like, the lucky moment seize,
Gain what ye ask, and ask what'er ye please!

Thus the immortal Amazons of yore,
In *Mar's* red field, the palm of conquest bore;
Even he, whose labours filled earth's circuit wide,
Here first in arms a foe superior try'd.
To pining youths, who left the myrtle bough,
And plucked the laurel from the warrior's brow!'

582. May 23, 1780 Carlisle House, Ladies Only
'Is not the hope of reclaiming a Libertine a principal cause of conjugal unhappiness?'
Gazetteer May 22

583. May 24, 1780 University for Rational Amusement, Theological Question
'The following text will be investigated: "Thou oughtest therefore to have put my money to the exchangers; and then, at my coming, I should have received mine own, with usury." St. Matt. ch xxv. v. 27.'
Gazetteer

584. May 25, 1780 Carlisle House School of Eloquence
'Is Great Britain verging more toward an absolute Monarchy or a Republic?'
Gazetteer May 22

585. May 27, 1780 Coachmakers Hall
'Is the man who never marries, or he who marries merely for pecuniary advantage, the greater enemy to the fair sex?'
Gazetteer May 25

586. May 27, 1780 La Belle Assemblee
'Whether are the elegant Amusements of the Town, or the simple Pastimes of the Country, more agreeable?'
Gazetteer

587. May 28, 1780 University for Rational Amusement, Theological Question
St. Matthew, chap. xxv, vers 27. 'Thou oughtest therefore to have put my money to the exchangers, and then at my coming I should have received mine own with usury.'
Morning Chronicle May 27

588. May 28, 1780 Religious Association
'And the smoke of their torment ascendeth up for ever and ever.'
London Courant May 27

589. May 29, 1780 Tusculanum, or the Rural Assembly for the Discussion of Moral, Political, Commercial, and Miscellaneous Questions at Smith's Tea Gardens, Vauxhall
'1. Which is the greater requisite in a Commander, courage or caution?
2. Is there a greater prospect of happiness in married or single state?
Those who are desirous of visiting Vauxhall Gardens, may here find an agreeable variety in their evening's entertainment, and the early hour at which the debate will conclude will be no impediment.'
Admission one shilling.
It was decided that caution was the greater requisite in a Commander.
Gazetteer

590. May 29, 1780 The Summer Lyceum or Liberal Assembly, for Free Debate, Lectures, and Oratorical Exercises, Smith's Tea Gardens, Islington
'Does the too prevailing aversion to matrimony in the present day, arise from a defect in the morals of the people, or a deficiency in the laws of our country?
The discussion of the most interesting and entertaining subjects by the people at large, is a recreation not only rational in itself, but particularly adapted to the taste of an English audience. To accommodate the public with an amusement that has received the sanction of the sentimental and polite, Mr. Smith has opened his great room, under the direction of a person of literary talents, where moral and political questions will be investigated, lectures regularly delivered, and orations on eminent characters occasionally pronounced.'
Gazetteer

591. May 29, 1780 Westminster Forum
'Would it not have been highly proper in the present state of naval affairs to have appointed Sir Hugh Palliser to the command of the Channel fleet, notwithstanding the popular clamour against him?'
Decided that this would have been highly improper.
London Courant May 27/Short History of the Westminster

592. May 30, 1780 Carlisle House, Ladies
'Is gallantry in men, or coquetry in the female sex, the most censurable?'
Gazetteer

593. June 1, 1780 Carlisle House School of Eloquence
'Has the King a right to make peace with America without the consent of Parliament?'
Gazetteer

594. June 2, 1780 La Belle Assemblee
'In the failure of a mutual affection in the married state, which is to be preferred, to love or be loved?'
London Courant

595. June 4, 1780 Religious Association
St. Mark vers. 15, 'There is nothing from without a man that entering into him can defile him; but the things which come out of him: those can defile him.'
Morning Chronicle June 3

596. June 6, 1780 Tusculanum
'Does the account of the late engagement in the West Indies, contained in the Gazette, justify the encomiums passed therein on the French Officers? Do not the late official dispatches throw too general a reflection on the officers of the British Fleet?'
Morning Chronicle

597. June 12, 1780 Tusculanum
'Does modern Matrimony offer a greater prospect of happiness than a single life?'
Morning Chronicle

598. September 7, 1780 Coachmakers Hall
'Are the military associations now forming in the metropolis, more likely to be productive of advantage or disadvantage to the community?'
Gazetteer September 2

599. September 7, 1780 King's Arms Society, for Free and Candid Debate, removed from Coachmaker's Hall
'Were the late Riots the effect of Accident or Design?'
Admittance sixpence; ladies may either sit separate or with their friends.
London Courant August 26

600. September 8, 1780 London Courant
Mitre Tavern, Fleet Street
'A Society of Gentlemen, who propose to meet weekly, during the Winter, at the Mitre Tavern, Fleet Street, for the discussion of Political, Moral, and other Interesting Subjects, take this opportunity of announcing to the public, that the following important question will be debated Monday next [September 11]:

"Has the general conduct of the Ministry in the last Parliament, entitled its Members to the Suffrages of the people on this election?" Admittance TWO SHILLINGS.'

601. September 14, 1780 King's Arms Society
'Would the electing members to serve in Parliament, by ballot, tend more to lessen undue influence, than the present mode of election?' London Courant September 9

602. September 21, 1780 Coachmakers Hall
'Ought the right of electing Representatives to serve in Parliament to depend on the property, or to be considered as the personal privilege of every Englishman?'
Gazetteer

603. September 21, 1780 Debating Society, King's Arms-tavern, Cornhill
'Would it not be conducive to the happiness of the marriage state, that no woman should have a marriage portion?'
Gazetteer September 20

604. September 23, 1780 London Courant
'THE MIDDLESEX FORUM, for the exercise of public Speaking, will be opened on Wednesday next, the 27th inst. at the superb and elegant Room, known by the name of the
MUSEUM, SPRING GARDENS.
The Question to be debated will be, "Is it likely, that the People of England will receive any benefit from the general re-election of their Representatives in Parliament?"
The chair will be taken precisely at eight o'clock; and as it is meant that the Middlesex Forum should be conducted upon the most liberal plan, as an incitement to Elocution, and an honourable testimony thereof,
A most capital GOLD MEDAL
will be given to the best Speaker, to be delivered to him at the close of the evening by the Moderator, upon the vote of the company present.
Ladies will be admitted, though it is intended that none but Gentlemen shall be permitted to speak upon the question, as it is meant to set an evening sport for the female part of the forum.
Previous to, and during the time of debate,
The WAXWORK
which has so much excited the public curiosity and resort, will be exhibited, representing a Court of Justice in full display of all their oratorical proceedings; together with many more capital characters.
Price TWO SHILLINGS.'

605. September 25, 1780 Westminster Forum

'If uniformity of conduct, and tried abilities, render a Member of Parliament truly valuable, will not the rejection of Alderman Sawbridge be highly dishonourable to the Livery men of London?'
London Courant September 21

606. September 26, 1780 London Courant
'The intention of presenting the best speaker of the *Middlesex Forum* next Wednesday with a *Gold Medal*, seems to meet with the general idea and approbation of the public, who have long thought some mark of distinction necessary on such occasions, as an incitement to oratory and elocution, than which nothing can more conduce to the reputation of an individual, or the honour of the state.'

607. September 27, 1780 Gazetteer
'The debating Society at Coachmakers'-hall was opened on Thursday evening last to a genteel and respectable auditory, when the Chairman, with great propriety, addressed the company in the following well delivered speech:
GENTLEMEN,
Little needs to be said in commendation of public disputation conducted upon a liberal plan: it is as ancient as the days of Demosthenes and Cicero; for it was then, and ever since has been considered in a most advantageous light.
A liberal discussion of subjects political and philosophical must tend to increase the stock of human knowledge, and to open and expand the ideas of mankind. A mutual exchange of sentiments, in a friendly society, can only be productive of advantage; such an intercourse pleases while it instructs, and in the end the mind is furnished with that firmness and cool stability which can only be acquired in public debate.
Public disputation was revered as an invaluable blessing at a time when Rome was at the highest pitch of greatness: Philosophers and Politicians of all ages have ever considered it of the greatest consequence to mankind. For to dispute candidly, to discuss liberally, what means it? but that a society of friends have met for the very laudable purpose of discovering truth. Human genius cannot wish for a superior field to exercise in: it draws forth ideas which would never have arisen in the closet, and stimulates to such discoveries as would ever have been buried in retirement. Public disputation acts on genius as the flint does on steel – they both produce rays which would ever have been hidden, but for collision and friendly intercourse.
Be it our care then, gentlemen, to conduct this Society on such a plan – the assistance of every individual is necessary.
Much indeed ought to be said as an apology for your Chairman – but as it is his sincere intention to act with care and with impartiality, he deems it unnecessary to apologize for his want of abilities in a society of gentlemen, met for no other purpose but candid and liberal disputation. He will, therefore, not trouble you any further, conscious that he shall experience that candour which has ever so particularly distinguished this respectable Society.'

608. September 27, 1780 Morning Chronicle
'On a late Decision, by the King's Arms Society, "That the Abolition of Portions would be conducive to Matrimonial Happiness."

As 'twas lately determin'd, that no one from hence,
When taking a wife, should accept of few pence;
'Tis presum'd, that the ladies in gratitude ought
To prefer the poor lover, who's not worth a groat:
That thus destitute both, they both may be sure,
Themselves are alone, not their purses the lure.
Then contemplate ye lads, and ye lasses, the blisses!
When sans bread and cheese, you exist but on kisses!
And if love, in nine months, a fine boy should compleat,
They who live but on love, sure its produce may eat!
So cherish your wives, all as much as you're able,
As you value the sight of a joint at your table.
M. R.'

609. September 27, 1780 King's Arms
'Are those nations of Europe justifiable, who, in the critical moment of danger in which this country stands, have formed a maritime confederacy, under the pretense of preserving the neutrality of the seas?'
Morning Chronicle

610. September 28, 1780 Coachmakers Hall
'Are the military associations now forming in the metropolis, more likely to be productive of advantage or disadvantage to the community?'
Gazetteer September 27

611. September 29, 1780 Morning Post
'One of the first objects of consideration of the new Parliament, it is said, will be, a restriction upon public debating societies, particularly those in which theological questions are discussed. It cannot be doubted, but that such assemblies are exceedingly productive of both religious and political profligacy.'

612. October 1, 1780 Christian Society, at Mr. Greenwood's room
St. Matthew 5th, verse 34, 'Swear not at all.'
London Courant September 29

613. October 2, 1780 Westminster Forum
'Which do most injure civil society, the absolutely indolent or the actively vicious?'
London Courant September 29

614. October 2, 1780 Middlesex Forum, Cox's Museum, Spring Garden
'Which of the two is the worst character, the absolutely indolent or the actively vicious?'
London Courant

615. October 4, 1780 Middlesex Forum
'Which of the two is the worst character, the Member of Parliament that bribes the elector, or the Minister that corrupts the Member of Parliament?'
Morning Chronicle

616. October 5, 1780 Coachmakers Hall
'Would it not tend to the happiness of mankind, if women were allowed a scientific education?'
Gazetteer October 3

617. October 5, 1780 King's-Arms Society
'Is the general charge of depravity of manners more applicable to the male or female character?
The room is conveniently adapted for the accommodation of the ladies.'
Gazetteer October 3

618. October 7, 1780 Christian Society
'They that are whole need not a physician but they that are sick.'
Morning Chronicle

619. October 9, 1780 Westminster Forum
'Does the Morning Post, or the General Advertiser, deserve the greater share of reprobation?'
London Courant October 5

620. October 11, 1780 Middlesex Forum
'Who of the two suffered the hardest case, Lord George Gordon or Mr. Laurens?'
London Courant October 9

621. October 12, 1780 King's Arms Society
'Ought the Hon. Henry Laurens, late President of the American Congress, to be treated as a rebel, or as a prisoner of war?'
Gazetteer October 10

622. October 12, 1780 Coachmakers Hall
'Are not the Representatives of the Commons in Parliament bound to obey the instructions of their particular constituents?'
Gazetteer October 11

623. October 14, 1780 La Belle Assemblee
'Ought not the women of Great Britain to have a voice in the election of Representatives, and be eligible to sit in Parliament as well as the men?'
London Courant

624. October 14, 1780 Christian Society
'And it repented the Lord that he had made man on the earth.'

Morning Chronicle

625. October 16, 1780 Westminster Forum
'Whether the practice of admitting strangers into the Gallery of the
H—e of C—ns is likely to produce greater advantages or disadvantages
to the nation?'
London Courant October 14

626. October 18, 1780 Middlesex Forum
'Would it be right for the legislature to lay a tax on all batchelors after
a given age?'
London Courant

627. October 18, 1780 Morning Post
'On Saturday evening *La Belle Assemblee* opened for the winter season,
and were honoured with a very brilliant and respectable audience. The
debate was admirably supported, and many pointed good things said
which would be no discredit to a much higher assembly. Several Ladies
who evidently came as auditors with no intent to speak, could not
refrain from favouring the audience with their sentiments, in a language
remarkably chaste, elegant and convincing. – A well wisher to this
nouvelle and rational amusement, recommends to the Proprietors to
make three prices instead of one, and have boxes, pit, and gallery, for
which the place is well calculated. Thus would the pockets and persons
of each class be more agreeably accommodated.'

628. October 19, 1780 Kings Arms
'Would it not have been of great advantage to mankind, if, in the
construction of Civil Governments, rewards had been decreed for
Virtue as well as Punishments for Vice?'
Morning Chronicle October 18

629. October 19, 1780 Coachmakers Hall
'Would it not be for the honour and interest of Great Britain to release
immediately the Hon. Henry Laurens, late President of the American
Congress, who was taken on his embassy to the States of Holland?'
Gazetteer October 17

630. October 21, 1780 Morning Post
'A correspondent says he was last Saturday night at the opening of *La
Belle Assemblee*. The speeches of the Ladies now, in general, are well
delivered; but, like some tavern wines, have too much *Perry* in their
composition; and others seem to *Hunt* after humour. The *President*
recapitulated the arguments of the speakers in such a manner, that
the auditors were like poulterers' turkies, first fed with corn, and then
afterwards crammed with *Pollard*.'

631. October 21, 1780 La Belle Assemblee

'Would it not be for the benefit of society, if the plan of female education was extended to the arts and sciences?'
Places may be taken for the boxes 3s., Pit 2s., Gallery 1s.
London Courant October 19

632. October 22, 1780 Christian Society
Romans chap. ix, vers. 13 'He hath mercy on whom he will have mercy, and whom he will, he hardeneth.'
Admission 6d.
Morning Chronicle October 21

633. October 23, 1780 Westminster Forum
'Whether a good citizen would be justified in acting with his patron and friend, though he should seem to him to oppose the interest of his country?'
London Courant October 19

634. October 26, 1780 King's Arms Society
'Would it be proper at this crisis, considering our late successes, to allow independence to America?'
Gazetteer October 24

635. October 26, 1780 Coachmakers Hall
'Whether if on an investigation of the claims of private sufferers by the rioters in June last, damages should be recovered against the Chief Magistrate of this City – he ought to be reimbursed by the inhabitants of this metropolis?'
Gazetteer October 24

636. October 27, 1780 Morning Post
'A correspondent observes with pleasure, that the wise resolution of the Common Council to exclude their wives from the Lord Mayor's feast, is to become the subject of debate and ridicule of the Ladies of *La Belle Assemblee*. He should not be surprized, if it should turn out that the question originated with one of the offended Ladies, that they might have an opportunity of making reprisals. There is no doubt but that it will afford ample scope for laughter and ridicule, and should Mrs. —, who has been a constant patroness of *La Belle Assemblee*, take it into her head to communicate her sentiments on the subject, she will undoubtedly be able to give the most highly-finished picture of the Aldermanic body, as she is certainly more acquainted with the *constitution* and abilities of the Court than all the Poets or Poetesses of England.'

637. October 28, 1780 La Belle Assemblee
'Was it consistent with justice or politeness to think of excluding the ladies of the Common Council from the Lord-mayor's feast?'
London Courant October 26

113

638. October 29, 1780 Christian Society
Acts ch. 8, vers. 36 & 37 'And as they went on their way, they came unto a certain water; and the eunuch said, see here is water; what doth hinder me to be baptized. And Philip said, if thou believeth with all thine heart thou mayest. And he answered and said, I believe that Jesus Christ is the Son of God.'
Morning Chronicle October 28

639. October 30, 1780 Westminster Forum
'Whether the Corporation of London ought to defend their Magistrates in the action brought against them by an eminent Trader, who sustained great damages in the late riots?'
London Courant October 28

640. November 2, 1780 Coachmakers Hall
'Which is to be preferred in the choice of a wife, beauty without fortune, or fortune without beauty?'
Gazetteer October 31

641. November 2, 1780 King's Arms Society
'Is Love or Ambition more predominant in the human breast?'
Gazetteer

642. November 4, 1780 Christian Society
Revelations 22 chap. vers 14 'Blessed are they that do his commandments.'
Morning Chronicle

643. November 4, 1780 La Belle Assemblee
'Whether, in the present difficult situation of public affairs, a tax upon old batchelors would not only be just but equitable?'
London Courant November 2

644. November 5, 1780 School for Theology, Museum, Spring Garden
'It is easier for a camel to go through the eye of a needle, than for a rich man to enter into the kingdom of God.' St. Mark, chap. x, ver. 25.
'And they were astonished out of measure, saying among themselves, who can be saved.' ver. 26.
Gazetteer November 4

645. November 6, 1780 Westminster Forum
'Whether the Law of Solon, which makes it a capital offence for any citizen to take a part in a civil dissension, is calculated for the security of a society and consonant with sound policy?'
London Courant November 2

646. November 7, 1780 Coachmakers Hall

'Can Administration be justified in the dismission of the late Speaker of the House of Commons?'
Morning Chronicle November 6

647. November 9, 1780 King's Arms Society
'Would a law to restrain extravagance in dress and the table, be of advantage or detriment to the morals and trade of this kingdom?'
Morning Chronicle November 8

648. November 11, 1780 La Belle Assemblee
'Can the Rev. Mr. Madan's doctrine of a plurality of wives be justified either by the laws of policy or religion?'
London Courant November 9

649. November 12, 1780 Christian Society
Matt. xxvi, vers 52 'All they that live by the sword, shall perish by the sword.'
Morning Chronicle November 11

650. November 12, 1780 School for Theology, Spring Gardens
' King Agrippa said unto Paul: Almost thou persuadist me to be a Christian.'
Admission 1s.
Morning Chronicle November 11

651. November 13, 1780 Westminster Forum
'Whether the late advertisement of persons calling themselves a Committee of Association for a certain great city, signed by a Right Honorable Member of the H—e of C—ns, is the effect of real patriotism and calculated to promote the interest of the country?'
London Courant November 9

652. November 16, 1780 King's Arms Society
'Can the doctrine of a celebrated Divine, in his treatise in behalf of a plurality of wives, be justified upon the principles of religion, reason, or sound policy?'
Gazetteer November 14

653. November 16, 1780 Coachmakers Hall
'Is it the love of the mental or personal charms of the fair sex, that is more likely to induce men to enter into the married state?'
Gazetteer November 14

654. November 18, 1780 La Belle Assemblee
'Can the Rev. Mr. Madan's doctrine of a plurality of wives be justified either by the laws of policy or religion? and, Whether is the man of learning, fortune, courage, or politeness, most acceptable to the ladies?'
London Courant November 16

115

655. November 19, 1780 Christian Society
Genesis iv. vers. 19 'And Lamech took unto him two wives.'
Morning Chronicle November 18

656. November 20, 1780 Westminster Forum
'Whether the advertisement of a Committee of Association of the City
of Westminster, signed by the Hon. Charles Fox, dated Nov. 3, is the
effect of real patriotism, and calculated to promote the interest of this
country?'
London Courant November 16

657. November 22, 1780 Forum of Eloquence, borough of Southwark
'Whether it had been better for this nation, that the Earl of Mansfield
had never existed?'
After a debate of three hours, it was carried in the affirmative by a very
large majority. 'It was determined that "neither in his *professional* nor
political character had his very enlightened understanding occasioned
so much good as evil to this country".'
London Courant November 23

658. November 23, 1780 Coachmakers Hall
'Would not the Commander in Chief in America have promoted the
Royal cause more, had he delivered up General Arnold, and thereby
have saved the brave, but unfortunate Major Andre?'
Gazetteer November 21

659. November 23, 1780 King's Arms Society
'Has the discovery of America been productive of more good or evil
consequences to mankind?
N.B. This is the question for the solution of which the Royal Academy
of Arts and Sciences at Lyons have offered a premium of a thousand
livres.'
Gazetteer November 21

660. November 25, 1780 La Belle Assemblee
'Whether the marriage act is consistent with sound policy?'
London Courant November 23

661. November 26, 1780 Christian Society
'Woe unto the world because of offences, for it must needs be that
offences come: but woe to that man by whom the offence cometh.'
Morning Chronicle November 25

662. November 27, 1780 Westminster Forum
'Would it have been consistent with honour and humanity in Sir Henry
Clinton to have given back General Arnold if he could thereby have
saved Major Andre?'
London Courant November 23

663. November 30, 1780 Coachmakers Hall

'Is not the deliberate seduction of the fair, with an intention to desert, under all circumstances worse than murder?'
Gazetteer November 28

664. November 30, 1780 King's Arms Society
'Can friendship subsist between the sexes without the passion of love?'
Gazetteer November 28

665. December 2, 1780 La Belle Assemblee
'Whether the sports of the field are proper amusements for the Ladies?'
London Courant November 30

666. December 3, 1780 School for Theology, Coxes Museum
'Indeed I baptize you with water unto repentance, but he that cometh after me is mightier than I, whose shoes I am not worthy to bear; he shall baptize you with the Holy Ghost, and with fire.' St. Matthew ch. iii, vers. 11.
Admission 1 shilling.
Gazetteer December 2

667. December 3, 1780 Theological Society, High Holborn
Jam. cha. v, ver. 12 'But above all things, my brethren, swear not, neither by heaven, neither the earth, neither by any other oath, but let your yea be yea and your nay nay lest ye fall into condemnation.'
Morning Chronicle December 1

668. December 3, 1780 Christian Society
Job chap. 14 vers. 5 'See his days are determined, the number of his months are with thee; thou hast appointed his bound that he cannot pass.'
Morning Chronicle November 31

669. December 4, 1780 Westminster Forum
'Would it not be prudent to suffer the Convocation to sit, in order to consider the dangerous Doctrines contained in the late Publication of the Rev. Mr. Madan?'
London Courant November 30

670. December 7, 1780 Coachmakers Hall
'Ought not Great Britain immediately to recognize the independence of America, and open a treaty of general pacification?'
Gazetteer December 5

671. December 7, 1780 Carlisle House School of Eloquence
'Is the misconduct in the Council of a State an excuse for the desertion of a soldier from the standard he has inlisted under?'
Decision affirmative.
Morning Chronicle December 5

672. December 7, 1780 King's Arms Society
'Would not solitude in prison be a better mode of punishing criminals for capital offences, than that universally practiced in this kingdom?'
Gazetteer December 5

673. December 9, 1780 La Belle Assemblee
'A noble Lord having stated in the House of Commons, with his usual accuracy, that the decrease of people in this country within the last ninety years has been one million eight hundred thousand; therefore the question is, "Whether this decrease is more owing to the manners of the Ladies or of the Gentlemen?" '
London Courant December 7

674. December 10, 1780 Religious Society of Theological Enquiry, Coachmakers Hall
Second verse of 3rd chap. of first epistle of St. Paul to Timothy, 'Let a Bishop be the husband of one Wife.'
Morning Chronicle December 9

675. December 10, 1780 School of Theology, Coxe's Museum, Spring Garden
'Wherefore they are no more Twain, but one Flesh.' St. Matthew ch. xix, vers. 6. 'This text is selected as a Critique upon Mr. Madan's Defense of Polygamy.'
Admission 1 shilling.
Daily Advertiser December 9

676. December 11, 1780 Robin Hood, Butcher Row, Temple bar
'Whether any encrease of population on the Rev. Mr. Madan's plan would compensate for the confusion, Polygamy would create in society? And (if time permits) Would not the present aspect of American affairs justify Parliamentary thanks to the Ministry for their PERSEVER-ANCE in the national cause?
Admittance (men only) Six-pence, liquor included.
This undertaking is at the instance of many gentlemen desirous of renovating the old constitution of debating societies.'
Adjourned.
Morning Chronicle

677. December 11, 1780 Westminster Forum
'Is the frequency of corruption any excuse for the acceptance of a bribe?'
London Courant December 7

678. December 12, 1780 The Female Congress, Great Room, at the late King's Arm Tavern, Cornhill, for Ladies only
'Was Adam or Eve the more culpable in Paradise?'
Admittance One Shilling.
London Courant December 5

679. December 12, 1780 London Courant
'A Society of Gentlemen, whose views are to the Senate and the Bar, and whose studies are principally employed on the constitution of this country, has been for some time under the direction of the Rev. David Williams. The design of the society is to acquire the art of composing, and delivering Orations, &c. by such exercises, as an intimate knowledge of the human heart, by a study of its passions, alone can suggest. This design does not interfere with the purposes of those who are usefully occupied in removing defects of pronunciation, or improving the ear and modulating the voice for declamation. The business of the Society commences when the members have availed themselves of any assistances they may have wanted on such accounts; and its exercises, though in the circumstances they were first entered upon they had the fullest claim to originality, are similar to those which were given in Athens and Rome, in the periods of their highest lustre.

Though there are some reasons which induce the Society to make its design known; though it may be desirous to increase the number of its members, by the first and noblest youth of this country; yet the importance of its views, the harmony which prevails in it, and the satisfaction arising from the proper direction of its pursuits, are circumstances not to be hazarded merely to become numerous. Every nobleman or gentleman, therefore, must be proposed, in order to be admitted, if two black balls do not appear against him.

The Society will have public acts; but as no pecuniary advantages will arise from them, no persons will be admitted who is not introduced by the members.'

680. December 13, 1780 London Courant
'Last night the Pantheon society met for the discussion of the adjourned question, 'Can the conduct of Lord George Gordon respecting the Protestant Association be construed into High Treason?' . . . After a full discussion, it was moved and unanimously agreed to, that in respect that most of them who spoke against him, meant only to afford an opportunity to his friends, of clearing him from any shadow of guilt, the question should be dismissed unanimously in his favour.'

681. December 13, 1780 Carlisle House, The School of Eloquence
'Can an officer, whose military service is peculiarly essential to the service of the state, excuse himself in honour from such duty, on account of a conceived affront or injury received from the rulers of its councils?'
The decision was, that 'the true patriotic hero will abate every feeling of interest or resentment to venture himself totally in the service of his country; at the risque not only of his life but fame.'
It was impossible, in the course of the debate, tho' contrary to the general rules of the School, to avoid some reprehension being made on the voluntary retirement of Admiral Keppel from his public character, which was seconded by the general opinion of the room, amidst many

pleasing compliments to his personal courage and abilities and private
virtue.'
Morning Chronicle

682. December 14, 1780 Coachmakers Hall
'Whether, if the idea of indelicacy, which custom has affixed to any
advances of the fair sex, to enter into the married state, was abolished,
it would not tend to the happiness of both sexes?'
Gazetteer December 12

683. December 14, 1780 King's Arms Society
'Would not a tax on Maids and Bachelors, after a certain age, be of
public utility?'
Gazetteer December 12

684. December 14, 1780 School for Theology, Spring Gardens
'Who can say, I have made my Heart clean, I am pure from Sin?'
Proverbs, ch. xx, vers 9.
Daily Advertiser December 13

685. December 14, 1780 Morning Post
'Last Tuesday evening a society for debate by *Ladies only* was opened
at the late King's Arms Tavern, Cornhill, under the name of the *Female
Congress*. The company was splendid and respectable, and so very
numerous, that there was a considerable overflow. The chair was taken
by a Lady, who made an elegant exordium, which lasted near twenty
minutes. She traced the practice of eloquence through the medium of
the debating societies, till at length Ladies were admitted to speak. She
paid a delicate compliment to the *Belle Assemblee*, as the first institution
in which women were restored to their natural rights, and declared the
Female Congress was not opened from any spirit of rivalry or opposition, but solely to accommodate the Ladies of the east and south ends
of the town, whom the distance of the Haymarket deprives of hearing
Ladies debate so frequently as they might wish. She then mentioned
the common objections, or rather cavils, against women speaking in
public, and very ably defended the propriety of it, as well as the character of such who spoke. During the whole evening she maintained the
dignity of the chair, and filled it with astonishing ability, so as to convince all present, that where a woman can be found equal to the task,
a *woman alone* ought to preside over a *female society*. The debate that
ensued was carried on with great spirit and vivacity. Some of the Ladies
were capital in wit, humour, and eloquence, and all were agreeable,
though it was apparent that *three* of them spoke under the disadvantages
consequent on a first attempt: in short, the company were entertained
with twelve pleasing speeches, and departed after giving every mark of
general approbation.'

686. December 16, 1780 Morning Post

'The numerous *disputing societies and forums for harangue* have had such an effect on public opinion, that peoples of abilities and knowledge are now likely to be determined by the fluency of speech. But if we may believe a judicious writer, the common fluency of speech in many men, and most women, is owing to a scarcity of matter; for whoever is a master of language, and hath a mind full of ideas, will be apt in speaking to hesitate upon the choice of both; – whereas *common speakers* have only one set of ideas, and one set of words to cloath them in, and these are always ready at the mouth; so people come faster out of a church, when it is almost empty, than when a croud is at the door.'

687. December 16, 1780 La Belle Assemblee
'Whether is the inclination greater in spinsters to be married or in married men to be single?'
London Courant December 14

688. December 17, 1780 Christian Society
Colossians chap. 3, vers. 20, 21. 'Children obey your parents in all things.'
Morning Chronicle December 16

689. December 17, 1780 School for Theology, Spring Gardens
'All Scripture is given by Inspiration of God, and is profitable for Doctrine, for Reproof, for Correction, for Instruction in Righteousness.' 2 Timothy, ch. iii. vers 16.
Daily Advertiser December 16.

690. December 18, 1780 Robin Hood, Butcher Row, Temple Bar
'Whether any encrease of population on the Rev. Mr. Madan's plan would compensate for the confusion polygamy would create in society? The vote was almost nem. con. negative.'
Morning Chronicle

691. December 18, 1780 Westminster Forum
'Is publick examination of prisoners, and afterwards publishing the same, proper or improper?'
London Courant December 14

692. December 19, 1780 Female Congress, King's Arms Tavern, Cornhill
'Does Jealousy in Women more frequently arise from Love or Pride?'
Admission One Shilling.
Gazetteer December 16

693. December 21, 1780 Coachmakers Hall
'If the Legislature of these kingdoms were to frame a law concerning marriage agreeable to the system recommended by the Rev. Mr. Madan, in a late publication, would it not tend to prevent the ruin of

the female sex, in all its horrid consequences, both to the public and individuals?'
Gazetteer December 19

694. December 21, 1780 King's Arms Society
'Would it not be of advantage to the fair sex, that every man who had seduced a woman, should be obliged to marry her?'
Gazetteer December 19

695. December 21, 1780 Carlisle House, The School of Eloquence
'Can a member of the British Legislature absent himself from his attendance in Parliament, consistently with the duty he owes his country and constituents?
From an accident of a Gentleman mistaking the question as "Whether the Member was obliged strictly to pursue the mandates of his constituents." The question, in the midst of a very spirited and entertaining argument, was carried away for the remainder of the night with a torrent of wit and humour, from out of its proper channel; but being thought worthy of a more serious discussion, a motion was made and consented to, that it should stand over.'
Morning Chronicle

696. December 21, 1780 La Belle Assemblee
'A celebrated Dutchess having invited the nobility to attend her route at 12 o'clock at night, which, in the vulgar regulation of time, is considered rather as an unseasonable hour for the beginning of an entertainment; therefore the question to be discussed is, Whether a Woman of Fashion can do wrong?'
Morning Chronicle

697. December 24, 1780 School for Theology, Museum, Spring Gardens
'Who can say, I have made my Heart clean, I am pure from Sin?'
Proverbs ch. xx, vers 9.
Daily Advertiser December 23

698. December 25, 1780 Robin Hood
'Is the declaration of hostilities by the Court of London, against the States of Holland commendable at this crisis?'
Morning Chronicle

699. December 26, 1780 Female Congress, King's Arms Tavern
'Who is the more condemnable, the young woman who marries an old man, or the old woman who marries a young man?'
A Lady in the Chair.
'After the close of the Debate, the Lady in the Chair will commence a Series of Characters of Living Ladies. – That for Tomorrow night, the Character of Miss Hannah More, Authoress of the Tragedy of Percy, &c. &c.'
Gazetteer December 25

700. December 27, 1780 Carlisle House, School of Eloquence
'Can a member of the British Legislature absent himself from his attendance in Parliament, consistently with the duty he owes his country and constituents?'
The Question 'was renewed in debate with much precision and judgment, to the great amusement of the company. In short, no argument ever gave more pleasure in its discussion. It was determined in the negative.'
Admittance 3s. Tea, Lemonade, Capillaire and Orgeat, included.
No Gentleman can be permitted to speak in Masque.
Morning Chronicle

701. December 28, 1780 King's Arms Society
'Doth not the present mode of educating females in boarding schools greatly prejudice their rising morals?'
Gazetteer December 26

702. December 28, 1780 Coachmakers Hall
'If the Legislature of these kingdoms were to frame a law concerning marriage agreeable to the system recommended by the Rev. Mr. Madan, in a late publication, would it not tend to prevent the ruin of the female sex, with all its horrid consequences, both to the public and individuals?'
Gazetteer December 27

703. December 31, 1780 Christian Society
Hebrews chap. 10, vers. 25 'Not forsaking the assembling of ourselves together, as the manner of some is, but exhorting one another; and so much the more, as ye see the day approaching.'
Morning Chronicle December 30

704. December 31, 1780 School For Theology, Spring Gardens
'Jesus took Bread, and blessed it, and brake it, and gave it to the Disciples, and said, Take, eat, this is my Body.' St. Matthew, ch. xxvi, vers. 26.
'Previous to the Investigation, by particular Desire, will be delivered a moral Lecture.'
Daily Advertiser December 30

705. December 31, 1780 La Belle Assemblee
'Whether, during the continuance of the war, it is becoming in the ladies to encourage the produce, manufacture and fashions of France? and, Whether the recent legal decision in the Court of Chancery, "That without an equality of fortune there can be no just basis for wedlock" is consistent with the laws of nature, reason and equity?'
London Courant December 30

706. December 31, 1780 Religious Society for Theological Enquiry, at Coachmakers Hall
16th verse of the second chapter of St. Paul to the Galatians 'That we might be justified by the faith of Christ, and not by the works of the law; for the works of the law shall no flesh be justified.' And James 2nd, 24th verse 'Ye see then how that by works a man is justified, and not faith alone.'
Admission 6d.
Gazetteer December 30

707. January 1, 1781 Robin Hood
'Whether enquiry into the state of the nation ought not to have preceded the commencement of the Dutch war? and, Whether accused culprits should be put into irons?'
Adjourned.
Morning Chronicle January 8

708. January 2, 1781 Athenian Society, High Holborn, near Little Queen Street
'Is the Spy, who acts through principle for the good of his Country, to be considered a contemptible character?'
Boxes 1s., Pit 6d.
Morning Herald

709. January 4, 1781 Coachmakers Hall
'Has not the conduct of the Dutch justified the steps taken by Administration?'
Morning Chronicle January 3

710. January 4, 1781 King's Arms Society
'Are Administration justifiable, at this crisis, in their conduct towards the Dutch?'
Morning Chronicle

711. January 4, 1781 Carlisle House The School of Eloquence
'In case the Dutch should offer to renew their former treaty with this country, would it be for its interest, at this crisis, to accept such a proposal?
The great object of the Proprietors of this House being the introduction of the arts and sciences in entertainment of the Public, as a specimen of an infant school of Music, established on a new system and principle, a child of five years old will play several solos, and other pieces on the violin previous to the Debate, for the Public's approbation of the undertaking.'
The Question 'was debated with great spirit, vigour of argument, and compliment to the present Ministry for their animated resentment of the perfidy of so treacherous an ally; and carried in the negative.
A very interesting observation was thrown out that by the present quarrel with the Dutch, it were to be hoped Great Britain would reas-

sume her native rights of Fishery upon her own coasts, which is a mine of wealth encircling her shores, besides being so natural a nursery for our seamen and navy.'
Question decided in the negative.
Morning Herald January 9

712. January 7, 1781 Christian Society, Haymarket
James, chap. v. ver. 16 'Confess your faults to one another.' 'Intended to enquire into the utility, or necessity of auricular confession.'
Morning Chronicle January 6

713. January 7, 1781 Religious Society, for Theological Enquiry, Coachmakers Hall
Epistle to the Hebrews, chap. 2, vers 14 'Are they not all ministering spirits, sent forth to minister to them, who shall be heirs of salvation.'
Morning Chronicle January 6

714. January 7, 1781 Theological Society, High Holborn
Revelation Chap xix ver 10, 'And I fell at his Feet to worship him. And he said unto me, see thou do it not: I am thy Fellow-Servant, and of thy Brethren that have the Testimony of Jesus: worship God: for the Testimony of Jesus is the Spirit of Prophecy.'
Morning Herald January 2

715. January 7, 1781 School for Theology Spring Gardens
'And the Lord God said, It is not good that the man should be alone; I will make him an help-mate for him.' Genesis chap 11, ver. 10.
'N.B. Previous to the investigation, by particular desire, will be delivered a MORAL LECTURE.
Admission One Shilling.'
Morning Herald January 6

716. January 8, 1781 Robin Hood
'Would it not be proper and becoming in the belligerent powers to proclaim a temporary suspension of hostilities in the West India Islands?'
Morning Chronicle

717. January 8, 1780 Westminster Forum
'Whether the practice of examining persons accused of crimes publicly before Magistrates, and afterwards publishing the examinations and evidence before trial, ought to be discontinued?'
London Courant

718. January 9, 1781 Athenian Society
'Is it the business of a soldier to be convinced of the justice of a war, before he consents to take an active part in it?'
Lecture on Elocution, by a Lady.
Morning Herald January 5

719. January 11, 1781 Carlisle School of Eloquence
'Which object of pursuit is most advantageous to an infant State, the Culture of its Natural Productions, or the Establishing of Manufactures?'
Morning Herald January 9

720. January 11, 1781 Coachmakers Hall
'Supposing a parent, or a guardian will, to cross the wishes of the lover, which ought to resign their pretentions?'
Morning Chronicle

721. January 12, 1781 La Belle Assemblee
'Whether the recent legal Decision in the Court of Chancery, that "Without an Equality of fortune there can be no just Basis for Wedlock" is consistent with the Laws of Nature, Reason, and Equity?'
Morning Herald January 10

722. January 14, 1781 Christian Society, Haymarket
Ecclesiastes, Chap. xl. ver. 9 'Rejoice, O young man, in thy youth, and let thy heart cheer thee in the days of thy youth; and walk in the ways of thy heart, and in the sight of thine eyes: but know thou, that for all these *things,* God will bring thee unto judgement.'
Morning Herald January 13

723. January 15, 1781 Westminster Forum
'Whether the present rupture with the Dutch, can be defended, either in point of policy or practice?'
London Courant

724. January 15, 1781 Morning Chronicle
'A correspondent earnestly requests of the managers of La Belle Assemblee that the following important question may be proposed for discussion on Friday, the 26th current. Five *Gentlemen*, three of whom with cockades, and the other two with gold loops and buttons in their hats, (from which it is inferred, they are either in a *military* or *naval* capacity) being seated in the boxes, and also one person in the pit, on Friday evening, at La Belle Assemblee, after a very polite remonstrance from the President in the chair, and a general disapprobation of their conduct being signified by the audience, were all so void of good manners, as to wear their hats during the entertainment for that evening. The question therefore offered for discussion will be – "Is it consistent with the principles of politeness, or either laws of good breeding for the Gentlemen to wear their hats in the presence of the Ladies?" As the question seems proper to be handled by those to whom this small share of respect is generally thought due, it is hoped the managers will be so kind as [to] allow it to be ascertained by the voice of the impartial fair.'

725. January 16, 1781 Athenian Society, High Holborn

St. Luke, chap xii, ver 4,5 'Suppose ye, those Eighteen, upon whom the Tower of Siloam fell, and slew them, think ye that they were Sinners above all men, that dwelt in Jerusalem? I tell ye, nay, but except you repent, ye shall all perish likewise.'

'The Proprietor of the Room is the more forward to hope for the appearance of a numerous assembly on the above night, as he is to derive no advantage from the emoluments, which are to be deposited in the bank of Messrs. Drummond, for the humane and pious purpose of relieving our unfortunate fellow subjects, whose distresses, in consequence of the late hurricane in the West Indies call loudly upon the opulent and humane, for relief. If he can be instrumental in any measure in alleviating their suffering, and supplying their wants, the sacrifice he makes of his own interest on the above night, can bear no comparison with the luxuriant pleasure, which the motives that produced that sacrifice, must afford him, if they meet with the hoped for success. ADMITTANCE TWO SHILLINGS AND SIXPENCE.'
Morning Herald January 15

726. January 18, 1781 Coachmakers Hall
'Is that part of our criminal law just, which prevents a prisoner from making a *full defence*, as well to matters of *fact*, as to matters of law by Council?'
Morning Chronicle, January 17

727. January 18, 1781 Carlisle House School of Eloquence
Her Majesty's Birth day
'Is Royalty, in the female line, more highly ornamented by a display of the domestic Virtues, or an exertion of political accomplishments?'
Following 'will be recited an Ode, interspersed with Airs and Duettos, and accompanied with a complete Band of Wind Instruments, the Vocal parts by a GENTLEMAN and LADY, (being their first performance in Public). The Music to the Ode entirely new, and composed for the occasion by Dr. ARNOLD.
Admittance 3 shillings.'
Morning Herald January 16

728. January 21, 1781 Christian Society, Haymarket
Exodus chap. xxii. vers. 18. 'Thou shalt not suffer a witch to live.'
Morning Chronicle January 20

729. January 21, 1781 Religious Society, for Theological Enquiry, Coachmakers Hall
1st Cor. chap. xiv. ver. 34 'Let your women keep silence in the churches, for it is not permitted unto them to speak, but they are commanded to be under obedience. As also saith the law.'
Morning Chronicle January 20

730. January 21, 1781 School for Theology Spring Gardens

127

'But some man will say, How are the dead raised up, and with what body do they come?' St. Paul's 1st Epist. to the Corinthians, chap. xv. ver. 35.

'N.B. The intention of this text is a scriptural and philosophical enquiry into the Resurrection of the dead.'
Morning Herald January 19

731. January 22, 1781 Westminster Forum
'Is self-love the universal motive of human action?'
Morning Herald

732. January 25, 1781 Carlisle House School of Eloquence
'Is the prevailing custom in the fair sex, of rigidly precluding from their company (and consequently from every opportunity of reformation) such persons who have deviated from the strict path of virtue, more favourable or prejudicial to virtue itself?'
Morning Herald January 24

733. January 25, 1781 King's Arms Society
'Does that infamy annexed to female deviations from Chastity, operate more in keeping the sex virtuous, or in rendering them desperately vicious?'
Morning Chronicle

734. January 25, 1781 Coachmakers Hall
'Whether in cases of Trial for High Treason, the Sheriffs, by returning an extraordinary number to serve on Juries, may not deprive the prisoner of the advantage of his challenge?'
Morning Chronicle

735. January 28, 1781 School for Theology Spring Gardens
'What doth it profit, my brethren, though a man say he hath faith, and have not works; can faith save him?'
Morning Herald January 26

736. January 28, 1781 Religious Society for Theological Inquiry, Coachmakers Hall
'For therefore we both labour and suffer reproach, because we trust in the living God, who is the Saviour of all men, especially those that believe.' 1st Tim. chap. iv ver. 10
Morning Chronicle January 27

737. January 28, 1781 Christian Society, Haymarket
Ecclesiastes, chap. ix, ver. 11 'I returned, and saw under the sun, that the race is not to the swift, nor the battle to the strong, neither yet bread to the wise, nor yet riches to men of understanding, nor yet favour to men of skill, but time and chance happeneth to them all.'
Morning Chronicle January 27

738. January 29, 1781 Westminster Forum
'Have the frequent acts of parliament made for the relief of Insolvent Debtors been more productive of good or evil?'
Morning Chronicle

739. February 1, 1781 Coachmakers Hall Society
'Which of the two characters are more likely to make the best husband, the Rake, or the Sot?'
Morning Herald

740. February 1, 1781 King's Arms Society
'Which is the greater enemy to society, the crafty Hypocrite, or the open Debauchee?'
Morning Chronicle

741. February 4, 1781 Religious Society for Theological Inquiry, Coach Makers Hall
Text: 1 Cor. chap. vii ver. 27 'Art thou bound unto a wife, seek not to be loosed; art thou loosed from a wife, seek not a wife?'
Morning Chronicle February 3

742. February 4, 1781 Theological Academy, Spring Gardens
Ad Dei gloriam, & salutem Animarum.
'The School introduces the following System: Metaphysics, Ethics, Pulpit Oratory, Church History, School Divinity and Cannon Law
'As you have heard that Anti-Christ is come' 1 John, II. 18. Query, Is not the Pope the man of sin? Also, was there not a Pope Joan?
N.B. The Proprietor of this elegant Room (desirous to make those mental improvements as extensive as possible to the public) has divided it into seats at 1s each, and seats at 6d. each.'
Morning Herald February 3

743. February 5, 1781 Westminster Forum
'Have the frequent Acts of Parliament made for the relief of insolvent debtors been more productive of good or evil? and, Can oppression in rulers justify resistance in the ruled?'
Morning Herald

744. February 7, 1781 Carlisle House School of Eloquence
'The Proprietors to the Public.
The original Plan of the institution of a School of Genius, to be formed into several classes, under a Scientific Society, was adopted by a Proprietor of this House, so long ago as the year 1777: which was to have been supported by such public entertainments, as the House was peculiarly capable of exhibiting. A School of eloquence is one branch running from that original stem, which opened last year, for the candid discussion of such questions, as might be therein proposed, for the improvement of young orators, and the entertainment of the public, both which ends were fully answered; but from the natural warmth of the temper

129

and mind of man, when raised into debate by the powers of oratory, most of the questions relative to the policy of the state, were thought by the more serious class of people to have been treated with a freedom, that proves the danger of such assemblies in any form of government whatever. For this reason, and lest other assemblies now constituting themselves into such power of state disquisition, or examination of religious or theological subjects, to the hazarding that respect to religion amongst the populace which is due to it; – should think themselves screened under the umbrage of the School of Eloquence, the proprietors have resolved, that the mode of debate in the said school should be changed into a more correct display of eloquence for the entertainment of the public in delivering orations of either sex, as the subject may require.'
Morning Herald

745. February 8, 1781 Coachmakers Hall
'Will a revision by the House of Commons, of certain late Courts Martial, upon two of its Members be productive of real advantage to the nation?'
Morning Chronicle

746. February 11, 1781 Theological Academy Spring Gardens
' "La Theologie est elle la plus solide de toutes des Sciences, comme elle est la plus parfait." St. Augustine
1st John, chap ii, ver 18 "As you have heard that Antichrist cometh, now there are become may Antichrists." Query, Is not the Pope a man of sin?
Ecclesiast. chap. ii "If the tree shall fall to the North, or to the South; in what place soever it shall fall, there it shall be." Query, What proof hath the Papists of Purgatory?'
Morning Herald February 10

747. February 11, 1781 Christian Society, Haymarket
St. Matthew, chap. vii, vers. 20 'By their fruits ye shall know them.'
Morning Herald February 10

748. February 11, 1781 Religious Society for Theological Inquiry, Coachmakers Hall
Rev. xx and 6th verse 'Blessed and holy is he that has part in the first resurrection: On such the second death hath no power, but they shall be priests of God and of Christ, and shall reign with him a thousand years.'
Morning Chronicle February 10

749. February 12, 1781 Westminster Forum
'Can Oppression in Rulers justify Resistance in the Ruled?'
Tea Rooms open at Six.
Morning Herald

750. February 15, 1781 King's Arms Society
'Does travelling into foreign countries tend more generally to improve or corrupt the traveller?'
Morning Chronicle

751. February 15, 1781 Coachmakers Hall
'Which is the more difficult to obtain in Marriage, an old Maid, or a Widow?'
Morning Chronicle January 14

752. February 16, 1781 La Belle Assemblee
'Whether the preference, that is now given, at the Opera House, to dancing over music, and the infatuation in favour of Vestris, is the result of refined, or of vitiated taste?
Amidst the decline of political Debate, the institution known by the name of La Belle Assemblee, stands distinguished by public patronage and fashion. Their debates are uncontaminated with epithetical abuse, and with personal invective. They leave these to higher assemblies, where the privileges of the gentlemen, may justify the intemperance of the orator. The Ladies, knowing nothing of the affairs of state, do not interfere with them; but while the debating societies, appropriated to gentlemen, are lamenting ever the disasters, or boasting of the successes of the empire, content themselves with subjects of a lighter nature, arising from the morals, or the character of the age. In this harmless, at least, if not valuable entertainment, they trust in the continuance of that approbation, with which they have so long been honoured.'
Previous to the Debate, Collin's celebrated Ode on the Passions, will be recited by a Lady.
Morning Herald February 13

753. February 18, 1781 Theological Academy Spring Gardens
'Ecclesiast. chap. xi. "If the tree shall fall to the North, or to the South; in what place soever it shall fall, there it shall be." Query, What proof hath the Papists of Purgatory?'
Morning Herald February 17

754. February 18, 1781 Religious Society for Theological Inquiry, Coachmakers Hall
1st Cor. 14th ch. 31 'For ye may all prophesy one by one, that all may learn, and all may be comforted.'
Morning Chronicle February 17

755. February 19, 1781 Westminster Forum
'Whether the late-advanced Doctrines of having two or more Wives, and the Legitimation of Bastards, will tend to promote or discourage Matrimony?'
Morning Herald

756. February 22, 1781 King's Arms Society, Cornhill

131

'Is the woman of superior beauty, or of ample fortune in more danger from flattery?
The room is conveniently adapted for the accommodation of the ladies.'
Morning Chronicle

757. February 22, 1781 Coachmakers Hall Society, Foster lane, Cheapside
'Which is to be preferred for Youth – a Public or Private Education?'
Morning Chronicle

758. February 23, 1781 La Belle Assemblee
'Is that part of the Turkish faith true, which declares "That Women have no souls"?
After the Debate a lady will (for the second time) Recite Collin's celebrated Ode on the Passions.
Admittance 3s., 2s. and 1s. The Room will be lighted with Wax. Places for Boxes may be taken.'
Morning Herald February 21

759. February 25, 1781 Theological Academy Spring Gardens
'Romans, viii. 29 "To whom he did foreknow, he also did predestinate."
Doth the present Church of England maintain her seventeenth Article of Unconditional Predestination?'
Morning Herald February 24

760. February 25, 1781 Religious Society for Theological Inquiry, Coachmakers Hall
Isaiah, 58 ch. v. 6 'Is not this the fact that I have chosen, to lose the bands of wickedness, to undo the heavy burdens, and to let the oppressed go free, and that ye break every yoke.'
Morning Chronicle February 24

761. February 26, 1781 Westminster Forum
'Which is most praiseworthy, Fortitude in Adversity, or Benevolence in Prosperity? and, if time will permit, the following: Is Sense, Beauty, or Wealth, the most desirable Quality in a wife?'
Morning Herald

762. March 1, 1781 Coachmakers Hall Society
'Are Laws made for restraining Minors from marrying without the consent of Parents or Guardians, founded in Reason and public Convenience?'
Morning Chronicle

763. March 1, 1781 King's Arms Society
'Would it not be more for the honour and interest of this Nation, to admit the Independence of America, than to adopt the sanguinary mode

recommended by Mr. Wraxall, to involve the empire of Germany in war?'
Morning Chronicle

764. March 2, 1781 La Belle Assemblee
'The Ladies intend to open the BUDGET for the Service of the Current Year, in humble Anticipation of that of the Premier. And will conclude with COLLINS's beautiful ODE on the PASSIONS. By a LADY.'
Morning Herald March 1

765. March 4, 1781 Theological Academy, Spring Garden
'1st chap. of 2nd Epistle to Timothy, ver. 6 "Therefore I put thee in remembrance, that thou fill up the gift of God, which is in thee, by the putting on of my hands." Query, Is Ordination essential to the Ministerial Office? And is the Ordination in the Church of England valid?'
Morning Herald March 2

766. March 5, 1781 Westminster Forum
'Are the present Laws in force, for restraining Minors from Marriage without the consent of Parents or Guardians, founded on Reason or public Utility?'
Morning Herald

767. March 8, 1781 King's Arms Society
'Is not that custom founded on false delicacy, which forbids the ladies making the first overtures for a matrimonial union with the man they love?'
Morning Chronicle

768. March 8, 1781 Coach-Makers Hall
'Which is the more blameable character, a tyrannical husband, or a perverse wife?'
Morning Chronicle

769. March 9, 1781 La Belle Assemblee
'The Opening of the BUDGET, and the Debate that ensued upon the taxes that were proposed by the female Premier, afforded such high and uncommon entertainment to the numerous and splendid Company in the Rooms, that a general request was made, that on the subsequent Friday the Ladies should resume the consideration of the Budget, in preference to the Question given out from the Chair.
In obedience therefore to the desire of the Public, the Ladies mean, This Evening, to resume the Debate on the following taxes:
1. On all Old Maids and Batchelors above a certain age.
2. On Men-milliners, Men-mantua-makers, Men-marriage-brokers, &c.
3. On female Fox-hunters, female Dragoons, female Playwrights, and Females of all descriptions who usurp the occupations of the men.
4. On Monkies, Lap-dogs, Butterflies, Parrots, and Puppies, including those of the human species.

5. On made-up Complections.
6. On French Dancers, French Frizeurs, French Cooks, French Milliners, and French Fashion-mongers.
7. On Quacks and Empirics, including those of the State, the Church, and the Bar.
8. On Intrigues, Elopements, and Divorces of Quality and Fashion. And,
9. On a Weekly Fast to be observed by the Bishops and Aldermen.'
Morning Herald

770. March 12, 1781 Westminster Forum
'Have the News Papers been of greater Service or hurt to Society?'
Morning Herald

771. March 13, 1781 Coach-Maker's-Hall Society
'The Managers of the Society for free debate, assembling at Coach-Maker's-Hall, Foster-lane, Cheapside,' will change date of weekly meeting.
'If a tax was to be laid on Old Batchelors, and the produce was to be given as a marriage portion to young Maidens, would it not tend to the advantage of the community?'
Morning Chronicle

772. March 16, 1781 La Belle Assemblee
'Whether it would not be for the benefit of both Countries, if a Law was established to prevent TRIPS TO SCOTLAND, and also to prevent TRIPS FROM SCOTLAND?'
Morning Herald March 14

773. March 18, 1781 Christian Society, Haymarket
St. Matthew, chap. x, vers 19 'But when they shall deliver you up, take no thought how or what you shall speak, for it shall be given you in that same hour, what ye shall speak.'
Morning Herald March 17

774. March 18, 1781 Religious Society for Theological Inquiry, Spring Garden
'For I know that my Redeemer liveth, and that he shall stand at the latter day upon the earth. And though my skin worms destroy this body, yet in my flesh shall I see God, whom I see for myself, and my eyes shall behold, and not another, though my reins be consumed within me.' Job 19 chap., 25, 26, 27 vers.
'N.B. With a view to enquire concerning the surviving of the material body, and whether the proofs are not equal to those respecting the comfortable doctrine of eternity.'
Morning Chronicle March 17

775. March 19, 1781 Westminster Forum
'Is it consistent with propriety that women should perform men's characters on the stage?'
Morning Herald

776. March 20, 1781 Coach-Makers Hall Society
'Which is the more useful character, the Divine, the Physician, or the Lawyer?'
Morning Herald

777. March 23, 1781 La Belle Assemblee
'Whether it would not be for the benefit of this Country, if Females had a Voice in the Elections of Representatives, and were eligible to sit in Parliament, as well as the Men?'
Morning Herald March 20

778. March 24, 1781 London Courant
LA BELLE ASSEMBLEE
'By various arts the love of fame's confess'd,
In various shapes, by ruling passions dress'd:
To various objects levell'd is its aim,
Now 'tis the love of fun, and now of fame.
Sportsmen have oft with wonder gaping stood,
Aeneas like, at Venus in a wood;
With modern instruments of death pourtray'd,
O'er hedge, thro' copse, will dash the sporting Maid;
Some, thro' the thirst of fame, love nobler deeds,
Proud o'er high bars to urge the flying steeds.
Such sports as these, to rural maids confin'd,
By city dames, of glory more refin'd,
Are heard with pit, or with scorn proclaim'd,
Who boast themselves with nobler thirst inflam'd.
Aid me, thou spirit of satyric *Young!*
New whims declare how well he whilom sung;
The beauteous sex how well did he display,
Their peccadillos, and their modes *outre.*
  Where Frenchmen and Italians dance the Hayes,
Hence the Haymarket call'd in modern days,
There stands a Dome, where auctioneers have roar'd,
Loud hammers rapp'd, and puffers have encor'd –
No more the spendthrift's all, to sight brought forth,
Shall trust to Christie to proclaim its worth;
A female senate now with pleasure see
Flowing alike with eloquence and tea:
The hammer now yon President shall hold,
By whom the ardent orators are told
How far, with reason, and with wit, the theme
Runs glibly o'er the tongue; and when they dream –
Hard task indeed! restraining female wit;
What clown so rough, what beau would judge it fit?
But hark! yon President his hammer rears,
And, with sonorous hem, the theme declares –

135

A theme, replies the critic, with a sneer,
Just suited to the judgment of the fair:
No doubt some fashionable whim will seem
The justest object for a female theme;
No doubt, some new amendment on their dress,
Some new punctilio, or politesse –
These themes will suit the orators and place,
Which gay Flirtilla shall with joy embrace.
Cease, barb'rous critic! cease thy taunts profane;
Wrong thy conjectures, and thy sneers are vain;
Patriots and demagogues, with spirits bold,
There in Night's empire shall their converse hold,
From themes most trifling noble thoughts shall rise,
Whilst Burke would wonder, Fox would stare surprise:
The Muse with pleasure the debate shall sing,
And shew, from trifles what vast things can spring.'

779. March 25, 1781 Christian Society, Haymarket
'A Man to whom God hath given riches, wealth, and honour, so that
he wanteth nothing for his soul of all that he desireth, yet God giveth
him not power to eat thereof, but a stranger eateth it; this is vanity,
and is an evil disease.' Ecclesiastes, chap. vi, ver. 2.
Morning Herald March 24

780. March 25, 1781 Religious Society for Theological Inquiry, Coachmakers Hall
1st Tim. chap. 2 ver. 5 'For there is one God, and one Mediator
between God and men. The Man, Christ Jesus, who gave himself a
ransom for all to be testified in due time.'
'N.B. With a view to inquire into the divinity, humanity and office of
Jesus Christ. Particularly to shew, that Deism is not consistent with true
religion?'
Morning Chronicle March 24

781. March 26, 1781 Westminster Forum
'Will the taking of St. Eustatia be more likely to continue the War with
Holland and America, or produce a Peace?'
Morning Herald

782. March 27, 1781 Morning Herald
'ORATORY. Gentlemen, whose views are directed to the Bar, the
Pulpit, the Senate, or any other condition of life, in which early and
confirmed habits of eloquent delivery are so essentially necessary, are
respectfully acquainted, That a select and respectable Society for Instituting ORATORICAL EXERCISES, upon Subjects of LAW,
POLICY, and LEGISLATION, is now forming under the immediate
direction of several Gentlemen of the Temple, and other Inns of Court,
at the superb Edifice lately built by the Incorporated Society of Artists
of Great Britain, between Catherine-street and Exeter 'Change, in the

Strand; where a NEW GRAND AMPHITHEATRE is just now completed for the purpose, laid out in the most commodious manner for public Speaking, and ornamented in the highest taste.

And, as it is a principal object in this plan, that it should bear the nearest resemblance to the House of Commons, as well with respect to the accommodations for SPEAKING, HEARING, and SEEING to the greatest advantage, as to the rules and orders observed in the debates and proceedings of that august assembly, none but Subscribers are to be admitted into the lower part of the Amphitheatre; and no money is on any account to be accepted for admission into the gallery, which is raised upon a most elegant construction, and appropriated for ladies only, and the Subscribers by whom they are introduced.

The chair to be elective, the election in the Subscribers at large, and every other method adopted, that can secure an authority in the Chairman, a regularity in the proceedings, a respect in the company, and a dignity in the debates, suitable to so liberal an institution, and the elegant style of the place, which is prepared for so genteel an assembly. Subscriptions for this Society are taken in at the Office of the Amphitheatre, No. 350 Strand, at ONE GUINEA each, for the first Hundred and Fifty members, and at TWO GUINEAS for each who shall subscribe after that number is completed.

The Society are to meet every Saturday evening, or oftener, as may be determined at their first meeting, which will be on Saturday the 7th of April next; when their first business will be to elect a Chairman, and then to consider of the Rules and Orders, to be prepared by a Committee, consisting of those who subscribe before Saturday the 31st March; when such as shall have then subscribed, are to meet at the Amphitheatre for that purpose, at eleven o'clock in the forenoon.'
.

783. March 27, 1781 Society for free debate, Coach-makers Hall
'Whether the Court of Common Council acted properly in rescinding at their late meeting, the resolutions which had formerly passed, relative to the Delegates from the petitioning Counties?'
Morning Herald

784. March 29, 1781 King's Arms Society
'Is it more probable, that our late successes against the Dutch will produce a peace, or tend to the continuance of the war?'
Morning Chronicle

785. March 30, 1781 Morning Herald
'To the Students of law, and others zealous of Improvement in Eloquence. As many classes in life are justly emulous of acquiring an easy Elocution, which is principally the result of habit, and as the several places, which have been opened with a view to improvement in Eloquence, were too remote from the seminaries, to which they ought to be subordinate – the Inns of Court: It is proposed to open a Room contiguous to the Temple for the purpose of public debate, upon principles the most reasonable; the admittance only One Shilling, as it is

intended to reap no pecuniary advantage by it, but barely the expence of the room, lights, &c. Yet as some expence must be incurred in the first instance, it is proposed to admit subscribers to this plan, paying Half-a-Crown to the Fund for carrying on this Society, and Six-pence each and every night.

It is designed to open it experimentally this Evening at the Mitre Tavern, in Fleet Street, and continue it eighteen nights by adjournment.

"Have the Associations or their delegates any right to demand a restoration of triennial parliaments?

Is it agreeable to the maxims of sound policy, to tolerate Popery in a Protestant government?" '

786. April 1, 1781 Christian Society, Haymarket
St. Luke, 24 chap. ver 37 'But they were terrified and affrighted, and supposed that they had seen a spirit.'
Morning Herald March 31

787. April 1, 1781 Religious Society for Theological Inquiry, Coach-makers Hall
1st Tim. chap. ii, ver. 9 'In like manner also, that women adorn themselves in modest apparel, with shamefacedness and sobriety, not with broidered hair, or gold, or pearls, or costly array.'
Morning Chronicle March 31

788. April 3, 1781 Society for free Debate Coach-Makers Hall
'Is the wife who usurps the husband's authority; or the husband, who permits it, the more blameable?'
Morning Herald

789. April 5, 1781 King's Arms Society
'Is it possible to foretell future events, which is commonly call'd fortune-telling, by the position of the stars?'
Morning Chronicle

790. April 6, 1781 Students of Law, and others, zealous of IMPROVE-MENT IN ELOQUENCE Mitre Tavern Fleet-street
'Some gentlemen met on Friday last, and with learning and precision debated, on legal and constitutional ground, the following adjourned and amended question: "Have the Associations or their Delegates, an unlimited right to apply to their representatives for a restoration of triennial Parliaments? And the following, if time will permit, Is it consistent with the principles of sound policy to tolerate Popery in a Protestant Government?"
Every Gentleman may introduce a lady, free from additional Expence.'
Morning Herald

791. April 6, 1781 (For ONE NIGHT ONLY) by Particular Desire

'This Evening at Greenwood's Rooms, Hay-market, THE FEMALE DELEGATES will meet to consider on a Petition to Parliament for a redress of Female Grievances.'
Morning Chronicle

792. April 8, 1781 Religious Society for Theological Inquiry, Coach-makers Hall
'But he was wounded for our transgressions, he was broiled for our iniquities: the chastisement of our peace was upon him, and with his stripes we are healed.' Isaiah, 53 chap. ver 5.
Morning Chronicle April 7

793. April 10, 1781 Society for free debate, Coach-makers hall
'Which would more promote the interest of Religion – A Clergy supported by voluntary contributions, or by compulsive tythes?'
Morning Herald

794. April 12, 1781 King's Arms Society
'Is it possible to foretell future events (which is commonly called fortune-telling) by the position of the stars?'
Morning Chronicle

795. April 15, 1781 Christian Society, Mr. Greenwood's Rooms, Haymarket
'Investiga[tion of] the following text, Ephesians, chap.iv, ver. 5, "One Lord, one Faith, one Baptism"; intended to enquire whether it would not be more for the happiness of society, if every person was obliged to subscribe to the established religion of the country.'
Morning Chronicle April 14

796. April 15, 1781 Religious Society for Theological Inquiry, Coach-makers Hall
'Investiga[tion of] the following text, St. Matthew chap xxvii, ver. 521 – "And the graves were opened; and many bodies of the Saints which slept arose, and came out of the graves after his resurrection, and went into the holy city, and appeared to many."
Admittance to Gentlemen and Ladies Sixpence.'
Morning Chronicle April 14

797. April 22, 1781 Christian Society
'Text, Joshua chap. vii, ver. 19 "And Joshua said unto Achau, my son give, I pray thee, glory to the Lord God of Israel, and make confession unto him, and tell me now what though hast done; hide it not from me." Designed to enquire into the possibility of the salvation of a convicted criminal, who falsely proclaims his innocence at his execution.'
Morning Chronicle April 21

798. April 24, 1781 Society for free debate, Coach-Makers hall

'Whether the doubts that have been suggested on the case of the late Capt. Donellan, are well founded?'
Morning Herald

799. April 28, 1781 Students of Law, and other Gentlemen, associated in order to institute, upon a Plan hitherto unattempted, a SELECT SCHOOL OF ELOQUENCE, Law, Policy and Legislation [hereafter called the Lyceum]
'To-morrow Evening's Debate will be grounded on a Subject lately mentioned by a Member, to a certain August Assembly, relative to the Grant of a Bounty from Parliament on Scotch Linens; which will of Course introduce an enquiry into the relative legal and constitutional rights of the three Nations, as well as the Policy of the British Government.'
Morning Herald April 27

800. April 29, 1781 Christian Society
'Text, Malachi, chap. 3, ver. 8, 9 "Will a man rob God? Yet ye have robbed me, but ye say, wherein have we robbed thee? In tithes and offerings. Ye are cursed with a curse, for ye have robbed me, even this whole nation." Intended to enquire into the rights of giving tithes.'
Morning Chronicle April 27

801. May 1, 1781 Coach-Makers Hall
'Whether the doubts that have been suggested on the case of the late Capt. Donellan are well founded?'
Morning Herald

802. May 3, 1781 LYCEUM INTELLIGENCE
'After what we have seen of the numerous places opened for public debate, we should not have thought it of sufficient importance to take notice of any new institution of that nature, if the annunciation of a plan upon an new and select principle, for students and literary gentlemen; by subscription only, at the late exhibition room in the Strand, had not given a fresh edge to an almost blunted curiosity; and it is but justice to confess, that the experiment afforded us very ample gratification.

From the first features of this infant institution, it is not easy to pronounce upon the probability of its success; but there certainly appears no small degree of merit in the design of the undertaking, which appears to be intended as a school for the *Senate* as well as the *bar*; and in the debates of last Saturday evening, when the society met, for the first time, an attention was paid to parliamentary forms, which would have done credit to a much more matured institution; but what appeared most to claim our attention, was the striking symmetry and convenient construction of the amphitheatre, the elegance of the throne for the president, and the beautiful simplicity with which the whole was fitted up, which gave it an air of dignity superior to the bare appearance of either house of Parliament.

We can say but little for the arguments made by the different speakers, as the disputation was engrossed early in the evening by a few long-winded orators, who did not seem to know when they ought to leave off; but we must acknowledge that the young gentleman who officiated as chairman, displayed the greatest abilities in that situation (into which it appeared he was surprised by an unexpected election) and gave evident proofs of an early genius directed by the most mature judgment.'
Morning Herald

803. May 6, 1781 Christian Society
'Text Heb. chap. 13, v. 18 "We trust we have a good conscience." Intended to enquire whether what is termed conscience is natural or acquired.'
Morning Chronicle May 4

804. May 8, 1781 For One Night only, This Evening . . . at the Assembly Room, King's arms, Cornhill, the Ladies of the Belle Assemblee will join the Ladies of the Female Congress
'Can the Rev. Mr. Madan's doctrine of a plurality of wives be reconciled to reason, religion, or policy?'
Admittance One Shilling.
Gazetteer

805. May 8, 1781 Coachmakers-Hall Society
'Whether the doubts that have been suggested on the case of the late Captain Donnellan are well founded?'
Gazetteer

806. May 9, 1781 King's Arms Society
'If the Evidence contained in the Defence of Mr. Donellan, as published by Mr. Webb, had been produced on the Trial, is it probable that he would have been convicted?'
Gazetteer

807. May 16, 1781 King's Arms Society
'Whether the preventing the public investigations of religious subjects, is not a breach of civil and religious liberty?'
Gazetteer

808. May 19, 1781 Lyceum
'This Evening, pursuant to Notice given on Saturday last, certain Propositions will be moved by a Member, upon the following prize subject given out this Year by the Academy of Lyons, viz. Whether the Discovery of America has been productive of Benefit or Injury to Europe? – If, of benefit; what are the best means to preserve and encrease it? – if, of injury, What are the best means to remedy it?
In order to associate Genius, and give every Encouragement to an Institution founded on the most liberal Principles, that ever gave rise

to any Society in this Country, the Select Committee have resolved, that those who may wish to subscribe for the remaining Nights of this Season, shall not be obliged to pay the full subscription, as if they had been Members from the Beginning. – But, to preserve a proper Degree of Respect in the Company, the Subscription will never be lower than HALF A GUINEA.'
Morning Herald

809. May 29, 1781 La Belle Assemblee and the Female Congress, united for one evening at Coachmakers Hall
For the Benefit of a Family in Distress
'Is the Turkish article of faith true, that says women have no souls? and, Is the man of learning, courage, fortune, or politeness, most acceptable to the ladies?'
Admittance 1s.
Morning Chronicle

810. September 6, 1781 The Societies for Free Debate, lately held at Coach-maker's hall, and at the King's Arms, Cornhill, being united, will commence their Debates at Coach-maker's Hall
'Can any circumstances render the character of a Spy honourable?'
Gazetteer August 29

811. September 13, 1781 Coach-maker's Hall
'Is the encouragement given to the present mode of performing the Beggar's Opera, a proof of *refined* or *vitiated* taste?'
Gazetteer September 11

812. September 20, 1781 Coach-maker's Hall
'Which of the present candidates to represent the city of London in Parliament, has from his *public* character and conduct, the best claim to that honour?'
Question 'was carried in favour of the Lord Mayor.'
Gazetteer September 19

813. September 27, 1781 Coach-maker's Hall
'Can the Ministry be justified in not having furnished Admiral Parker with a greater force when he went against the Dutch?'
Gazetteer September 26

814. October 4, 1781 Coachmakers Hall
'Is the boasted superiority of the male over the female sex founded in justice?'
Gazetteer October 2

815. October 11, 1781 Coachmakers Hall
'Which is the more ridiculous character, a crusty old bachelor or a peevish old maid?'
Morning Chronicle October 10

816. October 12, 1781 Morning Chronicle
A LECTURE
'In a large and elegant Room, at the THREE TURKS, Fleet Street, near St. Dunstan's Church, THIS PRESENT EVENING, at Eight o'clock, will be delivered,
By the Reverend E.B. M.D.
A LECTURE on Dr. GRAHAM's Efforts to improve the Works of Nature; with a few remarks on the CELESTIAL BED.
After which the subject will be continued, by the following question, 'Whether the Works of Nature be not superior to the Works of Art?'
N.B. The Lecture and Debate will be conducted with the utmost decorum and decency; particularly since Ladies, as well as Gentlemen, are most respectfully invited.'
Admission One Shilling.'

817. October 18, 1781 Coachmakers Hall
'Is it probable, that if rewards were given for the encouragement of matrimony, it would tend to the general good?'
Gazetteer October 16

818. October 19, 1781 Three Tuns
'Which is the greatest incitement to Virtue, the dread of punishment, or hope of Reward?'
Preceded by 'a Lecture . . . by the Reverend E.B . . . on the alarming and dangerous VICES of the present TIMES; with seasonable and pathetic Remarks on the dreadful execution of yesterday.'
Morning Chronicle

819. October 25, 1781 Coachmakers Hall
'Is there any reality in the Doctrine of Apparitions?'
Morning Chronicle October 24

820. October 26, 1781 Morning Chronicle
Sir,
'Being at Coachmaker's Hall last Thursday night, I was sorry such a numerous auditory found so little entertainment there, from the discussion of a subject so interesting, as, *How far a reward for the encouragement of matrimony would operate for the benefit of the State,* or some such words: wanting the confidence of delivering my sentiments there, and thinking that a few hints on that head will be much more diffused coming through the channel of your paper, Mr. Printer, I submit them to your candour.
Mankind in general have it much more in their own favour to encourage matrimony than any interference of Government can possibly effect. Would they, in the same manner as the freeman of a city, have the alternative of being employed in that city, in preference to aliens, more especially married masters, should not engage single while married men are to be had; their business likewise would not suffer from the frequent changing of servants, the tie being much greater on the

married man to continue in his place; instead of this, at present it is an insuperable objection to a man's getting a place; and what can be a greater discouragement to the married state among dependent men, than its incapacitating him to procure employment. If it is true that the gentlemen orators at Coachmaker's Hall are paid for opening their mouths; the idea makes some keep theirs shut, if sounded, their interest would be better answered, to improve, than to bandy their wit from each other so much.'

Your's, &c.,
D.G.

821. October 31, 1781 Coachmakers Hall
'Are there any circumstances which would render the expulsion of an Alderman by his brother justifiable?'
Morning Chronicle

822. November 8, 1781 Coach-makers-hall
'Does the passion of Love operate more for its happiness, or that of its objects, from the age of 15 to 25, or from 25 to 50?'
Gazetteer November 6

823. November 15, 1781 Coachmakers-hall Society
'Which of the extremes is likely to be attended with the more injurious consequences, a *severe* restraint over all the actions of youth, or an unlimited indulgence of every wish and inclination?'
Gazetteer November 13

824. November 22, 1781 Coachmakers Hall
'Would it not be for the benefit of both sexes, if the law were made to prohibit marriage, where a great disproportion of years subsists?'
Morning Chronicle November 21

825. November 29, 1781 Coachmakers-hall
'Do dreams foretell future events?'
Gazetteer November 27

826. December 6, 1781 Coachmakers-hall
'Is the capture of Lord Cornwallis more likely to accelerate a peace, or prolong the war?'
Gazetteer December 4

827. December 13, 1781 Coachmakers-hall
'Is the residence of Jews in this country of advantage or detriment to the state?'
Gazetteer December 11

828. December 20, 1781 Coachmakers Hall
'Which is more likely to die a Maid, the Coquet or the Prude?'
Morning Chronicle December 19

829. December 27, 1781 Coachmakers Hall
'Are the fair Sex more generally ruined by their own folly, or the treachery of the men?'
Morning Chronicle December 26

830. January 2, 1782 Coachmakers Hall
'Is it consistent with Christian charity for the Minister of St. James's, Clerkenwell, to prosecute the preachers at Lady Huntingdon's chapel?'
Morning Chronicle January 1

831. January 10, 1782 Coachmakers Hall
'Is the love of power more prevalent in the male or female sex?'
Morning Chronicle January 9

832. January 17, 1782 Coachmakers Hall
'Has a British King more to fear from the flattery of his supposed friends, or the open attacks of his enemies?'
Morning Chronicle January 16

833. January 24, 1782 Coachmakers Hall
'Ought the 30th of January to be kept as a feast or a fast?'
Morning Chronicle January 23

834. January 31, 1782 Coachmakers Hall
'Which is more to be lamented, the union of a man of sense with a frivolous woman, or of a woman of understanding with a frivolous man?'
Morning Chronicle January 30

835. January 31, 1782 Westminster Forum, Hampshire Hog, Piccadilly
'Would not the revisal and simplification of the Laws of this kingdom be of benefit to the People?
The known candour and impartiality of the gentlemen debaters of this Primitive Society need no comment; suffice it to say, that gentlemen of the first abilities, both in education and eloquence, honour this meeting; and auditors who resort for knowledge and instruction, are sure of gratifying their most sanguine wishes in their very laudable pursuit.'
Admission only Sixpence, refreshment included.
Morning Herald

836. February 7, 1782 Coachmakers Hall
'Is the reading even of the best novels likely to improve either the morals or understanding of the fair sex?'
Morning Chronicle February 6

837. February 14, 1782 Coachmakers-hall
'Is the late enquiry into the conduct of the First Lord of the Admiralty likely to be productive of any good consequences to the State?'
Gazetteer February 12

838. February 21, 1782 Coachmakers-hall
'Is there any truth in the opinion that reformed rakes make the best husbands?'
Gazetteer February 19

839. February 21, 1782 Westminster Forum. Hampshire Hog, Piccadilly
'Which is the greatest trial to the human mind, Prosperity or Adversity, both considered in the extreme?
The public are respectfully desired to attend as early as possible, that the many ingenious gentlemen (who honour this Society) may have an opportunity of speaking within the usual time.'
Morning Herald

840. February 28, 1782 Coachmakers-hall
'Ought not women to vote for Members of Parliament, and be eligible to sit there themselves?'
Gazetteer February 26

841. March 1, 1782 Westminster Forum, Hampshire Hog, Piccadilly
'Was it an improper Exertion in the Prerogative to make Lord George Germain a Peer?'
Morning Herald

842. March 7, 1782 Coachmakers-hall
'Does the moral drawn from the solemnity of Tragedy, or the levity of Comedy, make the more lasting impression on the Audience?'
Gazetteer March 5

843. March 8, 1782 Westminster Forum, Hampshire Hog, Piccadilly
'Is the late Majority in the House of Commons likely to prove advantageous to this Kingdom?'
Admittance 6d. Porter and Tobacco included.
Morning Herald

844. March 14, 1782 Coachmakers-hall
'Is the late decision in Parliament in favour of peace likely to produce the desired effect?'
Gazetteer March 13

845. March 21, 1782 Coachmakers-hall
'If a man be in a boat with his mother, his wife, and his daughter, when the boat oversets, and he can save but one, which ought he to save?'
Gazetteer March 19

846. March 21, 1782 Westminster Forum, Hampshire Hog, Piccadilly
'Is it likely, that a change in Administration, at this juncture, would be attended with particular Benefit to this Kingdom?'
Morning Herald

847. March 28, 1782 Coachmakers-hall
'The Society for Free Debate will resolve itself into a *Committee of Ways and Means*, to consider of *new Taxes* to raise the supply granted to his Majesty, in preference to those proposed at the opening of the BUDGET.'
Gazetteer March 26

848. March 30, 1782 Lyceum
'Is not the total change in Administration, which has taken place this week, essential to the salvation of this nation; and what measures are most expedient to be adopted by the new Administration at home and abroad, to extricate Great Britain out of her present difficulties?
In the present critical and alarming State of public affairs in this country, so deeply affecting to every honest mind, and so indispensably requiring the exertion of every good Citizen, it is of the highest importance to the collective interest of the state, and perhaps to the peace and welfare of every individual, that a correct, temperate, and sound judgment should be formed concerning the measures of Government . . . By particular desire, Mr. Smeathman will take the chair, as Moderator.
N.B. The house is well aired, and the Great Room and the galleries are matted throughout, the seats are covered with green baize, and likewise the folding doors, which shut the entrances to the lobbies, and the Green Room will be illuminated [with] wax lights. Admittance 2s.
Near one thousand ladies and gentlemen, many of them of the first rank and fashion, were present at the debates; when it was determined "That a total change in administration, which took place last week, was absolutely essential to the salvation of this nation".'
Gazetteer/Morning Herald April 5

849. April 4, 1782 Society for Free Debate Coachmakers-hall
'Will again resolve itself into a *Committee of Ways and Means*, farther to consider of some other new Taxes to raise the supply granted to his Majesty, in preference to those proposed at the opening of the BUDGET.'
Gazetteer April 2

850. April 6, 1782 Lyceum
'Whether that art, called STRATAGEM, is most predominant over the minds of the male, or female sex?
Whether the prerogative of the Crown, as it stood before the Revolution, or the influence of the Crown, as it hath arisen since, and as exercised by the late administration, be the more dangerous and alarming to the constitution of this country?'
Morning Herald April 5

851. April 10, 1782 Lyceum
'Has Great Britain any reason to be alarmed at the resolutions or proceedings of the Volunteers of Ireland?

Debated with great spirit in the presence of a numerous and respectable assembly of both sexes and determined in the negative.'
Morning Herald April 10

852. April 11, 1782 Coachmakers-Hall
'The Committee appointed to consider of Ways and Means will report their proceedings; after which the following Question will be debated: – Is a bad Wife better than no Wife?'
Gazetteer April 9

853. April 17, 1782 Lyceum
'Whether a fair representation of the People in Parliament would not be the best security of a virtuous Administration against evil Advisers of the Crown? and Whether the Union of England and Scotland has proved advantageous to this country?'
Morning Herald April 13

854. April 18, 1782 Coachmakers-Hall
'Are the demands of the Irish founded more on justice than on a consciousness of their own strength?'
Gazetteer April 16

855. April 24, 1782 Lyceum
'Would a legislative union between Great Britain and Ireland be more beneficial to both kingdoms; than the Independent Legislature claimed by the Irish?
Morning Herald April 22

856. April 25, 1782 Coachmakers-Hall
'Is that indifference, which too generally takes place after marriage, to be attributed more to the fault of the husband or wife?'
Gazetteer April 23

857. April 29, 1782 Lyceum
'Is mankind happiest in a state of nature or refinement? and Can true love admit of jealousy?'
Pit 1s. Gallery 2s.
'The success which Mr. Smeathman has met with in his School of Eloquence, induces him to offer to the Public a new species of Entertainment at the Lyceum, for the improvement of speaking on the Stage. It is his object, in the present decline of Theatrical Talents, to lay, if possible, the foundation of future excellence, and he submits himself to the candour of the public for that indulgence which an infant undertaking requires. He flatters himself a little experience will demonstrate the utility of his plan, and he looks forward to the encouragement of all lovers of dramatic representations, with the assurance of the propriety of his intentions, however feeble may be his first essay. The Students of the Inns of Court, and all others who aspire to eminence in reading, pleading, preaching or public speaking, may have an opportunity of

acquainting themselves with his method of teaching Elocution, which must with the utmost certainty lay the foundation of true eloquence, by attending at his private oratorical exercises.'
Gazetteer

858. May 2, 1782 Coachmakers-Hall
'Which of the two passions has contributed most to the unhappiness of mankind, LOVE OR AMBITION?'
Gazetteer April 30

859. May 8, 1782 Lyceum
'Can true love admit of jealousy?'
Gazetteer

860. May 22, 1782 Lyceum in the Strand School of Eloquence
'Whether slavery, as enforced by the European Nations, is to be defended on any principle? and, Which is of most immediate consequence to the People of England at this juncture, that they should learn the use of Arms, or obtain a real Representation in Parliament?'
Pit 1s., Gallery 2s.
Parker's General Advertiser May 21

861. May 29, 1782 Lyceum
'Whether the fashionable infidelities of married couples are more owing to the depravity of the Gentlemen, or the inconstancy of the Ladies?'
Parker's General Advertiser May 27

862. June 5, 1782 Lyceum
'Whether slavery, as enforced by the European Nations, is to be defended on any principles?'
Parker's General Advertiser June 3

863. June 12, 1782 Lyceum
'Would a good Citizen be justifiable in supporting his Patron and Friend, though he should appear to him to entertain principles inimical to the interests of his Country?'
Parker's General Advertiser

864. September 19, 1782 Coachmakers Hall
'Has the conduct of the present administration sufficiently corresponded with their former professions to merit the confidence of the people?'
Morning Post

865. September 26, 1782 Coachmakers Hall
'Is the *late mode* of executing criminals, immediately after conviction, a *just* and *beneficial* measure?'
Morning Post

866. October 3, 1782 Coachmakers Hall

'Is the wife who usurps the authority of the husband, or the husband who permits it, the more contemptible character?'
Morning Post

867. October 10, 1782 Coachmakers-Hall
'Whether, at the present crisis, the Resources of the City of London would be best applied towards raising a regular and effective Militia, or in building a Ship of the Line for the use of the Government?'
After the debate 'will be delivered an EULOGY to the memory of the much esteemed and lamented Gentleman, who lately fell in the service of the Military Association, interspersed with solemn music, composed for the occasion, and selected from the best masters.
Admittance, this night ONE SHILLING.'
Morning Chronicle

868. October 17, 1782 Coachmakers Hall
'Is it consistent with justice and sound policy to punish Adultery with Death?'
Parker's General Advertiser October 16

869. October 24, 1782 Coachmakers-Hall
'Would it not greatly contribute to the promotion of virtue, and to the benefit of society, if merit at all times took precedence of birth and fortune?'
Gazetteer October 22

870. October 31, 1782 Coachmakers Hall
'Does the youth who is early introduced into the pleasures and amusements of life, or he who is totally with-held from them, bid fairest to shun the vices of the age?'
Morning Post

871. November 7, 1782 Coachmakers Hall
'Would it not greatly promote matrimony, if every single person, after 25 years of age, was to pay an annual sum towards the portioning of the daughters of the poor?'
Morning Post

872. November 14, 1782 Coachmakers-Hall
'Has political or religious enthusiasm done more mischief in the world?'
Gazetteer November 12

873. November 21, 1782 Coachmakers-Hall
'Can a man be justified in entering into the marriage state, from any other principle than that of love?'
Gazetteer November 19

874. November 28, 1782 Coachmakers Hall

'Does jealousy ever subsist between the sexes, but through the influence of real love?'
Morning Post

875. December 5, 1782 Coachmakers Hall
'Which have been more injurious to Society, Trading Justices or Methodist Preachers?'
Parker's General Advertiser December 4

876. December 12, 1782 Coachmakers Hall
'Which is the more desirable in a wife, *beauty* without *fortune*, or *fortune* without *beauty?*'
Morning Post

877. December 19, 1782 Coachmakers Hall
'Does Quackery abound more in Law, Physic, or Divinity?'
Morning Post

878. December 26, 1782 Coachmakers-Hall
'Can either sex a second time enter into the marriage state from a principle of love?'
Gazetteer December 24

879. January 2, 1783 Coachmakers Hall
'Ought the Bashful or the Impudent Man to succeed best in his pretensions to Love and Fortune?'
Parker's General Advertiser January 1

880. January 4, 1783 Gazetteer and New Daily Advertiser
'*Hostis honori invidia*
AN APPEAL TO THE PUBLIC
When the Conductors of the AMICA COLLATIO ACADEMY, held at the Reverend Mr. Pennington's Chapel, Paul's-alley, Barbican first adopted the plan on which their new institution is formed; they were aware of the objections which the prejudiced and interested would raise against such a liberal establishment; but as they expect support only from the wise and judicious, they mean to act in such a manner as shall not disappoint the sanguine wishes of their friends; and while they regret the ungenteel behaviour of those concerned in a neighbouring Society, they find consolation in the assurances of the party alluded to, who have signified their intention of giving no further interruption to the Amica Collatio, provided their Monday debates were confined to religious subjects; they shall be obliged – therefore, for the future, every Monday will be appropriated for the purpose alluded to, by way of debate, comment and delineation; and in order to remove the jealousy of interested opponents, as well as to satisfy the wishes of those who minds are enlarged, every Thursday evening is fixed on for the discussion of Political and Miscellaneous Topics, by way of debate only; thus, by attending to approved and popular subjects, the same night that the

opponents of this place transact their business, they cannot complain of an attempt to gain their devoted admirers; but should they lose any attendants, it is presumed they will have more sense than to shew any resentment at a preference given to merit. The conductors hire no speakers to prostitute their sentiments,or to tickle the ear for the sake of temporary applause, so that every person who attends will have liberty to speak his mind, and will also be heard with that candour becoming rational beings.

Next Monday, being Twelfth-Day, the question intended for that evening is postponed to the Monday following . . . Overtures on the organ. Galleries for the Ladies. Admittance 6d. Subscribers to the chapel pay half price.'

881. January 7, 1783 Amica Collatio Academy
'Is it right, at this crisis, for the Protestant Association to petition Parliament (or in any other manner to concern themselves with the laws) relative to Popery?'
Gazetteer

882. January 9, 1783 Amica Collatio Academy
'Are parents justified in preventing their children from marrying agreeable to their inclination?
N.B. For the future, Mondays will be appropriated for religious, and Thursdays for political and miscellaneous subjects. Please to note, a peculiar emulating encouragement is given to those who write approved pieces on any question . . . young people will be easily taught the manner of public speaking, and be freed from that awkward diffidence ever attending modest merit – an encouragement not to be found in any prejudiced or partial society.'
Gazetteer January 7

883. January 9, 1783 Coachmakers-Hall
'Which is the more injurious member of society, the busy fool, or the ingenious villain?'
Gazetteer January 7

884. January 13, 1783 Amica Collatio Academy
'At half price, *for this evening only*
"Which is the greatest foe to virtue, the disguised hypocrite; or the professed libertine?"
N.B. The conductors particularly invite all such as are, or may be prejudiced against this society (by false reports, malicious insinuations, and the artful suggestions of incendiaries, and disturbers of tranquillity) to attend, as some matters relating to certain individuals, will be explained, and every other satisfaction given that cannot fail to be highly acceptable to every candid and liberal mind. For this evening only, subscribers to the chapel will be admitted gratis, and every other person for three-pence.'
Gazetteer

885. January 16, 1783 Coachmakers Hall
'Ought the Quakers, on account of their religious principles, to be excused from taking part in the defence of their country?'
Gazetteer January 14

886. January 20, 1783 Amica Collatio Academy
'Whether the Moral Writer, or the Divine Preacher, contributes more to the instruction and amendment of Society?
N.B. The Rev. Mr. Pennington, being unanimously elected perpetual President, will take his seat at eight precisely. It is also agreed, that ladies, as well as gentlemen, shall speak and vote in this Society; and that all who mean to support this institution, pay only threepence for admission. For the information of strangers, the late President will, at the conclusion of the debates, relate every particular of this Society from its commencement; explain the reasons for his own conduct, and impartially investigate the behaviors of certain persons, who have clandestinely opposed the proprietor of this place.'
Gazetteer

887. January 23, 1783 Coachmakers Hall
'Are not Women made more abandoned by the Contempt of their own Sex after the slightest deviation from Virtue, than by the Inconstancy of the Men?'
Parker's General Advertiser January 22

888. January 30, 1783 Coachmakers Hall
'Was the Execution of King Charles Murder, or an Act of Justice?'
Parker's General Advertiser January 29

889. February 6, 1783 Coachmakers Hall
'Are the Conditions of Peace such as this country ought to accede to in its present situation?'
Gazetteer

890. February 13, 1783 Coachmakers Hall
'Can a wife be reformed by correction?'
Gazetteer

891. February 20, 1783 Coachmakers Hall
'Ought the King to have given Independence to America without the concurrence of the other branches of the Legislature?'
Gazetteer

892. February 26, 1783 Coachmakers Hall
'Are the Arguments advanced against the Peace sufficient to arraign the Conduct of Ministers in acceding to it?'
Parker's General Advertiser February 25

893. March 3, 1783 Amica Collatio Academy for Universal Investigation
'In which of the sexes is the love of power most predominant?'
The Ladies (having the same liberty as the Gentlemen to speak and vote . . .)'
Admittance threepence.
Gazetteer

894. March 6, 1783 Coachmakers Hall
'Is not a Man culpable in making any Advances to the Fair Sex, if he has not Intention of Matrimony?'
Parker's General Advertiser March 5

895. March 10, 1783 Amica Collatio and Academy for Universal Investigation
'Which character causes the greatest increase of vice and irreligion, the Atheist who performs every moral duty, or the Professor of the Gospel who leads an immoral life?
A question that claims the attention of every age and description . . .'
Gazetteer

896. March 13, 1783 Coachmakers Hall
'Would a sumptuary law to restrain different orders of the people with respect to diet and apparel (similar to that which has lately taken place in Denmark) be more beneficial for its prudent tendency, or detrimental on account of its arbitrary principle?'
Gazetteer

897. March 17, 1783 Amica Collatio
'Whether it is for the advantage of a state to suffer an unrestrained liberty in the press?'
Gazetteer

898. March 20, 1783 Coachmakers Hall
'Are there any just grounds for supposing that the understandings of the female sex are in any respect inferior to those of the men?'
Gazetteer

899. March 27, 1783 Coachmakers Hall
'Is the present mode of reducing the price of Bread consistent with fair trade, and likely to produce any public good?'
Parker's General Advertiser March 26

900. March 31, 1783 Amica Collatio
'Whether the doctrine of predestination or chance is most consistent with religion and reason?'
Gazetteer

901. April 3, 1783 Coachmakers Hall

154

'Ought not the word *obey* to be expunged from the marriage ceremony?'
Gazetteer

902. April 10, 1783 Coachmakers Hall
'Is it probable that any good will be derived to this country from an Administration that differed so widely on essential constitutional points?'
Parker's General Advertiser April 9

903. April 17, 1783 Coachmakers Hall
'Is it consistent with the Character of a Woman of Virtue to undertake the Profession of an Actress?'
Parker's General Advertiser April 16

904. April 24, 1783 Coachmakers Hall
'Has Methodism done more Good or Harm to this Country?'
Parker's General Advertiser April 23

905. May 1, 1783 Coachmakers Hall
'Has Methodism done more Good or Harm to this Country?'
Parker's General Advertiser April 30

906. May 5, 1783 Amica Collatio
'Whether the artist who occupies his trade and calling for the support of his family, or a clergyman who preaches on a Sunday, only for the sake of getting money, is the worse character?'
Gazetteer

907. May 8, 1783 Coachmakers Hall
'Hath a parent the natural right to restrain a child's inclination to marriage?'
Gazetteer

908. May 15, 1783 Coachmakers Hall
'Does the passion of love operate more powerfully in the male or female breast?'
Gazetteer

909. May 22, 1783 Coachmakers Hall
'Can duelling be justified upon the principles of reason and true courage?'
Gazetteer

910. May 29, 1783 Coachmakers Hall
'Was the Restoration of Charles the Second, on the 29th of May, such an event as will justify the keeping it a Festival?'
Gazetteer

911. September 11, 1783 Coachmakers Hall
'Will not the *Receipt Tax* tend to interrupt the course of Commerce and promote litigious Suits at Law?'
Morning Post September 9

912. September 18, 1783 Coachmakers hall
'Is a Court of Law a fit place for an Officer to settle a point of honour?'
Morning Herald

913. September 25, 1783 Coachmakers Hall
'Is the excess of Dress and Fashionable Amusements more prejudicial to the Morals, or beneficial to the Commerce of this Country?'
Morning Herald

914. October 2, 1783 Coachmakers Hall
'Would a Law to prevent Persons divorced from marrying again, be a just and beneficial Measure?'
Morning Herald

915. October 9, 1783 Coachmakers Hall
'Ought not Women to be permitted to preach in our Churches as well as Men?'
Morning Herald

916. October 16, 1783 Coachmakers Hall
'Do Riches, independent of Vice, tend more to produce Happiness or Infelicity?'
Morning Herald

917. October 23, 1783 Coachmakers Hall
'Would punishing the crime of seduction with death be a just and beneficial measure?'
Gazetteer

918. October 30, 1783 Coachmakers Hall
'Can Misfortune without the concurrence of Vice, effectually destroy our Happiness?'
Morning Herald

919. November 13, 1783 Coachmakers hall
'Is Love productive of Happiness equivalent to the anxiety ever inseparable from that Passion?'
Morning Herald

920. November 20, 1783 Coachmakers Hall
'Have the different Sectaries in this Country contributed more to Injure or promote the cause of Religion?'
Morning Herald

921. November 27, 1783 Coachmakers Hall
'Would it be consistent with Justice for Government to infringe upon
the Charter of the East India Company?'
Morning Herald

922. December 4, 1783 Coachmakers Hall
'Would it be consistent with justice for Government to infringe upon
the charter of the East-India Company?'
Gazetteer

923. December 11, 1783 Coachmakers Hall
'Does money or merit tend more to recommend a lady to a husband?'
Gazetteer

924. December 18, 1783 Coachmakers Hall
'Does Virtue tend more to promote or impede our success in life?'
Morning Herald

925. December 26, 1783 Coachmakers Hall
'Is not the interference of the Crown to influence the decisions of Parlia-
ment, an unconstitutional Measure?'
Morning Herald December 25, 1783

926. January 1, 1784 Coachmakers Hall
'Is not the interference of the Crown to influence the decisions of Parlia-
ment an unconstitutional measure?'
Gazetteer

927. January 8, 1784 Coachmakers Hall
'Are not the defects greater than the advantages of Boarding-school
Education?'
Gazetteer

928. January 15, 1784 Coachmakers Hall
'Is a wife to be commended who receives into her family the illegitimate
children of her husband?'
Gazetteer

929. January 22, 1784 Coachmakers Hall
'Is the opinion well founded, which says we ought sometimes to hold a
Candle to the Devil?'
Morning Herald

930. January 29, 1784 Coachmakers Hall
'The anniversary of the death of King Charles the First being usually
attended by conversations relative to the distinct constitutional powers
of the different branches of the Legislature, the subsequent question is
appointed for debate: For the predominance of which part of the

Legislature have the people most to fear, the Crown, the Lords or the Commons?'
Gazetteer

931. February 5, 1784 Coachmakers Hall
'Ought not the violation of *any condition* in the marriage ceremony to dissolve the *whole?*'
Gazetteer

932. February 12, 1784 Coachmakers Hall
'Does not a Minister, who holds his place contrary to the sense of the Commons, deserve the public censure of the people?'
Gazetteer

933. February 19, 1784 Coachmakers Hall
'Does not a Minister, who keeps his place without the confidence of the House of Commons, deserve the public censure of the people?'
Gazetteer

934. February 26, 1784 Coachmakers Hall
'The question announced from the chair for this evening's debate being coldly received, the managers trust the public will see the propriety of substituting the following, which immediately adverts to the grand constitutional points at present the objects of general attention.
Would the Commons be justifiable in with-holding the *supplies*, because his Majesty has appointed a Ministry who has not their confidence?'
Gazetteer

935. March 4, 1784 Coachmakers Hall
'Would a Dissolution of Parliament be likely to promote the public peace?
At this Juncture, when every true Friend to the Constitution is anxiously wishing for some mode of fixing the now unsettled state of public affairs, the . . . [above] question . . . must appear a proper subject of investigation.'
Morning Herald

936. March 11, 1784 Coachmakers Hall
'If the present differences are attended with fatal consequences, who ought to be called to an account for them, the present Administration or Opposition?'
Morning Herald

937. March 18, 1784 Coachmakers Hall
'In the present struggle, has the Minister or Opposition shewn the greater regard for the Constitution?
The interruption produced by the heat of party zeal on Thursday last induced the author of the above question to withdraw it; but as it must

be infinitely superior to any trivial matter at this important crisis, the managers trust it will be deemed a proper subject for discussion.'
Gazetteer

938. March 25, 1784 Coachmakers Hall
'Was not the treatment of the late motion for a more equal representation in Parliament a convincing proof that the House of Commons have not the good of their country at heart?'
Gazetteer

939. April 1, 1784 Coachmakers Hall
'Ought the right of electing Representatives to serve in Parliament to depend on the property, or to be considered as the personal privilege of every Englishman?'
Gazetteer

940. April 8, 1784 Coachmakers Hall
'Ought a Representative in Parliament to follow the dictates of his own conscience, or implicitly to obey the instructions of his constituents?'
Gazetteer

941. April 15, 1784 Coachmakers Hall
'Ought a Member of Parliament to follow the dictates of his own conscience, or the instructions of his constituents?'
Gazetteer

942. April 22, 1784 Coachmakers Hall
'Does the confusion in which the people are involved result more from a well-grounded fear of their late Representatives, or from popular phrenzy, excited by ministerial artifice?'
Gazetteer

943. April 29, 1784 Coachmakers Hall
'Is the unpolished country girl, or refined town lady, best calculated to render the matrimonial state truly happy?'
Gazetteer

944. May 6, 1784 Coachmakers Hall
'Is it consistent with decency for the female sex to interfere in elections?'
Gazetteer

945. May 13, 1784 Coachmakers Hall
'Can any motive justify a person of either sex passing through life in a state of celibacy?'
Gazetteer

946. May 20, 1784 Coachmakers Hall
'Which is the greater virtue, constancy in love, or sincerity in friendship?'
Gazetteer

947. May 27, 1784 Coachmakers Hall
'Can friendship subsist between two ladies who have placed their affections upon the same gentleman?'
Gazetteer

948. September 7, 1784 Ciceronian Society for Free Debate, Chapel, Margaret Street, Oxford Market
'Would not an union with Ireland, similar to that with Scotland, be productive of the greatest Advantages to both Kingdoms?
The money arising from this Institution, after defraying the necessary Expences, will, on the first Tuesday of every Month, be voted to such Public Charity as the Majority of the Company shall think proper. The constant Attendance which many of the most shining Characters in the Senate, at the Bar, and in the Church, have given to well-regulated Societies of this Nature, best speak their publick Utility; but when charitable Purposes are likewise intended to be promoted by the present Institution, it is presumed no further inducement need to be held forth to a free and generous People for their Countenance and Support.'
Admittance 6d., gallery 1s.
Daily Advertiser

949. September 7, 1784 Westminster Society for Free Debate, One Tun in the Strand
'Would the retail Shopkeepers be justifiable in refusing Payment of the Shop tax?
As this Society is instituted upon the most liberal Principles, its Object being to open and improve the Mind, to remove early-contracted Prejudice, to enable timid Merit to dismiss its Fears, and accustom the Mind to the useful Talent of publick Speaking, such Gentlemen as may be disposed to deliver their Sentiments at this Society will be heard with candid Attention; every Indulgence will be given to young Speakers, and no Pains spared for the Preservation of good Order and Harmony.'
Daily Advertiser

950. September 9, 1784 Coachmakers Hall
'Is it probable that the advantages arising from the Act to restrain smuggling will compensate for the heavy burden of the new Window Tax?'
Morning Herald

951. September 14, 1784 Ciceronian Society
'Whether Constancy in Love is most predominate in the Male or Female Sex?'
Daily Advertiser

952. September 16, 1784 Coachmakers Hall

'The verdict of the Jury on the Bishop of St. Asalph's Trial having justly called the public attention, to those matters the following Question (as the most entertaining and useful) will be debated 'Ought Jurors to be Judges of LAW as well as FACT?'
Morning Herald

953. September 23, 1784 Coachmakers Hall
'Ought Jurors to be Judges of LAW as well as FACT?'
Morning Herald

954. September 30, 1784 Coachmakers Hall
'Is the extraordinary attention of the public to Air Balloons, a proof of the folly, or superior science, of the present age?'
Morning Herald

955. October 7, 1784 Coachmakers Hall
'Is the vanity of the Women, or the depravity of the Men, the greater cause of female ruin?'
Morning Herald

956. October 12, 1784 Ciceronian Society
'Has the System of Deism, or the Doctrine of Predestination, been most detrimental to the Morals of Mankind?'
Daily Advertiser October 11

957. October 14, 1784 Coachmakers Hall
'Is it consistent with justice and sound policy that the elder child should inherit more than an equal portion of the parent's property?'
Gazetteer

958. October 19, 1784 Ciceronian Society
'Would the Subject be justifiable in refusing to pay the additional Tax on Windows, the Price of Tea not being reduced in Proportion, from the Idea that the Tax is a Commutation?'
The society 'reprobated the additional Tax on Windows [and] their Prime Minister, lest the Revenue should suffer, did then propose for Discussion . . . another tax . . .'
Daily Advertiser October 18

959. October 21, 1784 Coachmakers Hall
'Which is the wisest man, he who marries, or he who lives single?'
Gazetteer

960. October 26, 1784 Ciceronian Society
'Would it be sound Policy in Government to lay a Tax on old Batchelors, apportioning the Tax to their respective Circumstances?
And being an enemy to secret Influence, he, in Conjunction with his Brother Ministers, give this publick Notice, not even wishing that a new

Tax should be debated and passed in a thin House, with a Majority of ministerial Members.'
Daily Advertiser October 25

961. October 28, 1784 Coachmakers Hall
'Would not a Tax upon Batchelors be a just and beneficial measure?'
Morning Herald

962. November 2, 1784 Ciceronian Society
'Can any Thing be politically good which is morally evil?'
Daily Advertiser November 1

963. November 4, 1784 Coachmakers Hall
'Does Pride tend more to support or destroy female virtue?'
Gazetteer

964. November 4, 1784 Gazetteer
'Orator – Now a man possessed of great fluency of speech, who can dwell for *two hours* on that which does not require *ten minutes*, and convinces none but his dependents. FORMERLY, one who could stem the current of public licentiousness, and being known to be a man of sincere integrity himself, could, by argument, make his greatest enemies his most contrite converts.'

965. November 9, 1784 Ciceronian Society
'Has the Increase of Methodism in this Country been friendly to the Interests of Morality?'
Daily Advertiser November 8

966. November 11, 1784 Coachmakers Hall
'Is the opinion that dreams foretell good or bad fortune, more deserving of censure or justification?'
Gazetteer

967. November 16, 1784 Ciceronian Society
'Is the existence of Witches and Apparitions probable?'
Daily Advertiser November 15

968. November 18, 1784 Coachmakers Hall
'Is a wild or studious youth the more likely to make a good husband?'
Gazetteer

969. November 23, 1784 Ciceronian Society
'Does a domestick or Boarding School Education best qualify a young Lady for the social and other necessary Purposes of Life?
The Directors of this Society entertain the most pleasing Hopes of its publick Utility, from the very respectable Company of both Sexes, who repeatedly honour it with their Presence, and cannot help thus publickly to thank them for that decent, orderly and genteel Behaviour observed

in general; but also for that candid indulgence uniformly shewn to young Speakers in particular.'
Daily Advertiser November 22

970. November 25, 1784 Coachmakers Hall
'Would it be for the interest of this country to take any part between the Emperor and the Dutch?'
Gazetteer

971. November 30, 1784 Ciceronian Society
'Which ought a Man to prefer in the Choice of a Wife, Money, Sense, or Beauty?'
Daily Advertiser November 29

972. December 2, 1784 Coachmakers Hall
'Was women designed to be *equal* or *inferior* to man?'
Gazetteer

973. December 7, 1784 Ciceronian Society
'Can a Roman Catholick, consistent with the Principles of his Religion, be a good Subject to a Protestant Prince?'
Daily Advertiser November 29

974. December 9, 1784 Coachmakers Hall
'Does not the frequency of capital punishments tend to increase offenders?'
Gazetteer

975. December 16, 1784 Coachmakers Hall
'Are the men of the present age more dissipated than the women?'
Gazetteer

976. December 21, 1784 Ciceronian Society
'Has the Discovery and Progress of the Arts and Sciences been serviceable to Mankind?'
Daily Advertiser December 20

977. December 23, 1784 Coachmakers Hall
'Does the usual observance of Christmas tend more to the general levity of manners, or to promote the cause of Christianity?'
Gazetteer

978. December 28, 1784 Ciceronian Society
'Would it not be good Policy for the Legislature to appoint the married Clergy (for certain Salaries, and under certain Obligations) to receive Proposals from Lovers of either Sex, and negotiate all Matrimonial Agreements?'
Daily Advertiser December 27

979. December 30, 1784 Coachmakers Hall
'Has the Tragedy of George Barnwell tended more to improve the morals of youth; or the Beggar's Opera to injure them?'
Gazetteer

980. January 4, 1785 Ciceronian Society, Margaret Street Chapel, Oxford Market
'Is it consistent with Female Delicacy for a Lady, under any Circumstances, to make the first Proposals of Marriage?'
Daily Advertiser January 3

981. January 6, 1785 Coachmakers Hall
'Is a Maid or a Widow of the same age, and in the same circumstances, to be preferred in the choice of a Wife?'
General Advertiser January 5

982. January 11, 1785 Ciceronian Society
'Is Flattery a necessary Ingredient to conduct Mankind in the Affairs of Life?'
Daily Advertiser January 3

983. January 13, 1785 Coachmakers Hall
'Which should a woman prefer as essential to her happiness in the marriage state, the FOOL on the pinnacle of fortune, or the man of SENSE in the vale of indigence?'
Gazetteer

984. January 18, 1785 Ciceronian Society
'Is a private or a publick Education preferable, when the Circumstances of the Parents will admit of the former?'
Daily Advertiser January 10,

985. January 20, 1785 Coachmakers Hall
'Whose feelings are most poignant, the mariner expecting shipwreck, the criminal on the point of execution, or the lover informed of the desertion of his mistress?'
Gazetteer

986. January 25, 1785 Ciceronian Society
'Which Form of Government is best calculated to secure the Liberty of the Subject, that of a Republick, or that as by Law established in this Kingdom?'
Daily Advertiser January 17

987. January 27, 1785 Coachmakers Hall
'Has a man unjustly sentenced to a shameful and painful death, a right to avoid the infamy and torture of the same, by putting a period to his own existence?'
Gazetteer

988. February 1, 1785 Ciceronian Society
'Is the Christian Church authorized from Scripture to observe the first Day of the Week, in Preference to the Seventh, as the Sabbath?'
Daily Advertiser January 24

989. February 3, 1785 Coachmakers Hall
'Ought not every man to be considered as an enemy to his country that attempts to oppose a Reform in Parliament?'
Gazetteer

990. February 8, 1785 Ciceronian Society
'Is not the Caledonian Society that meets in Pall-Mall, and profess to encourage one another only in the Way of Trade, a dangerous Combination?'
Daily Advertiser February 7

991. February 10, 1785 Coachmakers Hall
'Ought not that Man who attempts to oppose a Reform in Parliament, to be esteemed as an enemy to his Country?'
General Advertiser February 9

992. February 17, 1785 Coachmakers Hall
'Ought not any one who attempts to oppose a Reform in Parliament to be esteemed an enemy to this Country?'
Gazetteer

993. February 23, 1785 Debating Society, The Crown, Cranbourn Passage, Leicester Fields
'Are the decisions of the Commons, respecting the Westminster Election, to be attributed more to Justice or Party prejudice?
Tickets to be had at the bar, at 6d. each, to be spent in manner most agreeable to the purchaser.'
Gazetteer February 22

994. February 24, 1785 Coachmakers Hall
'Has not the Westminster Scrutiny been carried on more to gratify party views, than to produce justice to the contending candidates?'
Gazetteer

995. February 29, 1785 Ciceronian Society
'Does the love of Liberty, the love of Life, or the love of Ladies, predominate most in the breast of Man?'
General Advertiser February 28

996. March 3, 1785 Coachmakers Hall
'Which profession (in the hands of bad men) is most injurious to mankind, Law, Physic or Divinity?'
Gazetteer

997. March 10, 1785 Coachmakers Hall
'Would it be for the interest of this country to coincide with the resolutions of the Irish Parliament respecting the commerce of both countries? As it is expected that upon a subject so materially interesting to trade, the company will be uncommonly numerous . . .'
Gazetteer

998. March 17, 1785 Coachmakers Hall
'Would it be for the interest of this country to coincide with the resolutions of the Irish Parliament respecting the commerce of both countries?'
Gazetteer

999. March 22, 1785 Ciceronian Society
'Can the eternal Salvation of every Individual of the human Race be proved from Scripture and Reason?'
Daily Advertiser March 21,

1000. March 24, 1785 Coachmakers Hall
'Will it be for the benefit of this country to confirm the resolutions of the Irish Parliament, respecting the commerce of both countries? The Question on the Irish Resolutions was carried last Thursday by a very large majority against them . . .'
Morning Herald

1001. March 25, 1785 Theological Society, Margaret Street Chapel
'Heb. ii vers. 9 "He tasted Death for every Man." Are not the Doctrines of Election and Reprobation depreciating the Sacrifice of Christ, and derogatory to the Honour of God?'
Daily Advertiser

1002. March 29, 1785 Ciceronian Society
'Do the Diversions of the Stage tend most to improve or contaminate the morals of Mankind?'
Admittance for the future 3d. to the Body of the Chapel, 6d. to the Gallery.
Daily Advertiser March 28

1003. March 31, 1785 Coachmakers Hall
'Which stands the best chance for a Husband, the Prude, or the Coquette?'
The Question 'was determined in favour of the latter'.
Morning Herald

1004. April 1, 1785 Theological Society, Margaret Street Chapel
'Heb. ii. 9. "He tasted Death for every Man." Are not the Doctrines of Election and Reprobation depreciating the Sacrifice of Christ, and derogatory to the Honour of God?'
Admission 3d. to the body of the Chapel and 6d. to the galleries.
Daily Advertiser

1005. April 7, 1785 Coachmakers Hall
'Has a minister of this country a right to make any concessions, or bring forward any measure which may affect Great Britain, without consulting the British Parliament?'
It was (almost unanimously) determined 'against the minister's actions.'
Morning Herald

1006. April 14, 1785 Coachmakers Hall
'Which ought a Woman most to avoid, in the choice of a Husband – Deformity of Body, – or Weakness of Mind?
Company were almost unanimous that weakness of mind ought to be more avoided.'
Morning Herald

1007. April 15, 1785 Theological Society
1 Pet. iv. 12 'Is not the Roman Catholick Doctrine of Purgatory agreeable to Reason and Revelation?'
Daily Advertiser

1008. April 21, 1785 Coachmakers Hall
'Which is the more desirable situation, to be alive to all the feelings of sensibility, or totally indifferent to every thing that does not immediately concern ourselves?'
It was 'determined (by a great majority) that it was more desirable to be alive to all the feelings of sensibility.'
Morning Herald

1009. April 28, 1785 Coachmakers Hall
'Which is the greatest object of pity, the Woman who is tied to a Drunken Husband, or the Man who is tied to a scolding Wife?'
Company decided that a woman with a drunken husband was more to be pitied.
Morning Herald

1010. May 5, 1785 Coachmakers Hall
'Are the bold manners of the Women, or the fopperies of the Men, more censurable in the present day?'
Determined that the fopperies of the men were more censurable.
Morning Herald

1011. May 12, 1785 Coachmakers Hall
'Which, during the course of his Administration, has given the greater proof of Patriotism, Mr. FOX or Mr. PITT?'
Morning Herald

1012. May 19, 1785 Coachmakers Hall

'Which, during the course of his Administration, has given the greater proof of Patriotism, Mr. FOX or Mr. PITT?
It was after a most spirited debate, determined by a very great majority, that the patriotism of Mr. Fox in and out of office, was far superior to that of Mr. Pitt.'
Morning Herald May 26

1013. May 26, 1785 Coachmakers Hall
'Does the Minister deserve more credit or censure for the contents of his Budget?'
Morning Herald

1014. September 1, 1785 Coachmakers Hall
'Is it constitutional to oppose an act of Parliament which is generally admitted to be partial and oppressive?'
The vote was carried, by a small majority, in the negative.
Daily Advertiser

1015. September 8, 1785 Coachmakers-hall Society
'Would it be political in Administration to prosecute further the Irish propositions?'
The question 'was debated before a very respectful and numerous audience; but so ill an impression have these propositions left on the minds of the public, that scarcely an advocate appeared for their further prosecution, it was therefore carried almost unanimously in the negative.'
Gazetteer September 15

1016. September 8, 1785 Westminster Forum, at the One Tun, Strand
'Would the retail Shopkeepers be justifiable in refusing Payment of the Shop Tax?'
Admittance 6d., beer included.
Daily Advertiser September 7

1017. September 8, 1785 The original Society for free debate, lately held at Coachmakers-hall, is now removed to the Assembly Room, at the Mitre Tavern, Fleet-Street
'Would not a union of this country with Ireland, similar to that with Scotland, be likely to quiet the jealousies subsisting between the two nations?
After a most spirited debate, it was unanimously agreed to adjourn the further discussion of this interesting subject to this evening, to give those Gentlemen an opportunity of speaking who could not be heard for want of time.'
Gazetteer

1018. September 15, 1785 Coachmakers-hall Society
'Have the present Ministry discovered a disposition more favourable or inimical to the liberties of the people?'

Audience decided that ministry was inimical, by a great majority.
Gazetteer

1019. September 15, 1785 Society for free debate, Mitre Tavern
'Would not a union of this country with Ireland, similar to that with Scotland, be likely to quiet the jealousies subsisting between the two nations?
N.B. the Managers most respectfully inform the public that they have no connection whatever with any society now held at Coachmaker's-hall as the whole of the persons concerned in the Society lately held there have left that place (except the person who rents the Hall).'
Gazetteer

1020. September 22, 1785 Coachmakers-hall debating Society
'Is the assertion of Mr. Pope true, that every woman is at heart a rake?
When after a very ingenious and lively debate, conducted with becoming deference to female delicacy, the dictum of that eminent poet was almost unanimously declared to be false.'
Gazetteer September 29

1021. September 22, 1785 Society for Free Debate, Mitre Tavern
'Whether Ambition or the passion of Love had been productive of more injury to society?
At a large and respectable meeting of both sexes, it was determined that Ambition' had caused most injury.
Gazetteer September 29

1022. September 29, 1785 Coachmakers-hall debating Society
'Which is the more useful member of society, the Divine, the Physician, or the Lawyer?
When, after several ingenious gentlemen had displayed their abilities in support of the several learned characters, the audience was pleased, by their almost unanimous decision, to declare the Divine to be the most useful member of society.'
Gazetteer

1023. September 29, 1785 Society for Free Debate, Mitre Tavern
'Which of the two statesmen, Mr. Fox or Mr. Pitt, from his past conduct, has given the greater proof of ABILITY to rule this country in its present situation?'
Gazetteer

1024. October 6, 1785 Coach Maker's-Hall Debating Society
'Is not the delicate sensibility of females the principal cause of their own misfortune?'
The Question 'was introduced by a gentleman of distinguished abilities in an elegant speech, replete with sterling sense, and delivered with a laudable regard to the chastest ear of the female part of the audience, and afforded a very interesting debate, in which the sensibility of the fair sex was ably defended as the guardian of feminine virtue; the

seductive arts of gallantry justly reprobated; and many seasonable observations thrown out, tending to the general promotion of virtue, and the discouragement of vice: it was decided by a considerable majority in the negative.'
Gazetteer

1025. October 10, 1785 London Theological Society for Free Debate, Queen's Arms Tavern, Newgate street
'Will Scripture or Reason support the Doctrine of eternal Punishment? In this enlightened and enquiring Age, it is presumed that a Society instituted for the investigation of Theological and Metaphysical Subjects will meet with universal Approbation.'
The Question was determined in the affirmative.
Admittance to Ladies and Gentlemen 6d. each.
General Advertiser October 13

1026. October 13, 1785 Coachmakers-Hall Debating Society
'Did the present Administration come into office upon constitutional grounds? and has their conduct since been such as to entitle them to the support of every true friend to his country?'
The Question, 'after a most animated debate (before a crowded audience) was determined in favour of the Ministry'.
Daily Advertiser

1027. October 17, 1785 London Theological Society for Free Debate
'Can man by his conduct shorten or prolong his own life?
It was determined in the affirmative by a large majority.'
General Advertiser October 13

1028. October 20, 1785 Coach-maker's Hall Debating Society
'Does not suicide originate in cowardice?
Many different opinions were ably maintained, as the source from whence it originates; but they all united in the laudable purpose of exposing its heinous deformity, and recommending religion and virtue as the only effectual shield against it. It was decided in the negative.'
Daily Advertiser

1029. October 21, 1785 Times
To the Editor of the *Universal Register*
'Sir,
Every plan or institution designed to disseminate knowledge, to improve the taste, and advance eloquence, merits attention and encouragement. I was led to this remark by the weekly meetings of several societies, in which questions relative to religion and morality, to government, policy, and legislation, have been, or are to be proposed for discussion.
By attending assemblies of this sort, such an emulation may be raised, as shall stimulate to read, and to investigate useful subjects. May not gentlemen, who speak on points which have been proposed, acquire an

easy correct manner of expressing themselves, or at length gain such an acquaintance with polite literature, as shall prove highly useful and ornamental through the whole of life?

Precision and perspicuity in reasoning may thus be learned, or arguments properly arranged, and just conclusions drawn. In disquisitions of this sort, a relish for what is manly and liberal must be acquired, the narrow and contracted will be banished, and a generous cultivation take place: the dogmatical and petulant will be avoided, nor will vague assertions be admitted to supply the place of evidence and argument.

I therefore add, that these disinterested literary societies may be considered as nurseries for several of the departments in life, particularly the senate, the bar, and the pulpit, in which places the wish of clearness and precision of spirit and rhetoric, as well as of classical elegance, is too often discernible.

If the fine arts be favourable to virtue, certainly a person's preparing himself to speak with propriety in public (if he feel as he ought) cannot but cultivate the understanding, and mend the heart: and, when what is spoken comes from an individual marked by purity of manners, joined to a refined taste, it is received with respect, and makes a suitable impression.

Though a celebrated writer says, "that eloquence leads men by the ears", yet it is hoped that the mere tinsel and jingle of words, or dressed out sentences, without any thing solid and convincing, will not be received as oratory. Eloquence is the art of persuasion; its most essential requisites are sound reasoning, perspicuity, and an appearance of sincerity in the speaker; with such graces of style and utterance as shall invite and command attention; good sense must be its foundation. Without this no man can be truly eloquent: fools can persuade none but fools; a man of sense must be convinced before he is persuaded.'

RHETORICUS

1030. October 24, 1785 London Theological Society
'If the generally received doctrine of eternal punishment be true, are not the brute creation happier than the human race?'
General Advertiser

1031. October 24, 1785 Debate at Mr. Kinloch's, the Newcastle upon Tyne, Broad street Square
'Would it tend to the Aggrandizement of the State were Debt expunged, and the Stock-Holders to receive Annuities?'
Daily Advertiser December 22

1032. October 27, 1785 Coachmakers Hall
'Have theatrical entertainments a general tendency to improve or prejudice the morals of the people, and was it prudent to grant a license to Mr. Palmer for opening a new place of publick exhibition?'
Question 'was carried in favour of the Stage by a small majority; but against Mr. Palmer's intended new Theatre, by a great Majority.'
General Advertiser November 3

1033. October 27, 1785 Free Debate, Mitre Tavern
'Whether the friendship of individuals should, at all times, give place to the love of their country?'
The Question was 'determined by a small majority, in favour of the love of their country'.
Morning Herald November 3

1034. November 2, 1785 Theological Debate, Oratory, Surry Bridewell, St. George's-fields
'Upon what Ground can the Doctrine of Universal Salvation be supported?'
Admission three-pence only.
Times

1035. November 3, 1785 Mitre Tavern
'Does pride tend more to protect or to destroy female virtue?'
The Question was debated 'before a polite and numerous auditory of Ladies and Gentlemen . . . The business was opened by a well-informed speaker, in an elaborate and accurate speech. He touched upon all the leading points, that were connected with the subject. He spoke fully upon the nature of pride, as it affected both sexes, and all classes of mankind. He gave a number of instances from domestic and public history of the fatal consequences of pride upon the female sex, but reserved his final decision upon the question till a further period of the debate.
He was succeeded by a number of able disputants, who generally contended, that pride was an enemy to the virtue of the fair.
There were not wanting, however, ingenious advocates to support a contrary doctrine, who argued, that pride from a sense of shame they must endure, if they swerved from virtue, would induce those who were governed by it, to guard against a loss of honour; and that though deviations from chastity were, from their elevated situations more glaring among the higher orders of the people, than among the latter; yet, unfortunately, they were infinitely more frequent among the latter. After a well-conducted debate, more connected than diffusive, and more argumentative than elegant, it was decided, that "Pride tends more to destroy than to protect female virtue." In the course of the business, a short altercation arose on some misconceived expressions used by one of the speakers, which, however, was soon reconciled by the judicious moderation of the Chairman, and the polite forbearance of the gentlemen who uttered them.'
General Advertiser November 8

1036. November 3, 1785 Coachmakers Hall
'Are the understandings of men naturally superior to those of women, or does education constitute the difference?
It was determined by a majority, nearly amounting to a unanimity, that men have no claim to a native superiority of understanding.'
General Advertiser

1037. November 10, 1785 Coach Maker's Hall Debating Society
'Is it justifiable in Creditors to detain their Debtors in prison, who have surrendered up the whole of their Property – and would it be a measure of Wisdom in the Legislature, at the present Period, to pass a general Act of Insolvency?'
First part of Question was decided to be unjustifiable 'by a considerable majority'; second part of Question 'by a small majority'.
General Advertiser

1038. November 10, 1785 Mitre Tavern Society for Free Debate
'Whether the Discontent of the People of this country, during the present reign, has arisen more from real or imaginary evils?
It was determined by an almost united vote of all present, that there were real evils enough in the present reign, without recurring to imaginary ones.'
Morning Herald November 17

1039. November 14, 1785 London Theological Society
'Whether the present is the only state of probation?
Afforded a very entertaining and interesting Debate. The Speakers entered minutely into the subject, and by reference to Jewish, Pagan, and Christian authority, displayed admirable learning, ability, and force of reasoning, on both sides of the question; although the decision was almost unanimously in favour of the present being the only state of probation.'
General Advertiser November 21

1040. November 17, 1785 Coach Maker's Hall Debating Society
'Have the late Lord Chesterfield's Letters to his Son, been injurious to the morals of society?'
The audience voted in the affirmative by a small majority.
Times

1041. November 17, 1785 Mitre Tavern Society for Free Debate
'Is an Old Maid a proper object of Ridicule?'
Morning Herald

1042. November 21, 1785 London Theological Society
'Which was the most criminal, Adam or Eve, in eating the forbidden fruit?
General Advertiser

1043. November 24, 1785 Coachmakers Hall
'Does conjugal affection most prevail among the lower, the middling, or the higher ranks of people?
Many Gentlemen distinguished for their oratorical powers, wit and ingenuity, employed their admired talents in exploring the various cause, which embitter the marriage state, and in recommending virtue and the improvement of the mind as the surest bond of connubial happi-

ness. It was determined by a considerable majority, that the middling orders of the people enjoyed the greatest share of conjugal happiness.'
General Advertiser December 1

1044. November 24, 1785 Mitre Tavern Society for Free Debate
'Are Theatrical Representations more conducive to vice or to virtue?'
Determined that theatre more conducive to virtue.
Morning Herald December 1

1045. November 28, 1785 Lyceum Free Debating Society
'Whether Mr. Pitt, by his dereliction of the cause of Whiggism, has not rendered it more essential service than his eloquence could have done, if he had persevered in its support?'
Question originally proposed by the Right Hon. C. J. Fox.
'This society is instituted under the patronage of several gentlemen, distinguished for rank and ability, and its conductors hope, that by maintaining a respectability in its resort, and a delicate propriety in the subjects of discussion, this institution will deserve the support of the public in general.'
Morning Herald

1046. December 1, 1785 Coachmakers Hall
'Which ought we most to prefer in the choice of a Wife, personal beauty, or mental accomplishments?'
The Question 'was decided by a considerable majority in favour of mental accomplishments.'
General Advertiser

1047. December 1, 1785 Mitre Tavern Society for Free Debate
'Which is more likely to make the better Husband to a woman of sensibility, a Miser or a Spendthrift?
Determined by a small majority, in favour of the Spendthrift.'
Morning Herald

1048. December 5, 1785 Society for Free Debate, Lyceum, Stand
'Whether the male or female sex be more infected with the fashionable foibles of the present day?'
Morning Herald

1049. December 8, 1785 Coachmakers Hall
'Which is the more essential qualification for a Prime Minister, great abilities, or strict integrity?
After an animated contest, conducted with becoming candour and liberality, it was determined by a small majority, that strict integrity is the most essential qualification in a Prime Minister.'
Times

1050. December 8, 1785 Mitre Tavern Society for Free Debate

'Which is the best situation for the display of Eloquence, the Pulpit, the Bar, or the Senate?'
Morning Herald

1051. December 12, 1785 Free Debating Society, Lyceum in the Strand
'Are the Intellectual Faculties of the Male, naturally superior to those of the Female Sex; or does Education constitute the difference?'
Admission 6d.
Morning Herald

1052. December 15, 1785 Coachmakers Hall
'Which is the more beneficial to youth of both sexes, a public or private education?
Determined by a small majority in favour of a public education for boys, and almost unanimously of a private one for females.'
Morning Herald December 22

1053. December 15, 1785 Mitre Tavern Society for Free Debate
'Is not an Old Bachelor a contemptible character?
As no criminality appeared to belong to celibacy, unless accompanied with guilt, he was, on the shew of hands, unanimously acquitted (one hand only excepted).'
Morning Herald

1054. December 19, 1785 Lyceum Debating Society
'Is Learning a desirable Qualification in a Wife?
After a debate in which nervous eloquence and poignant wit were happily combined, was decided in the affirmative.
The conductors of this Society return thanks to the Public for the encouragement by which it has already been distinguished, and to the many eloquent and ingenious Gentlemen who have favoured their Assemblies with their entertaining discussions.'
Morning Herald

1055. December 22, 1785 Coachmakers Hall
'Would an Act of Parliament, empowering a family alliance between this country and France, be consistent with prudence and sound policy?'
Morning Herald

1056. December 22, 1785 Mitre Tavern Society for Free Debate
'Which has the best claim to our Affections, our Parent, Wife, or Child?'
Morning Herald

1057. December 26, 1785 Lyceum Debating Society
'Whether the operation of the Marriage Act has tended to the encrease of Conjugal Felicity?'
Morning Herald December 22

1058. December 29, 1785 Coachmakers Hall Debating Society
'Should the Ladies encourage the English Silk Manufacture?'
This Question 'called forth the abilities of many judicious and well informed Speakers: Though every Speaker commiserated the distressed condition of the unemployed Weavers, yet several of them ably pointed out the mischievous consequences that would probably follow to the Cotton Manufacture, by the proposed encouragement of the Silk Weaving Business. After a variety of ingenious arguments, in which the Speakers on both sides displayed equal candour, liberality, and humanity, it was determined, almost unanimously, that it would be highly laudable and patriotic in the Ladies to encourage the Silk Manufacture.'
General Advertiser January 4, 1786

1059. December 29, 1785 Mitre Tavern Society for Free Debate
'Whether the principles of Honour practiced by the Great, tended more to promote Vice or Virtue?'
The Question 'after many excellent arguments, both for and against Duelling, which appeared to be the leading feature of the question, it was determined that every species of modern Honour tended to promote Vice rather than Virtue.'
General Advertiser January 4

1060. January 2, 1786 Free Debating Society, Lyceum
'Which is more Happy, the Person possessed of Sensibility, or he who is a Stranger to it?'
Morning Herald

1061. January 5, 1786 Coach-Makers-Hall Debating Society
'Would it not be for the interest of the community, to impose a tax on Old Batchelors, and give the produce thereof, as marriage portions, to Young Maidens?
It was almost unanimously carried in favour of the tax.'
General Advertiser January 4

1062. January 5, 1786 Mitre Tavern Society for Free Debate
'Can that Wife be truly said to love a Husband, who frequently disobeys him?
It was at length determined by a small majority, that a wife might disobey her husband and still love him.'
General Advertiser January 4

1063. January 12, 1786 Coachmakers Hall
'Do not the principles of methodism tend to blind the judgment and contract the heart?'
Morning Herald

1064. January 12, 1786 Mitre Tavern Society for Free Debate

'Which bids fair to make the best member of Society, the youth who is early introduced to the follies and vices of the age, or he who is carefully kept from them till he has arrived to years of maturity?'
Morning Herald

1065. January 19, 1786 Coachmakers Hall
'Do not the principles of methodism tend to blind the judgment and contract the heart?'
Question 'was decided in favour of the persons under that denomination. The speakers on both sides, having proved themselves able and ingenious debaters, received from a most numerous and genteel audience (excepting a few zealots) those tributes of applause which are ever attendant on the effusions of manly eloquence, and true genius, joined to knowledge.'
Morning Herald January 26

1066. January 19, 1786 Free Debating Society, Mitre Tavern
'Whether it was not false Delicacy which forbid the fair sex making the first advances to the man they love?
It was determined at the close, by a great majority, against the ladies making the first advances.'
Morning Herald January 26

1067. January 26, 1786 Coachmakers Hall
'Is not the conduct of those parents who abandon their daughters, for the loss of honour, a principal cause of the increase of prostitution?
After a debate replete with the most salutary lessons of moral instruction, strength, and precision of reasoning, elegance of language, and chastity of sentiment, [the question was] by a considerable majority of a most respectable auditory, decided in the affirmative.'
Morning Herald

1068. January 26, 1786 Free Debating Society, Mitre Tavern
'Which of the two characters in the course of his political Conduct has given the better proof of his being a real Friend to his Country, Mr. Fox or Mr. Pitt?
On the chairman's giving his opinion on the shew of hands, a great part of the company objected to it: in consequence of the exceeding crowded state of the room, and neither party being disposed to yield, we decline saying anything farther as to the decision.'
Morning Herald

1069. February 2, 1786 Coachmakers Hall
'Have the people more reason to believe that the present opposition to Government proceeds from a sincere regard for the interest of the nation, or a desire only to get into power?'
Morning Herald

1070. February 2, 1786 Society for Free Debate, Mitre Tavern

'Is that maxim founded on truth which says, a reformed rake makes the best husband?'
Question was determined in the negative.
Morning Herald

1071. February 6, 1786 New Westminster Forum or School for Elocution, King St. St. James
'Do Ladies by going to India, for the purpose of obtaining Husbands, deviate from their characteristic delicacy?'
The Question was 'almost unanimously decided in the affirmative'.
Morning Herald

1072. February 9, 1786 Coachmakers Hall
'Have the people more reason to believe that the present opposition to Government proceeds from a sincere regard for the interest of the nation, or a desire only to get into power?'
The Question 'was decided against the Opposition'.
Morning Herald

1073. February 9, 1786 Society for Free Debate, Mitre Tavern
'Which of the three virtues is most easy to be found, Honesty in a Lawyer, Disinterestedness in a Physician, or Practical Piety in a Divine?'
Question 'determined in favour of the Divine'.
Morning Herald

1074. February 13, 1786 New Westminster Forum
'Does the present state of Parliamentary Eloquence, tend to retard or promote the Public Welfare?'
Morning Herald

1075. February 16, 1786 Coachmakers Hall
'Is Jealousy a Proof of Love?
The adjournment of this subject was, by desire of the majority of one of the most crouded and brilliant audiences that ever honoured a Society for National Entertainment with their presence, in order to afford an opportunity to several Gentlemen distinguished for their oratorical abilities, who were desirous to, but could not for want of time . . . take part in the debate . . .'
Morning Herald

1076. February 16, 1786 Society for Free Debate, Mitre Tavern
'Is it not the aim of the present Minister rather to please the Sovereign than the People?
It was determined, that the Minister's aim was to please both King and People.'
Morning Herald

1077. February 20, 1786 New Westminster Forum or School for Elocution, King Street, St. James's Square
'Which is more painful to a Woman of Sensibility – to be obliged to marry a man she disliked, or not allowed to marry the man she loved?'
Times

1078. February 23, 1786 Coachmakers Hall
'Is Jealousy a Proof of Love?'
Question was 'decided in the affirmative'.
Morning Herald

1079. February 23, 1786 Society for Free Debate, Mitre Tavern
'Which bids fair to make the best Husband, a Knave or a Fool?'
The Question was 'determined in favour of the Fool'.
Morning Herald

1080. February 27, 1786 New Westminster Forum
'Is Suicide an Act of Courage?'
Morning Herald

1081. March 2, 1786 Coachmakers Hall
'Which is to be preferred for a Wife, an Old Maid or a Widow?
The debate being instructive as it was entertaining, and the advocates for the two female characters having equally distinguished themselves for strength and precision of reasoning, and that chastity of sentiment which is the companion of good sense, drew from a very crouded and brilliant assembly of Ladies and Gentlemen those tributes of applause which a liberal audience never denies to genius and ability.'
Question determined in favour of the widow.
Morning Herald

1082. March 2, 1786 Society for Free Debate, Mitre Tavern
'Are not Newspapers, as they are at present conducted, of greater Injury than Benefit to Society?'
The Question was determined in favour of the Newspapers.
Morning Herald

1083. March 6, 1786 New Westminster Forum
'Which is the most ridiculous Character, a Man Milliner or a Military Fop?
The two characters were pourtrayed, and commented on, by the different Speakers in a style far superior to that which usually characterises public assemblies of this description. – The question being put, there appeared a very small majority against the Man Milliner.'
Morning Herald

1084. March 9, 1786 Coachmakers Hall
'Are not the Pleasures of Imagination superior to those of Possession?'

The question was, 'by a small majority of a brilliant assemblage of Ladies and Gentlemen, decided in favour of possession. The debate was distinguished for much sound argumentation, true philosophical reasoning, and pleasantry of wit . . .'
Morning Herald

1085. March 9, 1786 Society for Free Debate, Mitre Tavern
'Is it not an Instance of great Partiality and Injustice, to exclude the Ladies from the Knowledge of Free Masonry?
It was determined against the Ladies being made acquainted with the secret.'
Morning Herald

1086. March 13, 1786 New Westminster Forum
'Are personal Charms more likely to obtain a Woman a Husband, than Mental Accomplishments?'
Morning Herald

1087. March 16, 1786 Coachmakers Hall
'Which is the most exceptionable Character, the Trading Justice, the Quack Doctor, or the Methodist Teacher?'
Morning Herald

1088. March 16, 1786 Society for Free Debate, Mitre Tavern
'Which is the happier State, Marriage, or a single Life?
But so far will a judicious audience be prejudiced in favour of wedded love, that though much merit was due to the great ingenuity of the Speakers, on the other side, they gave it in favour of Matrimony by a great majority.'
Morning Herald

1089. March 20, 1786 New Westminster Forum moved to Squibb's Auction Room, Saville Row
'Is that proverb founded in truth, which describes Adversity to be the School for Wisdom?'
The Society has moved 'in order to accommodate its truly polite supporters; for which purpose they have engaged the above room, as being more central, elegant, convenient, and in every respect better adapted for the display of public elocution . . .'
Morning Herald

1090. March 23, 1786 Coachmakers Hall
'Which is the most unexceptionable Character, the Trading Justice, the Quack Doctor, or the Methodist Teacher?
From the crouded state of the hall, and other concomitant circumstances, it could not be ascertained whether the Trading Justice or Methodist Teacher was the character against whom the majority decided.'

April 13; a note acknowledges a mistake on the outcome: 'there was an evident majority against the Methodist Teacher.'
Morning Herald

1091. March 23, 1786 Society of Free Debate, Mitre Tavern
'Which stands the best chance to get a Husband, a Prude or a Coquet? Less criminality, or hypocrisy appearing in the Coquet than the Prude, it was carried in her favour.'
Morning Herald

1092. March 27, 1786 New Westminster Forum
'Is it just, in this enlightened age, to preclude Ladies from voting in Elections, or sitting in the Senate?
It is utterly impossible, for the limits of an advertisement in a due degree to express, the exquisite entertainment the debate on the above question afforded; serious argument, sterling wit, and genuine humour, powerfully contended for the approbation of a splendid and numerous assemblage of persons, by whom the question was decided in the affirmative'.
Morning Herald April 3

1093. March 30, 1786 Coachmakers Hall
'Is that Opinion founded in Truth, which says, That the First Impression of Love on the Heart is the strongest, and seldom or never erased?'
The Question 'was, by a considerable majority, decided in the Affirmative'.
Morning Herald

1094. March 30, 1786 Society for Free Debate, Mitre Tavern
'Are the boasted Liberties of England Real or Imaginary?
The company in general appeared not willing to think their liberties were imaginary, (though many striking observations were made use of to prove them so) therefore determined in favour of their being real.'
Morning Herald

1095. April 3, 1786 New Westminster Forum
'Can a Woman expect to find Sincerity in a Man who has proved inconstant to the first object of his Love?'
Morning Herald

1096. April 6, 1786 Coachmakers Hall
'Has the Publication of Mrs. Bellamy's Apology for her Life been friendly or injurious to the Cause of Virtue?'
It was decided that Publication 'was more injurious than friendly to the cause of virtue'.
Morning Herald

1097. April 6, 1786 Society for Free Debate, Mitre Tavern

181

'Do the laws of nature give any Privileges to the Husband, that may not equally be claimed by the Wife?'
Question was determined in the affirmative.
Morning Herald

1098. April 10, 1786 New Westminster Forum
'Notice was last Monday given, in the presence of an exceedingly numerous and elegant auditory, by a gentlemen who frequently displays his abilities in this institution, that he would this day open his Budget of Taxes; has authorized the proprietors to lay them before the public the following objects which he intends to propose for taxation; man-milliners; walking jockies, male and female; geese vended in the Metropolis on Michaelmasday; dull sermons; old maids; pinns and needles; corks; music-paper; engravings; transplanted teeth; cradles; wigs; night-caps; walking-canes; umbrellas; rings; silentees of both Houses of Parliament; the wit of aldermen and common council; female false protuberance; clerical charity; wet nurses, &c.'
Morning Herald

1099. April 13, 1786 Coachmakers Hall
'Is the Decrease of Mr. Pitt's Popularity to be imputed more to the Misconduct of his Administration, or to the Inconsistency of the People?
It was determined, by a great majority, that the decrease of that Gentleman's popularity was to be attributed to the inconsistency of the people, and not to any misconduct in his administration.'
Morning Herald

1100. April 13, 1786 Society for Free Debate, Mitre Tavern
'Which contributes most to impoverish the lower class of people, the Publican, the Pawnbroker, or the Trading Justice?
The company appeared to view them all as objects beneath the notice of either wit or ridicule; but, on the shew of hands, a majority appeared against the Trading Justice.'
Morning Herald

1101. April 17, 1786 New Westminster Forum
'Continued discussion of the Budget of Taxes . . . the remaining contents are,
Cradles, Walking Jockies, both Male and Female, Wigs, Night Caps, Clerical Charity, Hobby Horses, Beards, Female false Protuberances, Wit of Aldermen and Common Council, Silentees of both Houses of Parliament.'
Morning Herald

1102. April 20, 1786 Coachmakers Hall
'Which is the more blameable Character, the Parent who exacts too rigid an Obedience from his Children, or he who leaves it altogether to the Child for a Return of Duty and Affection?'

It was determined 'that the parent exacting too rigid an obedience from his children, is less blameable than he who leaves his offspring for a return of duty and affection'.
Morning Herald

1103. April 20, 1786 Society for Free Debate, Mitre Tavern
'Which recommends a Man most to the Fair Sex, Wit, Courage or Politeness?'
The Question was determined in favour of Politeness.
Morning Herald

1104. April 24, 1786 New Westminster Forum
'In which consists the greater pleasure, conferring or receiving a Benefit?'
The Question 'was, by a small majority, decided in favour of the person who confers the benefit'.
Morning Herald

1105. April 27, 1786 Coachmakers Hall
'Which is the most injurious to Society, a knavish Attorney, an illiterate Schoolmaster, or the keeper of a Register Office?
A considerable majority declared the knavish Attorney to be the most injurious to society.'
Morning Herald

1106. April 27, 1786 Society for Free Debate, Mitre Tavern
'Is more happiness to be expected from the marriage of a Young Man with an Old Woman, or from that of a Young Woman with an Old Man?
Many Gentlemen of distinguished abilities declining speaking, who were present, thinking neither had any claim to happiness where a reciprocal state of affection must be wanting; but, on the shew of hands, a majority appeared in favour of the old Man with the Young Woman.'
Morning Herald

1107. May 1, 1786 New Westminster Forum
'Which is the more disagreeable, a jealous or a scolding Wife?'
Morning Herald

1108. May 4, 1786 Coachmakers' Hall, Debating Society
'Is not the deliberate Seduction of the Fair, with an intention to desert, under all circumstances, equal to murder?
After a debate, in which several learned and highly respected characters took a part, and which afforded equal pleasure and improvement to a very respectable audience, was decided in the negative.'
Morning Herald

1109. May 4, 1786 Society for Free Debate, Mitre Tavern
'Is Learning a desirable Accomplishment in a Wife?'

183

The Question 'produced a debate explete with sound argument, solid reasoning, and in the person of some gentlemen, an elegance of stile, which would have done honour to the first assembly in the nation, but it was out of the power of those collected excellences themselves to convince the company that learning was requisite for happiness in the marriage state, therefore they determined against it.'
Morning Herald

1110. May 8, 1786 New Westminster Forum
'Is the recent proposed plan for discharging the National Debt, compatible with the true spirit of Taxation, and the future safety of the Empire? The Members of the above Institution deem it incumbent at this important political crisis to bring forward that question, which has already engaged the attention of the senate, and called forth different opinions from men of high rank, enlightened learning, and political penetration; the subject that involves the prosperity of the present race, and their succeeding generations. . .
After it had undergone the most profound and unprejudiced discussion, it was, by a respectable majority, decided against the Minister's scheme of National Redemption.'
Morning Herald

1111. May 11, 1786 Coachmakers' Hall, Debating Society
'Are not the Restraints contained in the Marriage Act, and every other Restriction on the Matrimonial Contract, contrary to the natural Rights of Mankind, and injurious to Conjugal Felicity?'
It was 'decided by a considerable majority, that the restraints contained in the marriage act are neither contrary to the natural rights of mankind, nor injurious to conjugal felicity'.
Morning Herald

1112. May 11, 1786 Society for Free Debate, Mitre Tavern
'Would not the Marriage State be much happier, if Divorces could be obtained when the Parties are tired of each other?
The question relative to divorces being granted, where the parties were tired of each other, was, after a most ingenious and entertaining debate, determined in the negative.'
Morning Herald

1113. May 15, 1786 New Westminster Forum
'Whether Incontinence in a Wife ought to be a Reproach to her Husband?'
Morning Herald

1114. May 18, 1786 Coachmaker's Hall, Debating Society
'Is either of the following assertions of the two Poets founded in truth and experience: – Mr. Otway's, – "That man is, by nature, false, cruel, and inconstant;" or Pope's, – "That every woman is at heart a rake".'

184

The debate found that the assertions of both Otway and Pope were 'contrary to truth and experience.'
Morning Herald

1115. May 18, 1786 Society for Free Debate, Mitre Tavern
'Which is more culpable, the man who attempts to seduce the Wife of his Friend, or the Woman whose levity of manners encourages and affords him the strongest assurances of success?'
The debate found the seducer of the wife more culpable than the woman.
Morning Herald

1116. May 25, 1786 Coachmakers Hall
'Which has reflected more disgrace on human nature, Slavery in Foreign Countries, or the frequency of Public Executions in our own?
N.B. As this debate will comprehend the most important enquiry, why the punishment of women for certain offences should be severer than that of men, Ladies are particularly requested to attend early. . .'
Morning Herald

1117. May 25, 1786 Society for Free Debate, Mitre Tavern
'Which has been the greater disgrace to humanity, the perpetual slavery of foreign countries, or the frequent executions of our own?'
Morning Herald

1118. May 29, 1786 New Westminster Forum
'Which is likely to make the better Wife, an Old Maid or a Widow?
The Conductors of this Institution, sensibly impressed with the strenuous support which has constantly accompanied their exertions, take leave to thank a polite, candid, and liberal public, for that peculiar patronage; and as the motives which formed this institution were infinitely remote from those of a mean or mercenary nature, the proprietors presume they have a superior claim to the countenance of a nation famed for patronizing every laudable effort, capable of contributing to the instruction and amusement of mankind.'
Morning Herald

1119. June 1, 1786 Coachmakers Hall
'Which has reflected more disgrace on human nature, Slavery in Foreign Countries, or the frequency of Public Executions in our own?
It was almost unanimously decided . . . that the frequency of public executions in this country, is more disagreeable. . .'
Morning Herald, June 8

1120. June 8, 1786 Coachmakers Hall
'Whether it would not be consistent with justice, and for the good of society, to admit the solemn affirmation of the people called Quakers, to able of equal testimony, in all ways, with an oath?'
Morning Herald

1121. August 31, 1786 Coachmakers Hall
'Would it not be highly necessary in the Legislature to pass an act for the perpetual confinement of all Lunatics who have either attempted or committed murder?'
Debated decided in negative, by a considerable majority.
General Advertiser

1122. September 7, 1786 Coach-Makers-Hall Debating Society
'Whether Virtue is its own reward?'
The Question 'after a very ingenious, profitable, and entertaining debate, determined almost unanimously in the affirmative'.
Daily Advertiser September 13

1123. September 7, 1786 Mitre Tavern Society for Free Debate
'Is it proper for the British Parliament to permit the Heir Apparent's going into a state of retirement unworthy of his rank?'
The Question 'produced one of the most spirited debates ever heard in any society of a like nature. A great number of Gentlemen of the first ability came forward on the occasion, and repeatedly received the warmest tribute of applause from a crowded and brilliant audience. It was at length determined, at a late hour of the evening, that the Parliament were no ways censurable for that transaction.'
General Advertiser September 14

1124. September 13, 1786 Coach-makers-Hall, Debating Society
'Which is more injurious to the real happiness of society, the want of Piety in the Divine, the want of Integrity in the Lawyer, or the want of Patriotism in the Ministry?'
Daily Advertiser

1125. September 14, 1786 Mitre Tavern Society for Free Debate
'Which is more powerful in the human breast, Interest or Pleasure?'
General Advertiser

1126. September 20, 1786 Coachmakers Hall
'Does the Misconduct of Husbands or the negligent Behaviour of Wives lead to conjugal infidelity?'
Decided against the husband.
Gazetteer

1127. September 21, 1786 Society for Free Debate, Mitre Tavern
'Whether a great disproportion of years, or a total contrariety of disposition, ought to be most avoided?'
The Question 'afforded much wit, humour and keen satire, and was attended by a crowded audience of Ladies and Gentlemen. It was determined that a great disproportion of years ought to be more avoided, than a total contrariety of disposition.'
General Advertiser September 28

1128. September 28, 1786 Society for Free Debate, Mitre Tavern
'Does the late frantic attempt at Regicide furnish sufficient reason for
the numerous Addresses to the Throne?'
General Advertiser

1129. September 28, 1786 Coachmakers Hall
'Would it be consistent with the safety of the British Constitution to
grant to the Roman Catholics and Dissenters all the privileges civil and
religious that are enjoyed by members of the established Church?'
The decision was against granting such privileges to Roman Catholics,
and in favour, by a very large majority, of granting them to Dissenters.
Daily Advertiser

1130. October 2, 1786 Westminster Forum, Spring Garden
'Is the intended Transportation of Convicts to Botany Bay disgraceful
to a civilized Community?'
Times

1131. October 5, 1786 Coachmakers Hall
'Would it be a wise law to compel every unmarried Man to marry the
woman he had seduced and every married Seducer to allow that female
maintenance for life?'
A very large majority of the audience voted against the proposal.
Daily Advertiser October 4/General Advertiser October 11

1132. October 5, 1786 Society for Free Debate, Mitre Tavern
'Whether a woman of sensibility would feel more pain on the loss of a
lover by Death, Banishment or Marriage?'
Audience decided on death.
General Advertiser October 12

1133. October 9, 1786 Westminster Forum, late Coxe's Museum,
Spring-Gardens
SORROWS OF WERTER
'Was the conduct of Charlotte, in admitting the visits of Werter, after
her Marriage, consistent with female delicacy?
This subject is particularly interesting to the Fair Sex.'
Five hundred people were present; the vote went against the conduct
of Charlotte.
Times

1134. October 12, 1786 Coachmakers Hall
'Which has a greater claim to our compassion; the Man reduced to a
state of distress by unavoidable misfortunes in trade; or the Man in a
similar situation, by the exercise of his humanity?'
The debate was decided in favour of the charitable man.
General Advertiser October 11

1135. October 12, 1786 Society for Free Debate, Mitre Tavern

'Which has threatened the Constitution of England with greater danger, the attack of Prerogative in and before the reign of James the Second; or the power of Secret Influence since the Revolution?'
The audience voted that the former was the greater threat.
General Advertiser

1136. October 14, 1786 Morning Herald
'We experienced infinite satisfaction last Monday evening at the Westminster Forum, during the discussion of Charlotte's conduct in admitting the visits of Werter after her marriage; the splendour of the company, we may assert, without having recourse to the illusive and notorious *shift of puffing*, merited the approbation of *La Belle Assemblee*, and with equal truth it may be remarked, that the debate throughout was animated, shrewdly argumentative, humourous and satirical; the behaviour of Charlotte subsequent to the hymeneal consummation was finally reprobated by a decided majority. The question which was given out to be investigated next Monday evening is, we understand, postponed; and the subject substituted is taken from the celebrated Tragedy of Jane Shore, suggested and to be introduced by a gentleman whose oratorical powers have ever deservedly met the marked approbation of this very popular assembly – Is the sentiment contained in the following lines *unjustly* severe on the fair sex?

> If poor weak woman swerves from Virtue's rules,
> If strongly charm'd she leave the thorny way,
> And in the softer paths of pleasure stray,
> Ruin ensues, reproach and endless shame.
> In vain with tears the loss she may deplore,
> In vain look back to what she was before,
> She sets, like stars, that fall to rise no more.'

1137. October 18, 1786 Coachmaker's Hall, Debating Society
'Is the love of power more predominant in the Male or Female Breast?'
Question determined 'That the love of power of more predominant in the Female Breast.'
Daily Advertiser October 25

1138. October 19, 1786 Mitre
'Whether Beauty or Fortune was the best recommendation in a Woman to a Husband?'
General Advertiser

1139. October 23, 1786 Westminster Forum, Spring Gardens
'Was Charlotte correct, in admitting the visits of Werter, after her marriage?'
The Question was 're-investigated in the presence of five hundred persons, amongst whom were several of rank and fashion . . . on the question being put, it was almost unanimously decided against Charlotte.'
Morning Herald October 30

1140. October 26, 1786 Coachmaker's Hall, Debating Society
'Are the sentiments of the late Dr. Johnson founded in truth, that contained in his Rambler, "That the married are generally unhappy," and that in his Prince of Abyssinia, "That celibacy has no pleasure"?'
Decided that Dr. Johnson's sentiments 'are not founded in truth'.
Daily Advertiser October 25

1141. October 26, 1786 Society for Free Debate, Mitre Tavern
'Which is more likely to recommend a woman to a husband, beauty without fortune, or fortune without beauty?'
Four hundred were present, yet many were turned away.
'By a show of hands, at a very late hour, it was determined in favour of Fortune.'
General Advertiser/Morning Herald November 2

1142. October 30, 1786 Westminster Forum
'Which has the greater claim on our Compassion, the distressed Divine, the discouraged Mechanic, or the needy Poet?'
Declared in favour of the distressed Divine.
Morning Herald

1143. November 2, 1786 Coachmaker's-Hall Society for Free Debate
'Is it justifiable for a Man to fight a Duel, in vindication of the honour of the Lady he loves; to resent the injury done to his seduced Wife or Sister, or under any provocation whatsoever?
The fashionable Custom of determining Disputes by duelling, has given birth to many letters directed to the managers of this Society, requesting a public discussion of the subject . . . The doctrines laid down by an eminent and learned Counsel, on a recent and popular transaction, occupies a considerable part of public attention, and will probably excite a desire in many Gentlemen of abilities, anxious for the good order and happiness of society, to take a part in a debate in which those great objects are involved.
A considerable majority decided, that no provocation will justify that practice.'
Daily Advertiser November 1

1144. November 2, 1786 Society for Free Debate, Mitre Tavern
'Can the African Slave Trade be justified on the principles of Equity, the policy of Nations, or Christianity?
It was at length determined against the Slave Trade, almost unanimously; the Policy of nations only had a few hands in its favour.'
Morning Herald

1145. November 3, 1786 Westminster Forum, Spring Garden
'Is the Maxim of the celebrated Moralist, Monsieur de la Rouchfaucault, that "Marriage is sometimes convenient but never delightful" true?'

189

The Question 'underwent a very elaborate and entertaining discussion
. . . in the presence of Six Hundred Persons, whose liberal approbation
of the different Speakers proved the pleasure and satisfaction they
experienced at the investigation of the above Maxim, which they finally
adjudged was not founded in truth.'
Times November 10

1146. November 6, 1786 Westminster Forum
'The truth of the moral reflection of Rochefaucault that "Il y a de bons
marriages, mais il n'y'en a point de delicieuse." Marriage is sometimes
convenient, but never delightful.'
Morning Herald

1147. November 9, 1786 Society for Free Debate, Mitre Tavern
'Which is the most injurious to Society, a Quack Doctor, a Trading
Justice, or a Methodist Teacher?'
Question 'carried against the Methodist Teacher by a great majority'.
Morning Herald

1148. November 10, 1786 Coachmakers Hall
'Which of the two married ladies has the greater claim to our pity, she
who, by the ill treatment of her husband has been induced to separate
from him, and is obliged to live on a scanty pittance, or she who braves
her misfortune and continues with him?'
It was decided 'that the Married Lady who continues with her Husband,
notwithstanding his ill treatment, is more to be pitied'.
Morning Herald

1149. November 10, 1786 Westminster Forum, Spring Gardens
'Whether the Prime Minister ought to enter the connubial state in order
to set a good Example to the Batchelors of Great Britain?'
Morning Herald November 9

1150. November 13, 1786 Westminster Forum
'Which is a more dangerous Seminary for female Education, an English
Boarding School, or a French Convent?
It was by a small majority decided in favour of the French Convent.'
Five hundred people present.
Morning Herald November 20

1151. November 16, 1786 Coachmakers Hall
'Which of the three public characters in the present situation of this
Country, is most qualified by his abilities and integrity to fill the office
of Prime Minister, Lord North, Mr. Fox, or Mr. Pitt?
It is the constant endeavour of the Managers to render this Society
extensively useful to Gentlemen designed for the bar, and others whose
future prospects may render the habit of public speaking indispensably
necessary. Young speakers, therefore, who may demand an indulgent

attention on the above or any other subsequent Question, may rest
assured of having their claims allowed.'
Morning Herald

1152. November 16, 1786 Society for Free Debate, Mitre Tavern
'Which of the three passions has done most injury to mankind, Love,
Avarice or Ambition?
Determined, that Ambition has done more harm than Love or Avarice.'
Morning Herald

1153. November 20, 1786 Westminster Forum
'Which is most injurious to Society, the Quack Doctor, the Trading
Justice, or the Methodist Preacher?'
Morning Herald

1154. November 23, 1786 Society for Free Debate, Mitre Tavern
'Does the Commercial Treaty with France, reflect Credit or Disgrace
upon our present Minister?
This being a subject in which the commercial interest of this country is
concerned, hope every gentleman capable of speaking to it, will come
forward on the occasion. . .'
The debate 'attracted the attention of a numerous and elegant company
of both sexes; a few Gentlemen distinguished themselves on the occasion, but the greater part acknowledged themselves to wish for information, rather than express their opinion on the subject; the company
seemed rather to hope than to feel themselves by any means on a
certainty, and determined by a small majority in favour of the Treaty.'
Morning Herald

1155. November 23, 1786 Coachmakers Hall
'Which of the three public characters in the present situation of this
Country, is most qualified by his abilities and integrity to fill the office
of Prime Minister, Lord North, Mr. Fox or Mr. Pitt?
Decided in favour of Mr. Pitt.'
Morning Herald

1156. November 27, 1786 Westminster Forum, Spring Gardens
'Which is most injurious to Society, the Quack Doctor, the Trading
Justice, or the Methodist Preacher?'
Determined against the Trading Justice.
Morning Herald

1157. November 30, 1786 Coachmakers Hall
'Which is the most injurious to the interest of Religion and Virtue,
Hypocrisy, Bigotry, or avowed Infidelity?'
The Question 'was decided against the hypocrite'.
Morning Herald

1158. November 30, 1786 Society for Free Debate, Mitre Tavern

'Do the Comforts of Matrimony counterbalance its Cares?
It was at length determined in favour of the comforts of wedlock, by a great majority.'
Morning Herald

1159. December 4, 1786 Westminster Forum
'Who is best qualified to be Prime Minister, Lord North, Mr. Fox, or Mr. Pitt?
It was decided by a considerable majority, that Mr. Fox was best qualified to be Prime Minister of this Country.'
Morning Herald

1160. December 7, 1786 Coachmakers Hall
'Can true Love subsist without Jealousy?
It was the opinion . . . of a majority of a very crowded and brilliant audience, that true Love may subsist without Jealousy.'
Morning Herald

1161. December 7, 1786 Society for Free Debate, Mitre Tavern
'Which is the greatest Proof of Courage, to accept or refuse a Challenge?
N.B. 'Tis with concern, the Managers hear that more than a hundred persons were disappointed the last evening for want of room. . .
By a shew of hands, the company were almost unanimous in favour of its being a greater proof of Courage, to refuse than to accept a Challenge.'
Morning Herald

1162. December 11, 1786 Westminster Forum
'Which contributes most to the unhappiness of Married Life: – Obstinacy in the Parents, Caprice in the Wife, or Arrogance on the part of the Husband?'
Morning Herald

1163. December 14, 1786 Coachmakers Hall
'Is the common saying true, that there is no medium in the Marriage State, but that it must be either extremely Happy, or extremely Miserable?'
Debate voted in the negative.
Gazetteer December 13/Daily Advertiser December 20

1164. December 14, 1786 Society for Free Debate, Mitre Tavern
'Which is to be preferred, the lasting comforts of Friendship, or the captivating joys of Love?'
Morning Herald

1165. December 18, 1786 Westminster Forum
'Is the recent Treaty of Navigation and Commerce with France, likely to benefit the Trading and Political Interests of the British Empire?

It being the earnest Desire of several Persons of eminence, both in the political and mercantile world, that the subject of the French Treaty, which has so much excited the remarks and speculations of the public, should undergo an impartial and dispassionate investigation. . .'
A very large majority voted in the negative.
Morning Herald

1166. December 21, 1786 Coachmakers Hall
'Would it be a wise Law to annex the Punishment of Death in all Cases to wilful and corrupt Perjury?'
Debate decided in the negative.
Daily Advertiser December 20

1167. December 25, 1786 Westminster Forum, Spring Gardens
'Is the sentiment of Mr. Pope's, that "Every Woman is at heart a Rake" founded on truth?
Decided by a great majority . . . that the sentiment of Mr. Pope['s] . . . was founded in truth.'
Morning Herald January 1, 1787

1168. December 27, 1786 Society of Free Debate, Mitre Tavern
'Whether the spirited girl who elope[s] for love, or the dull insipid female who marries for money, was most blameable?'
The Question 'was after a most animated debate, replete with wit, humour, and sound argument, determined in favour of the spirited girl.'
Gazetteer January 3, 1787

1169. December 27, 1786 Coachmakers Hall
'Which is the more exceptionable character, the Man Milliner, the Libertine or the Miser?
It was observed by one of the speakers at Coachmaker's hall ". . . that one of the characteristics of the present times was, for the sexes to exchange situations with each other, and that notwithstanding the numerous tribe of man milliners, mantua-makers, &c. the women seemed to be more remarkable for the adoption of the masculine characters. We had not only female jockeys, but female *shavers*, and that they had gone so far as even to take our soldiers by the *nose*, and give them a *lathering*."
Question determined that Man Milliner was most exceptionable.'
Gazetteer January 3,4, 1787

1170. January 1, 1787 Westminster Forum, Spring Gardens
'Which is more painful to a Woman of Sensibility, to be obliged to marry the Man she dislikes, or debarred the man she loves?'
Morning Herald

1171. January 4, 1787 Society for Free Debate, Mitre Tavern
'Which has been productive of more real injury to Society, Political or Religious Prejudice?

The above subject opened so extensive a field for historical information, it is hoped those Gentlemen who have stored their minds with this useful science will avail themselves of this opportunity.'
The Question 'produced a most animated debate, replete with historical information, which afforded much entertainment to a numerous and polite audience of both sexes, particularly of ladies, which reflected the highest credit on their taste: the question was determined against the effects of religious prejudice almost unanimously.'
Gazetteer January 3

1172. January 4, 1787 Coachmakers Hall
'Which is more blameable, the man who deliberately seduces a female, and then deserts her – or, the father who abandons his child so seduced?'
Gazetteer

1173. January 8, 1787 Westminster Forum, Spring-Gardens
'Would not a resistance to the Measure of removing the Incumbrances of the Heir Apparent, be a disgrace to Ministers, and an impeachment of the characteristic liberality of the British Empire?'
Question, 'after a very animated debate, [was] unanimously decided in the affirmative'.
Morning Herald

1174. January 11, 1787 Society for Free Debate, Mitre Tavern
'Which is the more contemptible character, the surly old Batchelor, or the peevish old Maid?'
The Question, 'after a most animated debate, before a crowded audience of both sexes, determined in favour of the old Maid'.
Gazetteer January 10

1175. January 11, 1787 Coach-Makers Hall Debating Society
'Which is more blameable, the man who deliberately seduces a female, and then deserts her, or the father who abandons his daughter so seduced?'
The discussion of the Question contained 'persuasive eloquence [which] was laudably employed in the cause of virtue. Several young speakers distinguished themselves on the occasion, proving their claims to the flattering plaudits they received from a very numerous, polite, and liberal auditory. A majority fixed the greater blame on the Parent.
The managers trust, that every Gentleman who enters this assembly, will perceive the propriety of submitting to the sense of the majority of it, remembering that true liberty is to act as we ought, and that decorum is the companion of good sense.
Upon these principles young speakers may rest assured of receiving the most encouraging indulgence, from that disinterested candour and liberality, which the audience at this society have ever manifested.'
Morning Herald

1176. January 15, 1787 Westminster Forum, Spring Gardens
'Which quality in a husband is most disagreeable, ill-founded jealousy, stupidity, or neglect?'
Morning Herald

1177. January 18, 1787 Coach-makers Hall Debating Society
'Which more deserves our censure, the Divine, who for the sake of a good Living, preaches a Doctrine he does not believe; or the Counsel, who for a Fee, pleads a Cause he knows to be repugnant to Justice?'
Audience voted that the Divine was the most censurable.
Morning Herald

1178. January 18, 1787 Society for Free Debate, Mitre Tavern
'Which is the most dangerous to the possessor, Wit in the Male, or Beauty in the Female Sex?
The above question being of an interesting nature, it is expected much entertainment will be derived from its discussion.'
The Question 'produced a most animated debate, replete with sound argument, wit, and humour, and was attended by a numerous and polite audience of both sexes; it was determined, that Beauty was more dangerous, by a considerable majority'.
Gazetteer January 24

1179. January 22, 1787 Surry Debating Society, Three Tuns Tavern, St. Margaret Hill
'Which will more probably become a great Character in Society, the Youth early introduced into Public Life, or he who is secluded from it till the years of maturity?
As this Society will be conducted under the inspection of Gentlemen of literary ability, to whom some of the most popular Speakers, both of the Mitre and Coach-makers-hall Societies, have promised their assistance; the Managers hope it will not be deemed unworthy the attention of those Ladies and Gentlemen who reside in, or near the Borough: And beg leave to assure those who may honour it with their support, that no subjects, either immoral, irreligious, indelicate, or trivial, shall be introduced for discussion; but that their utmost efforts shall be exerted in the selection of those questions, which may tend to enlighten the understanding, and amend the heart, while they expand the imagination and exercise the fancy.
A great majority determined, that the youth secluded from public life till the years of maturity was the more likely to become a great character. . .'
Gazetteer

1180. January 22, 1787 Westminster Forum
'Can the practice of DUELLING be justified by any circumstance in Civilized Society?'
The World

1181. January 22, 1787 Theological Society, Brownlow Street, Drury Lane
'Was universal redemption, by one act, intended by St. Paul?' 2 Thn. ii, 6. 'Who gave himself a ransom for all, to be testified in due time.'
The World

1182. January 23, 1787 Mitre Tavern Society for Free Debate
'Is the Distress into which Men of Genius too often fall, more owing to their own impudence, or a want of Patronage in the Public?
The above Meeting will be for the purpose of relieving a distressed individual, formerly a member of the Robinhood and Queens-arms Societies; the Gentlemen who support the Three Public Debating Societies have promised their assistance on this occasion. . . As the sum generally paid for admission is only designed to defray the necessary expence, tis thought expedient to make the admission for that evening (only) ONE SHILLING, otherwise the distressed objected would reap little advantage from it.'
Gazetteer January 22

1183. January 25, 1787 Mitre Tavern Society for Free Debate
'Which is more deserving censure, the Assassin who . . . the just punishment of the Law, or the Wretch who, from the motives of self-interest, secretly ruins his Friend?'
The Question was 'after a most animated debate, replete with many good arguments, determined against the false Friend'.
Gazetteer January 24

1184. January 25, 1787 Coachmakers Hall
'Do the vices and follies of mankind mostly proceed from too much indulgence in early life, from an improper education afterwards, or from the native temper and disposition of the mind?'
Debate decided that vices most from improper education.
Gazetteer

1185. January 29, 1787 Surry Debating Society
'Are the calamities of the present reign more to be attributed to the mal-administration of his Majesty's servants, or to the opposition made to their measures in the House of Commons?
It was determined that the present calamities of the reign were more attributable to his Majesty's Ministers than to the Opposition in the House of Commons.'
Gazetteer

1186. January 29, 1787 Westminster Forum, Spring Gardens
'Ought the practice of duelling to be totally abolished, or permitted within certain restrictions?'
The Question 'attracted a crowded house, and a polite assembly, when, after the most argumentative and entertaining debate, that has ever

been witnessed in this institution, it was by a great majority given in favour of the practice of duelling'.
Morning Herald February 5

1187. February 1, 1787 Mitre Tavern Society for Free Debate
'Which is the more disagreeable situation to a man of sensibility, to be subject to the caprice of a Coquet before marriage, or to be obliged to live with a Scold afterwards?
The above subject being of an interesting nature to the feeling of mankind, it is expected much entertainment will be given by the Chair to young speakers, to make this institution a school for their improvement, as well as for public entertainment.'
The Question 'after a most animated debate, before a numerous and polite audience determined in favour of the Coquet'.
Gazetteer January 31

1188. February 1, 1787 Coachmakers Hall Debating Society
'Are the Male or Female Sex more constant in Love?'
It was determined 'that the Female Sex are more constant in Love than the Male'.
Morning Herald February 8

1189. February 5, 1787 Westminster Forum, Spring Gardens
'Whether absolute power in the hands of a wise Monarch be preferable to the British system of Government, under the perversion of a corrupt Parliament?
This question has been communicated to the conductors of this institution by a Member of Parliament. . .'
The Question was, 'after an ingenious and truly entertaining debate, decided in favour' of the British system.
Morning Herald

1190. February 5, 1787 Surrey Debating Society
'Which is the greater domestic evil, a drunken husband or a scolding wife?'
It was determined that the scolding wife was the greater evil.
Gazetteer

1191. February 8, 1787 Coachmakers Hall Debating Society
'Is the opinion of Mr. Fox, that the jealousies and prejudices which animated and directed the Councils of our Ancestors ought still to exist, and continue to be cherished against France, consistent with the Political and Commercial Interest of this Country?
This popular Society, universally allowed to be a most rational entertainment, as well as a school of eloquence for young Gentlemen, will, it is hoped, be attended by the real friends of their country, in which its interest is materially concerned.'
Morning Herald

1192. February 8, 1787 Society for Free Debate, Mitre Tavern
'Does that Infamy which follows a Female's first deviation from Chastity, operate more to keep the sex Virtuous; or to render the Seduced more desperate in Vice?
The above subject having for its object the cause which too fatally leads to female ruin, it will of course be considered highly deserving public attention.
The Question was, after a most animated debate, before a crowded audience, determined that it made them more desperate in vice.'
Morning Herald

1193. February 12, 1787 Westminster Forum
'Whether the British system of Government under the perversion of a corrupt Parliament, be preferable to absolute Power, in the hands of a wise Sovereign?'
Question decided in favour of the former.
Morning Herald February 19

1194. February 12, 1787 Surrey Debating Society
'Have the Doctrines of Christianity been enlightened, or the Morals of the People amended, by the introduction of Methodism into this Country?
As it has been a matter of complaint from several respectable characters among the Methodists, that they are seldom brought forward fairly in public debates, but generally yoked with the most detestable characters, whereby their opponents take the advantage of criminating them by comparison, the Managers of this Society have, at the request of a gentlemen of well-known public abilities among that sect, instigated this enquiry; and hope they have thereby steered clear of enthusiasm on the one hand, or illiberality on the other.'
Gazetteer February 10

1195. February 15, 1787 Society for Free Debate, Mitre Tavern
'Which by their Conduct have discovered the greater share of Ability and public Spirit, the Persons at present in Power, or those in Opposition?'
The Question 'was debated before a large and respectable audience, of both sexes; – when, after a most spirited and animated debate, wherein many striking errors on the part of Administration were pointed out, it was determined, by a very great majority, in favour of the Opposition'.
Morning Herald

1196. February 15, 1787 Coachmakers Hall Debating Society
'Which is more censurable, the Female who is vain of her Beauty, or the Man who is proud of his Learning?'
The Question was decided 'by a great majority, that the man' was more censurable.
Morning Herald

1197. February 19, 1787 Society for Free Debate, Large Room, Three Tuns Tavern, St. Margaret's Hill
'Have the Doctrines of Christianity been enlightened, or the Morals of the people amended by the introduction of METHODISM into this country?'
Question 'was decided in favour of the Methodists'.
Gazetteer February 17

1198. February 19, 1787 Westminster Forum, Spring Garden
'Which is the more reprehensible in a seduced Female, deserted by her Lover and Friends, Suicide or Prostitution?
The rising eminence of this Society is an unequivocal proof of the entertainment it constantly affords; graced on all occasions by the presence of an amiable and elegant part of the fair sex, and honoured by the frequent attendance of persons of rank and fashion, it has become as much an object of public patronage, as of private conversation.'
At this debate 'every person present testified their approbation to the several arguments adduced, and after hearing a considerable display of ingenuity on both sides of the question, they decided, that Prostitution is the more to be condemned.'
Morning Herald

1199. February 22, 1787 Coachmakers Hall Debating Society
'Is an English Boarding School, or a French Convent, the more eligible for the education of young Ladies?
The education of the female sex is acknowledged to be an object of the greatest importance to their future happiness in life. A public discussion, therefore, of a subject of such magnitude, will doubtless meet the approbation of the numerous friends of this liberal institution.'
Morning Herald

1200. February 22, 1787 Society for Free Debate, Mitre Tavern
'Which is the most desirable in a Wife, – Wit, Beauty, or Good-nature?'
The Question 'produced a most spirited debate, and was attended by a crowded and polite audience of Ladies and Gentlemen. Several Speakers distinguished themselves much, particularly a young Gentleman, who declared it his first essay, who delivered a speech of considerable length, replete with sound argument, and an excellent flow of reasoning; though some of the first talents were employed in behalf of wit (and little or nothing said in favour of beauty) such were the strong prepossessions in behalf of good-nature, that it was carried in its favour by a great majority.'
Gazetteer February 28

1201. February 26, 1787 Westminster Forum
'Whether Dramatic Entertainments tend to improve or dissipate the Morals of Youth: – and is the licensing Mr. Palmer's Theatre, to be applauded or censured?

By the particular Desire of several Gentlemen of eminence in the literary world, the above question stands for discussion This Evening; – and it is requested, that young Gentlemen will not suffer themselves to be intimidated in the delivery of their sentiments, as the liberality which has continually appeared in the persons who have composed this Assembly, has always removed the scruples which young speakers are apt to entertain.'
Morning Herald

1202. February 26, 1787 Surry Debating Society
'Which it to be preferred for a Wife, an old Maid, or a Widow?'
Majority decided that a widow was preferable.
Gazetteer

1203. March 1, 1787 Society for Free Debate, Mitre Tavern
'Whether the decrease of Mr. Pitt's popularity was owing to his maladministration, or the caprice of the people?'
The Question 'was determined against him by a great majority'.
Morning Herald March 8

1204. March 1, 1787 Coachmakers Hall Debating Society
'Is an English Boarding School, or a French Convent, the more eligible for the education of young Ladies?
It was decided . . . by a considerable majority that the English boarding school is more eligible.'
Gazetteer March 8

1205. March 5, 1787 Surry Debating Society
'Which is the most injurious character to Society, a knavish attorney, an illiterate school-master, or the keeper of an insurance lottery-office?'
It was determined against the knavish attorney.
Gazetteer March 3

1206. March 8, 1787 Society for Free Debate, Mitre Tavern
'Ought not the word OBEY to be struck out of the Marriage ceremony?'
The Question 'was debated before a most crowded and brilliant audience of both sexes, who testified the highest satisfaction at the entertainment it produced. Many Gentlemen distinguished themselves on the occasion; a sound argument, wit, and humour, were successfully blended throughout the whole – when, after all parties had exerted themselves with much honour and credit to themselves, the audience, by a shew of hands, determined that the word OBEY ought to continue in the Marriage Ceremony.'
Gazetteer March 14

1207. March 8, 1787 Coachmakers Hall Debating Society

'Which would be more disagreeable to a lady of fine sensibility, to be compelled to marry the most aukward rustick, or the compleat modern fop?

The managers feel themselves highly honoured by the numerous questions of a political, moral and sentimental nature, they have received from the public, accompanied with the warmest eulogiums on the liberality and utility of this institution. No pains will be spared to secure a continuance of this approbation by the maintenance of good order, and the selection of such questions only as lead to mental improvement, mingled with entertainment.'

It was decided that a complete fop is most repugnant.

Gazetteer

1208. March 12, 1787 Surry Debating Society

'Has Love or Money most influence in forming the Matrimonial Connection?'

It was determined 'by a crouded and polite assembly, that love is a greater inducement to marriage than riches'.

Gazetteer March 10

1209. March 12, 1787 The Ancient London Society for Free Debate, lately the Theological, held at the Queen's Arms Tavern, Newgate Street

'Was the opposition of Lord George Gordon to the Mandate of the Ecclesiastical Court consistent with the Character of a Christian, or a Patriot?

The Managers of this Society, at the repeated solicitations of many respectable characters, have now agreed to resume their Weekly Deliberations. The utility and importance of such an institution, conduced on liberal principles, is so apparent, that they flatter themselves it is unnecessary here to enumerate its various advantages.'

Gazetteer

1210. March 15, 1787 Society for Free Debate, Mitre Tavern

'Which by his public conduct has most deserved censure, Lord North, Mr. Fox, or Mr. Pitt?

The Managers hear, with concern, that above a hundred Ladies and Gentlemen were prevented getting in last Thursday evening for want of room. . .'

In the debate 'several warm advocates stood forward for all three of the characters; but the chief of the arguments were directed against Lord North and Mr. Pitt; and on the shew of hands it was determined against the former by a considerable majority.'

Gazetteer March 14

1211. March 15, 1787 Coachmakers Hall

'Is the sentiment of Dr. Johnson founded in truth, That neither education nor reason secures the female sex against the influence of example,

201

but that they are for the most part good or bad, as they fall among those who practice vice or virtue?'
It was decided that Dr. Johnson's opinion is founded in truth.
Gazetteer

1212. March 19, 1787 Westminster Forum
WAYS AND MEANS
'Budget of Taxes, to be brought forward by the Chancellor of the Utopian Exchequer, at the Westminster Forum, Spring Gardens, this present evening . . . pursuant to his intimation on a former night, resolve the House into a Committee, for the purpose of taking into consideration the present state of the Utopian Revenue; –
when, to make good its deficiencies, the following taxes will be submitted for general investigation:
Courting Licences   Second Marriages
Snuff-takers   Smoakers
Smoak   Beautiful Women
Men Milliners   Female false Protuberances
The proceedings of the Forum will be conduced on this occasion according to the usage of a great assembly, but they hope to claim a distinction, from their superior politeness and decorum.'
Morning Herald

1213. March 19, 1787 Surry Debating Society
'Would it be consistent with the safety of the British constitution to allow the Roman Catholics and Dissenters of every denomination the same privileges enjoyed by the members of the Church of England?
The above question is brought forward at the request of a dignitary in the Catholic communion.'
The Question was 'determined in favour of Dissenters of every denomination; but carried against the Roman Catholics'.
Gazetteer

1214. March 22, 1787 Society for Free Debate, Mitre Tavern
'Which must be the more dreadful reflection to a Father, to have a seduced Daughter exist by Prostitution, or commit an act of Suicide?'
Gazetteer March 21

1215. March 22, 1787 Coachmakers Hall
'Which is more injurious to Family Prosperity, a Careless Indolent Husband, or a Wasteful Extravagant Wife?
Flattered by the very polite and numerous assemblage of Ladies, with whose presence this Society is constantly honoured, and by whom many questions of a moral and sentimental nature have been proposed, the Managers take permission to assure them, that the most respectful attention will be taken to every subject Female Generosity can suggest; and that no exertions will be wanting to secure a continuance of that strict order and decorum, which it is hoped will never be absent in an audience, of which Females compose a part.'

Audience decided that an indolent husband was worse.
Gazetteer

1216. March 26, 1787 Surry Debating Society
'Which is the greater affliction to a man of sensibility, the loss of a good wife, or the plague of a bad one?'
Determined that the plague of a bad wife was the greater affliction.
Gazetteer March 24

1217. March 26, 1787 Ancient London Debating Society
'Which is most injurious to the possessor, forwardness in the female, or bashfulness in the male sex?'
It was thought forwardness is more injurious in the female sex.
Gazetteer April 2

1218. March 26, 1787 Westminster Forum
WAYS AND MEANS
'The Chancellor of the Utopian Exchequer, in the presence of a very crowded House . . . brought forward his budget of taxes, and having taken his seat at the Treasury Bench, the Chairman of the Committee read the order of the day, when the Utopian Chancellor rose, and began by lamenting the necessity of serving fresh burthens on the people, but assured the House at the same time, that the exigency of the state still rendered extraordinary exertion necessary, in order to renovate to its former splendour and prosperity the Utopian Empire. The taxes which were negatived, were Courting Licenses and Smoak; and those carried in the affirmative, were Men-milliners and Snuff-takers. The House broke up at ten o'clock, and agreed to take the remainder of the budget into consideration this evening, viz.
Musical Amateurs   Beautiful Women
Dancers   Second Marriages
Smokers   Female False Protuberances'
Morning Herald

1219. March 29, 1787 Coachmakers Hall
'Whether is the Husband or the Wife more disgraced, when the Wife assumes the government over her Husband?'
Wife more blameable.
Morning Herald April 5

1220. April 2, 1787 Surry Debating Society
'Do Theatrical Entertainments tend more to improve or deprave the Morals of Mankind?'
Question determined in favour of the theatres.
Gazetteer March 31

1221. April 2, 1787 Ancient London Debating Society, Queen's Arms Tavern, Newgate Street

'Have Administration by instituting the Board of Controul, and abolishing Trials by Jury, proved themselves enemies to British Liberty?'
Gazetteer

1222. April 5, 1787 Society for Free Debate, Mitre Tavern
'With whom would a woman of sense be likely to be most happy with; married to the man that loved her, but that she disliked, or the man she loved, but who disliked her?'
Decided that 'woman of sense was more likely to be happy with the man that loved her.'
Morning Herald April 12

1223. April 5, 1787 Coachmakers Hall Debating Society
'Whether it is not a duty the Dissenters owe themselves as subjects of a free Country, to renew their application to Parliament, for the repeal of the Sacramental clauses in the Corporation and Test Acts?
It is the wish of several respectable Gentlemen in the dissenting interest, that the above question should undergo a liberal discussion . . . they throw down the gauntlet to the enemies of the Repeal of the Sacramental test, and meet them in the fair field of argumentation: impartiality, order and decorum therefore it is hoped will characterize every person who may attend on this occasion.
The most respectable characters both in the Dissenting interest and of the establishment, honoured this Society with their presence. . . The audience, sensible of the importance of the subject, expressed their desire of its being adjourned till this evening, when it is hoped that every Gentleman of abilities, animated with a desire to promote the real interest of society, will avail himself of the liberty this institution affords, freely to deliver his opinion.'
Morning Herald

1224. April 9, 1787 Surry Debating Society
'Is there any Probability of Happiness by a Marriage between an Old Maid and an Old Batchelor?'
The Question was decided in the affirmative.
Gazetteer April 7

1225. April 9, 1787 [Ancient London Debating Society] Queen's Arms Tavern, Newgate Street
'Which is the stronger basis of friendship, similarity of disposition, or reciprocity of interest?'
The Question 'was determined by a great majority in favour of the former. The Society take this opportunity of acknowledging their obligation for the great information they received upon the subject from the ingenious visitors who spoke in the course of the debate.'
Gazetteer April 16

1226. April 12, 1787 Society for Free Debate, Mitre Tavern

'Do the measures at present carried on against Mr. Hastings in the House of Commons, originate in private pique or public justice?' The Question 'after affording a most animated debate, in which several distinguished characters took a part, was determined that the persons who have preferred the prosecution against Mr. Hastings are actuated by public justice and not private pique.'
Gazetteer April 18

1227. April 12, 1787 Coachmakers Hall Debating Society
'Is it not a duty the Dissenters owe to themselves as subjects of a free Country, to renew their applications to Parliament, for the repeal of the Sacramental clauses in the Corporation and Test Acts?'
Debate decided in the affirmative.
Morning Herald

1228. April 16, 1787 Surry Debating Society
'Which Character is to be preferred by a Lady for a Husband, the Man of Wit, Courage or Politeness?'
Gazetteer April 14

1229. April 16, 1787 [Ancient London Debating Society] Queen's Arms Tavern, Newgate Street
'Is the present alarming increase of divorces to be attributed more to neglect in the male, or levity in the female sex?'
Gazetteer

1230. April 16, 1787 Theological Society, Holborn Hill
'Are the Torments of Hell Eternal?
The Proprietors having nothing in view, but to promote religious knowledge, piety and virtue among themselves and others, and not any pecuniary advantage.
Admission is only two-pence.'
Gazetteer

1231. April 19, 1787 Society for Free Debate, Mitre Tavern
'Which is the more blameable conduct in parents towards their children, severity or indulgence?
As the manners in which parents conduct themselves towards their children contribute to make them in a great measure the characters they afterwards fill in life, it is expected much entertainment, as well as moral improvement, will be derived from its discussion.
Every encouragement will be given to those gentlemen who are not in the habit of public speaking, as this society is intended for their practice and improvement.'
Gazetteer April 18

1232. April 19, 1787 Coachmakers hall

'Are the letters of the late Lord Chesterfield to his Son more injurious to the Morals of the Youth of the Male Sex, or the Reading of Novels to the Female Sex?'
Determined that reading Lord Chesterfield most injurious.
Morning Post

1233. April 23, 1787 Surry Debating Society
'Is it not a Duty the Dissenters owe to themselves, as subjects of a free country to renew their application to Parliament for a repeal of the sacramental clauses in the Corporation and Test Acts?
It is hoped the necessity of accompanying candour, order, and decorum, with the freedom of debate, on a question of material concern to every British subject, will be felt by Gentlemen on both sides.'
Gazetteer April 21

1234. April 26, 1787 Society for Free Debate, Mitre Tavern
'Ought a Husband to be despised for the infidelity of his Wife?'
The Question was 'determined that the Husband ought not to be despised. . .'
Morning Herald May 3

1235. April 26, 1787 Coachmakers Hall Debating Society
'Is it expedient to imprison people for Debt?'
The Question 'was productive of a very instructive debate, in which several young Law Students took a part, whose speeches afforded the most flattering prospects of their future eminence in that learned profession. The decision was doubtful, but it appeared to the President, to be in favour of Imprisonment for Debt.'
Morning Herald May 3

1236. April 30, 1787 Surry Debating Society
'Which is more injurious to domestic felicity, jealousy on the part of the husband, or inconstancy on the part of the wife?'
Gazetteer

1237. May 3, 1787 Society for Free Debate, Mitre Tavern
'Would it reflect Credit, or Disgrace on the Minister to oppose the present Motion in the House of Commons, for Relief of the Heir Apparent?'
The Question led 'to a most spirited debate which continued 'till near Eleven o'Clock, before a crowded and brilliant audience'. Decided that Minister would deserve censure if he opposed motion.
Morning Herald

1238. May 3, 1787 Coachmakers Hall Debating Society
'Whether it is more dangerous to Female Virtue, for the Fair Sex to repose too much confidence in their own, or the Male Sex?
As several of the most celebrated writers have made the above question a subject of their deliberations, it is presumed it will meet the approba-

tion of the polite and respectable assembly, with whose presence this institution is constantly honoured.'
It was decided 'that the Fair Sex ought to repose less confidence in the male than in their own sex'.
Morning Herald

1239. May 10, 1787 Society for Free Debate, Mitre Tavern
'Would it have been consistent with the safety of the British constitution, for the Legislature to have complied with the late Petition of the Dissenters for the repeal of the Test and Corporation Acts?'
The debate 'determined that the Test Act ought not to be repealed'.
Morning Herald

1240. May 10, 1787 Coachmakers Hall Debating Society
'Whether it is a greater crime for a man to seduce the wife or unmarried daughter of his friend?'
It was decided '(almost unanimously) that it is a greater crime to seduce the wife of a friend, than his unmarried daughter'.
Morning Herald

1241. May 17, 1787 Society for Free Debate, Mitre Tavern
'Is it not necessary for the preservation of the constitution of this country, that a reform should take place in the representation of the people, and the duration of Parliament?
It was at length determined, by a small majority, against any alteration, at present, taking place in Parliament.'
Morning Herald

1242. May 17, 1787 Coachmakers Hall Debating Society
(Messrs. FOX and BURKE)
'Is it more desirable that Messrs. Fox and Burke should be entrusted with a share of the government of this country – or continue out of office, as a check upon administration?'
Morning Herald

1243. May 24, 1787 Society for Free Debate, Mitre Tavern
'Is the Opinion of Lord Chesterfield true, that the Reputation of Veracity is more necessary in a Man, than that of Chastity in a Woman?'
Morning Herald May 23

1244. May 24, 1787 Coachmakers Hall
'Is it more desirable that Messrs. Fox and Burke should be entrusted with a share of the government of this country – or continue out of office, as a check upon administration?'
The debate decided against the admission of Fox and Burke to government.
Gazetteer

1245. May 31, 1787 Coachmakers Hall Debating Society

'Which is more likely to produce conjugal unhappiness, too early or too late Marriages?'
Morning Herald June 14

1246. June 7, 1787 Coachmakers Hall Debating Society
'Which is more likely to produce conjugal unhappiness, too early or too late Marriages?
So immediately concerned have a number of Gentlemen considered themselves in the discussion of the above question, that the time alloted for debate in two evenings, has been found too short to hear many, in whose minds the *cacoethes loquendi* has been excited.'
Morning Herald June 14

1247. June 14, 1787 Coachmakers Hall Debating Society
'Which is more likely to produce conjugal unhappiness, too early or too late Marriages?'
Morning Herald

1248. September 3, 1787 Westminster Forum
'Have the Managers of the Theatres Royal forfeited their claim to Public Patronage, by their Opposition to the Royalty Theatre?
The opposition to Mr. Palmer is by some considered as replete with the illiberal spirit of monopoly, while others consider it as only a justifiable and necessary restraint, and a proper vindication of a prudent law. This is a public cause, and should be publicly decided. . .
The Question, after a display of spirited eloquence, was almost unanimously decided in the affirmative.'
The World September 1

1249. September 6, 1787 Coachmakers Hall Debating Society
'Does the conduct of the licensed Managers towards the Royalty theatre, merit the censure of the public?'
The Question was decided in the affirmative.
This Society is 'an Institution calculated to prevent the Loss and Misapplication of Time, by providing for the leisure hours of both Sexes an entertainment calculated to instruct and lead the Mind to Reflection.'
Morning Herald September 13

1250. September 6, 1787 Society for Free Debate, Mitre Tavern
'Who has done most political injury to the cause of liberty?'
It was decided 'that the reputed patriots of the present reign, had done more injury than service to the cause of liberty'.
Morning Herald September 13

1251. September 10, 1787 Westminster Forum
'Is the Law which prevents the ROYAL FAMILY from MARRYING without the consent of PARLIAMENT, founded in Justice and sound Policy?'
The World September 8

1252. September 10, 1787 Westminster School of Eloquence, Panton Street, Haymarket
'Which of the three characters has rendered the most essential service to his country, Lord Heathfield [General Elliot] as a Warrior, Mr. Pitt as a Minister, or Mr. Fox as a Patriotic Senator?
The liberty of Public Debate is the envied privilege of this distinguished nation; the bulwark of a free people. Those who feel the laudable ambition of acquiring the art of public speaking, will find this Society calculated to facilitate that useful and admired accomplishment. A free enquiry after truth, naturally tends to liberate the mind from pernicious prejudices; to expand and warm the heart with benevolence. In the variety of subjects that meet discussion, the treasured wisdom of departed Philosophers, Divines and Moralists, is explored and brought to public view, while the thoughtless imperceptibly receive instruction mingled with entertainment.
It was determined by a small majority that Mr. Fox had rendered the most essential services to his country.'
The World

1253. September 13, 1787 Coachmakers Hall Debating Society
'Is it not dangerous to the constitutional Liberties of the Subject to preclude a Jury from judging of the Law in Cases of Libel?
The above question concerns the life, liberty and property of every British subject. Its importance will doubtless animate the friends of the constitution to speak their sentiments upon it with that freedom which this Society, designed to cherish the laudable ambition of public speaking, affords to every man.'
The question was decided in the affirmative.
Morning Herald

1254. September 13, 1787 Society for Free Debate, Mitre Tavern
'Is it probable that the shutting up every place of public entertainment on the Sunday, will produce the good effects designed by his Majesty's late Proclamation?'
Morning Herald

1255. September 17, 1787 Westminster Forum
'Are not the ROMAN CATHOLICS, in consequence of their behaviour since the last Act of Parliament passed in their favour, entitled to the same privileges as the PROTESTANT DISSENTERS?'
The World September 15

1256. September 17, 1787 Westminster School of Eloquence
'Is not the assertion of the late Lord Chesterfield, that every Woman, who is not absolutely ugly, thinks herself handsome, a libel upon the Sex?
It was decided . . . that Lord Chesterfield's opinion of the Fair Sex, is fallacious.'
The World

209

1257. September 20, 1787 Coachmakers Hall Debating Society
'Which has greater Influence upon the Actions of Mankind, the Hope of Good, or the Fear of Evil?'
Debate decided mankind more moved by hope of good.
Gazetteer September 19

1258. September 24, 1787 Westminster Forum
'Are not the ROMAN CATHOLICS, in consequence of their behaviour since the last Act of Parliament passed in their favour, entitled to the same privileges as the PROTESTANT DISSENTERS?
By a very small majority, determined in favour of the Roman Catholics.'
The World September 22

1259. September 24, 1787 Westminster School of Eloquence
'Which are more deserving Public Censure, Messrs. Palmer and Bannister, by withdrawing themselves from Drury-lane; or the Licenced Managers, in their opposition to the Royalty Theatre?'
Decided almost unanimously in favour of Palmer and Bannister.
The World

1260. September 27, 1787 Coachmakers Hall Debating Society
'Have Messrs. Palmer and Banister acted with Propriety in withdrawing themselves from the Theatre Royal in Drury Lane?'
Question answered in the affirmative.
Gazetteer September 26

1261. October 1, 1787 Westminster Forum
'Can the Necessity of the State, at the approach of War, justify the issuing of Press-Warrants?
It is but just to declare the discussion was doubtful.'
The World September 29

1262. October 3, 1787 Westminster School of Eloquence
'Which has proved himself the most firm and constant friend to the civil and religious liberties of this country, Alderman Wilkes or Mr. Fox?
Men of the public prints having pointedly accused Mr. Wilkes of deserting those patriotic principles, which raised him to the summit of popularity, the friends of that once celebrated character will have a fair opportunity of vindicating his public conduct: – at the same time those Gentlemen, who are advocates for the consistency of Mr. Fox, may obviate the charges of inconsistency, so frequently brought against that great statesman.'
The World

1263. October 4, 1787 Coachmakers Hall Debating Society
'Can Friendship subsist among Young Persons of the Two Sexes, without being accompanied by the Passion of Love?'
Question answered in the affirmative.

1264. October 8, 1787 Westminster Forum
'Would it increase the happiness of the Marriage State, if Divorces were more easily obtained?
The preference given to the above Question is presumed to be a satisfactory answer to the letter lately sent by a Lady accusing the Managers with negligence to the interest of the Fair Sex.'
The World October 6

1265. October 11, 1787 Coachmakers Hall Debating Society
(FOX against FRANCE)
'Has not the conduct of France afforded sufficient proof of the truth of Mr. Fox's assertion in the House of Commons, that Great Britain ought ever to cherish a jealousy and distrust against that Country?
Every question with which the Managers have been favoured, which is correspondent with their plan of rendering this Society a mingled source of refined entertainment, and intellectual improvement, will receive due respect – to young speakers, who may be desirous to address a British audience on the above question, every encouraging support will be given.'
Gazetteer

1266. October 18, 1787 Coachmakers Hall Debating Society
'Has not the conduct of France afforded sufficient proof of the truth of Mr. Fox's assertion in the House of Commons, that Great Britain ought ever to cherish a jealousy and distrust against that Country?'
Mr. Fox's assertion was declared justified almost unanimously.
Gazetteer October 17

1267. October 25, 1787 Coachmakers Hall Debating Society
'In which Cause is it most noble for a man to Die? In saving the life of an affectionate Mother, A friend who has saved him from Ruin, or in the Defense of the Liberties of his Country?'
A considerable majority voted that it was most noble to die for one's country.
Gazetteer October 24

1268. October 29, 1787 Westminster Forum
'Was it worthy of Admiration in the Romans to sacrifice Social Duties and Family Affection to Patriotism and Public Spirit?
It was decided by a great majority in favour of the Romans.'
The World

1269. November 1, 1787 Society for Free Debate, Mitre Tavern
'Has Lord George Gordon . . . created more confusion in London and its environs?'
It was 'determined unanimously' that Lord George Gordon had created most confusion.

Morning Herald November 8

1270. November 1, 1787 Coachmakers Hall Debating Society
'May the encrease of Female Prostitution be imputed more to the treachery and falsehood of the Male Sex; or the misconduct of Parents in giving their Daughters an improper Education?
The audience considered this Question as it really is, a subject of infinite importance to the well-being of the community, and expressed the highest satisfaction, at the very able and becoming manner in which it was argued by the speakers on both sides.' It was adjourned.
Morning Herald November 8

1271. November 5, 1787 Westminster Forum
'Admitting the characters of Charles and Joseph Surface in the School for Scandal to be real, would not Charles be the more dangerous Member of Society?
The Comedy from which the above Question is taken, stands first upon the list of modern dramatic writings. The characters of Charles and Joseph are happily drawn. Heedless extravagance and inattention, almost utterly subversive of morality and inattention, are the leading features of the one; consummate hypocrisy, and a determined contempt of all social feelings, eminently distinguish the other. Notwithstanding the favour with which Charles is generally received, it has ever remained a doubt with the discerning few, whether the hypocrite is not less dangerous to society.'
The World

1272. November 8, 1787 Society for Free Debate, Mitre Tavern
(CATO, WERTER, or EUGENE ARAM)
'In which situation is an act of Suicide, most entitled to our compassion; the deserted Patriot, the despairing Lover, or the condemned Criminal?'
Morning Herald

1273. November 8, 1787 Coachmakers Hall Debating Society
'May the encrease of Female Prostitution be imputed more to the treachery and falsehood of the Male Sex; or the misconduct of Parents in giving their Daughters an improper Education?'
Debate found prostitution due to improper education.
Gazetteer November 7

1274. November 12, 1787 Westminster Forum
'Admitting the characters of Charles and Joseph Surface in the School for Scandal to be real, would not Charles be the more dangerous Member of Society?'
The World

1275. November 15, 1787 Coachmakers Hall Debating Society

'Has the conduct of Mr. Pitt as a minister been more consistent with the patriotic spirit and principles of the late Earl of Chatham or the Politics of the Earl of Bute?'
Gazetteer November 14

1276. November 19, 1787 Westminster Forum
'Would it not reflect honour on Mr. Pitt, to impose an additional Tax upon every Batchelor above the age of forty, and apply the produce thereof as marriage portions to poor young maidens?
The above Question was conveyed to the Managers of this Society in a letter, signed by a considerable number of married men, stating, that as Old Batchelors do not sustain an equal share with them of the burthen of the State, and as their celibacy is a principal cause of the misery and incontinence of many of the female sex, it is fit that the sense of the public should be taken upon the expediency of the above Tax.'
The World

1277. November 22, 1787 Society for Free Debate, Mitre Tavern
'Is Jealousy a Proof of Love, or of an ignoble Mind?'
Determined that Jealousy proof of ignoble mind.
Gazetteer November 29

1278. November 22, 1787 Coachmakers Hall
'Has the conduct of Mr. Pitt as a minister been more consistent with the patriotic spirit and principles of the late Earl of Chatham or the Politics of the Earl of Bute?'
Decided in favour of Administration.
Gazetteer November 29

1279. November 29, 1787 Society for Free Debate, Mitre Tavern
'Is that opinion founded in Truth, which says, a Minister of this Country ought to have Influence sufficient to secure a Majority in the House of Commons?'
Question determined in the negative.
Morning Herald December 6

1280. November 29, 1787 Coachmakers Hall Debating Society
'Is the virtue of the Fair Sex more endangered by the influence of Vanity, Love, or Avarice?'
Decided in favour of Vanity.
Morning Herald December 6

1281. December 4, 1787 Westminster Forum
'Is Jealousy a Proof of Love?'
The 'decision was almost unanimously in the negative.'
Morning Herald December 10

1282. December 6, 1787 Society for Free Debate, Mitre Tavern

'Is it a Duty incumbent on all Mankind, to enter into the State of Wedlock?
This subject was sent to the Managers, in a Letter, from three Ladies and a Gentleman, who are particularly interested in its discussion. . .'
Society moving to Capel-court, Bartholemew-lane, and to be called the London Debating Society.
Morning Herald

1283. December 6, 1787 Coachmakers Hall Debating Society
'Which has the greater Claim to our pity, the Female who has lost an affectionate Husband, or she who is married to one who is cruel and perfidious?'
Question sent by 'a Lady, signing herself "A Disconsolate Widow" . . .
Whatever concerns the Female Sex must be allowed to have a serious claim to public attention; and the discussion of the above Questions may be productive of arguments tending to alleviate misfortune on the one hand, and of Sentiments of Prudence and Morality, that may in some measure prevent the Female Sex from falling into a painful situation on the other.'
Decided that 'to be united in wedlock to a husband cruel and perfidious is a greater misfortune than the loss of one kind and affectionate.'
Gazetteer December 13

1284. December 10, 1787 Westminster Forum
'Has the parliamentary conduct of Mr. Fox, in admonishing Administration against the treachery and infidelity of France, or the measures lately adopted by Mr. Pitt, in consequence of the politics of that country, exhibited the greater proof of their wisdom as Statesmen?
The political situation of Great Britain, at the present important period, must render this subject highly interesting, and well worthy the inquiry of every well-wisher to his country; the managers of this institution therefore have every reason to suppose that some distinguished abilities will be exerted on the occasion; and they hope that no persons will decline, from diffidence or intimidation, to deliver their opinions, as that candour and indulgence which youth and inexperience have a claim to, are always liberally shewn, and constant attention is paid to the preservation of good order and decorum.'
Morning Herald

1285. December 12, 1787 Westminster School of Eloquence
A question on which quality most recommends a lady to a husband.
'Determined that Riches will more probably recommend a Lady to a Husband.'
The World December 19

1286. December 13, 1787 Free Debate, The Original London Society, removed from the Mitre Tavern, Fleet Street, to a commodious Room, in Capel-court, Bartholemew-lane

'Which is a more disagreeable companion, a Peevish Old Maid or a Crusty Old Batchelor?'
Determined that Old Maid was more disagreeable.
Gazetteer December 19

1287. December 13, 1787 Coachmakers Hall
'Is the present alarming increase of Perjury mostly to be imputed to the neglect of moral instruction and example in the Clergy, to the artifices of bad Lawyers, or the careless manner in which Oaths are administered?'
Debate decided that perjury due to bad lawyers.
Gazetteer

1288. December 19, 1787 Westminster School of Eloquence
'Do the Comforts of Matrimony counterbalance its Cares?
The Recital of this Evening will be Mr. Pope's Elegy upon an Unfortunate Young Lady.'
The World

1289. December 20, 1787 Free Debate, Capel Court
'Would it not increase the popularity of Mr. Pitt to repeal the Shop Tax, and supply the deficiencies it might occasion, by a Stamp Duty upon Tickets for Conventicles, and an obligation for Methodist Teachers to take out Annual Licenses?'
The Question 'was determined unanimously against Ministers laying any restrictions upon the Sectaries'.
Gazetteer December 19

1290. December 20, 1787 Coachmakers Hall
'May a Man, consistent with justice, though destitute of Family and Fortune, marry a Lady in possession of both?'
Answer in the affirmative.
Gazetteer December 27

1291. December 24, 1787 Westminster Forum
'Is it consistent with Female Delicacy, for an ACTRESS to appear on the STAGE in the DRESS of a Man?'
It was decided, 'that an Actress may, consistently with Female delicacy, appear on the Stage in the dress of a man'.
The World December 22

1292. December 26, 1787 Westminster School of Eloquence
'Which is the greater Criminal, the Villain who robs an innocent Man of his Reputation – or the Seducer who deprives an unsuspecting Female of her Virtue?
Prior to the Debate, *Collin's Ode on the Passions* will be recited.
N.B. In answer to the letter signed "One who wishes to attend the School of Eloquence", the Managers only request his attendance to satisfy his scruples, and he will then be convinced that the species of

double entendre, of which he complains, is banished at the School of Eloquence.'
The World

1293. December 27, 1787 Free Debate, Capel Court
'Would making the education of youth a national concern, be to the rising generation productive of the glorious consequence attributed to that plan by the late Dr. Goldsmith?
As education alone constitutes the distinctions in our riper years, and as the affection of parents too frequently counteracts the best precepts of tuition; several gentlemen of distinguished abilities have requested the above subject being brought forward, and as it is of a national importance much entertainment may be expected from its discussion.'
Gazetteer December 26

1294. December 27, 1787 Coachmakers Hall
BY DESIRE OF AN UNFORTUNATE YOUNG LADY
'Does not the Man who abandons an amiable Wife and Family to Poverty and Distress deserve the punishment of Death equally with him who has violated the Laws of his Country?'
It was decided 'that the husband abandoning his wife and family to poverty, is equally criminal with him who has violated the municipal laws'.
Morning Post January 2, 1788

1295. December 31, 1787 Westminster Forum
'Is the virtue of the female sex most in danger from their own natural frailty, parental restraint, or the defects of modern education?'
Debate decided that female sex most in danger from the defects of modern education.
Morning Post January 7, 1788

1296. January 3, 1788 Coachmakers Hall
'Is it probable that a reformed rake will make as good a husband, as the man whose life has been uniformly consistent with prudence and morality?
The fair Sex, from a native softness and generosity of mind, being often led to give credit to maxims laid down by the other sex, upon the truth of which their happiness or misery in wedlock may depend; a Gentleman, no less respected for his abilities, than beloved for his philanthropy, has proposed the above question, as a subject of sufficient importance to recommend to the attention of a liberal and enlightened audience.
It was almost unanimously decided . . . that a reformed rake would not prove so good a husband, as the man whose life has been uniformly moral.'
Morning Chronicle January 2

1297. January 7, 1788 Westminster Forum

'Was the Belief of the Existence of Apparitions by the late Doctor Johnson, an Impeachment of his Understanding?
The decision of the audience, by a small majority, justified Doctor Johnson's belief in the existence of apparitions.'
Morning Post

1298. January 10, 1788 Coachmakers Hall
'Does the confidence reposed by the people in Mr. Pitt proceed more from his wisdom and integrity as a Minister, or from an opinion that Mr. Fox and his party have acted inconsistently and forfeited the support of a free people?
A popular character, zealous in his attachment to Mr. Pitt, having declared that the people are now convinced that they are indebted to the Minister for the salvation of the Constitution, and a gentleman equally animated in the cause of Mr. Fox, insisting that this distinguished Senator still possesses the confidence of the friends to freedom, it has been agreed to refer the question to a public audience.'
Morning Chronicle January 9

1299. January 14, 1788 Westminster Forum
'Is the assertion of the Marchioness de Lambert true, that love improves a virtuous soul?
Agreeable to the request of a celebrated poetical character, whose publications have lately been the subject of much panegyric in various prints [the question is debated.] He has pledged himself on the present occasion, to make a public display of his talents in poetry, by opening and arguing the above question, with a composition in verse; and afterwards to close the debate of the evening, with a legendary tale, explanatory of his opinion on the enquiry for investigation.
The Managers of this Institution are happy to be able to say, that the poetical Composition of the Gentleman who opened the debate . . . met with the unanimous applause of a numerous and splendid audience. – The humourous versified Essay which followed, afforded the highest diversion; and the recitals of a gentleman belonging to the Bath Theatre, added to the subsequent spirit with which the whole debate proceeded, drew from the audience incessant marks of approbation.'
Morning Post

1300. January 16, 1788 School of Eloquence, Panton Street Haymarket
'Does not the amiable philanthropy of Mr. Howard, and the general conduct of the Dissenters, incontestably prove their loyalty, and demand a repeal of the corporation and test acts?'
Morning Post January 23

1301. January 17, 1788 Coachmakers Hall
'Does the confidence reposed by the people in Mr. Pitt proceed more from his wisdom and integrity as a Minister, or from an opinion that Mr. Fox and his party have acted inconsistently and forfeited the support of a free people?

The honest zeal which ever marks the character of Englishmen in support of the man they hold to be the greatest friend to freedom, was manifest during the whole of the debate. . . The friends of MR. PITT seem confident that the decision will be in his favour, while the advocates of MR. FOX declare they are not afraid to trust his cause to a British audience.'
Morning Chronicle January 16

1302. January 21, 1788 Westminster Forum
'Is it consistent with the principles of justice, or with the nature of the British Constitution, and real interests of the Community, to punish with death [any] crime except Murder?
The last Question . . . produced a debate, which gave a convincing proof of the liberal support with which this society is honoured. . . It was decided, that there are crimes besides murder which deserve the punishment of death.'
Morning Post

1303. January 23, 1788 School of Eloquence, Panton Street Haymarket
'Does not the amiable philanthropy of Mr. Howard, and the general conduct of the Dissenters, incontestably prove their loyalty, and demand a repeal of the corporation and test acts?'
Morning Post

1304. January 24, 1788 Coachmakers Hall
'Does the confidence reposed by the people in Mr. Pitt proceed more from his wisdom and integrity as a Minister, or from an opinion that Mr. Fox and his party have acted inconsistently and forfeited the support of a free people?
The audience . . . was almost unanimous in pronouncing the confidence reposed in Mr. Pitt, to be the effect of his wisdom and integrity as a Minister.'
Morning Chronicle January 23

1305. January 28, 1788 Westminster Forum
'Which is most likely to stimulate a man to great and worthy actions; the passion of love, the sentiment of friendship, or the principle of public spirit?
The managers of the Westminster Forum are happy to be able to speak of the increasing reputation of this institution.'
Morning Post

1306. January 30, 1788 [School of Eloquence] Panton Street, Haymarket
Question on the propriety of boxing.
'In a debate equally replete with severe irony and strong reasoning, Boxing was pointedly reprobated by almost every speaker. A numerous audience decided against the brutality of the practice.'
Morning Post February 6

1307. January 31, 1788 Coachmakers Hall
'Which is most dangerous to its possessor, Jealousy in a Lover, Profligacy in a Merchant, or Ambition in a Statesman?
A Lady, whose mental accomplishments can only be equalled by her personal beauty, is the proposer of the above question. A recent circumstance announced in the public prints, as one among the fatal train of consequences of which the passion of Jealousy has been the cruel parent, is the reason assigned by the fair querist for uniting that passion with the two other important branches of which the question is composed.'
The audience decided that profligacy in a merchant was most dangerous.
Morning Chronicle January 30

1308. February 6, 1788 [School of Eloquence] Panton Street, Haymarket
'Are the understandings of the fair sex inferior to those of the male, or does education alone constitute the difference?'
Morning Post

1309. February 7, 1788 Coachmakers Hall
'Would it be consistent with the political and commercial interests of Great Britain for the legislature to pass an Act for the total Abolition of the Slave Trade?
The above interesting subject drew to this Hall . . . a very numerous assembly of Citizens the most respectable, and much to the honour of the fair sex, a considerable number of them forsook the places of trifling and uninstructive amusement, to attend the grave investigation of a Question in which one of the most important branches of the Trade and Commerce of this country is involved.'
Morning Chronicle February 6

1310. February 11, 1788 Westminster Forum
'Are the assertions of Dr. Johnson true, That the married are seldom happy, and that celibacy has no pleasures?'
The discussion disproved the assertions of Dr. Johnson.
Morning Post

1311. February 12, 1788 Original London
'Is Disappointment in Love a sufficient Excuse for a Man remaining a Batchelor?'
The Question decided in the negative.
Daily Advertiser February 19

1312. February 13, 1788 School of Eloquence
'Can the Slave Trade be justified on the principles of Justice, Christianity, Policy or Humanity?
Many ingenious arguments were adduced in favour of the Slave Trade – many powerful appeals to the feelings were urged against it. – Among

the foremost were those of an ingenious African. He contributed much information on the subject (being the result of his own experience).'
Morning Post February 19

1313. February 14, 1788 Coachmakers Hall
'Would it be consistent with the political and commercial interests of Great Britain for the legislature to pass an Act for the total Abolition of the Slave Trade?'
Although vote adjourned, most speakers seemed in favour of abolition.
Morning Chronicle February 13

1314. February 18, 1788 Westminster Forum
'Can any abuse of the LIBERTY of the PRESS, justify a limitation of that constitutional privilege?
As no subject is more interesting to an Englishman than that which relates to his rights and privileges, the managers of the Westminster Forum trust, that the above question will be particularly welcome to an English audience; and the more so in the present period, as some recent events of a public nature have given rise to much disputation on this important topic.'
Morning Post

1315. February 19, 1788 Original London Society, Capel Court
'Which stands the better chance for Happiness, an Old Woman who marries a young Husband, or an old Man who marries a young Wife?'
Determined that old Man married to young Wife has best chance.
Daily Advertiser

1316. February 20, 1788 School of Eloquence
'Can the Slave Trade be justified on the principles of Justice, Christianity, Policy or Humanity?
Upon the adjourned question of the Slave Trade, besides several most animated speeches, [the Society was] honoured by a circumstance never before witnessed in a Debating Society. A lady spoke to the subject with that dignity, energy, and information, which astonished every one present, and justly merited what she obtained, repeated and uncommon bursts of applause from an intelligent and enraptured auditory. The question was carried against the Slave Trade.'
Morning Post February 19

1317. February 21, 1788 Coachmakers Hall
'Would it be consistent with the political and commercial interests of Great Britain for the legislature to pass an Act for the total Abolition of the Slave Trade?'
Morning Chronicle February 27

1318. February 25, 1788 Westminster Forum
'Can any political or commercial advantages justify a free people in continuing the Slave Trade?

A NATIVE OF AFRICA, many years a Slave in the West-Indies, will attend . . . and communicate to the audience a number of very remarkable circumstances respecting the treatment of the Negroe Slaves, and particularly of his being forcibly taken from his family and friends, on the coast of Africa, and sold as a Slave – of the manner in which he was treated while in captivity, and the means by which he obtained his emancipation; together with several interesting circumstances relative to the conduct of the Slave-holders towards the African women. Several popular Gentlemen, who have interested themselves in the petitions presented to Parliament, will also be present; and a LADY, whose intellectual accomplishments, and wonderful powers of eloquence, delighted a public audience on Wednesday last, and procured her the highest respect and admiration, is expected to honour the Society with her sentiments.
The advocates for the abolition argued, that no policy was well founded. No commercial advantages could be permanent that were gained by a departure from the indispensible obligations of justice, and that virtue alone was the true foundation of national honour, the source of harmony, order and happiness in society. These arguments were ably answered by the speakers on the other side.' Question adjourned.
Morning Post February 23

1319. February 26 Original London Society, Capel Court
'Which is most predominant in the Breast of Man, the Love of Life, the Love of Liberty, or the Love of the Fair Sex?'
Daily Advertiser

1320. February 27, 1788 School of Eloquence
'Which is more blameable, the Lady that condescends to be mistress to the man she loves, or marries the man she hates?'
Morning Post February 26

1321. February 28, 1788 Coachmakers Hall
'Would it be consistent with the political and commercial interests of Great Britain for the legislature to pass an Act for the total Abolition of the Slave Trade?
The friends to the abolition employed many ingenious arguments in favour of the extension of freedom to a race of beings hitherto wandering in ignorance, and groaning under despotism, while the cautious politician, professing equal love of humanity contended against an innovation that might lead to the ruin of the trade and commerce of his country, without any real benefit to the objects of emancipation.'
Morning Chronicle February 27

1322. March 3, 1788 Westminster Forum
'Can any political or commercial advantages justify a free people in continuing the Slave Trade?'
Morning Post March 1

1323. March 4, 1788 Original London Society, removed from the Mitre Tavern to Capel Court
'Which is most predominant in the Breast of Man, the Love of Life, the Love of Liberty, or the Love of the Fair Sex?'
Determined that Love of Life most powerful in the human breast.
Daily Advertiser

1324. March 5, 1788 School of Eloquence, Panton Street
'Which is the greater Calamity – the Loss of a good Wife, or the Plague of a bad One?
The audience decided . . . by a considerable majority' that the plague of a bad wife was the greater calamity.
Morning Post March 4

1325. March 6, 1788 Coachmakers Hall
'Would it be consistent with the political and commercial interests of Great Britain for the legislature to pass an Act for the total Abolition of the Slave Trade?
The majority [of the audience] . . . declared that a total abolition of the Slave Trade, would be inconsistent with the political and commercial interests of this country.'
Morning Chronicle March 5

1326. March 10, 1788 Westminster Forum, Spring Gardens
'Can any political or commercial advantages justify a free people in continuing the Slave Trade?'
Morning Post

1327. March 11, 1788 Original London Society
'Which has contributed most to the Disgrace of this Country, the Cruelty and Peculation practiced by Servants of the India Company in the East, or the Encouragement given to the African Slave Trade in our West-India Possessions?
As the Attention of the whole Nation appears to be at present engrossed by these two grand Objects, the Managers of this Institution have, at the Request of a Number of Respectable Characters, brought them forward in Contrast for this Evening's Entertainment.'
Daily Advertiser

1328. March 12, 1788 School of Eloquence
'Which must be more disagreeable to a Lady of delicacy, to be compelled to marry the most ignorant clown, or a complete modern fop?'
Morning Post March 11

1329. March 13, 1788 Coachmakers Hall
'Has the conduct of Mr. Pitt, respecting the affairs of India, merited the praise or censure of the Publick?
There appeared to be a small majority against the Minister's conduct in relation to the affairs of India.'
Morning Chronicle March 12

1330. March 17, 1788 Westminster Forum, Spring Garden
'Has Mr. PITT forfeited his claim to popularity by the introduction of the depending INDIA BILL?
The dangerous precedent which an infringement of chartered rights must afford, and the questionable propriety of placing unlimited power in a Board of Controul were topics which call for the serious attention of the Patriot and the Politician.'
The question was resolved, by a considerable majority, in favour of Mr. Pitt.
Morning Post

1331. March 17, 1788 La Belle Assemblee, Brewer Street, Golden Square
'(Under the Patronage of several Ladies of Distinction)
Do not the extraordinary abilities of the Ladies in the present age demand Academical honours from the Universities – a right to vote at elections, and to be returned Members of Parliament?
The refined nature of La Belle Assemblee being in itself an exclusion of any indiscriminate assemblage of mixed company; the Nobility and Gentry who may honour it by their presence, are humbly assured no attention shall be omitted to render its order and regularity equal to its elegance and entertainment.
The audience . . . was numerous and polite – the debate a brilliant assemblage of wit, elegance, and pleasantry – the decision terminated in favour of the affirmative of the question.'
Admission Half-a-Crown – Ladies permitted to speak in veils.
Morning Post March 15, 1788

1332. March 20, 1788 Coachmakers Hall
'Is it justifiable for a man to fight a duel to vindicate the honour of the lady he loves, or under any provocation whatsoever?'
Morning Chronicle March 19

1333. March 24, 1788 La Belle Assemblee
'Which was more culpable in eating the forbidden Fruit, ADAM or EVE?
The Lady who honoured the Managers by a letter subscribed CAUTION, is respectfully entreated to dismiss her apprehensions on the present question – Indelicacy, and much more infidelity, will ever be carefully banished.'
Morning Post March 21

1334. March 24, 1788 Westminster Forum, Spring Gardens, Charing Cross
'Can a Lady seduced, and deserted by her seducer, be justified in intermarrying with a man of honour, without previously acquainting him of her misfortune?

223

As it is no uncommon event for the female sex to form matrimonial connections under the circumstances mentioned in the question, and as the propriety of such marriages is a matter of much dispute, a sentimental Lady, well known to the literary world, has presented the above inquiry.'
Morning Post

1335. March 26, 1788 Westminster School of Eloquence
'Is the Male or Female Character more distinguished by Constancy in Love?'
Morning Post

1336. March 27, 1788 Coachmakers Hall
'Which is the more eligible for a wife, a lady of fortune without education, or a lady of education without fortune?
To obtain happiness in the marriage state has long been the study of mankind, but though a science with which every person would wish to be acquainted, but few comparatively have obtained it. A Question therefore that may lead the mind to avoid the steps of juvenile imprudence, and to pursue the paths of wisdom, as far as respects matrimonial felicity, is highly worthy the attention of a rational audience.
The decision was almost unanimous, that a Lady of Education, though destitute of Fortune, ought to be elected for a Wife, in preference to the Lady of Fortune, without the benefit of Education.'
Morning Chronicle March 26

1337. March 31, 1788 Westminster Forum
'Can a Lady seduced, and deserted by her seducer, be justified in intermarrying with a man of honour, without previously acquainting him of her misfortune?'
Determined that such a lady ought not to marry a man of honour, without previously informing him of her misfortune.
Morning Post April 7

1338. March 31, 1788 La Belle Assemblee, Brewer Street, Golden Square
'Which is the greatest calamity to a female of sensibility, the loss of a lover by banishment, death, or marriage?'
Morning Post March 29

1339. April 2, 1788 School of Eloquence, Panton Street
'Which is the most injurious member of society – a Quack Doctor – a Trading Justice – or a Methodist Preacher?'
Morning Post

1340. April 3, 1788 Coachmakers Hall
'Is the great Increase of Methodists more to be attributed to the great Zeal and Abilities of their Preachers, or to the Want of a proper Spirit and Exertion in the Clergy of the established Church?

A learned Divine, warmly attached to the Freedom of publick Debate, and particularly friendly to this Society as an Institution which encourages aspiring Genius, producing mental improvement and rational Entertainment, thus diverting the minds of Youth from the pursuit of licentious Pleasure, has proposed the above Question as a Subject calculated to call forth the Powers of Eloquence in the Discovery and Maintenance of Truth.'
Morning Chronicle April 2

1341. April 7, 1788 Westminster Forum
'Which are more likely to be productive of happiness to the possessor, the gifts of nature, or the gifts of fortune?'
Morning Post

1342. April 8, 1788 La Belle Assemblee, Rice's Rooms, Brewer Street, Golden Square
'Ought not those Ladies whose husbands are Peers, and Members of Parliament, to exert their influence over them for an abolition of the Slave Trade?
At a time when the eyes of all Europe are fixed on this country to observe the part she may take in diffusing that liberty to others, which for so many centuries has been her peculiar boast, the importance of this inquiry must be obvious.'
Admission half a Crown.
Morning Post April 7

1343. April 10, 1788 Coachmakers Hall
'Is the great Increase of Methodists more to be attributed to the great Zeal and Abilities of their Preachers, or to the Want of a proper Spirit and Exertion in the Clergy of the established Church?
In proportion as mankind discover and act consistently with truth, they pursue the path of wisdom. Freedom in debate serves to promote this desirable purpose. The clouds of prejudice must be dispelled, and the principles of angry bigotry removed before the mind will be expanded, and the heart warmed with benevolence.'
The vote was almost unanimous in favour of the great zeal and abilities of the Methodist ministers.
Morning Chronicle April 9

1344. April 16, 1788 School of Eloquence
'Which is most worthy the admiration of this country, Mr. Fox, for his opposition to the American war – Mr. Pitt for retrieving our declining finances, or Mr. Burke, for bringing to public investigation the cruelties and peculations practised in the East-Indies?
Now the spirit of party virulence seems nearly evaporated, it is presumed an enquiry into the three grand political characteristics of these illustrious statesmen may neither be unworthy of the abilities of the gentlemen who speak in the School of Eloquence, nor devoid of enter-

tainment to the public, who now seem peculiarly interested in the affairs of the East-Indies.'
Morning Post April 15

1345. April 17, 1788 Coachmakers Hall
'Is Jealousy in a Husband, or Inconstancy in a Wife, more destructive to matrimonial happiness?
Jealousy and Inconstancy in Wedlock never prevailed more than at the present period. A young lady of extraordinary abilities has proposed the [above] question. . .. The lady, it is said, has lately finished an elegant novel, intitled "The Fair Inconstant" which is mentioned in terms of the highest panegyrick, but whether she has confidence enough in her talents to address a large assembly on so singular a question as the above is, time only can discover.
It was the opinion of the audience . . . that inconstancy in a Wife is more destructive to conjugal felicity than jealousy in a Husband.'
Morning Chronicle April 16

1346. April 21, 1788 Westminster Forum
COURTSHIP
'Which of the Two Maxims is more likely to prove successful to a Lover, that of Lord Chesterfield, which recommends us to consider every word before we speak it; or that of Ovid, which says,
    "Speak boldly on, and trust the following word;
    It will be witty of its own accord."
In answer to the Letter of the Lady who honoured this Society with the above Question, the Managers beg leave to observe, that though it is not strictly conformable to their rules to permit Ladies to speak in this assembly; yet, as this seems a subject on which the Fair Sex are peculiarly qualified to decide, they are willing to indulge her, if she still retains a wish to open the debate.'
The audience 'were of opinion, that the boldness recommended by Ovid is more likely to prove successful to a Lover, than the caution suggested by the late Earl of Chesterfield'.
Morning Post

1347. April 23, 1788 Westminster School of Eloquence, Panton Street, Haymarket
'Which is more eligible for a Wife, an Old Maid, or a Widow?
It has been an invariable maxim with the Proprietors of the School of Eloquence to avoid as much as possible those questions which have been debated in other Societies; however, at the united request of several Ladies, they have in this instance relaxed their laws, trusting the eccentricity of the question – and the fund of risibility it must naturally occasion, will plead their apology.
A widow was almost unanimously declared to be more eligible for a wife than an old maid.'
Morning Post April 22

1348. April 24, 1788 Coachmakers Hall

'Is the following opinion of Lord Peterborough founded in truth, viz. – That the Fair Sex are so envious of each other if you praise two of them at once, though you give to each the beauty of Venus and the wisdom of Minerva, they would neither of them be pleased?

The audience . . . were of opinion that Lord Peterborough's description of female envy, was consonant with truth.'

Morning Chronicle April 23

1349. April 28, 1788 Westminster Forum

'Is the Assertion of Mr. Pope well founded, That every Woman is at Heart a Rake?

A Lady of distinguished abilities, an admirer of the celebrated Poet, from whose works the above Question is taken, has solicited the Managers to introduce it for public debate, in order that the true meaning of the Poet may be discovered, and the fair sex publicly vindicated from a charge, in which their moral character is materially concerned, if unjustly accused.'

Morning Post

1350. April 30, 1788 Westminster School of Eloquence

'Is it not contrary to justice and propriety, to compel Women to serve [as] Church-Wardens, Constables, Overseers of the Poor, and other Parish Offices?

The novelty of the present question joined to its temporary nature (it being evidently founded on an affair that has lately been much canvassed, of a Woman being declared eligible to the office of Constable) induced a numerous and polite audience . . . to vote its immediate discussion.'

Morning Post April 29

1351. May 1, 1788 Coachmakers Hall

'Is the assertion of the late Mr. Fielding in his novel of Tom Jones, founded in truth, viz. That if Libertinism was more severely censured by the FAIR SEX, a Libertine would be a rare Character?

As nature, for the wisest purposes, has adorned the Female Sex with the most attractive graces of personal beauty, and mental affability, so their influence upon the manners of the opposite Sex, has been in various respects felt, and evinced by a studied deference and complaisance towards female opinion. How far the behaviour of the Fair Sex has justified the sentiment contained in the above question is well worth an attentive examination.'

It was decided that Mr. Fielding was correct.

Morning Chronicle April 30

1352. May 7, 1788 Westminster School of Eloquence

'Is the common saying true, that there is no medium in the marriage state, but that it must always be extremely happy, or very miserable?

As this Society will close, for the summer season . . . the Proprietors wish to impress on the Public that sense they entertain of the patronage with which it has been honoured. The number of important questions communicated to them by correspondents, best speak the estimation in which the School of Eloquence is held by the learned and judicious.'
Morning Post

1353. May 8, 1788 Coachmakers Hall
'Is it not disgraceful to a free and enlightened nation, to exclude the Roman Catholicks from any Civil or Religious Liberties, which are exercised by Methodists, Arians and Socinians?
A celebrated Romish Priest, has informed the Managers that he has challenged a venerable and learned Gentleman of the Methodist persuasion, to meet him in the Fair Field of Public Debate, on the above Question, and that Coachmakers Hall has been mutually agreed on as the most respectable and popular assembly for free discussion of a subject, in the decision of which, every man who feels a respect for the majesty of truth, will acknowledge himself immediately concerned.'
Morning Chronicle May 7

1354. May 14, 1788 Westminster School of Eloquence
'Which is the more disagreeable Character – a surly Old Bachelor or a peevish Old Maid?
The various expences attendant on the School of Eloquence (for this Evening) being presented as a gift to an indigent Widow, its entire receipts will be appropriated to her relief. On this occasion, a Lady, who has honoured this Society with her sentiments, has graciously promised either to open or close the debate, or to speak in the course of it. Previous to the entertainment, a Gentleman will (for that night only) recite Collin's Ode on the Passions.'
Morning Post May 13

1355. May 16, 1788 Coachmakers Hall
'Is it not disgraceful to a free and enlightened nation, to exclude the Roman Catholicks from any Civil or Religious Liberties, which are exercised by Methodists, Arians and Socinians?'
Morning Chronicle

1356. May 22, 1788 Coachmakers Hall
'Is it not disgraceful to a free and enlightened nation, to exclude the Roman Catholicks from any Civil or Religious Liberties, which are exercised by Methodists, Arians and Socinians?'
The debate was marked by 'much pleasant but allowable sarcasm'. The affirmative 'appeared to be the sense of the majority'.
Morning Chronicle

1357. May 29, 1788 Coachmakers Hall
'Are the Ladies of this country most distinguished for their Virtues, Beauty or Mental Accomplishments?

An English Lady of Distinction, educated in France, but lately arrived from that country, has acquainted the Managers of this institution, that she has heard various opinions respecting the most prominent feature in the character of her fair country-women, and it therefore desirous to hear the above question publicly debated before a British audience.'
Times May 26

1358. July 2, 1788 Society for Free Debate, Great Room, Capel-court, Bartholemew lane
'Does that Wife who assumes a Domination over her Husband, render him or herself more conspicuously ridiculous?'
The World

1359. July 7, 1788 Society for Free Debate, Capel Court
'Is the Rev. Mr. Wesley censurable for publicly maintaining the Existence of Witches, the Doctrine of Apparitions, and Demoniac Possessions?
The report of a Man possessed by Seven Devils, at Bristol, caused this enquiry. The public will now have the opportunity of hearing, (at his own desire) an aged, venerable, and learned Methodist, defend his opinions concerning, and deliver a succinct account of these strange appearances. Several Gentlemen of the first ability have promised to attend. The Lady who spoke at the Mitre Society, and declared she had frequently conversed with an Apparition, may depend on a candid hearing.'
The World

1360. July 14, 1788 Capel Court Debating Society
'Is the Rev. Mr. Wesley censurable for publicly maintaining the Existence of Witches – the Doctrine of Apparitions, and Demoniac Possessions?'
The World

1361. July 21, 1788 Capel Court Debating Society
'Is the Rev. Mr. Wesley censurable for publicly maintaining the Existence of Witches, the Doctrine of Apparitions, and Demoniac Possessions?'
The debate 'after three evenings' investigation, terminated in Mr. Wesley's favour'.
The World

1362. July 28, 1788 Capel Court Debates
'Which is the strongest obligation in the Marriage Covenant, Love, Honour or Obedience?
Love was determined the most powerful obligation.'
The World

1363. August 4, 1788 Capel Court Debating Society
'Between which Characters is the resemblance most striking – Sir Robert Walpole and Mr. Pitt, or Mr. Fox and Oliver Cromwell?'
The World

1364. August 11, 1788 Capel Court Debating Society
'Between which Characters is the resemblance most striking – Sir Robert Walpole and Mr. Pitt, or Mr. Fox and Oliver Cromwell?'
The World

1365. August 18, 1788 Capel Court Debates
'Which is the greater Domestic Evil, a Drunken Husband or a Scolding Wife?'
The World

1366. August 25, 1788 Capel Court Debates
'Is the desire of an Husband generally more powerful and commendable in an Old Maid or a Widow?
A violent contest having taken place between a Maiden Lady and a Widow, upon their adverse claims to Matrimony, they agreed to determine it by the decision of this Society. . . As in this institution Ladies have the privilege of speaking, there will be nothing indecorous in either, or both, supporting their own opinions.'
The World

1367. August 28, 1788 Coachmakers Hall
'Has the conduct of MR. FOX, in the part he has taken relative to the late Westminster Election, reflected honour or disgrace upon him as a British Senator?'
The World September 4

1368. September 1, 1788 Capel Court Debates
'Is the Passion of Love more powerful from the Age of 15 to 30 – or from 30 to 50?'
The World

1369. September 3, 1788 Westminster School of Eloquence, Panton Street Haymarket
'Do the Electors of Westminster deserve the Praise, or Censure of the Real Friends of this Country, in rejecting Lord Hood, and chusing Lord John Townshend, for their Representative in Parliament?'
The audience decided that praise was deserved.
The World September 10

1370. September 4, 1788 Coachmakers Hall
'Has the conduct of MR. FOX, in the part he has taken relative to the late Westminster Election, reflected honour or disgrace upon him as a British Senator?
As the constitutional liberty of this country is the pride of its own subjects, and the envy of surrounding nations, every man will acknow-

ledge the importance of the above question, the immediate object of which is to refer the conduct of a British Senator touching the right of election, the foundation upon which all our civil and religious privileges are built, to the decision of the publick.'
Small majority favoured Fox.
Morning Chronicle September 3

1371. September 8, 1788 Capel Court Debating Society
'Which is the most dangerous Member of Society, a Quack Doctor, a trading Justice, or a Methodist Preacher?'
Daily Advertiser September 20

1372. September 10, 1788 Westminster School of Eloquence, Panton Street Haymarket
'Is it not a reflection on the Female Character, for Ladies to interfere in Elections for Members of Parliament?
As several illustrious Females have the last two Elections for Westminster, taken a very active part in behalf of their favourite Candidate, it has been requested, that the propriety of such conduct be submitted to a fair and candid discussion, in order to determine, whether it should subject them to praise or censure.
It was determined . . . that the Fair Sex deserved praise rather than censure, for their interference in Elections.'
The World

1373. September 11, 1788 Coachmakers Hall
'Has the conduct of MR. FOX, in the part he has taken relative to the late Westminster Election, reflected honour or disgrace upon him as a British Senator?
In answer to the Card of the Lady, who says "she feels herself peculiarly interested in the above question as a female canvasser for Lord John Townshend" the Managers respectfully inform her, that the gallery has a commanding view over every part of the Assembly Room.'
The Question was decided, 'by a small majority' in the negative.
Morning Chronicle September 10

1374. September 15, 1788 Capel Court Debating Society
'Which is the most dangerous Member of Society, a Quack Doctor, a trading Justice, or a Methodist Teacher?
Most of the Speakers, however, seemed rather too pointed to reprobate the Conduct of the Methodist Preacher.'
Daily Advertiser September 20

1375. September 17, 1788 Westminster School of Eloquence
'Is the Virtue of the Fair Sex most in Danger, from the Influence of Love, Vanity or Avarice?'
It was determined 'that Vanity more frequently contributes to Female Ruin, than either Love or Avarice'.
The World

231

1376. September 18, 1788 Coachmakers Hall
'Is it possible for a Lady who has lost the Husband that was the object of her first Love, to entertain as strong an affection for the second as the first?

As a number of ladies constantly honour this Society with their presence, the managers are happy in compliance with their requests, to introduce occasionally, such questions as more immediately interest the female heart. At the same time they embrace the hope that by a judicious treatment of these questions much rational entertainment will be produced, and the audience inspired with a right sense of social virtues–
"And Marriage be no more the jest of fools"
Audience voted a second love could not be as strong.'
Times/Gazetteer September 17

1377. September 22, 1788 Capel Court Debating Society
'Which is the most dangerous Member of Society, a Quack Doctor, a trading Justice, or a Methodist Preacher?'
Daily Advertiser September 20

1378. September 24, 1788 Westminster School of Eloquence, Panton street Haymarket
'Which is the greatest Object of Pity, the Man who is deceived by the Lady he loves, or he who is reduced to poverty by the treachery of a false Friend, or the Debtor deprived of his liberty by a merciless Creditor?'
The audience decided that the debtor was most to be pitied.
The World

1379. September 25, 1788 Coachmakers Hall
'Can an Advocate for the Slave Trade be justly deemed a real Friend to the Constitutional Liberties of this Country?
As the Exercise of Reason is the distinguishing characteristic of Man from the Brute Creation, so it is the duty of Rational Beings to lend an attentive ear to those who complain of "Man's Cruelty to Man". – In this Inquiry the Philosopher, the Orator and Politician have a theme on which their abilities may be honourably employed. It is to be hoped that gentlemen will speak with freedom, remembering that the invariable object of this Institution, is to cherish Genius, enlarge the Understanding, and
"To spread the Truth from Pole to Pole"
Question answered in the negative.'
The World

1380. September 29, 1788 Capel Court Debating Society
'Is it not a Duty incumbent on all Mankind to enter into the State of Wedlock?
The Importance of the above Subject does not cynically preclude the Sallies of Wit or Humour; elegant and forcible Reasoning, Jollity and Mirth, are equally deducible upon it. In short, its engaging Wit, as

the handmaid to Virtue, inclined the Managers to give it that early Investigation.'
Daily Advertiser September 27

1381. October 1, 1788 Westminster School of Eloquence, Panton Street, Haymarket
'Is it possible for a Lady who has lost the Husband that was the object of her first Love, to entertain as strong an affection for the second as the first?
Several Ladies of great respectability have heard that the above question was debated at Coachmaker's Hall, being prevented from indulging their inclinations to be present at the Debate, solicited the Managers of this Institution to introduce it for public discussion.'
It was determined 'that the first impressions of Love were stronger'.
The World

1382. October 2, 1788 Coachmakers Hall
'But every woman is at heart a Rake'
'Whether the above Sentiment of Mr. Pope's ought to be considered as a compliment to, or censure of the Female Sex?
Various are the opinions of the true meaning of the celebrated Poet, from whose works the above remarkable lines are selected; and as the moral character of the female sex is of the greatest importance, not only to their own happiness and honour, but to society at large, the above question will doubtless be considered by the public to merit a fair and free discussion.'
It was decided that Pope meant to censure the fair sex.
Times/Gazetteer October 1

1383. October 6, 1788 Capel Court Debates
'Whether a Lady, entertaining no tender Affection for a Lover (who attempted an Act of Suicide on her Refusal) would be justifiable in marrying him?
To make the Woes of others our own is the Duty of every intelligent Being. To determine the Line of Conduct to be pursued in such a critical Situation is an Employment worthy the Man of Sense and the Female of Susceptibility. As the Fair Sex are undoubtedly the most competent to investigate a Subject of this Nature, the Managers have prevailed with the Lady, to whose Exertions this Institution owes much of its Popularity to begin and conclude the Debate, a Debate which must interest every sympathetic feeling to bestow a Sigh on the Fate of an Hackman, a Werter, or an Elliott.'
Daily Advertiser October 4

1384. October 7, 1788 Daily Advertiser
'Religious Discourse. . . The Subject for this Week is "How are we to understand the Doctrine of the blessed Millennium, will it be before the general Conflagration, or upon the System of Dr. Burnet and others in the new Heavens and the new Earth?" A full description of this

scriptural, rational and highly profitable Entertainment, containing the Rules. . . To the discerning and religious Part of Mankind it can be no unpleasing Intelligence that a Society is forming of liberal, learned and sensible Christians, whose sole view is to glorify God, disseminate divine Knowledge, and reconcile those seeming Differences among the Parties. This being their plan, they do not permit any Atheist, Deist, nor Socinian, nor any Wit disposed to ridicule Internal Religion and Christian Experience to confer among them, lest a greater Crop of Errors than of Bible Truths should be reaped in their Association. The long complained evil tendency of religious debating Societies being thus remedied, we hope our Conference will be of real utility. Ladies and Gentlemen having any intention to become Members will apply soon, as the Number is limited to 72.' Strangers, however, will be admitted.

1385. October 8, 1788 Westminster School of Eloquence
'Is it a duty incumbent on Children always to consult their Parents previous to Marriage?'
It was determined that 'children ought at all times to consult their Parents previous to Marriage.'
The World

1386. October 9, 1788 Coachmakers Hall
'Is the encrease of bankruptcies more to be imputed to luxury and extravagance, or to the decline of trade?'
Audience thought due more to luxury and extravagance.
Morning Chronicle October 16

1387. October 13, 1788 Capel Court Debates
'Is the Practice of foretelling future Events (commonly called Fortune-Telling) founded on Truth, or authorized by Religion?
At the desire of several Professors of the Art, who have promised to vindicate and explain its Principles' the above Question is proposed. 'If we may venture to predict on this Subject, we perceive much Mirth and Entertainment in a Conjunction; Wit will be the Lord of the Ascendant; Reason may afford a benign Aspect, and several Luminaries of the first Magnitude will rise to the Occasion.'
Daily Advertiser October 11

1388. October 13, 1788 A CARD To the Conductors of the Westminster Forum
'Several Friends to rational Entertainment having called at Spring Gardens to know when this institution would open for the season, were informed that it is to be removed to the Great Room (late Patterson's) King-Street, Covent-Garden, and to be opened for public debate next Wednesday Evening. This is certainly a more central part of the city of Westminster, and consequently an accommodation to many who make this Society their favourite place of amusement. They beg to hint also, that as the melancholy encrease of female prostitution, must interest the feelings of every compassionate bosom, a question, enquiring into

the cause of so much beauty being consigned to infamy and public contamination, would be a subject on which the orator might speak with laudable animation, as it involves an evil, which it is the duty and interest of every community to attempt to remedy, in order to which, it is necessary to explore the cause from whence it proceeds.'
The World

1389. October 15, 1788 Westminster Forum for Free Debate (Removed from Spring Gardens, Charing Cross, to the Great Room, King-street, Covent Garden)
'Is the Prevalence of Female Prostitution more to be imputed to the Treachery and Falsehood of the Male Sex; or to the Misconduct of Parents, in giving their Daughters an improper Education?
Encouraged by the flattering approbation of numerous respectable friends, the Conductors are determined to spare no pains to render this Institution the most rational and instructive of any that can engage the attention of an enlightened public. Care will be taken to preserve the strictest order; and every Gentleman desirous of cultivating the art of Public Speaking, may rest assured of meeting in this Society with the most liberal support. The subjects for debate will be miscellaneous; but none will be admitted, which have not a probable tendency to inspire a love of our country; to represent Virtue in the most engaging dress, and Vice in the most odious colours; to delight while they reform; eradicate pernicious errors, and warm the heart with benevolence.'
Morning Post

1390. October 15, 1788 Westminster School of Eloquence
'Do Mankind in general exercise their Fancy or Judgment most, in the Choice of a Wife?
The Managers beg leave to inform the Public, that the disturbance which took place last Wednesday Evening, was intirely owing to the malevolence and illiberality of an individual, who will never in future be permitted to have any connexion with any Society to which they belong.'
It was decided 'that Mankind consult their judgment rather than their fancy, in choice of a Wife'.
The World

1391. October 16, 1788 Coachmakers Hall
'Whether the great number of Old Maids may be mostly imputed to a disappointment in love, to the treachery of the male sex, or to any peculiarity in their own temper and disposition?
The Lady who favoured the Managers with the above question has informed them she belongs to a Club of female literatae, some of the Members of which constantly attend Coachmakers Hall on all questions of a moral, sentimental or philosophical nature. She adds, that as the banishment of prejudice, and the improvement of the mind, are the sole objects of the sisterhood, they are desirous of receiving some

information on the above question, being one which for some time has engaged their attention.'
The audience attributed the generality of old maids to a disappointment in Love.
Morning Chronicle October 16/Daily Advertiser October 23

1392. October 20, 1788 Capel Court Debates
'Can a Man who really loves a Female deliberately seduce her?
Were the Ladies convinced of this important Truth, That the Seducer cannot really love, "So many of the Sex would not in vain, of broken Vows, and faithless Men complain." The philanthropist, the Moralist, and the Man of Genius will on this Subject have the happy Opportunity of affixing an indelible Impression of Virtue on the female Mind, which Accident can never impair, nor Artifice obliterate.'
Daily Advertiser October 18

1393. October 21, 1788 Christian Areopagus
'Whether the Rev. Mr. Huntington in preaching the rigid Decrees of Election, or the Rev. Mr. Winchester in insisting on the Doctrine of Universal Salvation, approaches nearer the true Character of a Gospel Minister?
The above Question will undergo a fair and free Debate. . . The Doctrines of these popular Preachers being considered by their respective Followers as unanswerable, though totally contradictory to each other, several Gentlemen who profess themselves sincere Enquirers after Truth have requested the Managers to bring forward the Question, it being a subject in which every Christian is immediately concerned.'
Daily Advertiser October 20

1394. October 22, 1788 Christian Conference
'What are we to think of particular and universal Redemption, which is most scriptural and rational, or are both so?'
Daily Advertiser October 21

1395. October 22, 1788 Westminster Forum
'Were a General Election to take place, would the Independent Electors of Westminster prove themselves Friends to the Constitutional Liberties of this Country, by re-electing Mr. FOX, and rejecting LORD HOOD?
An eminent Political Character, a Patron of Liberty, and of this Institution, is the author of the above Question. Its importance must unquestionably be felt. Mr. Fox is charged by many with having, in several instances, and particularly in the late Westminster Election, made an attack on the essence of the Constitution, of which he has professed himself the zealous Guardian; while on the other hand his conduct is said by others to entitle him to live in the warmest applause of every Friend to Freedom and Britain.'
The World

1396. October 22, 1788 Westminster School of Eloquence
'Is it justifiable for a Man to fight a Duel with the Seducer of his Daughter, or Sister, or in vindication of the honour of the Lady he loves?'
The World

1397. October 23, 1788 Coachmakers hall
'Does it not reflect Disgrace upon a People who boast of being free to preclude any of their Fellow Subjects from an equal Participation of Liberty on Account of their religious Principles?
The celebrated Dr. Price has maintained, that all Civil Establishments of Religion ought to be considered as "Boundaries placed by human Folly to human Investigation"; and that no free Country can without the Imputation of Injustice deprive a Subject of any part of his Liberty on Account of his religious Sentiments. Several other Learned Divines and Politicians having on the contrary contended, that the Roman Catholicks and some other Sectaries cannot, consistently with the Safety of a free State, be allowed an equal Share of Liberty with others.'
Daily Advertiser

1398. October 27, 1788 Free Debate, Capel Court
'Which is the greater Virtue, Sincerity in Friendship or Constancy in Love?
Impressed with a grateful Sense of that publick Patronage with which the Capel Court Debates have been honoured, the Conductors pledge themselves to select such Questions as join publick Utility and moral Improvement to rational Delight; no Indulgence will be withheld from young Gentlemen who wish to acquire the Habit of publick Speaking, and every Effort will be . . . to render the Utility of the Society equal to it Popularity.'
Times October 25

1399. October 28, 1788 Christian Areopagus
'Whether the Rev. Mr. Huntington in preaching the rigid Decrees of Election, or the Rev. Mr. Winchester in insisting on the Doctrine of Universal Salvation, approaches nearer the true Character of a Gospel Minister?'
Daily Advertiser October 27

1400. October 29, 1788 Christian Conference
'What are we to think of particular and universal Redemption, which is most scriptural and rational, or are both so?'
Daily Advertiser October 28

1401. October 29, 1788 Times
'It is a disgrace to the modesty of the sex, to see a woman debating a question among a parcel of idle apprentice boys, at a Sixpenny Assemblage, in so well regulated a city as that of London. The Lord Mayor should look to this matter, which certainly ought not to have permission, and thus under his very eye set his authority at defiance. The

debating ladies would be much better employed at their needle and thread, a good sempstress being a more amiable character than a female orator. A dissertation on *Mantua-Making*, if the ladies are to speak in public, must be of greater benefit than a dispute about Sincerity in Friendship, Constancy in Love – *Charlotte's* ideal grief, *Werter's* romancing tomb – *Albert's* mock matrimony.

1402. October 29, 1788 Westminster Forum
'Were a General Election to take place, would the Independent Electors of Westminster prove themselves Friends to the Constitutional Liberties of this Country, by re-electing Mr. FOX, and rejecting LORD HOOD?
An eminent Political Character, a Patron of Liberty, and of this Institution, is the author of the above Question. Its importance must unquestionably be felt. Mr. Fox is charged by many with having, in several instances, and particularly in the late Westminster Election, made an attack on the essence of the Constitution, of which he has professed himself the zealous Guardian; while on the other hand his conduct is said by others to entitle him to live in the warmest applause of every Friend to Freedom and Britain.'
The World

1403. October 29, 1788 Westminster School of Eloquence
'Is it justifiable for a Man to fight a Duel with the Seducer of his Daughter, or Sister, or in vindication of the honour of the Lady he loves?'
Decided that a man was justified in fighting such a duel.
The World

1404. October 30, 1788 Coachmakers Hall
'Does it not reflect Disgrace upon a People who boast of being free to preclude any of their Fellow Subjects from an equal Participation of Liberty on Account of their religious Sentiments?
The Mind of Man cannot be better employed than in the Discovery of Truth; free Debate tends to this noble Purpose, and is one of the Privileges of the British Nation.'
Daily Advertiser October 29

1405. November 3, 1788 Capel Court Debates
'Which is the greater Virtue, Sincerity in Friendship or Constancy in Love?'
Daily Advertiser November 1

1406. November 4, 1788 Christian Areopagus, Kings Arms Tavern, Grafton Street Soho
'Whether the Rev. Mr. Huntington in preaching the rigid Decrees of Election, or the Rev. Mr. Winchester in insisting on the Doctrine of Universal Salvation, approaches nearer the true Character of a Gospel Ministry?'

Debate terminated in favour of Mr. Huntington.
Daily Advertiser November 3

1407. November 5, 1788 Westminster Forum for Free Debate, King Street Covent Garden
'Does the Conduct of the Administration or the Opposition approach nearer to Revolutionary Principles?'
Decision favoured Administration.
Morning Post November 11

1408. November 5, 1788 Christian Conference, Blossom Street Chapel, Norton Falgate
'Is it possible to reconcile our Calvinist and Arminian Brethren? or may Election and the Perseverance of the Saints be made scripturally and reasonably to harmonize with the freedom of the Will and general Redemption?'
Admission in the Body of the chapel 6d. Outside the bars 2d.
Daily Advertiser November 4

1409. November 5, 1788 Westminster School of Eloquence
'Are we more indebted for our Liberties to the Revolution or to the Barons for obtaining Magna Carta?'
More indebted for our liberties to the Revolution.
Daily Advertiser November 11

1410. November 6, 1788 Coachmakers Hall
'Does it not reflect Disgrace upon a People who boast of being free to preclude any of their Fellow Subjects from an equal Participation of Liberty on Account of their Religious Sentiments?'
Audience decided 'against the policy of granting every denomination of Christian an equal participation of Civil Liberty'.
Daily Advertiser November 5/The World

1411. November 10, 1788 Capel Court Debates
'Is Mr. Pope's Assertion true, That Every Woman is at Heart a Rake? It is the Aim of the Conductors of these Debates to present the Publick with original Questions; but at the Solicitation of many Ladies, who wished to hear one of their own Sex defend them against the Sarcasm of the above celebrated Writer, they have dispensed with the Observance of their usual Custom.'
Daily Advertiser November 8

1412. November 11, 1788 Christian Areopagus
'Does Reason or Revelation countenance a Belief in the Appearance of Ghosts and Apparitions?'
Daily Advertiser November 10

1413. November 12, 1788 Christian Conference

'Is it possible to reconcile our Calvinist and Arminian Brethren, or may Election and the Perseverance of the Saints be made scripturally and reasonably to harmonize with the Freedom of the Will and universal Redemption?'
Daily Advertiser November 11

1414. November 12, 1788 Westminster Forum
SEDUCTION – ROWE'S FAIR PENITENT
'I swear I could not see the lovely false betrayer
Kneel at my feet, and sigh to be forgiven,
But my relenting heart would pardon all,
And quite forget 'twas he that had undone me.'

'Are the above lines expressive of the real feelings of the Female Heart under the misfortune of Seduction?
This question was received from a lady no less celebrated for her exalted rank, than her splendid abilities and distinguished patriotism.'
Morning Post November 11

1415. November 12, 1788 Westminster School of Eloquence
'Which is the greater Cause of Matrimonial Infelicity, the Neglect of Dress and Behaviour in the Wife, or the Want of Respect and Attention in the Husband?'
Daily Advertiser November 11

1416. November 13, 1788 Coachmakers Hall
'Is it not a Principal Cause of Conjugal Unhappiness that Gentlemen pay more Respect to the Ladies when in Courtship than after Marriage? Whatever has a tendency to explore the sources of matrimonial infelicity must be of concern to the public in general. To a cause of conjugal misery, the late death of an amiable young Lady has been attributed, to whom the words of an elegant Poet are justly applicable:

Soft as the Balm the gentle gale distills,
Sweet as the fragrance of the new mown Hills,
Her opening Mind a thousand charms reveal'd,
Proof of those thousand that were still conceal'd.'

Question determined in the negative.
The World

1417. November 17, 1788 Times
'To the Editor of the TIMES
Sir,
The following question being advertised in to-day's Paper, to be debated to-morrow evening in Capel-Court, Bartholomew Lane, I have suggested a few thoughts upon it, which, if you think worthy notice, you will please to insert, "Which is the most calculated to promote licentiousness, the desperate doctrine of predestination, propagated by the Calvinistic Methodists; the sale of indulgencies in the Church of

240

Rome; or the system of universal salvation, maintained by the Rev. Mr. Winchester?"

I consider the question as founded on three different principles, calculated to establish an assurance of future happiness, or certain eventual fate; but as they operate differently, our present enquiry is, which has the greatest tendency to promote licentiousness. Admitting mankind to be equally *well informed*, I can perceive no difference in the *consequences* of the positions; for the *ultimatum* of each, being irrevocably fixed, gives the fullest latitude to the gratification of vicious propensities: but to view their operations on the minds of the *ignorant*, who are seldom disposed to *think*; *that*, which strikes them in the most plain, easy, and forcible manner, will certainly have the greatest influence. As being told therefore, in plain terms, they shall be *saved*, is evidently calculated to make the strongest impression: the doctrine of "*general salvation*", appears to be the most fertile soil for *licentiousness*.

I cannot help expressing my concern to find clergymen interesting themselves in the disquisition of religious topics, in these *debating societies*, for of all the dangerous systems that may be adopted, none can be more truly calculated to promote *licentiousness* and *irreligion*.

R.'

1418. November 17, 1788 Capel Court Debates
'Which is most calculated to promote Licentiousness, the desperate Doctrine of Predestination, propagated by the Calvinistic Methodists, the sale of Indulgencies in the Church of Rome, or the System of Universal Salvation maintained by the Rev. Mr. Winchester?
To ascertain the truth or fallacy of the novel Doctrine of the above popular Preacher is an Office which must deeply interest every Believer in the Christian Religion. The Pious and well-disposed of all Persuasions are hereby invited to decide upon a Subject the most awfully important ever submitted to public consideration.'
Daily Advertiser November 15

1419. November 18, 1788 Christian Areopagus
'Do Reason or Revelation countenance a Belief in the Appearance of Ghosts and Apparitions?'
Daily Advertiser November 17

1420. November 19, 1788 Westminster School of Eloquence
'Is not the present State of this Country an incontestible Proof that Mr. Pitt better deserves the Support and Confidence of the People than any of his Competitors or Predecessors in Office?'
Daily Advertiser November 18

1421. November 19, 1788 Westminster Forum
'Would it not reflect honour on the Bench of Bishops, to use their efforts for the suppression of Field Preaching, and limit the number of Methodistical Chapels?

241

The Managers agree with the learned proposer . . . that a public investigation of subjects like these, may tend to tear in pieces the mask of hypocrisy; elucidate truths the most important; and display true Religion in its nature, grandeur and Divine Majesty.'
The World

1422. November 20, 1788 Coachmakers Hall
'Which is the most predominant in the mind of man, the Love of Life, the Love of Liberty, or the Love of the Fair Sex?'
Morning Chronicle November 27

1423. November 24, 1788 Capel Court Society
'Which is most calculated to promote Licentiousness, the desperate Doctrine of Predestination, propagated by the Calvinistic Methodists, the sale of Indulgencies in the Church of Rome, or the System of Universal Salvation maintained by the Rev. Mr. Winchester?'
Daily Advertiser November 22

1424. November 25, 1788 Christian Areopagus, Great Room, King's Arms Tavern, Grafton Street, Soho
'Whether the Rev. Mr. Lindsey, and the other Ministers who deny the Divinity of Christ, have not departed more from genuine Christianity than either the Roman Catholicks or Antinomians?'
Daily Advertiser November 17

1425. November 26, 1788 Christian Conference
'Amongst the different sects of Christians which has most truth and least errors?'
Daily Advertiser November 25

1426. November 27, 1788 Coachmakers Hall
'Which is the most predominant in the mind of man, the Love of Life, the Love of Liberty, or the Love of the Fair Sex?'
Audience determined in favour of the love of the fair sex.
Morning Chronicle November 27

1427. November 27, 1788 Times
'The *Debating Societies* will shortly undergo the same interdiction as the Sunday sacred music six-penny meetings – to the great grief or idle apprentices and industrious pickpockets – a new room is opened, contrary to an express act of Parliament, near Soho Square, for disputing on religion, and inculcating atheistical principles, against the true establishment of christianity. This practice it is trusted will be immediately stopped, and the hearers as well as the speakers, committed by the Magistrates in that division of Westminster. Indeed the Ecclesiastical Court should take up this matter, as religion is now the question at most of these societies of debate.'

1428. November 28, 1788 Capel Court Society

'Would a Plurality of Wives, as allowed by the Rev. Mr. Madan in his *Thelyphtora*, be more productive of Confusion or real Advantage to Society?'
Daily Advertiser November 22

1429. November 28, 1788 Times
'We must again notice, that, of all matters, religion is a subject which should not be made the sport of idle prentice boys and scripture madmen in a debating society. The Magistrates are therefore reminded, it is their duty to put a total stop to those nuisances by a public notice, interdicting such idle assemblages.'

1430. December 1, 1788 Capel Court Society
'Was not Charlotte censurable for admitting the Visits of Werter after she was the Wife of Albert?'
Daily Advertiser November 22

1431. December 2, 1788 Christian Areopagus
'Whether the Rev. Mr. Lindsey, and the other Ministers who deny the Divinity of Christ, have not departed more from genuine Christianity than either the Roman Catholicks or Antinomians?'
Daily Advertiser

1432. December 3, 1788 Christian Conference
'If none can be Saved without the Knowledge of the Truth, what will become of those who never heard of the Truth?'
Daily Advertiser December 2

1433. December 3, 1788 Westminster Forum, King Street Covent Garden
'Should any event displace the present Administration, and fix the leaders of opposition in the seat of power, would it be advantageous or injurious to the welfare of this country?
Were the managers permitted publicly to announce the name of the author of this question (who is expected to speak on it), public curiosity would indeed be highly stimulated. They, however, should hold themselves inexcusable not to throw out some hint, that the lovers of debate may not, through a want of information be disappointed of hearing perhaps one of the first orations ever expected in a society of this nature.'
Morning Post.

1434. December 4, 1788 Coachmakers Hall
'Are the Fair Sex capable of acquiring as much Wisdom and Knowledge as the Male?
As it is the object of this Society to mingle entertainment with mental improvement, and to draw the minds of both sexes from fashionable follies and pernicious pleasures to the salutary pursuit of wisdom and the chaste delights of virtue. Questions are proposed to suit the various

243

tastes of the multitude, in order that they may be induced by degrees, to prefer, and at length reap the benefits of a rational place of amusement.' The audience decided that the female sex were not as capable of acquiring so much wisdom and knowledge as the male.
Morning Chronicle December 3

1435. December 8, 1788 Capel Court Society
'Is it not a Violation of the boasted Liberties of Great Britain to tolerate Slaving in any part of her Dominions?'
Advertisement talks of 'the Arcana of this inhuman Traffick'.
Daily Advertiser December 6

1436. December 8, 1788 Coachmakers Hall
'Whether the Doctrine maintained by Mr. Fox in the House of Commons, respecting the Regency, justified Mr. Pitt in charging him with speaking little less than Treason against the Constitution of this Country?
In the Decision of this Question, every Man who has a Regard for the Constitution, to which he owes the Privileges of a Briton, must feel himself intimately concerned. A fair and free Debate upon Subjects which involve the dearest Rights of a free People cannot be held in a Place more eligible than a popular Institution, situated in the Heart of the Capital, in the Presence of an Assembly of Citizens, whose Judgment, and whose Interest upon the Event of every political Discussion, plead the Propriety of introducing the above Question at the Present important Crisis.'
Daily Advertiser

1437. December 10, 1788 Christian Conference
'What is the true Characteristick of a Christian?
Admission Inside the Bar 6d. where each Gentleman may introduce a Wife, Daughter, or Sister gratis.'
Daily Advertiser December 9

1438. December 10, 1788 Westminster Forum, Removed from Spring Gardens to King Street, Covent Garden
'Which would have the greater tendency to maintain the honour and advantage of this Country – a conjunct, or individual Regency?'
Morning Post

1439. December 11, 1788 Coachmakers Hall
'Whether the great Extent and Grandeur of the Metropolis is not a Proof of the Increase of Luxury, and injurious to the national Prosperity?
A Petition has been presented to the Managers by a Number of Poor but intelligent Peasants, complaining of the Injury to Agriculture by the Number of new Buildings about every Part of this Capital, and praying that the above Question may be publickly debated. . . As some of the brightest Ornaments of the Law and the Senate have acknow-

ledged their Obligations to this popular Institution, many Gentlemen of distinguished Rank and Abilities are expected to attend on this Occasion.'

The majority declared 'that the increase of the Metropolis was not injurious to national prosperity'.

Times December 10/The World December 12

1440. December 15, 1788 Capel Court Debates

'Which manifested himself the true Friend of the Constitution, Mr. Fox in asserting, That the Prince of Wales has a positive Claim to the Executive Power, as a Regent; or Mr. Pitt in maintaining, That his Royal Highness possesses no more Right to that Office than any other Subject?'

Daily Advertiser December 13

1441. December 17, 1788 Westminster Forum

'Which is more constitutional, the assertion of Mr. Fox, The Prince of Wales has the same right to the exercise of regal power as if his Majesty were really dead; or that of Mr. Pitt – His Royal Highness has no more right to such power than any subject within the realm?

Free Debate is one of the valuable privileges of the British constitution. To collect the public opinion upon subjects of the last importance, is the duty of those who conduct societies of this nature, the Managers have, therefore, in this crisis, submitted the above enquiry to the consideration of that Public, whose dearest interests are connected with its discussion.'

Morning Post

1442. December 18, 1788 Coachmakers Hall

'Whether the Doctrine maintained by Mr. Fox in the House of Commons, respecting the Regency, justified Mr. Pitt in charging him with speaking little less than Treason against the Constitution of this Country?'

Daily Advertiser December 17

1443. December 22, 1788 Capel Court Debates

'Should the Prince of Wales be appointed Regent, would his Royal Highness more essentially promote the Interests of this Nation by retaining Mr. Pitt as Prime Minister, or dismissing him from the Public Service?'

Daily Advertiser December 20

1444. December 23, 1788 Coachmakers Hall

'Whether the Doctrine maintained by Mr. Fox in the House of Commons, respecting the Regency, justified Mr. Pitt in charging him with little less than Treason to the Constitution of this Country?'

Question determined in favour of Mr. Pitt.

Daily Advertiser

1445. December 24, 1788 Westminster Forum
'In the present critical situation of affairs, would Mr. Pitt, by forming
a junction with Mr. Fox, attach to his character any of that particular
odium which the enemies of Mr. Fox attribute to him for his coalition
with Lord North?
From the well-known powers of humour possessed by some gentlemen
who have promised to attend the debate, much keen satire and ironical
remarks may be expected; at the same time the subject by no means
precludes the Patriot, the Orator, and the Man of Genius from displaying the advantages that may probably result to this country from
so conciliatory a measure.'
Morning Post

1446. December 29, 1788 Capel Court Debates
'Is it not an Instance of great Partiality, inconsistency, and Injustice, in
the Free Masons, to exclude the Fair Sex from a Knowledge of their
Secret?'
Question decided in favour of Free Masonry.
Daily Advertiser December 27

1447. December 31, 1788 Westminster Forum
'Which is the wiser Man – he who marries, or he who remains single?
The alarming situation of public affairs having lately engrossed the
attention of this Society, the Managers trust any apology for deferring
questions of a more entertaining, though less important nature, is altogether unnecessary.'
Morning Post

1448. January 1, 1789 Coachmakers Hall
'Is the Virtue of the Fair Sex most in Danger from the Influence of a
bad Education, their natural Vanity, or from the extreme Sensibility of
the Female Heart?'
The World

1449. January 5, 1789 Capel Court Debates
'Which is the true Characteristick of a Lady's Man, Wit, Courage or
Politeness?'
Daily Advertiser January 3

1450. January 7, 1789 Westminster Forum
DUELLING – DEATH OF COL. ROPER
'Does not the late fatal Event, and other Evils resulting from DUEL-
LING, demand the Interposition of the Legislature to abolish the
Practice?
Duelling is one of those Evils which arise from a Refinement of Man-
ners. To investigate that fatal Rashness, which, through a mistaken
Principle of Honour, has robbed Society of some of its brightest Orna-

ments, is an Employment which must display the Abilities of the Gentlemen who speak in the Westminster Forum to great Advantage.'
Morning Post

1451. January 8, 1789 Coachmakers Hall
'Ought the Regent, who shall be appointed to govern during the Incapacity of his Majesty, be invested with full or limited Powers?
The Conductors of this Institution have been informed by many of Mr. Fox's Friends, that notwithstanding the late Resolutions of the City of London, in favour of the Minister's late Conduct, they have the strongest Reason to believe that the Majority of the Citizens are inimical to the Measures he has adopted respecting the Regency; they are therefore desirous that this interesting Subject should undergo a fair and free Debate, and that the real Sense of the Publick be collected upon it.'
A considerable majority were in favour of limiting the powers of the Regent.
Daily Advertiser January 7

1452. January 12, 1789 Capel Court Debates
'Whether the Doctrines taught by the present Mr. Wesley, or the late Mr. Whitfield, Messr. Romaine, Rowland Hill, &c. are more agreeable with the true principles of the Christian Religion?'
Notes that the popularity of the society due to its discussion of religious questions.
Daily Advertiser January 10

1453. January 14, 1789 Westminster Forum
'Which is the most distressing situation, a shipwrecked mariner, a condemned Criminal, or a seduced female, abandoned by her Lover?
Debating Societies, when properly conducted, have been esteemed by the wise and intelligent as School of Morality. It is the aim of the Managers of the Westminster Forum to select Questions which, while they afford an opportunity to display the talents of the orator, affix some important moral truths in the human mind.'
Morning Post

1454. January 15, 1789 Coachmakers Hall
'Is the Passion of Love productive of more Happiness or Misery to its Possessors?
Love is a Passion whose effects have puzzled the wisest Philosophers; by some it has been called the Spring from whence Virtue is often conveyed into resisting Nature; that it renders the Coward brave; and melts the hardiest Soul into a sense of Social Duty.'
Daily Advertiser January 14

1455. January 19, 1789 Capel Court Debates
'Which was more culpable in eating the forbidden Fruit, Adam or Eve?'
It was deemed that Eve was more culpable than Adam.
Daily Advertiser January 17

1456. January 21, 1789 Westminster Forum
'Which is the most powerful obligation of nature, Parental Affection, Filial Duty, or Conjugal Love?'
Morning Post

1457. January 22, 1789 Coachmakers Hall
'Should the Regent dismiss Mr. Pitt from Administration, would he act consistently with his Duty, and the general Interest of this Country? It is hoped that every Citizen will publickly answer this question in the Negative.'
Daily Advertiser January 21

1458. January 26, 1789 Capel Court Debates
'Which will most probably recommend a Lady to a Husband, Beauty, Riches or Understanding?
Female Understanding was deemed to be the most powerful Recommendation to a Husband.'
Daily Advertiser January 24

1459. January 28, 1789 Westminster Forum
'This Evening, the Westminster Forum will resolve itself into a Committee of the Whole House, on
THE STATE OF THE NATION
It is the great, the invaluable Blessing of the British Constitution, that Englishmen enjoy the privileges to investigate all public Transactions. The present crisis of affairs commands universal attention. The actions of past Administrations – the present effects of their measures – the alarming situation of the nation – the danger or advantages which may probably result to the country, from the expected change in Administration – will constitute the theme of this Debate.
The Patriot, the Orator, and the Political Humourist, have each a wide field, in which they may display their respective talents.
The House on the last Evening had a numerous attendance, when JOHN BULL, Representative of the whole British Nation, was called to the Chair, and the Society resolved itself into a Committee of the whole House.'
Morning Post

1460. January 29, 1789 Coachmakers Hall
'Whether mankind respecting the marriage state is directed by free will, or under a presiding and uncontroulable *destiny*?
It is said, this question suggested itself to a Lady, while she was perusing the celebrated Doctor Priestly's system of unavoidable necessity.'
Times January 28

1461. February 2, 1789 City Debates
'Is not that Custom cruel and unjust, which forbids a Female to make the first advances in Courtship?'
Daily Advertiser January 31

1462. February 4, 1789 Westminster Forum
STATE OF THE NATION
'It is requested, that those Gentlemen who support Administration, particularly those who intend to speak, will take their seats on the Treasury Bench, on the right, and the Opposition on the left side of the Chairman.'
Morning Post

1463. February 5, 1789 Coachmakers Hall
'Is the admired Constitution of this country more in danger from encroachments of the executive power, or from a faction in the House of Commons?'
Times February 4

1464. February 9, 1789 City Debates
'Is the Vanity of the Women, or the Depravity of the Men, the greater Cause of Female Ruin?
This Question was taken from a Memorandum written by the late unfortunate Dr. Dodd in a blank leaf of his Magdalen Book.'
Daily Advertiser February 7

1465. February 11, 1789 Westminster Forum
THE STATE OF THE NATION
Morning Post

1466. February 12, 1789 Coachmakers Hall
'Is the admired Constitution of this Country more in danger from the encroachments of the executive Power, or a Faction in the House of Commons? and then, Which is more censurable, the Foppery of the Men, or the Boldness of the Women?
To inform the judgment – correct the taste – remove pernicious prejudices – and lead the enquiring mind to the love of Truth, and the practice of Virtue, is the principle and natural tendency of this institution.'
Times

1467. February 16, 1789 City Debates
'Are Dreams the effect of a roving Imagination, or the certain Indicators of future Events?
The Rev. Caleb Evans of Bristol, having mentioned in his Sermon an extraordinary Circumstance of a Lady's having dreamt she was dancing, died, and sunk into a Place of Torment (who upon going that evening to a Ball, actually died, as she had dreamt, induced the Managers to adopt the [above] Question. . .
A Letter from the Rev. Mr. Evans was . . . publickly read in this Society by his son.'
Daily Advertiser February 14

1468. February 18, 1789 Westminster Forum
'Mr. ROLLE'S motion on the rumoured Marriage of a certain GREAT PERSONAGE
This Evening this Society will be resolved into a Committee of the Whole House on
THE STATE OF THE NATION
When the following Resolutions will be discussed:
Resolution 1st. That as the Regent is to be considered as the representative of Majesty, all restrictions on his authority which the necessity of the case do not absolutely require, are indecent and improper.
Resolution 2nd. That considering the effectual precautions taken by our Ancestors to preserve the Constitution and religious Establishment of this Country, the revival of the Topic of a rumoured Marriage between the Prince of Wales, and a certain Personage, at this Juncture, can only tend to inflame the minds of the people, disseminate suspicion, and consequently demands the loudest censure from ever true friend to the interests of this country.'
Morning Post

1469. February 19, 1789 Coachmakers Hall
'Is it justifiable for a Lady to marry the man she loves, in opposition to the will of her Parents or Guardians?'
Question sent in by 'a Celebrated Female, who has lately obtained a Divorce from her Husband, with whom she was induced to intermarry, in obedience to the commands of her parents'.
Morning Post

1470. February 23, 1789 City Debates
'Are Dreams the effect of a roving Imagination, or the certain Indicators of future Events?
Dreams were decided to be the Effects of a roving Imagination.'
Daily Advertiser February 21

1471. February 25, 1789 Westminster Forum
'Has not Mr. Pitt, by his resolute and successful endeavours to restore the Regal Power unimpaired into the hands of his Royal Master, merited the unlimited confidence of the Sovereign, and the universal applause of the people?
After a most excellent debate, the numbers were nearly equal, when a small majority appeared in favour of Administration: however, after most of the Members had paired off from the Treasury Bench, Tellers were demanded by the Opposition. This was resolutely withstood by the Speaker; but at the particular request of several popular Characters, the subject will be resumed. . .'
Morning Post

1472. February 26, 1789 Coachmakers Hall
'Does Suicide proceed more from a noble contempt of *death*, or a cowardly fear to encounter the ills of life?

250

The unfortunate affair that lately happened in Greenwich-Park, is at present a general subject of conversation among all ranks of people; – that a man should deliberately become his own murderer, and thereby arraign the disposer of all events, for having conferred on him the privilege of human existence, is no less surprising than shocking, to those who believe in a state of future rewards and punishment. – There are however, many who have dignified this horrid act, by giving to it the virtue of courage. This has induced a worthy Clergyman to propose for public discussion the . . . [above] question.'
Daily Advertiser February 25

1473. March 2, 1789 City Debates
'Which demands the greatest Portion of polished Genius, and powerful Eloquence, the Pulpit, the Senate or the Bar?'
Daily Advertiser February 28

1474. March 4, 1789 Westminster Forum
'Has not Mr. Pitt, by his resolute and successful endeavours to restore the Regal Power unimpaired into the hands of his Royal Master, merited the unlimited confidence of the Sovereign, and the universal applause of the people?'
Morning Post

1475. March 5, 1789 Coachmakers Hall
'Does Suicide proceed more from a noble contempt of death, or a cowardly fear to encounter the ills of life?
A worthy clergyman who was in company with the unfortunate French Gentleman a few days before he committed the horrid act of suicide' proposed the question.
It was determined 'that Suicide proceeds more from cowardice than courage'.
Times

1476. March 6, 1789 English Notables, Panton Street Haymarket
'Did the English Majority in the House of Commons, that voted the Restrictions in Mr. Pitt's Regency Bill – or the Irish Delegates, who addressed his Royal Highness to accept the Regency with unlimited powers – act more consistently with true Principles of Patriotism?
The above subject is of the highest national importance. This institution (opened for a few nights, under the patronage of several eminent political characters) will be sacred to such enquiries alone. The persons who may probably speak, being such as seldom honour debating societies with their presence, the Managers hope no one will attend who cannot preserve his temper, and treat Gentlemen with that degree of candour and liberality due to those who publicly deliver their opinions in support of the constitutional rights of their native country.'
Admission 6d. – Gallery 1s.
Morning Post

1477. March 6, 1789 Times
'The respectability of the debating society, well known under the appellation of the Forum, may, in fact, be imagined by the riot which took place there on their last night but one of debate; and by the harangue of one of the most notorious black-legs in London.'

1478. March 9, 1789 City Debates
'Ought the alarming Number of Suicides in this Country to be attributed to the Progress of Infidelity, Disappointment in the tender Passion, or any Peculiarity in our Soil and Climate?'
Daily Advertiser March 7

1479. March 12, 1789 Coachmakers Hall
'A CURE FOR A BAD HUSBAND
(Proposed by a Lady)
Would a Lady that is married to a tyrannical husband be more likely to promote her own happiness by a spirited opposition, or a patient submission to his temper and conduct?

A young Lady, on perusing the Trial of Lady Strathmore, observed to a polite company of both sexes, that the most effectual mode of securing a tolerable life with a bad husband, was to "oppose him with becoming spirit". This remark occasioning much difference of opinion, the above Question was immediately framed, and conveyed to the Managers of this Society, who, in compliance with the wishes of their Fair Correspondents, readily adopt it.'
Times

1480. March 13, 1789 Westminster Forum, King St, Covent Garden, but will move to Panton Street, Haymarket
'Did the English Majority in the House of Commons that voted the Restrictions in Mr. Pitt's Regency Bill – or the Irish Parliament, who commissioned the Delegates to address his Royal Highness to accept the Regency with unlimited powers – act more consistently with the true principles of Patriotism?
The House have determined, that the LADIES shall in future vote in this Assembly.'
Times, March 12

1481. March 16, 1789 City Debates
'Ought the alarming Number of Suicides in this Country to be attributed to the Progress of Infidelity, Disappointment in the tender Passion, or any Peculiarity in our Soil and Climate?'
Daily Advertiser March 14

1482. March 17, 1789 Westminster Forum
'Which is the noblest principle of the human mind, Love, Gratitude or Friendship?'
Morning Post March 16

1483. March 19, 1789 Coachmakers Hall
'Do the married Ladies of this Country receive too little or too much Indulgence from their Husbands?
A Lady lately returned from the Continent has published an excellent Pamphlet on the Subject of Divorces, in which she has asserted that "the exclusive Privileges and Indulgence which the English married Ladies receive from their Husbands may be considered as a principal Cause of the Number of matrimonial Suits that are constantly instituted in Doctors Commons." This extraordinary Observation from the Pen of a Female has induced several Ladies to propose the . . . [above] singular question.'
Daily Advertiser March 18

1484. March 20, 1789 Westminster Forum
'Did the conduct of certain Servants of the Sovereign (lately dismissed) indicate a disinterested Patriotism superior to private Obligations; or a time-serving Inclination to promote their own Interests?
– The dismissal of the Marquis of Lothian, Duke of Queensberry &c. now engrosses general conversation. – A great Political Character, the Author of this Question, must pardon our not prefacing this Advertisement with the Title he sent us, "Dismission of the Rats". – Illiberality shall never be adopted by the Conductors of the Westminster Forum.'
Morning Post

1485. March 23, 1789 City Debates
'Which has more Blanks to a Prize, Marriage or the Lottery?
Were we to publish the letter in which the above question was inclosed, it must excite universal Risibility. The Writer appears to have lost large Sums in the Lottery, which produced some matrimonial Bickerings from his Wife; angered with her Taunts he has taken this publick and comical Method of Revenge.
Though not in the habit of publick Speaking, he signifies his intention of addressing the Chair. As at this Society one Lady has frequently spoken, we cannot help reminding him that his Wife may perhaps claim the same Privilege. The Managers are conscious of the Frivolity of the Question, but they have adopted it as a necessary Relief to the important Subjects lately debated.'
Daily Advertiser

1486. March 25, 1789 Westminster Forum
'Which is more conducive to Happiness in the Marriage State, Riches without Affection, or Poverty with it?'
Morning Post March 20

1487. March 26, 1789 Coachmakers Hall
'Does the tender Sensibility of the Female Heart lessen or increase the Happiness of the Fair Sex?
We are happy to find, although too many dissipate their Time in Gaming, brutal Diversions, and Frivolity, that this Society still possesses

the highest Degree of public Approbation. What can afford greater Pleasure to an ingenious Mind than to behold a Multitude of both Sexes assembled for the Purpose of rational Entertainment and mental Improvement.'
Daily Advertiser March 25

1488. March 27, 1789 Westminster Forum
'Has the Administration of Mr. Pitt been most influenced by Interest, Ambition, or Patriotism?
As it [the Question] involves the late Political Transactions of both Parties, they respectfully recommend Candour and Moderation to the various Gentlemen who may speak; and as the Decision, which must be publickly announced, will proclaim the Opinion of a polite and intelligent Audience upon the actions of the Minister in the Aggregate, they hope the Gentlemen of either Party will not quit the Room till the close of the Debate.'
Daily Advertiser

1489. March 30, 1789 City Debates
'In which State do the Fair Sex enjoy most Happiness, Virginity, Marriage or Widowhood?'
Daily Advertiser March 28

1490. April 1, 1789 Westminster Forum
'Is not that Law Cruel and Unjust which inflicts the Punishment of Burning alive upon a Woman for the same Offence which subjects a Man only to the usual Forms of Execution?'
Daily Advertiser March 27

1491. April 2, 1789 Coachmakers Hall
'Which of the Sciences most deserves the Attention and Cultivation of Englishmen, Eloquence, Poetry or Musick?'
Meeting 'will be opened in Rhime by a Gentleman, whose poetical Works are much admired.
Question was determined in favour of eloquence.'
Daily Advertiser April 1/World April 9

1492. April 3, 1789 Westminster Forum
'Has the Administration of Mr. Pitt been more influenced by interest, ambition, or patriotism?'
Morning Post April 1

1493. April 6, 1789 City Debates
'Which will more probably produce Happiness in the Marriage State, Riches without Affection, or Poverty with it?
The Lady who occasionally speaks in this Society will . . . at the particular Request of an illustrious foreign Nobleman, now on a Visit to this

254

Country, who was disappointed when she spoke to the following question at the Westminster Forum, again deliver her sentiments.'
Daily Advertiser

1494. April 7, 1789 City Debates
'Ought the Repeal of the Shop Tax to be ascribed to the strenuous endeavours of the citizens of London, the opposition of Mr. Fox in the House of Commons, or the condescension of the Prime Minister?'
Times

1495. April 8, 1789 Westminster Forum
'Ought the Repeal of the Shop Tax to be ascribed to Mr. PITT or Mr. FOX?
The repeal of the Shop Tax was determined to have been occasioned by the exertions of Mr. Fox.'
Morning Post

1496. April 9, 1789 Coachmakers Hall
'Is the Assertion of Mr. Addison true, That the pleasantest Days of a Man's Life are those which he passes in Courtship?
It is not a little extraordinary that the Lady, at whose Solicitation this Subject is to undergo a publick Discussion, has declared, that she married the Man of her Heart, who proved the most kind and affectionate Husband, she is inclined nevertheless to favour Mr. Addison's opinion.'
Daily Advertiser April 8

1497. April 10, 1789 Westminster Forum
'Which has occasioned more Mischief among Mankind, Political or Religious Prejudice?
The Managers flatter themselves that the above Question is perfectly suited to the decorum necessary to be observed on this festival. The evils of political prejudice may be strikingly exemplified by its banishing such characters as Messrs. Fox, Sheridan, Burke, &c. from active situations; religious prejudice may employ the talents of the orator, in depicting the horrors of persecution, and even call in the aid of the humourist to expose the folly and ridicule the absurdity of Methodism, Popery, and fanatic Hypocrisy.'
Times

1498. April 13, 1789 City Debates
'Which is the greatest Calamity to the Female Mind, the loss of a Lover by Banishment, Death or Marriage?'
Daily Advertiser April 11

1499. April 15, 1789 Westminster Forum
'Ought not the Magistrates to unite their Efforts to prevent the intended Battle between Humphreys and Mendoza, and to abolish the Practice of Boxing entirely?

The Advocates for the Advantages of Refinement and Civilization in Society, will have an Opportunity to declaim against a Practice repugnant to the Feelings of Humanity; while, on the other Hand, the Amateurs of Boxing may argue in Favour of the Science, as a constant Means of Self-defence, consistent with the naturally bold and hardy Characters of the ancient Race of Britons.'
Morning Post

1500. April 16, 1789 Coachmakers Hall
'Which is more censurable, the effeminate Foppery of the Men, or the masculine Boldness of the Women?'
The Question received in a 'Petition from several Ladies, who stile themselves Old Maids, complaining of the Foppery of the Men and the forward Boldness of the Women, which they say is a principal Cause of many modest Ladies being obliged to live in a State of Celibacy.'
Daily Advertiser

1501. April 17, 1789 Westminster Forum
'Has the Opposition to Mr. Pitt, during his Administration, arisen from the genuine Principles of disinterested Patriotism, or the envious Emotions of disappointed Ambition?'
Morning Post

1502. April 18, 1789 Morning Post
CIVIC WREATH
'On the Evening of Tuesday, April the 21st, the Great Room, at the Crown and Anchor in the Strand, will be opened by a set of Gentlemen for the discussion of the following interesting question:
'To which of the high Political Characters, Mr. PITT or Mr. FOX, may, on a review be annexed the sacred epithet of – PATRIOT?'
A Civic Wreath of silver, the reward conferred by ancient Rome on virtuous Citizens, will be transmitted to him who shall be adjudged the superior character, by the hands of that gentleman who, in the opinion of his own party, shall be considered as having best defended the cause he espoused.
A Medal will be the recompense of his abilities. The most decided impartiality will be observed.
Admittance, to Ladies and Gentlemen, Half a Crown.'

1503. April 20, 1789 City Debates
'To which Character (next to the Supreme Disposer of all Events) ought this Country to pay the greatest Tribute of Gratitude; her Majesty, for her amiable Conduct during the Royal Malady; Dr. Willis, for his unremitting Attention to retrieve the Health of our Sovereign; or Mr. Pitt, for his preserving the Regal Authority in that State most agreeable to the Constitution of this Country and the Inclinations of his Royal Master?

An Ode on his Majesty's Recovery' will be recited by a Gentleman after the debate.
Daily Advertiser April 18

1504. April 22, 1789 Westminster Forum
'Is not that Parent who controuls the Affections of his Daughter in Marriage chargeable with cruelty and injustice, and answerable for any fatal consequences that may arise from his prohibition?'
Question to be debated because of death of Earl Caithness from love.
Morning Post April 17

1505. April 23, 1789 Coachmakers Hall
'Which is the best Theme for popular Admiration, the Wisdom and Patriotism of the Minister, the unexampled Loyalty of the People, or the gracious Interference of Divine Providence?'
Daily Advertiser April 22

1506. April 24, 1789 Westminster Forum
'Do solemn Public Processions on popular occasions, tend more to keep alive the national importance and spirit of a people, or to produce inflammatory prejudice and provoke riot and confusion?'
Work April 22

1507. April 27, 1789 City Debates
'Can a Wife be reformed by Correction?'
Daily Advertiser April 25

1508. April 29, 1789 Westminster Forum
'To which of the high Political Characters, Mr. PITT or Mr. FOX, may, on a Review of their WHOLE Conduct, with the greatest Propriety be annexed the sacred Epithet of – PATRIOT?
Several Gentlemen, who were disappointed at the last meeting, called at the Crown and Anchor' [requested the above debate].
'We cannot promise either a Civic Wreath to the Victor in this Debate, nor a Medal to the Gentleman who best defends him; but we pledge ourselves strictly to observe the most decided Impartiality on the subject.'
Morning Post

1509. April 30, 1789 Coachmakers Hall
'A Club of Female Literature, composed of Ladies of all ages, is lately instituted; the object of which is to read together, and endeavour to explore the truth and meaning of all books of a sentimental nature, especially such as relate to the conduct and happiness of their own sex. In all doubtful or difficult cases, a question is to be framed and transmitted to the Society at Coachmaker's-Hall, for Public discussion. One of the Sisterhood at their last meeting, read the following couplet on Wit and Beauty:

Wit, like Beauty, triumphs o'er the heart,
When more of Nature's seen, and less of Art.

An elderly Lady conceived this to be too high a compliment to beauty, and begged leave to read the following elegant lines on good nature:

Love rais'd on Beauty, will like that decay,
Our hearts may bear its slender chains a day,
Good-nature binds more easy, yet more strong,
The willing heart, and only holds it long.

After some conversation, the following question was framed, and sent to Coachmaker's-Hall, viz. 'Which is the most attractive in the Female Sex, Wit, Beauty, or Good Nature?' . . . Most of the Club will attend.
At the Conclusion of the Debate a Gentleman will deliver a poetical Oration on the Recovery of our much beloved Sovereign.'
Morning Post/Daily Advertiser

1510. May 1, 1789 Westminster Forum
'Would the Wisdom of this Country be more conspicuous in totally abolishing the Slave Trade – or continuing it under certain Restrictions?'
Morning Post

1511. May 4, 1789 City Debates
'Are the Understandings of the Fair Sex inferior to those of the Male, or does Education alone constitute the Difference?'
Daily Advertiser May 2

1512. May 6, 1789 Westminster Forum
'In which state do the Fair Sex enjoy most Happiness – Virginity, Marriage or Widowhood?'
Morning Post

1513. May 7, 1789 Coachmakers Hall
'AN IMPORTANT APPEAL TO THE PUBLIC
Would not the Abolition of the Slave Trade be yielding to the principles of mistaken Humanity, and highly injurious to the Interests of this Country?'
Question 'proposed by a Society of Merchants . . . Without intending to detract from the merit of similar institutions, we must allow Coachmakers hall to be the most popular assembly for free debate, in this country. Several learned Divines, and other distinguished characters who have written for and against the Abolition of the Slave Trade, are expected to be present, and take a part in the Debate.
Several Gentlemen with great Ability reprobated the Slave Trade as totally repugnant to Humanity and the Principles of a free Country. One Gentleman only opposed the Abolition, which he did in a Speech of great Fluency and Strength of Reasoning. He was replied to by an

258

African (not Gustavus Vassa) who discovered much strong natural Sense, and spoke with wonderful Facility.'
Times May 6/Daily Advertiser May 14

1514. May 11, 1789 City Debates
'Can the Legislators of this Country, consistently with its true Interests, consent to the total Abolition of the Slave Trade?
The African Prince who lately spoke in this Society has promised to be present; the celebrated Ouladah Equiano, or Gustavus Vassa, who has lately published his Memoirs, will speak, and the Lady, whose abilities are the Ornament of this Institution and the Admiration of the Publick, positively will deliver her Sentiments.'
Daily Advertiser May 9

1515. May 14, 1789 Coachmakers Hall
'Would not the Abolition of the Slave Trade be yielding to the Principles of mistaken Humanity, and highly injurious to the Interests of this Country?
The Question was sent to the Coachmaker's Hall as a Society universally allowed to be the most respectable and popular for free debate in this country.'
The society was 'almost unanimous in favour of the abolition of the slave trade'.
Daily Advertiser

1516. May 18, 1789 City Debates, Capel Court, Bartholemew-lane
'Can the Legislators of this Country, consistently with its true Interests, consent to the total Abolition of the Slave Trade? then, Does the earnest Wish of the Dissenters for the Repeal of the Test and Corporation Acts appear to originate in a Spirit of Patriotism, or a Wish for those Honours and Emolument which their Ancestors the Puritans affected to despise?
As this Enquiry may probably cause the Attendance of several of the Dissenting Clergy, the Managers pledge themselves to observe that Impartiality due to Gentlemen of the sacred Character, when addressing a numerous and respectable Audience on Behalf of the religious and civil Rights of Mankind.'
Daily Advertiser May 16

1517. May 21, 1789 Coachmakers Hall
'Are not the sacramental Clauses of the Corporation and Test Acts, both as they respect Catholick and Protestant Dissenters, unjust and repugnant to the Spirit of the British Constitution?'
The Question was 'proposed by several Protestant Dissenters who are Advocates for universal Toleration. . . Some of the Dissenters say that several of their Ministers, and particularly those two celebrated Philosophers and Theologists, Doctors Priestly and Price, are capable of answering every Objection that has been made to a free and general

Participation of civil and religious Liberties; they will probably both attend.'
Daily Advertiser

1518. May 25, 1789 City Debates
'Do the strenuous Efforts of the Dissenters for the Repeal of the Test and Corporation Acts, appear to originate in a Spirit of Patriotism, or a Wish for those Honours and Emoluments their Ancestors, the Puritans, professed to despise?
It has long been Matter of Doubt, whether Ambition or Piety are the leading Motives of the Dissenters. Their Conduct during the Reign of Charles the First, and the Usurpation of Oliver Cromwell, will doubtless be alluded to.'
Daily Advertiser May 23

1519. May 28, 1789 Coachmakers Hall
'Are not the sacramental Clauses in the Corporation and Test Acts, both as they relate to Catholick and Protestant Dissenters, unjust and repugnant to the Spirit of the British Constitution?
As that great Reasoner and Friend to the Freedom of Debate, the Rev. Mr. Robinson, of Cambridge, is now in London, the Managers anticipate the Pleasure of receiving as much Instruction from him at Coachmakers Hall upon a Question which involves the Civil and Religious Rights of Mankind, as he never fails to communicate from the Pulpit upon Religious and Moral Obligations . . . Such is the acknowledged Utility of this popular Institution, that several Law Students, who bid fair to rise to the highest Honours in their Profession, intend, after the Example of those admired Barristers, Messrs. Dallas and Garrow, to make it their School for practical Improvement in the Art of publick Speaking.'
Daily Advertiser May 28

1520. June 1, 1789 City Debates
'Which will make a more disagreeable Companion in the Marriage State, a crusty old Bachelor or a peevish old Maid?
Indeed the Question is amazingly calculated to excite Risibility, provoke Mirth and create Entertainment at the Expence of Vanity, Affectation, and ill-Nature; nor is the Exercise of persuasive Eloquence totally excluded, a powerful Apology for the old Maid arising from the Treachery of the Male Sex, many of the fairest Blossoms of the Female Creation frequently being abandoned by their faithless Admirers, and left through Life to blush unseen, or waste their Fragrance on the desert Air.'
Daily Advertiser May 30

1521. June 8, 1789 City Debates
ROYAL DUEL
'Does a recent Affair of Honour reflect more Lustre on the Character

of his Royal Highness the Duke of York, or on that of the Hon. Colonel Lenox?
Many injurious Reflections on the above noble Characters have appeared in various Publications, at the particular Request of several Persons of Fashion and Distinction, the above Question is appointed for Free Debate . . . to convey to the Publick, through the Medium of this popular and respectable Institution, Facts as yet known but to few, and Circumstances which the Heat of Party Zeal has misrepresented, to the manifest Injury of both the noble Combatants.'
Daily Advertiser June 6

1522. August 17, 1789 City Debates
'Will the expected Revolution in French Politics promote or militate against the true Interests of this Country?
The Managers of this Society, impressed with a lively Sense of that distinguished Patronage they have received, respectfully apprize Gentlemen at and intended for the Bar, their various other literary Correspondents, their noble Patrons, and the Publick at large, that the Season will commence . . . with the above popular and important Question: The Revolution in States, the Declension of Slavery, the Progress of Liberty, their respective and united Effects on the Arts, Manufactures, and Commerce of Great Britain are involved in this Subject. The Managers respectfully thank the Duke D'— for his polite Intimation, and promise every Thing in their Power to render the Debate worthy so noble an Attendant.'
Daily Advertiser August 15

1523. August 24, 1789 City Debates
'Can Animal Magnetism as practiced by Drs. Yeldall and da Mainauduc, Mr. Loutherberg and others, be supported on the rational Principles of sound Philosophy, or is it, according to the Report of Dr. Benjamin Franklin, a mere Imposture, calculated to deceive the Credulous?'
Daily Advertiser August 22

1524. August 27, 1789 Coachmakers Hall
'Would the establishment of liberty in France, be likely to prejudice or benefit the general interest of Great Britain?
The Debating Society, at Coachmakers Hall, Foster Lane, Cheapside, an institution established near a century, and allowed to be the most instructive and agreeable entertainment of any in this metropolis.'
Daily Advertiser August 26

1525. August 31, 1789 City Debates
'Is that Brother justifiable who punishes with Death the Seducer of his Sister's Virtue?
The Author of this Question must pardon our erasing the Names of the Parties concerned in the late unhappy Catastrophe at Whitechapel; the Reason must be obvious to every Man of Feeling: a most splendid

261

Debate however may be expected on such a Subject, not a Father, Brother or Admirer of the Sex but must find himself interested in its Discussion; the elegant Assemblage of Ladies who lately honoured these Debates with their Attendance must animate the Speaker on such a Theme. . .

A most numerous Audience were decidedly of Opinion, that a Brother was not justifiable in punishing the Seducer of his Sister's Virtue with Death.'

Daily Advertiser August 29

1526. September 3, 1789 Coachmakers Hall
'Whether the late Destruction of the Bastile, and the spirited Conduct of the French, do not prove that the general Opinion of their being possessed by a slavish Disposition was founded in National Prejudice?'
Daily Advertiser September 2

1527. September 7, 1789 City Debates
'Which is more desirable, to be alive to all the Feelings of Sensibility; or, wrapt in a Stoical Apathy, to remain totally indifferent to the Miseries and Misfortunes of Mankind?'
Daily Advertiser September 5

1528. September 10, 1789 Coachmakers Hall
'Is it consistent with Reason or Religion to believe that Mr. Loutherbourg has performed any Cures by a Divine Power without any medical Application?
A great Number of Persons having declared they have been restored to Health by . . . [Mr. Loutherbourg], and that they are ready to attest the same, has induced a popular Clergyman [to request the above debate]. . . There is no Doubt, if any Person has actually received Relief in the Wonderful Manner reported, but that Gratitude of Mr. Loutherbourg, as well as to the Supreme Being, will induce them on this Occasion to appear and publickly to announce it.
A Gentleman . . . stood up and assured a crowded and most respectable Audience, that he himself had obtained a perfect Cure, by this extraordinary Character, without the application of any Medicine. Two Gentlemen defended Mr. de Loutherbourg upon Scriptural Principles with great Ability.'
Daily Advertiser September 9

1529. September 14, 1789 City Debates
'Can Animal Magnetism, as practiced by Drs. Yeldall and De Mainauduc, Mr. Loutherberg, and others, be supported on the rational Principles of sound Philosophy; or is it, according to the Report of Dr. Benjamin Franklin, a mere Imposture, calculated to deceive the Credulous?'
The Question is 'by particular Desire of several scientifick Gentlemen, who continually attend the Society. . . During the Course of the first Evening's Debates, Dr. YELDALL will defend the Principles and

262

explain several of the Mysteries of the Science. The Doctor has obligingly signified his Intention of demonstrating, upon his Apparatus, prepared for the Purpose, the Powers of the Magnetic Effluvia. The Curious and Philosophick will therefore have the Opportunity of receiving that Conviction upon the Subject, which an enlightened Publick may justly claim from the Managers of a literary Institution, favoured with general Support and unbounded Patronage. Several Gentlemen wishing to hear the Sentiments of Mr. Loutherberg, and Dr. De Mainauduc, Cards of Invitation will be dispatched to both those great Characters.
To describe Dr. Yeldall's Oration . . . would exceed the Bounds of any Advertisement. His Experiments demonstrated him a Master of his Arts, and impressed that Conviction on a numerous and brilliant Audience, which caused them almost unanimously to declare, that his Practice of Animal Magnetism was founded on the sound Principles of Philosophy.'
Daily Advertiser September 12

1530. September 17, 1789 Coachmakers Hall
'Is it consistent with Reason or Religion to believe that Mr. Loutherbourg has performed any Cures by a Divine Power without any medical Application?'
Decided against Mr. Loutherbourg.
Daily Advertiser September 16

1531. September 21, 1789 City Debates
'Can Animal Magnetism, as practiced by Mr. De Loutherberg, be supported on the rational Principles of sound Philosophy; or is it, according to the Report of Dr. Benjamin Franklin, a mere Imposture, calculated to deceive the Credulous?'
Daily Advertiser September 19

1532. September 24, 1789 Coachmakers Hall
'Is Dr. Gregory's Assertion in the Father's Last Legacy true, that in this Country a Lady has hardly any Chance of marrying for Love?
An amiable but distressed young Lady, who, in Obedience to the Commands of her Relations, married the Man she did not love, has requested that this Subject might be taken into Consideration, in hopes that its Discussion may prevent many of her Sex from suffering the Misery that is her unhappy Lot, and point out to Parents the Folly and Cruelty of forcing their Daughters to give their Hands, where they cannot bestow their Hearts.'
Daily Advertiser September 23

1533. September 28, 1789 City Debates
'Can Animal Magnetism, as practiced by Dr. De Mainauduc, be supported on the rational Principles of sound Philosophy; or is it, according to the Report of Dr. Benjamin Franklin, a mere Imposture, calculated

to deceive the Credulous?'
Daily Advertiser September 26

1534. October 1, 1789 Coachmakers Hall
'Does the Belief in Apparitions, the Influence of good and evil Spirits, and in judicial Astrology, discover a superstitious Ignorance, or a true Knowledge of Religion and Philosophy?
The Managers beg Leave to inform the Publick, that Information having been given to them of an Apparition lately appearing to a worthy Clergyman; and some wonderful Discoveries made a few Days since by a modern Astrologer, particularly to a Tradesman in Old-Street, who will attend, and a young Woman lately deceased, the Love of Truth, the grand actuating Principle of this Institution, has induced them to bring forward the above Question, to which they solicit the Attention of the Divine, the Philosopher, and every person who can speak from Experience on this Occasion.'
Daily Advertiser September 30

1535. October 5, 1789 City Debates
'Was woman created inferior, equal, or superior to man?
Several Ladies of fashion were lately discoursing of the extra-ordinary abilities of a Lady who spoke in the City Debates, (*for the information of some of our readers, it may be necessary to mention, that this is the original Debating Society, instituted more than half a century. . .*). This produced a violent altercation upon the abilities of the sex in general, the power they possess over the actions of mankind, and the situation in which the first woman was placed.'
Daily Advertiser October 3

1536. October 8, 1789 Coachmakers Hall
'Is it not the Duty of every Friend to Liberty to Support the Resolution of the Protestant Dissenters for the Repeal of the Test and Corporation Acts?'
Daily Advertiser October 7

1537. October 12, 1789 City Debates
'Which is more absurd, the Notion of the Turks, that Women have no Souls, or the Opinion of some Philosophers, that Brutes are immortal?
Several Arminian and Calvinistick Divines intend to vindicate the Immortality of Brute Creation, as held by the Leaders of both Persuasions, the Rev. Matthew Henry, Mr. Toplady, Mr. J. Wesley, and even those celebrated Philosophers Locke, Hume and Soame Jennings. A Gentleman, long resident in Turkey, has undertaken to defend the Mahometan Opinion, and to prove that Females have no Souls, upon the System of Plato, and other eminent Philosophers.'
Daily Advertiser October 10

1538. October 15, 1789 Coachmakers Hall

'Is it not the Duty of every Friend to Liberty to Support the Resolution of the Protestant Dissenters for the Repeal of the Test and Corporation Acts?'
Great majority of the audience determined Question in favour of the Protestant Dissenters.
Daily Advertiser October 14

1539. October 19, 1789 City Debates
'Supposing a Mariner to be Ship-wrecked, with his Wife, Mother and Child – he can only save one Person with himself – which of them ought to be the Object of his Attention?'
The Question 'was sent by a Captain's Lady from Mile-End, who with her Husband, his Mother and an Infant not two Years old, were wrecked on their Return from India. Fortunately they were rescued from their dreadful Situation by a French East-Indiaman, who carried them safe into L'Orient. They will all three be present; and as this Question is an Enquiry into the Force of parental Duty, filial Affection,and conjugal Love, a Debate equally important, and affecting, is expected.'
Daily Advertiser October 17

1540. October 21, 1789 Westminster Forum
Question on the validity of professors of Animal Magnetism.
Vote against them.
Daily Advertiser October 27/Times October 20

1541. October 22, 1789 Coachmakers Hall
'Is the Assertion true, That the greater Part of bad Husbands are made so by the Misconduct of their Wives?'
Daily Advertiser October 21

1542. October 26, 1789 City Debates
'Which will render a Married Lady more wretched – her Husband to be jealous of her fidelity, or she of his?
There appears to reign this season an uncommon spirit of emulation between the leading Debating Societies. The Westminster Forum opened last Wednesday with uncommon splendour; and the Managers of the City Debates, jealous of its success, announce a Lady of the first eminence in the literary world to speak this evening. . . Indeed, the amazing oratorical excellence of the above Lady, is the best reason that can be argued for [the amazing success of the Society].'
Daily Advertiser October 24

1543. October 28, 1789 Westminster Forum
'Is the Passion of Love more powerful from 15 to 30, or from 30 till 50?
Although much may be urged to prove the Force of juvenile Love, yet many Instances (particularly the Lady at Highgate, aged 70, who lately

married one of her Domesticks) evince its Power on the Sexes during the latter Period.'
Macklin attended this debate.
Daily Advertiser October 27

1544. October 29, 1789 Coachmakers Hall
'Does Mr. Pitt merit the Character of being a Friend to the Liberty and Welfare of this Country after having extended the Excise Laws by the Tobacco Bill and other Measures of a similar Tendency?
Among the numerous and very respectable Audience who attended to hear this truly interesting Subject . . . was a foreign Prince, supposed by many to be his Highness the Duke of Orleans. He was attended by several of the Nobility, and listened with great Attention to the Speakers on both Sides.'
Daily Advertiser October 28

1545. November 2, 1789 City Debates
'Which is most repugnant to Truth, the Heathen Notion of Transmigration, the Papists Doctrine of Purgatory, or the Rev. Mr. Winchester's celebrated System of Universal Salvation?
Several learned and popular Divines, of various Persuasions, perceiving with Regret the Increase of Mr. Winchester's Doctrine, have requested the Managers to announce the above Question for Debate, as they decidedly intend to prove Mr. Winchester's System is at best but a Protestant Purgatory. They have preferred this Society, as better adapted for such a Subject than the Pulpit, Mr. Winchester and his friends being here allowed to answer their Arguments, a Circumstance incompatible with the sacred Order of Publick Worship. Several leaders of Messr. Wesley and Whitfield's Communion have joined in the Requisition. The serious and well-disposed, whether Divines or Laymen, are hereby invited, either as Audience or Speakers, and the Managers sincerely hope the Gay and Volatile will either absent themselves for that Evening, or else hear with Silence and Attention a Debate instituted at the Request of some of the most sacred Characters that adorn the Pulpit, and turning upon that grand Theme of human Salvation, which struck even the Angelick Armies with Silence! The Hint of A.B. has been adopted, Cards of Invitation have already been sent to the Rev. Messr. Knight, Bradburne, and Browne. Several learned Catholicks have signified their Intention to attend, and vindicate the Doctrine of Purgatory by the Tradition of Ages, the Authority of the Church, and the Evidence of Scriptures.
The . . . Debate was peculiarly distinguished by the Speeches of two Gentlemen, one of whom supported Mr. Winchester's Doctrine with great Ability; and the other accused him of prematurely opening the Book of Divine Mercy (sealed to the Day of Doom) to loose one of which Seals would have been Presumption, even in an Archangel!'
Daily Advertiser October 31

1546. November 4, 1789 Westminster Forum

'Is the late alarming Number of Suicides to be attributed to Disappointment in the tender Passion, the Progress of Infidelity, or that gloomy Insanity which Foreigners ascribe to the effects of our Soil and Climate? The Duke of Orleans is said recently to have visited the Capel Court Society: His Royal Highness being expected . . . to honour the Westminster Forum with his Presence every Accommodation will be made preparatory to the Reception of such an illustrious Character.'
Fifty-three suicides were reported in the newspapers within the month.
Daily Advertiser

1547. November 5, 1789 Coachmakers Hall
'Does Mr. Pitt merit the Character of being a Friend to the Liberty and Welfare of this Country after having extended the Excise Laws by the Tobacco Bill and other Measures of a similar Tendency?
Mr. Fox, or some of the leading Men in Opposition, are expected to state the Grounds upon which they object to the late Extension of the Excise Laws. This is requested by many respectable Persons, who are convinced that a Question of this Nature ought only to be referred to an Assembly like this composed of a mixed Number of intelligent Citizens, and not to a Party convened at a Tavern, who come avowedly all on one Side.'
Audience 'determined almost unanimously that the Extension of the Excise Laws was inconsistent with the Liberty and Welfare of this Country'.
Daily Advertiser November 4

1548. November 9, 1789 City Debates
'Which is most repugnant to Truth – the Heathen Notion of Transmigration – the Papists Doctrine of Purgatory – or the Rev. Mr. Winchester's celebrated System of Universal Salvation?
From the Number of Gospel Ministers, Gentlemen Leaders in Messr. Wesley and Whitfield's Societies, Divines of the Baptist, Presbyterian and Romish Communions who have promised to attend, the Debate . . . will probably be one of the most important ever submitted to the Consideration of the Christian World.'
Daily Advertiser November 7

1549. November 11, 1789 Westminster Forum
'Did the late Extension of the Excise Laws originate in the Frauds committed on the Revenue by Smugglers and Dealers in Tobacco, or in the Schemes of artful Ministers to subvert the Liberties of a free People?'
On the Question of the Excise Laws, the Debate decided their extension 'originated in the Frauds of Smugglers and Dealers in Tobacco'.
Daily Advertiser November 10

1550. November 12, 1789 Coachmakers Hall
'Does Suicide proceed mostly from a Disappointment in Love, a State of Lunacy, or from the Pride of the human Mind?'

Question proposed 'by a young Lady, whose Friend lately put an End to her Existence from a Disappointment in Love. . . Those who have heard of the late Suicide committed by the unhappy young Girl who was in Love with the Mulatto, together with other similar Cases, and who also recollect many other recent Suicides, to which no other Cause can be assigned but Pride or Lunacy will allow this Subject to have a very high Claim to publick Attention.'
Daily Advertiser November 11

1551. November 16, 1789 City Debates
'Which is more blameable – the Disobedience of the Daughter who elopes with her Lover – or the Tyranny of the Father who compels her to marry contrary to her Inclination?'
Daily Advertiser November 14

1552. November 17, 1789 Marybone Debates, Spread Eagle, Charles Street, Middlesex Hospital
'Which is the most blameable, the Daughter who in Disobedience to her Father, elopes with her Lover, or the Father who obliges the Daughter to marry against her Inclination?
This Institution is founded on the same Principles, as the late Robin Hood Society, which was supported by the best Orators this Country had to boast of, and held in the highest Estimation for more than 40 Years; and the Managers of this Society flatter themselves that this Debate will be truly instructing and entertaining, as many Gentlemen of extraordinary Abilities have promised to be present.'
Admittance to Ladies and Gentlemen 6d. each.
Daily Advertiser

1553. November 18, 1789 Westminster Forum
'Ought the Number of old Maids to be attributed to their Aversion to Matrimony, Disappointment in Love, or any Peculiarity in their Persons or Tempers? and, Which is most absurd, the Notions of the Turks, that Women have no Souls, or the Opinion of some Philosophers, that Brutes are immortal?'
Question originated because 'several Ladies lately discoursing on the Merits of Mr. Haley's celebrated Essay on Old Maids, collected some of the leading Causes assigned by that Author for the Increase of these venerable Pieces of Antiquity.'
Daily Advertiser November 17

1554. November 19, 1789 Coachmakers Hall
'Does conjugal Infidelity proceed more from the Inconstancy of the Female Heart, or the improper Behaviour of Married Men to their Wives?
The late encreasing Number of Causes for crim. Con. having occasioned much Dispute in the polite Circles, as to the true Source of conjugal Infidelity, seven young Ladies were nominated to frame a Question . . . [and] will all be present.'

Daily Advertiser November 18

1555. November 23, 1789 City Debates
'Which is most defensible, the Plurality of Wives, permitted to Eastern Nations; confining the Clergy of Catholick Countries to Celibacy, or allowing Marriage to first, but denying it to second Cousins?'
Question sent in by a French Nobleman.
Daily Advertiser November 21/Times

1556. November 25, 1789 Westminster Forum
'Which is more absurd, the Notion of the Turks, that Women have no Souls, or the Opinion of Dr. Priestley, Soame Jennings, and other Philosophers, that Brutes are immortal?
It is not the Practice of this Society to adopt Questions that have been previously debated in other Institutions: But at the Request of many learned Gentlemen, wishing to investigate the philosophick Part of the Question (who were disappointed Admittance at the Capel-Court Society when this Question was debated there), at the Desire of many Families of Distinction resident in Westminster, and at the Solicitation of several Ladies anxious to hear what can be said on so curious a Subject, a Deviation from established Custom has been permitted.'
Daily Advertiser November 24

1557. November 26, 1789 Coachmakers Hall
'Whose feelings are likely to receive the greatest delight, those of the banished husband, restored to a beloved wife, the mariner saved from shipwreck, or the slave who has regained his liberty?
This pleasing subject of debate is adopted at the request of the joyful wife of a long banished husband, who, in the course of a checquered life, has been a witness both of the feelings of a distressed mariner, and those of the poor captive freed from the miseries of slavery. A Gentleman many years the unhappy companion of an affectionate husband, who was torn from his wife, and confined in the Bastile; has promised to take a part in the debate on the subject.'
Times

1558. November 30, 1789 City Debates
'Is Physiognomy a Science that discovers the Natural Disposition of Mankind by their Features – or merely a Visionary Speculation of Philosophick Enthusiasm?'
Daily Advertiser November 28

1559. December 3, 1789 Coachmakers Hall
'Is the Conduct of the French Assembly, in declaring the Possession of the Church to be the Property of the Nation, and their Care in providing for the inferior Clergy, worthy the Imitation of this Country?'
Question went in the affirmative.
Daily Advertiser December 2

1560. December 7, 1789 City Debates
'Is the Assertion of Ovid true, Love conquers all Things, and all must yield to Love?
The Lady's Oration . . . was the most astonishing display of real Eloquence ever heard in a Society of this Nature; the Audience was numerous and polite; among the bright circle of Beauties three Irish Ladies of Distinction shone conspicuous; they lamented that their departure for their own country, in the suit of his Grace of Westmoreland, would deprive them of carrying any more than this one Testimonial of Female Excellence to a kingdom famed for its admiration of Oratory.'
Daily Advertiser December 5, 14

1561. December 9, 1789 Westminster Forum
'Which is the greater Calamity, the Infidelity of a Beloved Wife, or the Seduction of an only Daughter?
The above Question . . . was handed to the Chair by an elegant Party of Females who accompanied the Lady who lately spoke in this Society. Not a Father nor a Husband but must be peculiarly interested in the subject, and from the various applications for places in the Gallery which we have received, a most numerous Assemblage of the Fair Sex is expected to be present. It is the earnest wish of the Gentlemen who conduct the Westminster Forum to tender it a School of moral Instruction as well as of polite Amusement. The Orator on this occasion will have every opportunity for the display of his talents, either to expatiate on the feelings of an injured Husband, robbed of the only blessing that could tolerate existence, or of an affectionate Father, encountering that dishonour and anguish in the last stage of life which would be insupportable even in the prime of manhood.'
Daily Advertiser December 8

1562. December 10, 1789 Coachmakers Hall
'Does Happiness in the Marriage State depend mostly on a Similarity of Disposition, Equality of Years, or on being possessed of the first Object of our Affections?
This Society is now universally allowed to be the best School of useful Knowledge, Eloquence and rational Instruction, as well as a Place of the most agreeable Entertainment of any of which this great Metropolis can boast. Scarcely a Week passes without its acquiring new Patrons and Admirers. A Lady, who has distinguished herself by her literary Productions, has promised to furnish the Managers with every novel Question, the Discussion of which may lead to the Happiness of her own Sex, or the Benefits of the Community at large. As an Earnest of her Friendship she has sent the above Question.'
Daily Advertiser December 9

1563. December 14, 1789 City Debates
'Are Ladies in the Choice of a Husband, most frequently actuated by Interest, Caprice or real Affection?

270

This Society is the first in public estimation, both for the numbers and respectability of its Auditors, the Excellency of its Speakers, and the time it has been established.'
Daily Advertiser December 12

1564. December 16, 1789 Westminster Forum
'Which is the greater Calamity, the Infidelity of a beloved Wife, or the Seduction of an only Daughter?
The late heavy damages given by the Court of King's Bench to the injured Captain Parslow, and many recent instances of Matrimonial Infidelity, render the above Question at this time peculiarly interesting. . . Indeed this Society seems now to have regained the ancient splendour it enjoyed, when those bright luminaries of the Law, Messrs. Erskine, Dallas, and Garrow shone in a conspicuous degree ornaments of the Institution. The numerous attendance of Ladies . . . and the many application for reserved seats . . . prove the estimation in which they and the Publick hold these Societies, as Schools of Morality, Wisdom and Entertainment.'
Daily Advertiser December 15

1565. December 17, 1789 Coachmakers Hall
'Is there not a greater Degree of Guilt in the married Lady who consents, than in the unmarried Man who seduces her to Adultery?
The Prevalence of Adultery is now a Subject of Conversation among all Ranks of People, and what is a little extraordinary, many Ladies insist that the Women are more to blame than the Men.'
Daily Advertiser December 16

1566. December 19, 1789 City Debates
'Are Methodists Enthusiasts who deceive themselves – Hypocrites who deceive others – or Men of genuine Piety, who have revived the neglected Doctrines of Christianity?
It is to determine whether Methodists are what they themselves profess, or what their Enemies accuse them of being. . .. The Methodists have been frequently arraigned at the Bar of Ridicule; here they await the unbiassed Determination of Reason and Impartiality. We warn Gentlemen apt to relate Stories of Methodist Preachers (Numbers of which are promised) to be cautious; as there is scarcely one of those Rev. Gentlemen now in Town, upon whom these Tales have been raised, but is expected to be present. . .. A late ostentatious Advertisement is too contemptible for the serious Animadversion of the reputable Societies. We leave that Institution, whose empty benches require such adventitious Aid, to trumpet forth its own Praises through the dark Medium of Calumny: The Philosophers, Divines, Wits and Orators who speak in this Society, sufficiently promulgate its Merits, and unequivocally stamp it the leading School of Morality, Science, Instruction and Entertainment.'
The Decision of near 600 respectable Auditors was "The Methodists are Men of genuine Piety".'
Daily Advertiser December 18

1567. December 23, 1789 Westminster Forum
'Which is the greater Sufferer from unlawful Love, the Husband, whose Wife's Incontinence obliges him publickly to sue for Justice – the Lady, whose Crime is thereby published to the World – or the Seducer, against whom Damages are awarded to the Ruin of his Fortune?'
Daily Advertiser December 22

1568. December 24, 1789 Coachmakers Hall
'Is there not a greater Degree of Guilt in the married Lady who consents, than in the unmarried Man who seduces her to Adultery?'
Daily Advertiser December 23

1569. December 28, 1789 City Debates
'Which Line of Conduct ought a Father to pursue with a seduced Daughter, to banish her from his Family and Protection, as a necessary Warning to her Sisters; or nobly to forgive her Fault, in Hopes of her Repentance?
A young Lady, the unhappy Victim of Seduction, having in Vain supplicated Forgiveness of a once-indulgent but now inexorable Father, framed the above Question, and intreated him, as her last Request, to attend its Discussion in this Society. The Gentleman has written to the Managers, expressing a high Sense of the moral Influence of these Societies, and promising to bring his four other Daughters to hear the Debate, which, it is sincerely hoped, will not only tend to fortify the Female Heart against the Artifices of Seduction, but to relax that parental Rigour which dooms to a Life of Anguish and Infamy an unfortunate Daughter, who might be restored to Happiness, if not to Honour, could her injured Parent once conceive her Re-Admission to his Family not to be a dangerous Example.'
Daily Advertiser December 26

1570. December 30, 1789 Westminster Forum
'Ought not the Legislature of this Country, against the next General Election, to follow the Example of the French National Assembly in apportioning the Number of Representatives to the Number of Inhabitants in each District, and thereby preventing the rotten Boroughs from maintaining that Influence they at present hold in the British Parliament?
Capel Loft, Esq. (from the Revolution Society) rose, and addressed the Chair in a Speech of considerable Length, containing among other valuable Particulars, some Communications to that Society from the French National Assembly. The Evening concluded with voting unanimous Thanks (moved and seconded by two Law Students of eminence) to Capel Loft, for his excellent Oration.'
Daily Advertiser December 29

1571. December 31, 1789 Coachmakers Hall

'Is the common Practice of taking the Youth of both Sexes to Plays and similar publick Amusement in the Holidays, more likely to efface the moral and instructive Impressions from their Minds, or to enlarge and improve their Understanding?'
Daily Advertiser December 30

1572. January 4, 1790 City Debates
'Ought two Lovers (possessed of mutual Affection but devoid of Fortune) to marry, trusting to Providence and their own Industry for Support – or to separate, from Motives of Prudence?
Gentlemen who speak in this Society may depend on Candour and Politeness; every species of illiberality, and all improper allusions from one Speaker to another, are immediately silenced by the chair.'
Daily Advertiser January 2/World January 4

1573. January 6, 1790 Westminster Forum
'Ought not the Legislature, against the next General Election, to follow the Example of the French National Assembly, in apportioning the number of Representatives to the number of Inhabitants in each District, and thereby prevent the rotten Boroughs from maintaining that Influence they at present hold in the British Parliament?'
Daily Advertiser January 5

1574. January 7, 1790 Coachmakers Hall
'Is it not dangerous to the Press, and inconsistent with reason, to consider the publication of TRUTH as a LIBEL?
The Liberty of the Press is the most valuable of all the privileges which belong to a free people; because it is the great shield by which all the rest are defended, it is also the refuge of distressed innocence, and the trumpet of virtuous fame. – whatever aims at its destruction, directs a stab against the Constitution.'
Audience decided that Truth ought not to be deemed a libel.
Daily Advertiser January 6

1575. January 11, 1790 City Debates
'Who best deserves the Suffrages of the Electors of Great Britain, at the ensuing General Election, those Members who have supported Mr. Pitt, and Administration, or those who have adhered to Mr. Fox and Opposition?
Such an Investigation cannot be held with more Propriety than in a popular Assembly situated in the very Heart of this great Metropolis. . .
The Decision of this Question, which will be announced through the medium of publick Prints, may have no small Influence on many Votes of those respectable Citizens who decidedly patronize this Institution.'
Small majority supported Mr. Pitt.
Daily Advertiser January 9

1576. January 13, 1790 Westminster Forum

'Ought not the Legislature, against the next General Election, to follow the Example of the French National Assembly, in apportioning the number of Representatives to the number of Inhabitants in each District, and thereby prevent the rotten Boroughs from maintaining that Influence they at present hold in the British Parliament?'
Daily Advertiser January 12

1577. January 14, 1790 Coachmakers Hall
'Is the following assertion of the late Lord Chatham in the House of Lords, and quoted in the notes to Dr. Price's Revolution Sermon, founded in truth, viz. "That the Church of England has a Popish Liturgy, a Calvinistic Creed, and an Arminian Clergy"?'
If the above question should be decided in the affirmative, 'the following question will immediately follow, viz. "Is it not evident from the arguments of Dr. Price and others, that it is unjust and impolitic, to continue the restrictions on the Protestant Dissenters?"
The Society at Coachmakers Hall is held in such high estimation by the friends of mental improvement, that several members of the learned professions, and some of the leading men in the political world, have declared their intention of making it the place, for the free and public discussion of all questions which involve the constitutional rights, or in any wise concern the interest and happiness of society at large.'
Audience thought, by a small majority, that Earl of Chatham was wrong.
Daily Advertiser January 13

1578. January 18, 1790 City Debates
'Is that Indifference which frequently takes place after Marriage to be attributed to the Inattention of Husbands, the Misconduct of Wives, or to the Flattery usually paid to the Fair Sex in Courtship?'
Lady speaks to the question who, in past, spoke in favour of Methodism.
Daily Advertiser January 16

1579. January 20, 1790 Westminster Forum
'Ought a young Lady, whose Choice of a Husband clashes with the Choice of her Parents, to marry the Man of her Heart contrary to their Commands, against her own Inclinations to comply with their Injunctions, or to remain in a State of Celibacy?'
Daily Advertiser January 19/Gazetteer January 19

1580. January 21, 1790 Coachmakers Hall
'Is it an impeachment of the character of the Protestant Dissenters, as peaceable subjects to renew their applications to the ensuing Parliament, for the repeal of the Test and Corporation acts?
The Protestant Dissenters have been charged in several of the public prints with having acted inconsistently with the character of real christians and peaceable subjects, by their late and present exertions to obtain a repeal of the Test Laws. Convinced of the fallacy of this charge, and

274

that they ought to enjoy an equal participation of privileges with the rest of their fellow citizens, the Managers have been requested by some very respectable dissenters to bring forward the above question for a free, candid, and liberal debate before an enlightened audience. Many of the brightest ornaments both of the established church and in the dissenting interest, will it is expected be present.'
Daily Advertiser January 20

1581. January 25, 1790 City Debates
'Ought that Man who accidently discovers the Infidelity of his Friend's Wife to reveal it to, or conceal it from, her injured Husband?
Whether it is better to hazard the ruin of a Friend's Happiness by informing him of the fatal Discovery, or to suffer him in a false Slumber of Security (from which he may one Day terribly awake) to dream of that Virtue and Honour in a Wife which she does not possess, but has criminally lavished on the most depraved Character in Society, the Seducer of a married Lady.'
Daily Advertiser January 23

1582. January 27, 1790 Westminster Forum
'Which is the more likely to die an Old Maid – a Prude or a Coquette? The Managers have the more readily adopted . . . [the above question], as from the Wit, Humour, Satire it must produce in Debate, it will form a necessary relief to the fair auditors from the more important Questions which have lately engaged the attention of this Society.'
Daily Advertiser January 26

1583. January 28, 1790 Coachmakers Hall
'Are the principles of the Protestant Dissenters, such as to justify the Legislature in refusing to repeal the Test and Corporation Acts?
Truth will only be found by those who seek for it – it is earnestly recommended to every auditor to bear with dispassionate attention, and reflect with calm deliberation before they hold up their hands, remembering, that they sit as Judges in a Court of free Debate, for the trial of a most important cause.'
It was determined 'by a considerable majority of a very crouded and respectable audience, that the principles of the Protestant Dissenters are such as to justify the legislature in repealing the Test and Corporation Acts'.
Daily Advertiser

1584. February 1, 1790 City Debates
'Is the Observation founded in Truth, that a reformed Rake makes the best of Husbands?'
Daily Advertiser January 30

1585. February 3, 1790 Westminster Forum
'Are the Ladies of this Country most distinguished for their beauty, virtue or mental accomplishments?'

Audience were of the opinion that the British Fair were most distinguished by their virtue.
The World/Daily Advertiser February 9

1586. February 4, 1790 Coachmakers Hall
'Is the old adage, as quoted by Sir William Temple, true – That good men marry early – Wise men, seldom?
In compliance with the request of several respectable ladies, who constantly attend this society, and who refer ever doubted case, either of a moral or sentimental nature, to the decision of the very numerous and enlightened audience who attend it, the above question is introduced for public discussion.'
Daily Advertiser February 3

1587. February 8, 1790 City Debates
'Which is the happier State, Marriage or a single Life?
It is with pleasure the Managers behold the popularity of these Debates enabling them daily to extend the moral influence of their Society. The liberality observed here to young Speakers, and the utter exclusion of every improper allusion from one Gentlemen to another, has induced many persons of the most distinguished abilities to fix on this Society as a proper place for the exercise of their talents, and the cultivation of their genius. At the same time the delicacy of expression which the law of these Debates enjoins, has not only induced a Lady of high literary fame . . . frequently to speak in this Society, but has gained it a constant attendance and decided patronage of the most respectable Ladies in the City of London, and of several of the most celebrated Amateurs of Literature in the polite Circles.'
Daily Advertiser February 6/Gazetteer February 6

1588. February 10, 1790 Westminster Forum
'Is it possible for a Man who really loves a Female to deliberately plot her Seduction?'
Daily Advertiser February 9,

1589. February 11, 1790 Coachmakers Hall
'Is which situation of life is the greatest portion of happiness to be found, in the elevated walks of wealth and grandeur, the busy scenes of trade and commerce, or the humble paths of industry and retirement?'
The above question 'was politely transmitted to the managers by an intimate friend of the late Dr. Samuel Johnson, who frequently made it a subject of private conversation'.
Daily Advertiser February 10

1590. February 11, 1790 Temple of Eloquence, Upton's Rooms, Store Street, Tottenham Court Road
'In which Situation is the greatest Portion of Happiness to be found, in the elevated Walks of Wealth and Grandeur, the busy Scenes of Trade and Commerce, or in the humble Shades of Rural Retirement?

276

This Society is instituted at the request of several Ladies and Gentlemen resident in this Part of the Town. The Managers (although conscious of the powerful alliance promised them by Gentlemen in the habit of public speaking) think it their duty thus to publish a general invitation to Gentlemen of Ability in the honourable and literary Walks of Life; and to assure Ladies and Gentlemen who may honour this rising institution with their presence, that it shall be their constant aim to establish it by an attention to Merit, Liberality, and Public Utility.'
Daily Advertiser February 10/Gazetteer February 10

1591. February 15, 1790 City Debates
'Who best deserves the Suffrages of the Electors at the ensuing General Election – those Members who have supported Mr. Pitt and Administration – or those who have adhered to Mr. Fox and Opposition?
A Society like this, usually honoured with the Presence of from 400 to 600 respectable Citizens of this great Metropolis. . .'
Daily Advertiser February 13

1592. February 17, 1790 Westminster Forum
'In a late difference between the two Celebrated Leaders of Opposition on the subject of the French Politics, which appeared to be influenced by the soundest principles of Patriotism – Mr. Burke or Mr. Sheridan?'
Gazetteer February 16

1593. February 18, 1790 Coachmakers Hall
'Whether the sentiments of Mr. Burke or Mr. Sheridan, as delivered in the House of Commons upon the Revolution in France, are the more consistent with true principles, liberty, and the happiness and interest of mankind?'
Daily Advertiser February 17

1594. February 18, 1790 Temple of Eloquence, Upton's Great Room, Store Street, Tottenham Court Road
'Are the Corporation and Test Acts a real Infringement upon the Liberties of the Protestant Dissenters, or wholesome Restrictions necessary for the preservation of Church and State?
When we mention that arguments are promised to be delivered not only from Messrs. Madan, Wesley, and other Gospel Ministers, but that the Audience will likewise have the leading sentiments of Drs. Price, Priestley and Kippis, laid before them, any further intimation will be needless, than to solicit the opinion of the serious and well disposed of every denomination. We are under the absolute, though disagreeable necessity, of requesting the Rev. Mr. Huntington, if he delivers his Scriptures on the Arian Dissenter, to confine himself to the law of debate, and reflect who will be there to answer him.'
Daily Advertiser February 17

1595. February 22, 1790 City Debates

'Ought the Test and Corporation Acts to be repealed, as injurious to the Civil and Political Rights of the Protestant Dissenters, retained as necessary Barriers to preserve the Constitution in Church and State, or some other Form of Exclusion appointed to rescue the sacred Elements from that Prophanation to which they are at present liable?
. . . The Request of several popular Divines . . . that Dr. Priestley, Price or Kippis will . . . meet them . . . and prove (if they can) that Men who deny the first Principle of our Religion, the Divinity of Christ, are not dangerous to be admitted to any share of the Government of a Christian Country.'
Daily Advertiser February 20

1596. February 24, 1790 Westminster Forum
'Which is the strongest Obligation in the Marriage Covenant, Love, Honour, – or Obedience?'
Gazetteer February 23

1597. February 25, 1790 Temple of Eloquence
'Are the Corporation and Test Acts a real Infringement upon the Liberties of the Protestant Dissenters, or wholesome Restrictions necessary for the preservation of Church and State?'
Daily Advertiser February 24

1598. February 25, 1790 Coachmakers Hall
'Would it not be better if Young Men after the age of 18, and Young Women after the age of 16, could Marry without being subject to any censure from their Parents, their Friends, and the World?
Matrimony is described to be a state capable of the highest degree of human happiness, if hands are joined where hearts agree. Many are of opinion that the Marriage act is repugnant to the Laws of Nature, and has been a bar to the felicity of thousands.'
Daily Advertiser February 24

1599. March 1, 1790 City Debates
'Who best deserves the Suffrages of the Electors at the ensuing General Election – those Members who have supported Mr. Pitt and Administration – or those who have adhered to Mr. Fox and Opposition?
It was impossible last Evening to collect any Decision, as many Gentlemen very unfairly held up both Hands.' A celebrated nobleman laid a wager on the outcome.
In favour of Opposition.
Daily Advertiser February 27

1600. March 3, 1790 Westminster Forum
'Is the Conduct of Mr. Fox, in supporting, or of Mr. Burke in opposing the Repeal of the Test and Corporation Acts the better Proof of the Independence and Patriotism of their respective Principles?'
Gazetteer March 2

1601. March 4, 1790 Coachmakers Hall
'Is it consistent with Reason and the Christian Religion to believe that Dreams foretell any future Events, and that there are at the present Day any such Appearances as Spirits or Apparitions?'
The present Question 'comes with peculiar Propriety at a Time when Numbers are urged by a Confidence in their Dreams to risk their whole Property in the Lottery'.
Daily Advertiser March 3

1602. March 4, 1790 Temple of Eloquence
'Are there any just Grounds for supposing that any Intimation from departed Spirits are communicated to Mankind by way of Apparitions or other supernatural Tokens?
Besides the Arguments of Gentlemen who have made this their peculiar Study, the Publick will have an Opportunity of hearing some remarkable recent Cases. The Death of the Gentleman at Highgate, by the Appearance of the Woman lately murdered at Pancras, will be circumstantially related by a friend of his.'
Daily Advertiser March 3

1603. March 8, 1790 City Debates
'Which is more likely to die an Old Maid – a Prude or a Coquette?'
Daily Advertiser March 6

1604. March 10, 1790 Westminster Forum
'Which is the more criminal Conduct in a Lady – to condescend to become Mistress to the Man she loves, or to marry the Man to whom she has an Aversion?'
Gazetteer March 9

1605. March 11, 1790 Coachmakers Hall
'Is the assertion of Dr. Price true, that the Methodists have mistaken the service acceptable to God, for a system of faith souring the temper, and a service of forms supplanting morality?'
Daily Advertiser March 10

1606. March 11, 1790 Temple of Eloquence
'Are the calvinistical Doctrines taught by the late Rev. Mr. Whitfield and his Successors, Messrs. Knight, Huntington, and the Arminian tenets held by Mr. Wesley, or the novel System of Universal Salvation maintained by Mr. Winchester, the most consistent with Revelation, and most productive of moral Purity?'
Daily Advertiser March 10

1607. March 15, 1790 City Debates
'Which ought more to be avoided in the Marriage State, a great Disproportion of Years, or a total Contrariety of Temper and Disposition? The Audience in this Society never yet withheld their Approbation from a juvenile Speaker.'

Daily Advertiser March 13

1608. March 17, 1790 Westminster Forum
'Is the Assertion of Dr. Barry's late Letter to the King true, That Boxing is repugnant to the Laws and Maxims of a civilized State, evinces but little if any Courage, discovers much Barbarity, is not instrumental to any Service, but certainly productive of many Evils?
The Rev. Dr. Barry, A.M. Chaplain to the Lord Bishop of Kildare will open and close the debate.'
The decision was in favour of Dr. Barry's treatise.
Daily Advertiser

1609. March 18, 1790 Coachmakers Hall
'Is it true that a Married Woman ceases to Love her Husband after he becomes Jealous of her without a Cause?'
Daily Advertiser March 17

1610. March 22, 1790 City Debates
'Is there most Hypocrisy practiced in Love, Religion or Politicks?'
A cleric will argue (from the example of the Methodists and other sectaries) that most hypocrisy in religion. Methodists will come to disagree. Fox supporters (looking at Pitt) will say most in politics.'
Daily Advertiser March 20

1611. March 24, 1790 Westminster Forum
'Which is most absurd, a Belief in Apparitions, a Reliance on Dreams, or an implicit Faith in the Predictions of Judicial Astrology?'
Daily Advertiser March 23

1612. March 25, 1790 Coachmakers Hall
'Is the assertion true, that Men are more given to Inconstancy in Love, and that Women are more apt to assume the appearance of that passion when they do not feel it?
A young Lady who is shortly to be married has expressed an earnest wish to bring the matter to a public trial, and has therefore done, as Ladies now do (who have a taste for rational entertainment) sent the cause to Coachmakers Hall.'
Daily Advertiser March 24

1613. March 29, 1797 City Debates
'Has not Mr. Fox by coalescing with Lord Hood betrayed the Whig Interest, and deserted the Rights of the Electors of Westminster?'
Daily Advertiser March 27

1614. March 31, 1790 Westminster Forum
'Was the late Compromise of Candidates between Mr. Fox and the Minister a correct decision, or a Betrayal of the Rights of the Electors of Westminster?'

The audience 'upwards of 300' were decidedly of the opinion that the compromise was a betrayal.
Daily Advertiser April 2

1615. April 1, 1790 Coachmakers Hall
'Whether the Agreement to bring in Lord Hood and Mr. Fox for Westminster, ought to be deemed a disgraceful barter of the Rights of the whole body of Electors, or a measure of commendable Policy, to preserve the Peace of that City?
The Public are respectfully informed, that several Independent Electors of Westminster, feeling, as they ought, the importance of the Rights of Election, have, instead of listening to party invective, thought it the most fair and honourable way to submit the above question to the judgment of their fellow Subjects, after a full and free investigation of its merits.
The Question was determined Ten to One, in favour of Mr. Fox's late conduct.'
Daily Advertiser March 31

1616. April 3, 1790 Westminster Forum
'Which is the most dangerous Character, a faithless Lover, or a pernicious Friend?'
Daily Advertiser April 2

1617. April 5, 1790 City Debates
'Which implies the greatest Weakness, a Belief in Apparitions, a Reliance on Dreams, or an implicit Faith in the Predictions of Judicial Astrology?'
The Managers 'have invited Mr. Sibley and several other eminent Professors of the Astral Science, and . . . the celebrated Female Conjuror Mrs. Williams has now an Opportunity (consistent with Propriety) of publicly defending her claims to Foreknowledge.'
Daily Advertiser April 3

1618. April 7, 1790 Westminster Forum
'Was the Minister more censurable in offering, or Mr. Fox in accepting, the Proposal of nominating but one Candidate of each party?'
Audience thought the Minister was more censurable than Mr. Fox.
Daily Advertiser April 6

1619. April 8, 1790 Coachmakers Hall
'Which Character is the most truly amiable, the FRIEND – the PATRIOT – or, the CITIZEN OF THE WORLD?
This truly interesting Question was introduced at the request of a Friend of the ever memorable and godlike Mr. HOWARD, in hopes that some Gentlemen in the course of the debate, will take occasion to exhibit his virtue before a public audience – and that others animated by his glorious example may begin a life of beneficence of immortal honour, and unspeakable felicity.'
Daily Advertiser April 7

1620. April 12, 1790 City Debates
'Which implies the greatest Weakness, a Belief in Apparitions, a Reliance on Dreams, or an implicit Faith in the Predictions of Judicial Astrology?
The celebrated Dr. Ranger, Professor of the Astral Science, will explain and vindicate the Practice of foretelling future Events by the Position of the Stars.'
Daily Advertiser April 10

1621. April 14, 1790 Westminster Forum
'Would not the Electors of Westminster evince a becoming Spirit by rejecting at the next Election Lord Hood and Mr. Fox, and returning two independent Characters to Parliament?'
Daily Advertiser April 13

1622. April 15, 1790 Coachmakers Hall
'Has Mr. Pitt by introducing the Tobacco Act, and extending the Excise Laws, adopted Measures destructive of the Interests of Great Britain, and subversive of the inestimable Blessings of Liberty?
The Publick are respectfully informed that in compliance with the Solicitations of many respectable Electors, this very popular Institution will, for the remainder of the Season, be dedicated to the Discussion of a Series of important political Subjects, including a free investigation both of the public Conduct of the Minister and on the Opposition, in order that at the ensuing General Election the People may be the better able to know to whom they ought to give their Suffrages.
It was determined almost unanimously that Mr. Pitt, by introducing the Tobacco Act, and extending the Excise Laws, had adopted measures destructive of the interests of Great Britain.'
Daily Advertiser April 14

1623. April 19, 1790 City Debates
'Which implies the greatest Weakness, a Belief in Apparitions, a Reliance on Dreams, or an implicit Faith in the Predictions of Judicial Astrology?'
More than 300 Gentlemen voted for adjournment.
Daily Advertiser April 17

1624. April 21, 1790 Westminster Forum
'Is the Increase of Methodists to be ascribed to the Supineness of the Church of England Clergy, the Zeal and Ability of Methodist Preachers, or the Ignorance and Folly of their Hearers?'
Daily Advertiser April 20

1625. April 22, 1790 Coachmakers Hall

'Is unhappiness in the Marriage State more to be attributed to the exercise of too much power by the Men, or of too little obedience on the part of the Women?'
Daily Advertiser April 21

1626. April 26, 1790 City Debates
'Which implies the greatest Weakness, a Belief in Apparitions, a Reliance on Dreams, or an implicit Faith in the Predictions of Judicial Astrology?
Dr. Ranger and Mr. Urton, Astrological Professors, will explain the Science, and demonstrate from the Nativity of a Gentleman (who denied the Power of Astrology, and whose Hour of Birth they have taken) the Truth of the Science.' One of the largest attendances in the history of the institution.
Daily Advertiser April 24

1627. April 28, 1790 Westminster Forum
'Is the Increase of Methodists to be ascribed to the Supineness of the Church of England Clergy, the Zeal and Ability of Methodist Preachers, or the Ignorance and Folly of their Hearers?'
Gazetteer April 27

1628. April 29, 1790 Coachmakers Hall
'Which is the greater Affliction to a man of Sensibility, the loss of a Good Wife, or the plague of a Bad One?
As the great end of the Managers in every question they adopt, is to diffuse knowledge, correct the judgment, and amend the heart, it is hoped, from the well-known abilities and moral views of the Gentlemen who speak in this much esteemed Society, that the Debate will in some measure tend to lead some Married Ladies to review their conduct, and that good Husbands will learn to bear with Philosophic patience both the Afflictions to which the Question refers.'
Daily Advertiser April 28

1629. May 3, 1790 City Debates
'Is the following Assertion mentioned by Dr. Johnson in his Rambler true: That most Persons who marry repent their Engagement, and secretly repine at the Happiness of those who remain single?'
Daily Advertiser May 1

1630. May 5, 1790 Westminster Forum
'Which is the greater Disgrace to Humanity, the Ruffian who drags the Female African from her Family, her Kindred and her native Country, or the Monster who has lately wounded and terrified many Ladies in this Metropolis?'
Daily Advertiser May 4

1631. May 6, 1790 City Debates (open for a charitable purpose)
'Which is most consistent with Revelation and Reason, the Arminian tenets of the Rev. Mr. John Wesley, the Calvinistick Decrees upheld

by the Rev. Mr. Whitfield and his other Opponents, the theology propagated by late Emmanuel Swedenburgh under the Title of the New Jerusalem, or the Doctrine of Universal Salvation maintained by the Rev. Mr. Winchester?'
Mr. Winchester to conduct the debate.
Daily Advertiser May 1

1632. May 6, 1790 Coachmakers Hall
'Does not a late melancholy event, among many other fatal consequences of Duelling, tend to prove, that no point of honour can justify a Man's accepting a Challenge who has a Wife and Family?
The sentiments of mankind upon the practice of Duelling, are various; the rigid Moralist totally condemns it. Some Philosophers do not disapprove of it, many men of honour lament its necessity. A respectable family, some of whose relations belong to a profession, and are at the present moment under such peculiar circumstances as to render a challenge probable, have solicited the Managers to adopt the above Question.'
Daily Advertiser May 5

1633. May 10, 1790 City Debates
'Which is most consistent with Revelation and Reason, the Arminian tenets of the Rev. Mr. John Wesley, the Calvinistick Decrees upheld by the Rev. Mr. Whitfield and his other Opponents, the theology propagated by late Emmanuel Swedenburgh under the Title of the New Jerusalem, or the Doctrine of Universal Salvation maintained by the Rev. Mr. Winchester?'
Daily Advertiser May 8

1634. May 12, 1790 Westminster Forum
'Who best deserves the suffrages of the Electors of England at the ensuing General Election – those Members who have supported Mr. PITT and Administration – or those who have adhered to Mr. FOX and Opposition?'
Gazetteer May 11

1635. May 13, 1790 Coachmakers Hall
'Is Female Ruin most to be attributed to the Errors of Education, to the Treachery of the Male Sex, or the young People not being sufficiently guarded against the Consequences of their Passions?'
Daily Advertiser May 12

1636. May 17, 1790 City Debates
'Which is most consistent with Revelation and Reason, the Arminian tenets of the Rev. Mr. John Wesley, the Calvinistick Decrees upheld by the Rev. Mr. Whitfield and his other Opponents, the theology propagated by late Emmanuel Swedenburgh under the Title of the New Jerusalem, or the Doctrine of Universal Salvation maintained by the Rev. Mr. Winchester?

A most curious and interesting Enquiry will be made into Count Swedenburgh's Assertions "that for 14 Years he held Converse with the Angels, the Patriarchs and the Apostles; and that the Apostle Paul told him he repented having written certain passages in his Epistles", with matters equally mysterious'.
At this debate, there 'were upwards of 50 Divines of various Persuasions'.
Daily Advertiser May 15

1637. May 19, 1790 Westminster Forum
'Is that Brother justifiable, who punishes with Death the Seducer of his Sister's Honour?
Two alarming incidents, in the opposite walks of life, have occurred in less than a twelvemonth, of a Brother's avenging the wrongs of a Sister, by the death of her Betrayer. The one a Tradesman, near Whitechapel; the other in the late fatal duel between Mr. Reid and Mr. Ross.'
Gazetteer May 18

1638. May 20, 1790 Coachmakers Hall
'Which has the greater Reason the rejoice, the Widow who has lost a bad Husband, or the Lady who by marrying loses the reproachful appellation of Old Maid?
The Ladies who sent the above Question have done the Managers the Honour to say, that the Fair Sex consider this popular Society not only as an admirable School of Eloquence, but as a Court of Equity, in which the Causes of young Maidens, Wives, Widows, neglected Old Maids, and every other Subject that concerns the Happiness and Interest of Mankind, are fairly investigated and decided by a respectable and enlightened Audience.'
Daily Advertiser May 19

1639. May 24, 1790 City Debates
'Which is most consistent with Revelation and Reason, the Arminian tenets of the Rev. Mr. John Wesley, the Calvinistick Decrees upheld by the Rev. Mr. Whitfield and his other Opponents, the theology propagated by late Emmanuel Swedenburgh under the Title of the New Jerusalem, or the Doctrine of Universal Salvation maintained by the Rev. Mr. Winchester?'
Daily Advertiser May 22

1640. May 26, 1790 Westminster Forum
'Is it possible to foretell marriage – good or bad fortune – and other events in life, by the science of Judicial Astrology?'
Gazetteer May 25

1641. May 27, 1790 Coachmakers Hall
'Is the Assertion of Mr. Gibbon, the celebrated Historian, true, that Female Fortitude is commonly artificial, and seldom steady or consistent?'

Gazetteer May 26

1642. May 31, 1790 City Debates
'Which is most consistent with Revelation and Reason, the Arminian
tenets of the Rev. Mr. John Wesley, the Calvinistick Decrees upheld
by the Rev. Mr. Whitfield and his other Opponents, the theology prop-
agated by late Emmanuel Swedenburgh under the Title of the New
Jerusalem, or the Doctrine of Universal Salvation maintained by the
Rev. Mr. Winchester?'
Daily Advertiser May 29

1643. June 7, 1790 City Debates
'Which is most consistent with Revelation and Reason, the Arminian
tenets of the Rev. Mr. John Wesley, the Calvinistick Decrees upheld
by the Rev. Mr. Whitfield and his other Opponents, the theology prop-
agated by late Emmanuel Swedenburgh under the Title of the New
Jerusalem, or the Doctrine of Universal Salvation maintained by the
Rev. Mr. Winchester?'
Daily Advertiser June 5

1644. June 14, 1790 City Debates
'Which is most consistent with Revelation and Reason, the Arminian
tenets of the Rev. Mr. John Wesley, the Calvinistick Decrees upheld
by the Rev. Mr. Whitfield and his other Opponents, the theology prop-
agated by late Emmanuel Swedenburgh under the Title of the New
Jerusalem, or the Doctrine of Universal Salvation maintained by the
Rev. Mr. Winchester?'
In favour of Mr. Winchester's system.
Daily Advertiser June 12

1645. June 21, 1790 City Debates
'Will the Electors of Great Britain (from a Review of the whole publick
Conduct of the Rt. Hon. William Pitt) be justifiable in returning a
Parliament devoted to his Administration, or one in Opposition to his
Measures?
Conscious that the Debate in a Society like this, supported by Gentlemen of the most splendid abilities in the liberal professions, and numerously attended by the most respectable Merchants and Citizens of this
great Metropolis, must have considerable influence on the electors of
the kingdom in general . . . it is . . . necessary to acquaint the public,
that the grand outlines of the debate will be an examination into Mr.
Brook Watson's Pension, an investigation of the public principles of all
the city candidates, and a complete review of Mr. Pitt's whole administration, (including his extension of the Excise) by a Barrister of
eminence.'
Daily Advertiser June 19/Gazetteer June 19

1646. June 28, 1790 City Debates

'Do the well-known Facts of the Apparition of Julius Caesar to Brutus before the Battle of Philippi; that of Samuel to the Witch of Endor; and other Occurrences in Sacred and Prophane History, justify a belief in Witches and Apparitions?'
Daily Advertiser June 26

1647. July 5, 1790 City Debates
'Do the well-known Facts of the Apparition of Julius Caesar to Brutus before the Battle of Philippi; that of Samuel to the Witch of Endor; and other Occurrences in Sacred and Prophane History, justify a belief in Witches and Apparitions?
We have been sent a Relation of the extraordinary Case of George Lukins, the Bristol Daemoniack, out of whom the Rev. J. Wesley is said to have cast seven Devils. We are at a loss to express our Gratitude to a Gentleman who was present during a great Part of the Affair of the Cock-Lane Ghost, and who will . . . communicate many valuable particulars of that astonishing Transaction. . . The Apparition which was seen by the Rev. Mess. Madan, Whitfield and Wesley has already been mentioned but from such an authority as the Rev. Mr. K (the old Associate of the Rev. Mr. Whitfield) a second Relation by Way of Confirmation is certainly admissable.'
Daily Advertiser July 3/Times

1648. July 12, 1790 City Debates
'Did the late extraordinary Conduct ascribed to Rynwick Williams (commonly called the Monster) originate in an unfortunate Insanity – a diabolical Inclination to injure the Fair Part of the Creation – or in the groundless Apprehensions of some mistaken Females?'
Determined to come about because of a diabolical inclination.
Daily Advertiser July 10

1649. July 19, 1790 City Debates
'Ought not the Legislature (in protection of the Ladies of Great Britain) immediately to pass an Act rendering the Crime of Rhynwick Williams, commonly called the Monster, a capital Offense?'
Daily Advertiser July 17

1650. July 26, 1790 City Debates
'Which is the most distressing Situation, a Ship-wrecked Mariner, a condemned Criminal, or a seduced Female abandoned by her Betrayer?'
Daily Advertiser July 24

1651. August 2, 1790 City Debates
'Which is the more reasonable Conduct in an Old Maid past the Age of 40, patiently to bear the Reproach which the World annexes to her Situation, or run the hazard of marrying when Love cannot be supposed to be the Foundation of the Union?

There is in this Metropolis a Society of Spinsters called the Thoughtful Sisters; one of their Members received a Matrimonial Overture from a young Gentleman of 25; the Lady (as is customary among them) submitted her Case to the Society; but not being satisfied with their Decision, has boldly appealed to the publick Voice, through the Medium of this popular Institution. . . The whole Society of Thoughtful Sisters have signified their Intention of attending this Debate. . . The uncommon Extent of publick Patronage and literary Support we have received, compel us to continue these Debates during the whole Year.'
Daily Advertiser July 31

1652. August 23, 1783 City Debates
'Supposing a Father to have three Daughters, the eldest possessed of uncommon beauty, the next of superior understanding, and to leave his who fortune to the youngest, who is devoid of either – Query, which of the three Ladies stands the best chance for a Husband?'
Daily Advertiser August 21

1653. August 30, 1790 City Debates, Capel Court
'Are the religious Doctrines and general Practices of the People called Methodists consistent with or repugnant to the grand Tenor of Revelation, the Principles of Reason and Philosophy, and the Articles, Homilies and established Disciplines of the Church of England?
A calvinistick Divine of considerable Eminence has promised to answer a Gentleman's Oration against the Methodists, wherein he accused them of taking out licenses as Dissenters, and then professing themselves to be Churchmen. . . We think it our Duty . . . to acquaint the Rev. Mr. Forster, that it was asserted in the Debate by a Gentleman, that the words "Foster and Jesus Christ" were used as a Label on some of the Coaches of his Party at the late Clerkenwell Election.'
Daily Advertiser August 28

1654. September 2, 1790 Coachmakers Hall
'Would Mr. Pitt have acted like a wise and Patriotic Minister, if instead of submitting to a procrastinated negotiation, he had turned the Power and Arms of This Country against Spain, in vindication of our insulted Honour?'
Audience thought Mr. Pitt had acted like a wise and patriotic minister in regard to Spain.
Daily Advertiser September 1

1655. September 6, 1790 City Debates
'Are the religious Doctrines and general Practices of the People called Methodists consistent with or repugnant to the grand Tenor of Revelation, the Principles of Reason and Philosophy, and the Articles, Homilies and established Disciplines of the Church of England?'
Daily Advertiser September 4

1656. September 9, 1790 Coachmakers Hall
288

'Is the love of the *mental* or *personal* charms of the Fair Sex that is more likely to induce men to enter into the married state?'
Question sent by a 'a number of females who style themselves Ratiocinians; those Ladies hold a Lodge in the West End of the Town, and communicate to each other such observations as they have made upon the manners and conduct of both sexes, particularly when such conduct regards the married state.'
Daily Advertiser September 8

1657. September 13, 1790 City Debates
'Was the Assertion of Milton (when he parted from his Wife) true, that a confirmed Dislike is as just a Ground of Divorce as Infidelity?'
Daily Advertiser September 11

1658. September 16, 1790 Coachmakers Hall
'Has the preaching of the people called *Methodists* been productive of more good or harm to society?'
Almost unanimously determined that the preaching of the Methodists has been productive of good.
Daily Advertiser September 15/The World September 23

1659. September 20, 1790 City Debates
'In which Situation of Life do the Ladies enjoy most Happiness, Virginity, Marriage or Widowhood?'
A Lady who wishes to speak to this subject seems 'to doubt the Propriety of a Lady's addressing the Chair, she is respectfully informed that this Assembly having been honoured with many elegant Orations from several Females of great Character and Ability, her Sentiments may be delivered with the strictest Decorum, and will confer an Obligation.'
Daily Advertiser September 18

1660. September 23, 1790 Coachmakers Hall
'Do the Irish Jury who decided in opposition to the opinion of the Judge, that *Truth ought not to be deemed a Libel*, deserve the thanks of every friend to the Liberty of the Press, and the Rights of Mankind? A Question in which every man who values his life, liberty, or property is immediately concerned. . . English Juries have been called upon in the public prints to follow the late example of the Irish, and a great number of Jurymen are very anxious to know whether they would be justified in so doing.'
Carried by a very great majority in the affirmative.
Daily Advertiser September 22

1661. September 27, 1790 City Debates
'Which is the greater Deviation from real Manhood, the Effeminacy of a Man-Milliner, or the Brutality of the modern Boxer?'
Daily Advertiser September 25

1662. September 30, 1790 Coachmakers Hall

'Which is more conspicuous at the present day, the vanity of the Women or the treachery of the Men?
In compliance with the request of an amiable young Lady, whose sister fell a victim to the treachery of an officer in the army, this Question is appointed for debate. . . A young Gentleman complains to the Managers of the vanity of no less than six Ladies, to whom he has paid his addresses, and to which he imputes his celibacy.'
Daily Advertiser September 29

1663. October 4, 1790 City Debates
'Can any Motives justify a Person of either Sex in passing through Life in a State of Celibacy?'
Daily Advertiser October 2

1664. October 7, 1790 Coachmakers Hall
'Is it more distressing for a virtuous Lady to be in Love with an unworthy man, who has the same affection for her; or him who possesses honour and integrity, but cannot return her love?'
Daily Advertiser October 6

1665. October 11, 1790 City Debates
'Can any Motives justify a Person of either Sex in passing through Life in a State of Celibacy?'
Daily Advertiser October 9

1666. October 14, 1790 Coachmakers Hall
'Has Mr. Pitt proved himself possessed of sufficient Spirit, Wisdom and integrity, as a Minister to carry on a War with Spain, in a manner consistent with the dignity and safety of this country?'
Daily Advertiser October 13

1667. October 18, 1790 City Debates
'Is the present critical Posture of Affairs an Honour or a Disgrace to the Minister of this Country?
The political Hemisphere of Europe seems convulsed with Doubt and Irresolution, and the Fate of France apparently is still trembling upon the Balance.'
Daily Advertiser October 16

1668. October 21, 1790 City Debates, Kings Arms Building Cornhill
'Which is the more depraved and dangerous Character, a faithless lover or a perfidious friend?
This popular and much admired Society having long since obtained a decided Pre-eminence both in the Number and Abilities of the Gentlemen who support it, the Managers now felicitate the Publick in obviating the many complaints of Ladies and Gentlemen against the State of their late Room, its intolerable heat, from lowness of the Cieling, etc. It is with Pleasure they announce that Gentlemen of the first Ability will now have the Opportunity of addressing the Audience, at once

numerous and respectable, in an Hall (on the Decoration of which they have spared no Expence), the most elegant, capacious, and central in this great Metropolis. A most numerous company of Ladies, who may now depend on . . . Accomodations (the Room containing Seats for between 600 and 700 Persons). . .'
Daily Advertiser October 20

1669. October 21, 1790 Coachmakers Hall
'Has Mr. Pitt proved himself possessed of sufficient Spirit, Wisdom and integrity, as a Minister to carry on a War with Spain, in a manner consistent with the dignity and safety of this country?'
Decided that Mr. Pitt was possessed of sufficient wisdom and integrity.
Daily Advertiser October 20

1670. October 25, 1790 City Debates
'Ought not the Word Obey to be struck out of the Marriage Ceremony? It is now above two Years since the above Question was debated in this popular Society. A young Lady and Gentleman who accidently met commenced an Acquaintance from that Time, and are now upon the Tapis of Marriage; the Lady being ever since firmly of Opinion that the word Obey is entirely unnecessary, few of her Sex ever pronouncing it at the Altar, and still fewer practicing it after they become Wives, has made preliminary Condition with her Lover that he should, before she gives him her Hand, depend on her loving and honouring him as a Husband, but publickly renounce all Claims to the slavish System of Obedience.'
Daily Advertiser October 23

1671. October 28, 1790 Coachmakers Hall
'Ought Marriage to be considered as a Divine Institution, a meer Political Contract or an innovation of Priestcraft subversive of the natural liberty and happiness of mankind?
Several Students from the two Universities, after the example of those great and admired Advocates, Messrs. Dallas, Garrow, Serjeant Cockrell, &c. intend to make this Society their school for acquiring the useful art of addressing a public Assembly with ease and elegance.'
Daily Advertiser October 27

1672. October 28, 1790 City Debates, Kings Arms Building, Cornhill
'Which is the wisest Man, he who marries for Love, he who marries for Money, or he who runs the Hazard of dying an old Bachelor by remaining single till he meets with a Wife, in whom both Qualifications are united?
This Society being now the constant Resort of the Wise, the Intelligent and the Learned (the Successors of those brilliant Supporters of this Institution, when held in another Place, Messrs. Erskine, Dallas, Garrow, &c. the Honour of whose Assistance attaches itself to this Society . . . it is now become the fashionable Practice for private Per-

291

sons to refer any doubtful Case to the Gentlemen who support it for their Decision.' This question sent by three brothers.
Daily Advertiser October 27

1673. November 1, 1790 City Debates
'Has the Conduct of Mr. Pitt (from the time he was warned by Lord Stormont of the danger of not including Spain in the Treaty with France for disarming, down to the present Moment of Negociation) been such as merits the Confidence, or deserves the Indignation, of the Sovereign and the People?
This Society, which has been established more than Half a Century, the most ancient as well as the most respectable Institution for free debate in the Kingdom; cannot present the Publick with more decisive Proofs of its Superiority, than the Pretensions of others (who have instituted Societies in the Places from whence it has removed) to that Credit and Originality which a discerning Publick has long since rendered its exclusive Privilege.'
Daily Advertiser October 30

1674. November 4, 1790 Coachmakers Hall
'Do the Members of the English and Irish Whig Clubs, deserve to be considered as the friends and assertors of the Constitutional rights of the people – or as a body of men actuated by a party spirit, and who assemble to oppose the necessary measures of Government?'
Proper accommodation available for 'the Marchioness of L— and her daughter'.
Daily Advertiser November 3

1675. November 4, 1790 City Debates
'Has the Conduct of Mr. Pitt (from the time he was warned by Lord Stormont of the danger of not including Spain in the Treaty with France for disarming, down to the present Moment of Negociation) been such as merits the Confidence, or deserves the Indignation, of the Sovereign and the People?'
Attendance of the Cherokee Chiefs.
Daily Advertiser November 3

1676. November 9, 1790 City Debates
'Do Mr. Burke's reflections on the French Revolution, his comparison between Dr. Price and Hugh Peters, his strictures on the Doctor's sermon, on the meeting at the London Tavern, and the general tendency of the publication, breathe that spirit of freedom and liberality for which Mr. Burke has long been famous, or evince a total deviation from his former sentiments?
One of the Cherokee Chiefs who attended these debates on Thursday last . . . having expressed his intention by his interpreter of frequently visiting this Society during his stay in the metropolis, the Rev. Mr. B. must now retract his charge of deception; we never yet announced any circumstance in our advertisements that did not take place, nor are we

answerable for those Societies who advertise the attendance of exalted characters merely to deceive the public.'
Daily Advertiser November 6

1677. November 10, 1790 Westminster Forum, Panton Street
'Are the Reflections in Mr. Burke's pamphlet on the French National Assembly and the Protestant Dissenters, an insidious Attack on the Friends of the English Revolution of 1688, or the noble Emanations of a Heart anxious to preserve the Happiness of the People and the Honour of the Crown?'
Has undergone repair. Respectability of Society and decor 'is suited to Persons of Fashion and distinction'.
Daily Advertiser

1678. November 11, 1790 Coachmakers Hall
'Are the Observations in Mr. Burke's Pamphlet upon the sermon of Dr. Price and the French Revolution, consistent with his former professions and favourable to the just rights and liberties of mankind?
The public know too well that this institution is the only established and respectable one in the kingdom for free debate, to be deceived by the contemptible suggestions of falsehood and folly which disgrace the advertisements of an inferior mushroom Society.'
Times

1679. November 11, 1790 City Debates
'Is it consistent either with female prudence or delicacy to advertise for a husband?' [if the Lady who was to address the Society is well; if not]
'Can a man who really loves a female, deliberately seduce her?'
Daily Advertiser November 10

1680. November 15, 1790 City Debates
'Can a man who really loves a female, deliberately seduce her?'
A merchant and father of seven daughters, asks this question.
This Society is now frequented by Gentlemen of the first Independence and Ability: the Barrister here condescends to unfold the Arcana of Constitutional Knowledge; the Philosopher explores the latent Principles of Nature, whilst several Divines of popular Esteem quit the Pulpit of Instruction, and here communicate a System of Ethicks, diffusive as the vital Principle, and sacred as the hallowed Beam of Truth.
It is with reluctance we descend to notice the vulgar and contemptible attack of a sinking Society (once respectable by the orations of these dignified characters, who now confine their abilities to this Institution, and who, at our removal from thence, left nothing original but the stools and benches, together with some other wooden appurtenances.). . . The patronage of a generous public therefore compels us to assert our own dignity, to disclaim such a contemptible conduct as actuates our angry opponents, and to declare, we wage no war with Bedlam or the Mint.'
Daily Advertiser November 13/The World

1681. November 17, 1790 Westminster Forum
'Are the Reflections in Mr. Burke's pamphlet on the French National Assembly and the Protestant Dissenters, an insidious Attack on the Friends of the English Revolution of 1688, or the noble Emanations of a Heart anxious to preserve the Happiness of the People and the Honour of the Crown?
As the City Debates were honoured with the Presence of the Cherokee Chiefs, and we have received Intimation that they will probably attend us Tomorrow Evening, every necessary Preparation will be made for their Reception. This being a subject in which the Protestant Dissenters are peculiarly interested, and as Numbers of their Clergy are expected to be Present, no private Gentleman can be heard in preference either to the Divines of that Persuasion or those of the Establishment.'
Daily Advertiser November 16

1682. November 18, 1790 City Debates
'Is the Assertion of the celebrated poet, Prior, true, That after marriage Husbands sigh for liberty, and Wives for Power?
Such is the Celebrity of this Institution, that the Managers are happy in declaring the Tedium of a Pause is unknown in the Society, scarcely a Minute passing but what is occupied by Sentiments which, while they promote the Interests of Virtue, support the Dignity of Truth, and relieve the Mind in Proportion as they improve its Powers.'
Daily Advertiser November 17.

1683. November 18, 1790 Coachmakers Hall
'Is the Assertion of the celebrated poet true, viz. That after marriage the men always sigh for liberty, and their wives for Power?'
Daily Advertiser

1684. November 22, 1790 City Debates
'Which will make a Lady of Sensibility the worst Husband, a Spendthrift, a Miser, a Clown or a Fop?'
Daily Advertiser November 20

1685. November 24, 1790 Westminster Forum
'Which must be more irksome to a Female of Sensibility, Indifference from the Man she loves, or the most tender Assiduities of him whose Affection she is incapable of returning?
A Lady of literary Eminence, who frequently speaks in the City Debates' will speak on the topic.
Daily Advertiser November 23

1686. November 25, 1790 Coachmakers Hall
'Is the common observation true, that women love their first husbands, and men their second wives, with the strongest affection?'
Daily Advertiser November 24

1687. November 25, 1790 City Debates

'Which will render women of sensibility most unhappy, to be married to a spendthrift, a miser, a clown, or a fop?'
Daily Advertiser November 24

1688. November 29, 1790 City Debates
'To which of the following causes is Mr. Pitt most indebted for his present Popularity – his being the immediate Descendant of the immortal Chatham, his own Ability as a Minister, or that Folly and Credulity which Foreigners describe as the striking Characteristick of the British Nation?
It is expected the Address from the City on the Spanish Convention will be followed by most of the Corporate Bodies in the Kingdom. Several Gentlemen, however, who profess no other Design than to open the Eyes of the People, have signified their Intention of availing themselves of this Opportunity publickly to convince Persons who may be applied to for their Signatures to such Addresses . . . that the Whole of the Minister's Conduct deserves the Reprobation of every Friend of his Country.'
Audience concluded that Mr. Pitt owes his popularity to his own Abilities.
Daily Advertiser

1689. December 1, 1790 Westminster Forum
'Is the assertion of Mr. Addison (in the Spectator) true, that the happiest days of human life are those spent in courtship?
The managers have the honor to acquaint the public that this society is now frequented by persons of the first fashion and ability.'
Times

1690. December 2, 1790 City Debates
'Is it the fault of Husbands or of Wives, that there are so few applications for the Dunmow Flitch of Bacon?'
Daily Advertiser December 1

1691. December 2, 1790 Coachmakers Hall
'Which is the greater affliction to a man of virtue and sensibility; the infidelity of a *beloved wife*, or the seduction of an *only daughter*?
A free debate upon the above question will be productive of the end for which it is intended, namely, in guarding the unsuspecting and generous female against the arts of seduction, and to point out to the married of both sexes, that when they depart from conjugal fidelity they forsake the road to honour and real felicity; the subject was suggested to the managers by a worthy clergyman who lately witnessed the miserable fate of a beautiful young lady seduced under a promise of marriage, and whose death broke the heart of her affectionate father.'
Daily Advertiser December 1

1692. December 6, 1790 City Debates

'Which ought to be considered as the chief Authors of Female Misery, the artful Seducers of Virgin Innocence, or those inexorable Parents who abandon their unfortunate Daughters in Consequence of that Seduction?'
Daily Advertiser December 4

1693. December 6, 1790 Theological Society
'Ought the people called Methodists to be considered as Members of the Established Church – as Dissenters from it – or as a Religious Body of Men unconnected with either?'
Gazetteer December 4

1694. December 8, 1790 Westminster Forum
'Is the Assertion mentioned by Dr. Johnson in the Rambler true, that most persons who marry, repent their Engagement, and secretly repine at the happiness of those who remain Single?'
Gazetteer

1695. December 9, 1790 City Debates
'Which ought to be considered as the chief Authors of Female Misery, the artful Seducer of Virgin Innocence, or those inexorable Parents who abandon their unfortunate Daughters in Consequence of that Seduction?
The Grave and the Gay, the Aged and the Juvenile, joined in shedding the Tear of Sensibility for the unhappy Victim of Seduction.'
Daily Advertiser December 8

1696. December 9, 1790 Coachmakers Hall
'Has Dr. Price in his Revolution sermon published opinions injurious to the cause of the Protestant Dissenters, and contrary to the principles of the British constitution?'
Daily Advertiser December 8

1697. December 13, 1790 Theological Society, Capel Court, Bartholomew Lane
'Which is more consistent with the general Tenor of the Scriptures, that Tenets of Calvinism, that only a Part of the Human Race were elected to eternal Life, or those of the Arminians, that all Mankind were redeemed, and none but the Unbelieving or Disobedient will perish?
This Institution may be considered as a School of Theology, in which religious Knowledge will be promoted, Error detected, and Infidelity defeated. It has no Connection with a Society lately held in this Place, and will be conducted with Decorum; Levity and Ridicule will be discountenanced; the Doctrines of the Gospel will be treated with Reverence, and its Ministers with Respect.'
Daily Advertiser

1698. December 13, 1790 City Debates

'Which is the greater Object of Pity, the Lady left in a hopeless State of Virginity by the Perfidy of her Lover, or the married Man rendered an Object of Scorn through the Infidelity of his Wife?'
Daily Advertiser December 11

1699. December 15, 1790 Westminster Forum
'Which is more blameable, the disobedience of the daughter who elopes with her lover, or the tyranny of that father who compels her to marry contrary to her own inclinations?'
Gazetteer

1700. December 16, 1790 Coachmakers Hall
'Has Dr. Price in his Revolution sermon published opinions injurious to the cause of the Protestant Dissenters, and contrary to the principles of the British constitution?'
Daily Advertiser December 15

1701. December 16, 1790 City Debates
'A Mariner Shipwrecked (with his Mother, Wife and Child) was, after leaving the Vessel, in an open Boat, that unfortunately overset, unable to save more than one of them. Which ought to have been the Object of his Choice?'
Daily Advertiser December 15

1702. December 20, 1790 Theological Society
'Which is more consistent with the general Tenor of the Scriptures, that Tenets of Calvinism, that only a Part of the Human Race were elected to eternal Life, or those of the Arminians, that all Mankind were redeemed, and none but the Unbelieving or Disobedient will perish?'
Daily Advertiser

1703. December 20, 1790 City Debates
'Ought Mr. Horne Tooke's Petition to be considered as a libelous attack on the House of Commons, or a just statement of the defects of the British Constitution, arising from the unequal representation of the people?
Mr. Horne Tooke is a gentleman whose political sentiments have been the constant theme of misrepresentations and abuse both from Opposition and Administration. Several Gentlemen who wish impartially to investigate the merits of the petition, transmitted the above question to the managers, with the most positive assurance of the probability of Mr. Horne Tooke's attendance. The managers have the more readily adopted it, as they recollect, that Gentleman has formerly delivered his sentiments in these Societies; they take the liberty to add their most respectful solicitations for the honour of Mr. Horne Tooke's attendance. In the House of Commons he could not answer the invective levelled against his petition. In this Society (before a numerous selection of the most judicious part of the public) he may.'
Times

1704. December 22, 1790 Westminster Forum, Panton Street Haymarket
'Ought Mr. Horne Tooke's Petition to be considered as a libellous attack on the House of Commons, or a just statement of the defects in the British Constitution, arising from the unequal representation of the people?'
Times

1705. December 23, 1790 City Debates
'Ought two Lovers, possessed of mutual affection, but devoid of fortune, to marry, trusting to Providence and their own industry for support, or to separate on motives of prudence?'
Daily Advertiser December 22

1706. December 23, 1790 Coachmakers Hall
'Ought the Petition of Mr. Horne Tooke to be reprobated as an impudent Libel on the most important branch of the British Legislature, or supported by the people, as containing bold truths, and founded on constitutional principles?'
Daily Advertiser, December 22

1707. December 27, 1790 City Debates
'Every Woman is at Heart a Rake. Did Mr. Pope, in the above Sentence, utter an unwelcome Truth, or publish a scandalous Libel on the Fair Sex?'
Question determined as a libel on the Fair Sex.
Daily Advertiser December 25

1708. December 30, 1790 City Debates
'Is the present stagnation of matrimony owing to the levity of the women, the depravity of the men, or that want of harmony in those already married, which renders single persons of both sexes afraid to engage in the connubial state?'
Daily Advertiser December 29

1709. December 30, 1790 Coachmakers Hall
'Is the Passion of Jealousy stronger in the Breast of the male or the Female Lover?'
Daily Advertiser December 29

1710. January 3, 1791 City Debates, returned to Cornhill, opposite the 'Change
'Which ought a Lady to prefer for a husband, the man whom she regards who possesses no return of affection over he who tenderly loves her, but to whom she unfortunately has an aversion?'
Question by the 'request of a Lady, now a widow, who was circumstanced as this question described, and who unfortunately married the man of her heart, who did not regard her. . . Our fair correspondent attributes all her past misfortune to the election she made; and declares

that if she had, on the contrary, married the man who tenderly loved her, time and his merit would have altered her opinion, and assured her happiness.'
Daily Advertiser January 1

1711. January 5, 1791 Free Debates on a Superior Plan, Great Room, Maiden lane, Bedford Street Covent Garden
'Which opinion is more conformable to the true principles of the Constitution – Doctor Price's, who in his Discourse on the Love of our Country, says, that the King of Great Britain is almost the only lawful King in the world, because the only one who owes his Crown to the choice of his people – or Mr. Burke's, who, in his Reflections on the Revolution in France, asserts that this doctrine affects our Constitution in its vital parts? Amongst a People proud of their Free Constitution, and sensible of the vigilance with which it should be guarded, it is conceived, that whatever tends to instruct them in their rights, or remind them of their liberties, must meet attention and encouragement. Under this idea, a Society will be formed for the discussion of Political and Historical Questions.'
Admission one shilling.
The World January 3

1712. January 6, 1791 City Debates
'Which is the most agreeable to reason and revelation, the Arminian Tenets of the Rev. Mr. Wesley, the Calvinistic Decrees upheld by the Rev. Mr. Whitfield and other, the Swedenburgh Theology or the Doctrine of universal salvation maintained by the Rev. Mr. Winchester?'
Rev. Dr. Clarke opened the debate.
Daily Advertiser January 1

1713. January 6, 1791 Coachmakers Hall
'Which is the most injurious Character to Society, an ignorant Physician, a covetous Divine, or a dishonest Lawyer?'
Daily Advertiser January 5

1714. January 10, 1791 City Debates
'Which is the most agreeable to reason and revelation, the Arminian Tenets of the Rev. Mr. Wesley, the Calvinistic Decrees upheld by the Rev. Mr. Whitfield and other, the Swedenburgh Theology or the Doctrine of universal restoration maintained by the Rev. Mr. Winchester?'
Daily Advertiser January 8

1715. January 12, 1791 Free Debates on a Superior Plan
'Which Opinion is more conformable to the true principles of the Constitution – Doctor Price's, who, in the Discourse on the Love of our Country, says, that the King of Great Britain is almost the only lawful King in the World, because the only one who owes his Crown to the Choice of his People – or, Mr. Burke's, who, in his Reflections on the Revolution in France, asserts that this Doctrine affects our Constitution in its vital parts?'
The World January 11

1716. January 13, 1791 City Debates
'Which is the most agreeable to reason and revelation, the Arminian Tenets of the Rev. Mr. Wesley, the Calvinistic Decrees upheld by the Rev. Mr. Whitfield and other, the Swedenburgh Theology or the Doctrine of universal restoration maintained by the Rev. Mr. Winchester?'
Daily Advertiser January 12

1717. January 13, 1791 Coachmakers Hall
'Do the Cures, said to be performed by Animal Magnetism deserve to be credited, as the effect of a valuable discovery in nature – or to be considered as an imposition upon the credulity of mankind?'
Daily Advertiser January 12

1718. January 17, 1791 City Debates
'Which is the most agreeable to reason and revelation, the Arminian Tenets of the Rev. Mr. Wesley, the Calvinistic Decrees upheld by the Rev. Mr. Whitfield and other, the Swedenburgh Theology or the Doctrine of universal restoration maintained by the Rev. Mr. Winchester?'
Daily Advertiser January 15

1719. January 20, 1791 Coachmakers Hall
'Would either of the following Laws tend to prevent Seduction and Prostitution, viz. A Law to compel every Man to marry who has willfully remained single till the age of 30, or to allow those who are fond of Matrimony to have two Wives?
A Lady, who has lately perused the celebrated work of the Rev. Mr. Madan in favour of Polygamy, and who has made the causes of female ruin, a subject of her particular attention, has solicited the Managers of this Society to propose the above question for public debate. She is desirous of knowing the opinion of an enlightened assembly upon the consequence of allowing in this Country a plurality of wives.'
Daily Advertiser January 19/World January 20

1720. January 20, 1791 City Debates
'Which is the most agreeable to reason and revelation, the Arminian Tenets of the Rev. Mr. Wesley, the Calvinistic Decrees upheld by the Rev. Mr. Whitfield and other, the Swedenburgh Theology or the Doctrine of universal restoration maintained by the Rev. Mr. Winchester?'
Daily Advertiser January 19

1721. January 24, 1791 City Debates
'Which is the most agreeable to reason and revelation, the Arminian Tenets of the Rev. Mr. Wesley, the Calvinistic Decrees upheld by the Rev. Mr. Whitfield and other, the Swedenburgh Theology or the Doctrine of universal restoration maintained by the Rev. Mr. Winchester?'
Daily Advertiser January 22

1722. January 26, 1791 Free Debates on a Superior Plan
'Which would more promote the Interest of this Kingdom, the Aboli-
tion or Renewal of the East-India Company's Charter?'
The World

1723. January 27, 1791 City Debates
'Which is the most agreeable to reason and revelation, the Arminian
Tenets of the Rev. Mr. Wesley, the Calvinistic Decrees upheld by the
Rev. Mr. Whitfield and other, the Swedenburgh Theology or the Doctrine of universal restoration maintained by the Rev. Mr. Winchester?
Two Persons last Monday evening hissed a Reverend Gentleman who
defended the Universal Restoration. To prevent such unbecoming
Behaviour (a Debt due to our Reverend Attendants) proper Persons
will be appointed to conduct such offending Characters out of the Hall;
but we hope this Hint will be sufficient, as the Managers wish no Person
to attend this Institution, who (if unhappily not possessed the Charity
of a Christian) cannot behave with the Politeness of a Gentleman.'
Daily Advertiser January 26

1724. January 27, 1791 Coachmakers Hall
'Does the circumstance of the Queen of France, wearing a dagger to
prevent by suicide an ignoble assassination, argue more the fortitude
of ancient virtue, or the petulance of female pride?'
Times

1725. January 31, 1791 City Debates
'Which is the most agreeable to reason and revelation, the Arminian
Tenets of the Rev. Mr. Wesley, the Calvinistic Decrees upheld by the
Rev. Mr. Whitfield and other, the Swedenburgh Theology or the Doc-
trine of universal restoration maintained by the Rev. Mr. Winchester?
While two Gentlemen were pourtraying the striking Scene of a future
Judgement . . . that awful Silence reigned throughout the Assembly
which, while it was a just Tribute to the impressive Force of their Elo-
quence, proves, that even in an Age of Levity like the present, a popular
and numerously frequented Institution can be maintained sacred to the
Improvement of the mental Powers, the establishment of proper Opin-
ions in Divinity, and the Glory of that omnipotent Being who light up
Reason in the human Breast to examine his Works, to investigate his
Mercies, and to pay the Tribute of Adoration due to his inestimable
Bounty.'
Daily Advertiser January 29

1726. February 3, 1791 Coachmakers Hall
'Is it possible, by judicial Astrology, to prophecy or foretell any Event
that is to happen to the material World, or the good or ill Fortune of
Individuals?'
Daily Advertiser February 2

1727. February 3, 1791 City Debates

'Which is the most agreeable to reason and revelation, the Arminian Tenets of the Rev. Mr. Wesley, the Calvinistic Decrees upheld by the Rev. Mr. Whitfield and other, the Swedenburgh Theology or the Doctrine of universal restoration maintained by the Rev. Mr. Winchester?'
Daily Advertiser February 2

1728. February 7, 1791 City Debates
'Which is the most agreeable to reason and revelation, the Arminian Tenets of the Rev. Mr. Wesley, the Calvinistic Decrees upheld by the Rev. Mr. Whitfield and other, the Swedenburgh Theology or the Doctrine of universal restoration maintained by the Rev. Mr. Winchester?'
Daily Advertiser February 5

1729. February 10, 1791 Coachmakers Hall
'Is Beauty, Virtue, or domestick Prudence, the most amiable in a Wife?'
Daily Advertiser February 9

1730. February 10, 1791 City Debates
'Which is the most agreeable to reason and revelation, the Arminian Tenets of the Rev. Mr. Wesley, the Calvinistic Decrees upheld by the Rev. Mr. Whitfield and other, the Swedenburgh Theology or the Doctrine of universal restoration maintained by the Rev. Mr. Winchester?'
Daily Advertiser February 9

1731. February 14, 1791 City Debates
'Which is the most agreeable to reason and revelation, the Arminian Tenets of the Rev. Mr. Wesley, the Calvinistic Decrees upheld by the Rev. Mr. Whitfield and other, the Swedenburgh Theology or the Doctrine of universal restoration maintained by the Rev. Mr. Winchester?'
Daily Advertiser February 12

1732. February 17, 1791 Coachmakers Hall
'Is a Lady justifiable in admitting the Addresses of two Lovers at the same Time?'
Daily Advertiser February 16

1733. February 17, 1791 City Debates
'Would not Parliament's enacting the following Law totally annihilate all the baleful Effects arising from the Crime of Seduction – Government providing a proper Asylum for all the existing Objects of its fatal Influence – and obliging in future every single Seducer to marry the unfortunate Female – and every married Man guilty of the Crime to allow her a Maintenance till she enter into Wedlock?
The Publick has long, and perhaps too justly, complained of the Frivolity of many Questions which allude to the Female Sex. The Managers of this Society are determined (supported as they are not only by a numerous attendance of Ladies, but honoured with the Presence and Sentiment of the most wise and enlightened among their own Sex) to admit none but what (like the present) appeal powerfully to the Female

302

Heart in whatever Situation, and yet admit the Display of that Eloquence, and the reasoning Powers for which this Institution has long been held in Celebrity.'
Daily Advertiser February 16

1734. February 18, 1791 City Debates
'Which is the most agreeable to reason and revelation, the Arminian Tenets of the Rev. Mr. Wesley, the Calvinistic Decrees upheld by the Rev. Mr. Whitfield and other, the Swedenburgh Theology or the Doctrine of universal restoration maintained by the Rev. Mr. Winchester? This Question having continued 16 Evenings has of Course prevented the Managers obliging many Persons who have honoured them with other Subjects, they therefore found it impossible to adjourn it to any other Evening but for the following Circumstance: A Party of Calvinists took Possession of the Hall at an early Hour, their Speakers rose in Succession, and by that Means, and the Length of their Orations (which indeed were splendid) occupied almost the Whole of the Evening, one Rev. Gentleman only, and he with difficulty, being heard, who was of a different Opinion; they even took the Advantage of speaking till, by the Lateness of the Hour, the Gentleman, whose Right it was to close the Debate, was prevented replying, and then clamorously demanded the Decision: To prevent such unfair Advantages, and to obtain an unbiased Decision on this truly momentous Subject, the following Regulations will be observed this Evening, the Chair (to allow Time) will be taken at Half past Seven o'Clock; Preference of Hearing will be given to Divines; no Gentleman, except the Closer of the Debate, allowed to speak more than ten Minutes; and no two Speakers of the same Opinion, on any Account, permitted to follow each other.'
Decided in favour of Universal Restoration.
Daily Advertiser February 16

1735. February 21, 1791 City Debates
'Is the Obedience exacted by Husbands from their Wives a Punishment on the Sex for the first Woman's Transgression, or was Eve originally created in a State of Inferiority to Adam?'
The author [of the question] noted that the 'fair are in all respects equal to the males, that this Obedience is a Usurpation on the Part of Man and an Infringement on the natural rights of the Female World'.
Daily Advertiser February 18

1736. February 24, 1791 City Debates
'Is not the Eagerness with which Widows and Widowers enter again into Wedlock, a Proof of the superior Happiness enjoyed in that State, and of the folly of old Maids and Bachelors in remaining single?'
Daily Advertiser February 23

1737. February 24, 1791 Coachmakers Hall
'Are Ecclesiastical Establishments directed by Scripture, advantageous to Religion, or beneficial to civil Society?'

Decided in negative on all issues.
Daily Advertiser March 2

1738. February 28, 1791 City Debates, Kings Arms Hall, Cornhill
'Is not the eagerness with which Widows and Widowers enter again into Wedlock, a proof of the superior happiness enjoyed in that state, and of the folly of Old Maids and Batchelors in remaining Single?'
Daily Advertiser February 26

1739. March 3, 1791 City Debates
'Which has more Blanks to a Prize, Marriage or the Lottery?
This Subject on the first View appears to partake much of the ludicrous, doubtless many Ideas calculated to awake the risible Faculties of the Audience will be adduced on the Blanks in the matrimonial Lottery . . . but the chief End of the Conductors of this Society is to hold up in Terrorem the gloomy List of Blanks in the State Lottery, the Folly and Credulity of Dreamers, the Iniquity of Insurance Offices, kept open in Defiance of the Legislature, and the Evils which result to the Lower Orders of the People from a universal Spirit of Gambling being disseminated among them.'
Daily Advertiser March 2

1740. March 3, 1791 Coachmakers Hall
'Would the Passing the Bill now pending in Parliament for the Relief of the Roman Catholicks be consistent with the Security of the Protestant Religion, and with the Safety of the British Constitution?'
Decided that the bill could safely be passed.
Daily Advertiser March 2

1741. March 7, 1791 City Debates
'Are the cures attributed to Animal Magnetism performed by the operations of conceit in the patients, the power of Satanic influence, some occult principles in philosophy, or is the whole an imposition of interested persons to take advantage of the credulity of Mankind?
The audience was highly gratified by an Oration from that ingenious Lecturer Mr. Holloway, who, in an elegant Train of Reasoning, supported by numerous learned Authorities, proved himself a most powerful Advocate for the Science.' Dr. Stearn also spoke to the question.
Daily Advertiser March 5

1742. March 10, 1791 Coachmakers Hall
'Would it be consistent with Justice and sound Policy to grant relief to the Roman Catholicks, while the Protestant Dissenters are refused an equal Participation of civil and religious Liberties with the Members of the established Church?
It is proposed, with the concurrence of several eminent Catholick and Protestant Ministers, who consider free debate not only as the birthright of Englishmen, but, like the invaluable Liberty of the Press, the means by which truth is discovered, and error dispelled.'
Daily Advertiser March 9/The World

1743. March 10, 1791 City Debates
'Are the cures attributed to Animal Magnetism performed by the operations of conceit in the patients, the power of Satanic influence, some
occult principles in philosophy, or is the whole an imposition of interested persons to take advantage of the credulity of Mankind?'
Daily Advertiser March 9

1744. March 14, 1791 City Debates
'Are the cures attributed to Animal Magnetism performed by the operations of conceit in the patients, the power of Satanic influence, some
occult principles in philosophy, or is the whole an imposition of interested persons to take advantage of the credulity of Mankind?'
Five to six hundred people usually attend.
Daily Advertiser March 12

1745. March 17, 1791 Coachmakers Hall
'Are the Female Sex as capable of Sincerity in Friendship as they are
of Constancy in Love?'
Daily Advertiser March 16

1746. March 17, 1791 City Debates
'Are the cures attributed to Animal Magnetism performed by the operations of conceit in the patients, the power of Satanic influence, some
occult principles in philosophy, or is the whole an imposition of interested persons to take advantage of the credulity of Mankind?'
Daily Advertiser

1747. March 21, 1791 City Debates
'Which is the greater Calamity, either to a Lover or Husband, the Death
or Infidelity of the beloved object?
The many recent instances of infidelity in the conjugal state being lately
the subject of conversation in a polite assembly. Several married Gentlemen averred no evils could equal those resulting from falsehood and
inconstancy in a beloved Wife. This was opposed by a young Gentleman
as being no comparison to the distress of a fond Lover, whose warm
affections were fixed on a lovely and virtuous female and met a reciprocal return, but whom the cold hand of death had torn from his
embraces and buried with all his delightful expectations in the gloomy
sepulchre of mortality.'
Daily Advertiser March 19

1748. March 24, 1791 Coachmakers Hall
'Do the Cares of a Family, and the Confinement of a domestick Life,
afford a sufficient Excuse for those who wilfully remain in a single
State?'
Daily Advertiser March 23

1749. March 24, 1791 City Debates
'Is the Conduct of Mr. Pitt in appropriating the unclaimed Dividends to the publick Service, a patriotick Measure warranted by the Emergency of the State, or an Innovation on national Credit and private Property?'
Question raised by merchants and stockbrokers who think it inimical to the true interest of the nation.
Daily Advertiser March 23

1750. March 28, 1791 City Debates
'Does the real Religion that is conspicuous in many of the Followers of the late Messrs. Whitfield and Wesley compensate for the Hypocrisy and Enthusiasm which have been fostered under their venerable Names?
The Conductors return their unfeigned Thanks to the ingenious Mr. Hamilton Reid for his elegant Monody on the death of the late Mr. Wesley.'
Daily Advertiser March 26

1751. March 31, 1791 Coachmakers Hall
'Would it tend to prevent Adultery and Divorce if that Part of the Marriage Ceremony which says "As long as you both shall live" was expunged, and instead thereof the following Words inserted, "So long as you both can agree"?
This Society being universally considered as a Court of Equity as well as a School of Eloquence, every Question that concerns the Interests of the Community, the Happiness of Individuals, or that can affect the fine and laudable feelings of the Human Heart, will always meet with a welcome Reception. Upwards of 20 Ladies have united their Solicitations for a publick Debate upon this Subject; and as it is of great Importance to all who are or intend to be married, the Ladies as well as Gentlemen will be asked to express their Assent or Dissent to the proposed Alteration.'
Daily Advertiser March 30

1752. March 31, 1791 City Debates
'Has Methodism, as established by the Rev. Messrs. Whitfield and Wesley, promoted the interests of real Religion, or only increased the Number of Hypocrites and Enthusiasts?'
The 'Question was adjourned, and the Alteration made, at the particular Request of several Persons, who considered the Statement of last Evening as peculiarly partial to Methodism, and who pledged themselves to prove, by a Relation of various Examples (this Evening) of the Folly and Credulity of their Followers, that the Tenets of Messrs. Whitfield and Wesley have been more productive of Superstition and Enthusiasm than real religion.'
Daily Advertiser

1753. April 4, 1791 City Debates

306

'Has the Practice of giving large Fortunes with Daughters been more Productive of Good, in establishing the Credit and Happiness of the marriage State, or of Evil, by inclining Men to marry for Money rather than Love, and causing innumerable Disappointments in the tender Passions?'
Daily Advertiser April 2

1754. April 7, 1791 Coachmakers Hall
'Is the Passion of Love or Jealousy the more prevalent among the Female Sex?'
Daily Advertiser April 6

1755. April 7, 1791 City Debates
'Is Mrs. Gunning's Letter to the Duke of Argylle a sufficient Refutation of the Charges brought against her Daughter; or was the young Lady guilty of using Artifice with one Lover, in order to secure the Affections of another?'
The World

1756. April 11, 1791 City Debates
'Is the assertion of Dr. Johnson true, that the greater part of bad husbands are made so by the misconduct of their wives?
From this debate, the unhappy in the married world may be induced to amend their conduct, and the single of both sexes learn to avoid the evils and experience the comfort and happiness intended by the great author of our being to result from the sacred enjoyment of wedlock.'
Daily Advertiser April 9

1757. April 14, 1791 Coachmakers Hall
'Is it consistent with the Character of a Christian and a Man of Sense to believe that the Death of a Friend may be known by a supernatural Token, or that a departed Spirit ever appeared, and conversed with any Mortal?'
Daily Advertiser April 13

1758. April 18, 1791 City Debates
'If a Gentleman has gained the Affection of a Lady, and solemnly promises her marriage, but afterwards feels a stronger Passion for another, which ought he to marry?
The two ladies immediately concerned intend to be present; they as well as their sex in general who attend may expect much instructive entertainment from this interesting debate; they may learn to guard their hearts from giving too easy access to the seducing softnesses of love. How far a promise of marriage may be relied on, and whether happiness can be expected in wedlock, independent of a mutual and sincere regard for each other.'
Times

1759. April 21, 1791 Coachmakers Hall

'Is it not more difficult for a good Husband to reclaim a bad Wife [than] it is for a good Wife to reform a bad Husband?'
Daily Advertiser April 20

1760. April 21, 1791 City Debates
'Which is most consistent with Religion and Probability, a Reliance on the Predictions of judicial Astrology, an Opinion that Dreams foretell future Events, a Confidence in the powers of Animal Magnetism for the Cure of human Maladies, or the Belief that departed Spirits sometimes hold Converse with Mortals, and appear at the Moment of Dissolution by any supernatural Token, to absent Friends and Relatives?'
Daily Advertiser April 20

1761. April 25, 1791 City Debates
'Which is most consistent with reason and probability, a reliance on the predictions of judicial astrology, an opinion that dreams foretell future events, a confidence in the powers of animal magnetism for the cure of human maladies, or a belief that departed spirits sometimes converse with mortals, and appear at the moment of dissolution by any supernatural token, to absent friends or relations?
An eminent astrologer has requested permission to answer the observations of the celebrated magnetist who spoke on last evening. . . Either of the parties willing to demonstrate by example before the audience this evening the authenticity of their science, may depend upon every necessary accommodation.'
Times

1762. April 28, 1791 Coachmakers Hall
'Is the Conduct of Mr. Fox or Mr. Pitt, respecting a War with Russia, the more consistent with the Principles of the Constitution and the Welfare of the British Nation?'
Daily Advertiser April 27

1763. April 28, 1791 City Debates
'Which is the happiest State, a Maid, a Wife, or a Widow?'
Daily Advertiser April 27

1764. May 2, 1791 City Debates
'Which is the happiest state, a Maid, a Wife or a Widow?'
Daily Advertiser April 30

1765. May 5, 1791 Coachmakers Hall
'Would the Abolition or Continuance of the Slave Trade be more likely to promote the commercial Interests and national Dignity of Great Britain?
So interesting to the Feelings of Humanity, so important to the Honour and Character of this Country, to its Trade, Commerce and political Security, is this Question considered, that this Society . . . was visited by several Members of the House of Commons, Gentlemen at the Bar,

and a great Number of the most respectable trading and commercial Men in the Kingdom.'
Daily Advertiser May 4

1766. May 5, 1791 City Debates
'Which has been productive of most Misery among Mankind, unlawful and disappointed Love, inordinate Avarice, or unbounded Ambition?'
Daily Advertiser May 4

1767. May 9, 1791 City Debates
'Is the Assertion of Dr. Goldsmith on Seduction (in his celebrated Novel of the Vicar of Wakefield) true, that Women are much more unforgiving to female frailty than Men?'
Daily Advertiser May 7

1768. May 12, 1791 Coachmakers Hall
'Would the Abolition or Continuance of the Slave Trade be more likely to promote the commercial Interests and national Dignity of Great Britain?'
Daily Advertiser May 11

1769. May 12, 1791 City Debates
'Did the Sentiments of Mr. Burke on the French Revolution, in opposition to Mr. Fox (particularly his Assertion – "There are Men in this Country who have conceived the infernal Project of fundamentally overturning its Constitution" – and his Declaration – "He should from that Time excommunicate himself from the Party for ever –") indicate the patriotick Guardian of the British Constitution, or the enthusiastick Advocate for arbitrary Power?'
Daily Advertiser May 11

1770. May 16, 1791 City Debates
'What is the first Cause of Love?'
Daily Advertiser May 14

1771. May 19, 1791 Coachmakers Hall
'Would the Abolition or Continuance of the Slave Trade be more likely to promote the commercial Interests and national Dignity of Great Britain?'
Almost unanimously carried in favour of Abolition.
Daily Advertiser May 18

1772. May 19, 1791 City Debates
'What is the first Cause of Love?'
Daily Advertiser May 18

1773. May 23, 1791 City Debates
'Supposing a Father to have three Daughters, the eldest an uncommon Beauty, the next of a superior understanding, and to leave his whole

309

Fortune to the youngest (who is possessed of neither), which of the three stands the best chance for a Husband?'
Daily Advertiser May 21

1774. May 26, 1791 Coachmakers Hall
'Which of the three celebrated Characters has discovered the greatest Knowledge of the British Constitution, and appears to have its Welfare most at Heart, Mr. Fox, Mr. Burke or Mr. Pitt?'
Daily Advertiser May 25

1775. June 2, 1791 Coachmakers Hall
'Which of the three celebrated Characters has discovered the greatest Knowledge of the British Constitution, and appears to have its Welfare most at Heart, Mr. Fox, Mr. Burke or Mr. Pitt?'
Daily Advertiser 1

1776. June 9, 1791 Coachmakers Hall
'Can the Slave Trade be justified on any Principles of Humanity, Justice or sound Policy?'
Daily Advertiser

1777. August 22, 1791 City Debates
'Did the late Riots in Birmingham originate in groundless Apprehensions raised by the Tory Principles of Mr. Burke's Pamphlet, or from any improper Conduct of the Protestant Dissenters in celebrating the French Revolution in this Country?'
City Dissenters propose this debate.
Daily Advertiser August 20

1778. August 25, 1791 City Debates
'Did the late Riots in Birmingham originate in groundless Apprehensions raised by the Tory Principles of Mr. Burke's Pamphlet, or from any improper Conduct of the Protestant Dissenters in celebrating the French Revolution in this Country?'
Audience determined 'there being only six Hands held up in the negative' that Birmingham riots caused by Burke's principles.
Daily Advertiser August 24

1779. August 29, 1791 City Debates
'Was not the trial of Mr. Rose an evident proof of the political duplicity of Mr. Pitt, and of the absolute necessity of a Parliamentary Reform?'
The World

1780. September 1, 1791 Coachmakers Hall
'Is the Constitution of France, as now settled by the National Assembly, likely to prove beneficial to its inhabitants, and to promote the tranquility of Europe?
The signal Revolution in France, the subsequent labours of the National Assembly, and the numerous productions that contain sentiments

favourable or unfriendly to the proceedings of that Legislative Body, present a grand and extensive theme to the political speculator. A restless ambition directing the arms of France during its former system of Government, has been urged as the cause that has so frequently involved this country in the carnage and expences of war. How far the ancient enmity between the two kingdoms is likely to cease, and in what degree the tranquility of Europe may be promoted by the provisions of the French Constitution, are points that will doubtless be elucidated by the respective talents and information of the historian, philosopher and active politician.'
Daily Advertiser August 29

1781. September 1, 1791 City Debates
'Which is the happiest period of man's life, when courting a wife, when married to a wife, or when burying a bad wife?'
This Question is 'a relief from the more important subjects that have lately engaged their attention, and a suitable compliment to the fair part of the creation, by whom this institution is numerously attended'.
Daily Advertiser August 31

1782. September 5, 1791 City Debates
'Can any Circumstances justify a Lady of receiving the Addresses of more than one Lover at the same Time?'
Daily Advertiser September 3

1783. September 8, 1791 City Debates
'Which is the happiest state, marriage or a single life?
The Managers, thus honoured by the constant attendance of the beautiful, the gay, and the virtuous of one sex, and the learned, ingenious, and intelligent of the other, pledge themselves for perseverance in their usual conduct, particularly extending every possible indulgence to juvenile merit; cultivating on every opportunity those powers of female eloquence which they conceive to be the brightest ornament of British literature.'
Daily Advertiser September 7

1784. September 8, 1791 Coachmakers Hall
'Is the Constitution of France, as now settled by the National Assembly, likely to prove beneficial to its inhabitants, and to promote the tranquility of Europe?
In this ancient seminary of elocution the celebrated Mr. Paine (as well as some of the first characters at the bar) frequently spoke.'
Daily Advertiser September 7

1785. September 12, 1791 City Debates
'Which is the happiest state, marriage or a single life?'
Daily Advertiser September 10

1786. September 15, 1791 City Debates

'Does the Passion of Jealousy arise from an Excess of Love, or from the mean Suspicion of an ignoble Mind?
Indeed, such is the popular estimation of this (the oldest and most respectable Society for Free Debate) that those young Gentlemen who are anxious to attain the necessary, though difficult art of Public Speaking, will here have the opportunity of addressing a numerous, candid and intelligent audience; and at the same time, in the Orations which are delivered in this Seminary of Erudition, have placed before their observance, as models for juvenile elocution, talents of the most splendid nature, supporting the dignity of virtue, defending the principles of truth, and exploring the rugged path of Science.'
Daily Advertiser September 14/World

1787. September 15, 1791 Coachmakers Hall
'Is the Constitution of France, as now settled by the National Assembly, likely to prove beneficial to its inhabitants, and to promote the tranquility of Europe?'
Daily Advertiser September 14

1788. September 19, 1791 City Debates
'Supposing a Spirit (prior to its Existence in this World) had Knowledge of the peculiar Joys and Sorrows attendant on each Sex, and being left at Liberty to make its Choice, which would it probably prefer to inhabit, a Male or a Female Body?
We cannot help thus publicly soliciting . . . that the elucidation of this interesting subject may be adorned with the display of that female eloquence from which this society has already received so many obligations.'
Daily Advertiser September 17/The World

1789. September 22, 1791 City Debates
'Which has occasioned most Mischief among Mankind, Quack Doctors, Trading Justices, or Methodist Preachers?
This is a Society for free Debate. We cannot prevent those laughable Stories, told at the Expence of Methodist Preachers; all we can say is that our Institution is open to their Defence, particularly while they can boast such advocates as our learned Correspondent.'
Daily Advertiser September 21

1790. September 22, 1791 Coachmakers Hall
'Do not the comforts of matrimony more than counterbalance all the cares and anxieties attending it?'
Daily Advertiser September 21

1791. September 26, 1791 City Debates
'Ought the present Frequency of Divorce to be ascribed to the Depravity of Bachelors, the Inattention and Misconduct of Husbands, or the Levity and Folly of the Female Character?'
Daily Advertiser September 24

1792. September 29, 1791 Coachmakers Hall
'Which of the two Bodies of Men, the Members of the Church of England or the Dissenters, have rendered most Service to this Country, either as literary Characters or Supporters of the Constitution?'
Question brought about because of the letter of Dr. Tatham (of Oxford) to Woodfall's Diary of August 8th.
Daily Advertiser September 28

1793. September 29, 1791 City Debates
'In which Situation is most Happiness to be found, the elevated Walks of Wealth and Grandeur, the busy Scenes of Trade and Commerce, or humble Shades of domestick Ease and Retirement?'
Daily Advertiser September 28

1794. October 3, 1791 City Debates
'Which is the more pitiable Situation, a worthy Husband married to a bad Wife, or an amiable Wife married to a dissolute Husband?'
Daily Advertiser October 1

1795. October 6, 1791 Coachmakers Hall
'Which of the two Bodies of Men, the Members of the Church of England or the Dissenters, have rendered most Service to this Country, either as literary Characters or Supporters of the Constitution?'
Daily Advertiser October 5

1796. October 6, 1791 City Debates
'Ought not the Word Obey to be struck out of the Marriage Ceremony?'
Daily Advertiser October 5

1797. October 10, 1791 City Debates
'Which is more calculated for the Glory of the respective Nations and the Happiness of Individuals, the French or British Constitutions?
Several illustrious French refugees (now in this country) will be present; many of the first literary Characters of the Age are expected to speak; we forbear to particularize Names, however exalted. The Sentiments of Messrs. Mackintosh, Payne and Dr. Priestley will doubtless take the Lead in this important Investigation.'
Daily Advertiser October 8

1798. October 13, 1791 The World
A HINT TO SLEEPY MAGISTRATES
'It is a fact, that there is now a house in Brownlow-street, Drury-lane, where the following business is done – in the day, Fencing – in the evening a Hop, and private accommodations for Ladies and Gentlemen – and on Sunday, a hodge-podge inflammatory society of Arians, Socinians, Muggletonians, &c. &c. debating, and to use their own term, illustrating the Scriptures.'

1799. October 13, 1791 City Debates

'Which is more calculated for the Glory of the respective Empires, and the Happiness of Individuals – the French or British Constitution?'
Daily Advertiser October 12

1800. October 13, 1791 Coachmakers Hall
'Ought the different proceedings against the late Birmingham Rioters, and those of London in the year 1780 to be attributed to the unequal atrocities of the criminals, or to a narrow prejudice against the Protestant Dissenters?
As this Society is considered to be the organ of the public mind upon questions of great political concern, the greatest candour will be shewn to Gentlemen on both sides.'
Daily Advertiser October 12

1801. October 17, 1791 City Debates
'Is the assertion of that ancient Philosopher, Socrates, true, that "Women in Mischief are wiser than Men"?'
Decided Question in the affirmative.
Daily Advertiser October 15

1802. October 20, 1791 Coachmakers Hall
'Which of the three following events, is to be considered as the most striking instance of opposition to political tyranny, the exclusion of James the Second and his posterity from the throne of England, the independence atchieved by the States of America, or the late Revolution in the ancient Government in France?'
Daily Advertiser October 19

1803. October 20, 1791 City Debates, returns to Capel Court
'Which is the most depraved Character, the Betrayer of his Friend, the Alienator of a married Lady's affections from her Husband, or the Seducer of unsuspecting Virgin Innocence?'
Question sent by 'a Clergyman who was a Passenger from India in the Fitzwilliam, where the late unfortunate seduction of a young Lady terminated in the death of herself and her Seducer'.
The Fair Orator who often spoke at this society, published An Essay on the Ruin of Female Honour.
Daily Advertiser October 19

1804. October 24, 1791 City Debates
'Which is the most depraved Character, the Betrayer of his Friend, the Alienator of a married Lady's affections from her Husband, or the Seducer of unsuspecting Virgin Innocence?
The above Question . . . was proposed by a young Lady, about 25, who has two Sisters, one of whom by incautiously entering into Marriage is most unhappily united with a worthless Husband; the other (the eldest branch of the family) is, after discarding a numerous train of admirers, some for want of one perfection, some for want of another, left at the age of 45 in a state of hopeless virginity.

The Managers think it necessary to apprize the Ladies and Gentlemen who patronize this Institution, that there is not a Vestige of the Society left in Cornhill. All Annunciations . . . of the City Debates being held there, or in any other Place . . . are the Fabrications of necessitous and illiterate Persons to mislead the Publick.'
Daily Advertiser October 22

1805. October 27, 1791 Coachmakers Hall
'Which of the three following events, is to be considered as the strongest instance of opposition to political tyranny, the exclusion of James the Second and his posterity from the throne of England, the independence atchieved by the States of America, or the late Revolution in the ancient Government in France?'
Daily Advertiser October 26

1806. October 27, 1791 City Debates
'Can a Lady whose heart is entirely disengaged, expect Happiness, or her parents any justification, when, by their commands, she marries a man of opulence, for whom she has no real affection?'
Daily Advertiser October 26

1807. October 31, 1791 City Debates
'Are those Laws consistent with Justice, Humanity, and national Prosperity, which, by restricting the Blood-Royal intermarrying with the ancient Nobility of the Realm, compel them either to form continental Alliances, or remain in the single State?'
Daily Advertiser October 29

1808. November 3, 1791 Coachmakers Hall
'Have not Ecclesiastical Establishments in all Countries tended to the Support of Arbitrary Power?'
Daily Advertiser November 2

1809. November 3, 1791 City Debates
'Which most deserves the Ridicule of Mankind, the captious old Batchelor, the censorious old Maid, or the Widow who having buried a worthy Husband, marries again to the Prejudice of her infant Family?'
Daily Advertiser November 2

1810. November 7, 1791 Society for Free Debate, King's Arms, Change-Alley, Cornhill
'Is the Assertion of Rochefoucault true, which maintains that mutual Love is like Apparitions talked of by all, but seen by none?
The Conductors of this Institution respectfully acquaint the Publick, that the late Managers of the Society held here have no Concern in the present, which is principally composed of Law Students, who, emulous of several distinguished Barristers, are desirous of instituting a School of Eloquence, in which the Utile and the Dulce may be blended, render

315

the Auspices of a liberal and enlightened Audience, in the Beams of which alone modest Merit is found to expand.'
Daily Advertiser November 5

1811. November 7, 1791 City Debates, removed to Capel-court, Bartholemew-lane
'Is learning a desirable qualification in a Wife?'
Daily Advertiser

1812. November 10, 1791 Coachmakers Hall
'Have not Ecclesiastical establishments in all ages tended to the support of Arbitrary Power?'
Daily Advertiser November 9

1813. November 10, 1791 City Debates
'Did the French National Assembly act wisely in degrading Marriage from a Divine Institution to a Civil Contract?
The conduct of the National Assembly in rendering the Marriage Ceremony a mere Bargain between Party and Party, independent of all Divine Authority, justly begins to alarm all the European ladies.'
Daily Advertiser November 9

1814. November 14, 1791 City Debates
'Which have more widely deviated from the manly Character of our Male and virtuous conduct of our Female Ancestors, the Ladies of the present Age, by becoming Toxopholites, private Actresses, and whirling in all the Eccentricities of Fashion, or the modern fine Gentleman, in making themselves Crops, Boxers, Lobby-Loungers, etc.?'
Daily Advertiser November 12

1815. November 17, 1791 Coachmakers Hall
'Have not Ecclesiastical establishments in all ages tended to the support of Arbitrary Power?'
Daily Advertiser November 16

1816. November 17, 1791 City Debates
'Which have more widely deviated from the manly Character of our Male and virtuous conduct of our Female Ancestors, the Ladies of the present Age, by becoming Toxopholites, private Actresses, and whirling in all the Eccentricities of Fashion, or the modern fine Gentleman, in making themselves Crops, Boxers, Lobby-Loungers, etc.?'
Daily Advertiser November 16

1817. November 21, 1791 City Debates
'Which have more widely deviated from the manly Character of our Male and virtuous conduct of our Female Ancestors, the Ladies of the present Age, by becoming Toxopholites, private Actresses, and whirling in all the Eccentricities of Fashion, or the modern fine Gentleman, in making themselves Crops, Boxers, Lobby-Loungers, etc.?'
Daily Advertiser

1818. November 24, 1791 Coachmakers Hall
'Is the insurrection at Saint Domingo to be attributed to the declamations and writings of the advocates for the abolition of the Slave Trade, or to the cruelty and injustice of that species of traffick?
The question is introduced at the request of many respectable Gentlemen who consider, that at a period like the present, when the sun of Liberty is rising in every part of Europe, and when the hearts of millions are rejoiced, and their hands extended in warm congratulations upon the recovery of a great nation from slavery, a public enquiry into the causes of the late insurrection in the West India Islands, and the treatment of the negroes, as well as the justice and policy of the Slave Trade, must meet the cordial approbation of the public.'
Daily Advertiser November 23

1819. November 24, 1791 City Debates
'Whose Conduct ought more to be avoided by the Fair Sex in the Season of Courtship, the Lady's, who by taking too little Caution before Marriage, gets a bad Husband, or her's, by taking too much, dies an old maid?'
Daily Advertiser

1820. December 1, 1791 Coachmakers Hall
'Is the insurrection at Saint Domingo to be attributed to the exertions and writings of those who have interested themselves to procure an abolition of the Slave Trade, or to the cruelty and injustice of that species of traffick?'
Daily Advertiser November 30

1821. December 8, 1791 Coachmakers Hall
'Is not the war now carrying on in India disgraceful to this country, injurious to its political interests, and ruinous to the commercial interests of the Company?'
Times

1822. December 15, 1791 Coachmakers Hall
'Is not the war now carrying on in India disgraceful to this country, injurious to its political interests, and ruinous to the commercial interests of the Company?'
Decision almost unanimous that war is unjust, disgraceful and ruinous.
Daily Advertiser

1823. December 17, 1791 Westminster Debates, Queen of Bohemia, Wych Street, Drury Lane
'Which would a Man be most strenuous to preserve in case of imminent Danger, and without the Ability of saving more than one, his Wife, Mother or only Child?'
Daily Advertiser

1824. December 22, 1791 Coachmakers Hall
'Would it be most for the interest of this country, that the territorial possessions in India should still continue in the hands of the present East India Company, be taken under the sole and immediate direction of the Legislature, or be relinquished to the native inhabitants of the country?'
Daily Advertiser December 21

1825. December 29, 1791 Coachmakers Hall
'Would it be most for the interest of this country, that the territorial possessions in India should still continue in the hands of the present East India Company, be taken under the sole and immediate direction of the Legislature, or be relinquished to the native inhabitants of the country?'
Daily Advertiser December 28

1826. January 5, 1792 Coachmakers Hall
'Is it not the duty of the people of Great Britain, from a principle of moral obligation and regard to their national character, to abstain from the consumption of West India produce till the Slave Trade is abolished and measures are taken for the abolition of Slavery?
In addition to much sound reasoning and interesting narrative, a gentleman . . . exhibited to the audience the same iron mask that was produced in Court upon the memorable trial respecting Somerset the negro, and explained the manner in which it was used as an instrument to punish the unfortunate African Slave.
N.B. A pamphlet on the subject will, by desire of several respectable characters belonging to the Committee of the African Society be distributed (gratis) to the public by the door-keeper at the Hall.'
Daily Advertiser January 4/Times

1827. January 12, 1792 Coachmakers Hall
'Is it not the duty of the people of Great Britain, from a principle of moral obligation and regard to their national character, to abstain from the consumption of West India produce till the Slave Trade is abolished and measures are taken for the abolition of Slavery?
Almost unanimous vote of near six hundred persons in favour of our African brethren.'
Daily Advertiser January 11

1828. January 19, 1792 Coachmakers Hall
'To which of the two causes is to be attributed the present unequal representation of the people in the *Commons House of Parliament*, to a disinclination for any reform on their part, or to the influence of the executive government, as well as the present mode of *Election* as on the *Elected*?
Several Gentlemen . . . pointed out, with great zeal and ability, the defects in the present state of our Parliamentary Representation, and the undue influence exercised in the mode of Election.'
Times

1829. January 26, 1792 Coachmakers Hall
'Is the present unequal representation of the people in the Commons House of Parliament to be attributed to a disinclination for any reform on their part; to the influence of the Executive Government, as well as the present mode of Election as on the elected; or to the impracticability of procuring any reform whatever?'
Times

1830. February 2, 1792 Coachmakers Hall
'Would it reflect honour upon the people of Europe to withdraw their allegiance from those Princes, who shall attempt to oppose the liberties of France?
The character of this popular institution is to cherish genius, cultivate eloquence, and discover important truths.'
Times

1831. February 9, 1792 Coachmakers Hall
'Does the eulogium lately bestowed by Mr. Fox in the House of Commons on the character of Dr. Priestley, exonerate that celebrated character from the charges of holding principles hostile to the British Constitution?'
Daily Advertiser February 8

1832. February 16, 1792 Coachmakers Hall
'Which might be considered the most Criminal, the Merchants and Planters who carry on the Slave Trade; the British House of Commons, who have refused to abolish it, or the People who encourage it by the Consumption of Sugar and Rum?
To the Judgment, as well as the compassionate Feeling of the Fair Sex, an Appeal from the suffering Negroes will be made, in order to dissuade them from any longer consuming an Article of Luxury that is polluted with the Blood of innocent Fathers, Mothers and Children.'
Times

1833. February 23, 1792 Coachmakers Hall
'Which might be considered the most Criminal, the Merchants and Planters who carry on the Slave Trade; the British House of Commons, who have refused to abolish it, or the People who encourage it by the Consumption of Sugar and Rum?'
Times

1834. March 1, 1792 Coachmakers Hall
'Which ought to be considered the most Criminal, the Merchants and Planters who carry on the Slave Trade; the British House of Commons, who have refused to Abolish it, or the People who encourage it by the Consumption of Sugar and Rum?'
Times

1835. March 8, 1792 Coachmakers Hall
'Which might be considered the most Criminal, the Merchants and Planters who carry on the Slave Trade; the British House of Commons, who have refused to abolish it, or the People who encourage it by the Consumption of Sugar and Rum?'
Times

1836. March 15, 1792 Coachmakers Hall
'Has the conduct of Mr. Pitt in the late Negotiation with Russia, or that of Mr. Fox in opposing the Measure, and its Consequences, been more consistent with the true Policy and intitled to the Approbation of this Country?'
Times

1837. March 22, 1792 Coachmakers Hall
'Is it not a Dishonour to the British Nation to withhold from the Protestant Dissenters and English Catholics an equal Participation of Civil and Religious Liberties with the Members of the Established Church?'
Times

1838. March 29, 1792 Coachmakers Hall
'Is it not a Disgrace to the British Nation to withhold from the Protestant Dissenters and English Catholics an equal participation of Civil and Religious Liberties with the Members of the Established Church?'
Times

1839. April 5, 1792 Coachmakers Hall
'Has not the conduct both of Administration and Opposition been such, as to convince the people of this country, that they have no foundation for placing any confidence in either?'
Times

1840. April 12, 1792 Coachmakers Hall
'Is it justifiable in Creditors to detain their Debtors in prison after their whole property is surrendered, and would it be a measure of wisdom in the Legislature at the present period to pass a general Act of Insolvency?
The asserted impolicy of the laws between Debtor and Creditor, the crowded state of our prisons, and the exertions of Mr. Grey, and other public characters to procure a Reform in the Measure of Imprisonment for Debt, are circumstances which render the above question of great and immediate importance, in a commercial City its discussion must be peculiarly interesting, and will doubtless be conducted with that willingness to communicate and receive information, which distinguishes the liberal and enlightened manners of the age.'
Times

1841. April 26, 1792 Coachmakers Hall

'Have the Societies for Constitutional Information acted consistently with the character of wise and good Citizens, in publicly bestowing their approbation of the political conduct of Mr. Paine and John Horne Tooke?'
Times

1842. May 3, 1792 Coachmakers Hall
'Do those Members of the House of Commons who supported on Monday last the necessity of a Parliamentary Reform at the present crisis, merit the applause or censure of the people of this country?'
Times

1843. May 10, 1792 Coachmakers Hall
'Do those Members of the House of Commons who asserted the necessity of a Parliamentary Reform at the present juncture, merit the applause or censure of the people of England?'
Times

1844. May 17, 1792 Coachmakers Hall
'Do those Members of the House of Commons, who asserted the necessity of a Parliamentary Reform at the present juncture, merit the applause or censure of the people of England?'
Times

1845. May 24, 1792 Coachmakers Hall
'Are Associations for Political Purposes likely to promote the happiness of the people, by informing their minds, or to make them discontented without redressing their grievances?'
Gazetteer

1846. January 5, 1793 Select Association, Globe Tavern, Fleet Street
'Does NATURE or ART more contribute to form the perfect ORATOR?
Twelve Gentlemen Students of the Law, having announced their intention of establishing a Select Society for the discussion of Subjects that have a [claim] to public notice – the following Extracts from their Resolutions present the substance of a Plan, tending to combine Professional and Philanthropic Utility, and which is expected to obtain the concurrent support of those, whose liberal education and pleasures may induce them to assist in cultivating Oratory and the Belles Lettres.
2nd. That the number of persons to be admitted be limited to two hundred, paying one shilling each; and that those who may wish to secure admission, by sending for tickets previous to the evening of debate, shall be accommodated at the bar of the tavern.
3rd. That the Receipts which may arise from the encouragement given to this institution, be applied for the benefit of the Philanthropic Society.'
Morning Herald

1847. January 12, 1793 Select Association for Free Debate, Globe Tavern
'Is Imprisonment for Debt, consistent with the principles of a general Policy?'
Times January 11

1848. January 19, 1793 Select Association
'Is the London theatre, in its present state, conducive to the Interest of Morality?
It having been stated in a candid Manner, by the first Magistrate in the City, that a Number of Persons meeting for public Debate, cannot be prevented from making irrelevant Observations; the Society beg leave to inform the Public, that the discussion of Politics is not at this Time thought adviseable and that the President will restrain every improper digression.'
Times January 18

1849. January 26, 1793 Select Association
'Has Vanity or Interest a great Influence on the Conduct of Mankind?'
Times

1850. February 2, 1793 Select Association
'Would it not be for the commercial and political Advantage of Great Britain, if the Government would lay the Trade to India open, and take the territorial Possessions of the Company into their own Hands?'
Morning Herald

1851. February 9, 1793 Select Association
'Would it not be for the commercial and political Advantage of Great Britain, if the Government would lay the Trade to India open, and take the territorial Possessions of the Company into their own Hands?'
Morning Herald

1852. August 22, 1793 London Forum, Capel Court
'Does the Happiness of Mankind consist most in the Increase of Knowledge, Success in Trade, or the Enjoyment of social and domestic Felicity?
The Conductors of this Society . . . declar[e] that they shall ever be happy to receive and adopt such Questions as have a Tendency to polish the Manners and improve the Heart.'
Daily Advertiser August 21

1853. August 29, 1793 London Forum
'Does the Infelicity often attendant on the Marriage State most frequently arise from the Neglect of Husbands, the Misconduct of Wives, or the Flattery and Adulation usually paid to the fair Sex in Courtship?
The Questions of this Society are regularly advertised in this Paper . . . and announced to the Publick by large bills posted throughout the principal Streets of the Metropolis.'

Daily Advertiser August 28

1854. September 5, 1793 London Forum
'Which is the strongest Obligation, Gratitude to our Friends, Duty to our Parents, or Love for our Country?'
Daily Advertiser September 4

1855. September 12, 1793 London Forum
'Which Passion has the most powerful Influence upon Mankind, Ambition, Pleasure or Interest?'
Daily Advertiser September 11

1856. September 19, 1793 London Forum
'Is it consistent with Female Delicacy, manly Dignity, or a rational Prospect of connubial Happiness, for either a Lady or a Gentleman to advertise for a Partner in the Marriage State?
The strange Scenes of Courtship which must arise between Lovers whimsically introduced to each other by publick Advertisement, must afford in the Discussion of the above Question a Theme of Ridicule for the Humourist, a Field of Wit for the Satyrist, and an ample Range of Reflection for the speculative Philosopher.'
Daily Advertiser September 18

1857. September 26, 1793 London Forum
'Is it consonant with Reason, Philosophy, or Revelation, to believe in supernatural Appearances, or to suppose that a departed Spirit ever was seen by or conversed with Mortals?'
Daily Advertiser September 25

1858. October 3, 1793 London Forum
'Is it consonant with Reason, Philosophy, or Revelation, to believe in supernatural Appearances, or to suppose that a departed Spirit ever was seen by or conversed with Mortals?'
Daily Advertiser October 2

1859. October 10, 1793 London Forum
'In this expensive and elegant Age, which stands the better Chance of Respectability and Happiness in the conjugal State, the Man of middling Circumstances, who from prudential Motives marries for Money, or he who governed by the Dictates of the Heart marries for Love alone?
The Conductors of the London Forum respectfully inform the Publick, that in Consequence of the crowded Audience of the last Evening they have determined to reserve the elevated Seats for the Accommodation of Ladies.'
Daily Advertiser October 9

1860. October 17, 1793 London Forum

'Which has the greatest Influence on the Actions of Mankind, the Love of Life, the Love of Liberty, or the Love of the Fair Sex?'
Daily Advertiser October 16

1861. October 24, 1793 London Forum
'Which has the greatest Influence on the Actions of Mankind, the Love of Life, the Love of Liberty, or the Love of the Fair Sex?
It is with sensible Regret that the Conductors of this Society have to announce to the Publick, that the above Question, obviously calculated to afford and instructive and argumentative Debate, was adjourned on the last Evening in Consequence of the inflammatory and unconstitutional Principles which were avowed by an enthusiastick Individual, totally unconnected with the London Forum. Though the natural bias of an English Audience to the constitutional Rights of Liberty of Speech prevented that determinate Opposition which was made by the Chairman from procuring at first its usual and expected Effect, it affords the Managers peculiar Pleasure to declare, that the good Sense and Penetration of the Audience induced them at least to repel with Contempt Insinuations equally unsound and illiberal. When an Individual by a daring Obstinacy, as disrespectful as licentious, in Defiance of the established Order of the Society, will drag in by a studied Deviation from the Subject Opinions evidently hostile to the Happiness of Mankind, he may rest assured that neither an unblushing Front, nor a silly Affectation of Singularity, shall screen him from that publick Censure which such Conduct deserves. The Managers trust they shall receive the Support of every liberal and impartial Mind, when they declare, that, without Timidity on the one Side, or Temerity on the other, they are determined to support the Principles of the British Constitution, and never to countenance any Attempt to weaken that becoming Reverence for our holy Religion, which alone can secure the present and future Felicity of Man.'
Daily Advertiser October 23

1862. October 31, 1793 London Forum
'Ought the Man who submits to be governed by his Wife to receive Censure for his Weakness, or Praise for his Love of Peace?
The Reins of domestick Government, though apparently adapted by Nature for the Lords of the Creation, are frequently in Female Hands, guided with a Discernment and Propriety which evinces considerable Strength of Understanding, and great natural Goodness of Heart; on the contrary, various Misfortunes, and accumulated Distress, have been the result of a tame Submission in the Husband, and an unwarrantable Desire of Power in the Wife.'
Daily Advertiser October 30

1863. November 7, 1793 London Forum
'Is it from the Depravity of human Nature, or the wise Dispensations of an over-ruling Providence, that mutual Affection is so seldom found in the matrimonial State?'
Daily Advertiser November 6

1864. November 14, 1793 London Forum
'Which is the greater Trial of human Virtue, Prosperity or Adversity?'
Daily Advertiser

1865. November 21, 1793 London Forum
'Which is the more disagreeable Companion, a crusty old Bachelor, or a peevish old Maid?
Daily Advertiser November 20

1866. November 28, 1793 London Forum
'Which is the more blameable Character, the Seducer, who ruins unsuspecting Virgin Innocence, or the Father who abandons his Daughter in Consequence of such Seduction?
To one or other of the Causes mentioned in the above Question may justly be attributed the alarming Number of those unhappy Victims of Infamy who nightly parade the Streets of the Metropolis; it cannot therefore be uninteresting to the Woman of Sensibility, and the Man of Feeling; for however justly Censure may be merited there is a Sentiment of Compassion which pleads for the Unfortunate, and which it has long been the peculiar Boast of Britons to cherish and promote.'
Daily Advertiser November 27

1867. December 5, 1793 London Forum
'Is the Assertion of Socrates true, that Women in Mischief are wiser than Men?'
Daily Advertiser December 4

1868. December 12, 1793 London Forum
'Which is the greater Trial of human Fortitude: Treachery in a Friendship or Perfidy in Love?'
Daily Advertiser December 11

1869. December 19, 1793 London Forum
'Which is the greater Trial of human Fortitude: Treachery in a Friendship or Perfidy in Love?'
The audience decided 'that human Fortitude is put to a greater Trial by Perfidy in Love than by Treachery in Friendship'.
Daily Advertiser December 18

1870. December 26, 1793 London Forum
'Is the Assertion of Mr. Pope true, "Every Woman is at Heart a Rake"?'
Daily Advertiser December 25

1871. January 2, 1794 London Forum
'Is it from a prior Disappointment in Love, or delusive Principle of Avarice, or laudable Desire of rendering the connubial State happy, that so many Persons marry for Interest?'
Daily Advertiser January 1

1872. January 9, 1794 London Forum
'Has the Superstition of the Roman Catholicks or the Enthusiasm of the Methodists tended more to injure the general Interests of Religion? Religious discussion, when conducted with Liberality and Candour, is peculiarly to the reasoning Powers of Man.'
Daily Advertiser January 8

1873. January 16, 1794 London Forum
'Has the Superstition of the Roman Catholicks or the Enthusiasm of the Methodists tended more to injure the general Interests of Religion? The Charge of Plagiarism advanced against John Wesley from Dr. Johnson's Taxation no Tyranny, which gave such Offence to a clerical Character apparently of the methodistical Communion, will doubtless then be seriously investigated and correctly decided.'
Daily Advertiser January 15

1874. January 23, 1794 London Forum
'Has the Superstition of the Roman Catholicks or the Enthusiasm of the Methodists tended more to injure the general Interests of Religion?'
Daily Advertiser January 22

1875. January 30, 1794 London Forum
'Has the Superstition of the Roman Catholicks or the Enthusiasm of the Methodists tended more to injure the general Interests of Religion? The Question . . . was determined in favour of the Methodists.'
Daily Advertiser January 29

1876. February 6, 1794 London Forum
'Does the vast Body of Evidence recorded in sacred and prophane antient and modern History, combined with the Testimony of respectable living Characters, justify an Opinion that Dreams are sometimes Presages of future Events, or are they always to be accounted the Rovings of a bewildered Imagination?'
Daily Advertiser February 5

1877. February 13, 1794 London Forum
'Which is the greater Absurdity, to refuse a Divorce between Man and Wife when they are heartily tired of each other, or to dissolve a Marriage Covenant where mutual Affection subsists?'
Daily Advertiser February 12

1878. February 20, 1794 London Forum
'Ought the lamentable Fates of Rosamond and Jane Shore to be considered as memorable Instances of the Instability of all human Greatness, or to be held up to the Fair Sex as striking Examples of that just Punishment attendant on a Dereliction from Female Virtue?'
Daily Advertiser February 19

1879. February 27, 1794 London Forum
'Which is the greatest Nuisance to Society, a fraudulent Bankrupt, a pettyfogging Attorney, or a Lottery Shark who lives by illegal Insurance?'
Daily Advertiser February 26

1880. March 6, 1794 London Forum
'Is the Opinion of Mr. Pitt, last Week delivered in the House of Commons true, [that] the Decree of the French Convention for emancipating their Negroes in the West-Indies, a new and additional Reason for an immediate Abolition of the African Slave Trade?'
Daily Advertiser March 5

1881. March 13, 1794 London Forum
'Is the Opinion of Mr. Pitt, last Week delivered in the House of Commons true, [that] the Decree of the French Convention for emancipating their Negroes in the West-Indies is a new an additional Reason for an immediate Abolition of the African Slave Trade?
The Audience . . . were unanimous in expressing their Reprobation of the Slave Trade, and their Hope that the wise and virtuous Exertions of the British Parliament would speedily abolish in toto a Traffick so abhorrent to the Feelings of Humanity.'
Daily Advertiser March 12

1882. March 20, 1794 London Forum
'Is which Situation is most Happiness to be found, the elevated Walks of Wealth and Grandeur, the busy Scenes of Trade and Commerce, or the humble Shades of domestick Ease and Retirement?
Complaints of Unhappiness have so long been re-echoed from one Rank of Life to another that an Enquiry into the Source of such a general Failure in the universal Pursuit cannot but forcibly engage publick Attention.'
Daily Advertiser March 19

1883. March 27, 1794 London Forum
'In this expensive and fashionable Age ought two Persons possessed of mutual Affection, but destitute of Fortune, to marry, trusting in Providence and Industry for Support, or to separate from prudential Motives?'
Daily Advertiser March 26

1884. April 3, 1794 London Forum
'Which is most agreeable to Revelation, Reason and moral Virtue, Socinianism, as propagated by Drs. Price and Priestley; Arminianism, as preached by the late Rev. Mr. Wesley; absolute Predestination, as taught by Calvin; or the universal Restoration maintained by the Rev. Mr. Winchester?
The four opposing Systems of the present Question may be said to occupy almost the whole Circle of religious Opinion.'
Daily Advertiser April 2

1885. April 10, 1794 London Forum
'Which is most agreeable to Revelation, Reason and moral Virtue, Socinianism, as propagated by Drs. Price and Priestley; Arminianism, as preached by the late Rev. Mr. Wesley; absolute Predestination, as taught by Calvin; or the universal Restoration maintained by the Rev. Mr. Winchester?'
Daily Advertiser April 9

1886. April 17, 1794 London Forum
'Which is most agreeable to Revelation, Reason and moral Virtue, Socinianism, as propagated by Drs. Price and Priestley; Arminianism, as preached by the late Rev. Mr. Wesley; absolute Predestination, as taught by Calvin; or the universal Restoration maintained by the Rev. Mr. Winchester?'
Daily Advertiser April 16

1887. April 24, 1794 London Forum
'Which is most agreeable to Revelation, Reason and moral Virtue, Socinianism, as propagated by Drs. Price and Priestley; Arminianism, as preached by the late Rev. Mr. Wesley; absolute Predestination, as taught by Calvin; or the universal Restoration maintained by the Rev. Mr. Winchester?'
Daily Advertiser April 23

1888. May 1, 1794 London Forum
'Will the Laws of Conscience and Honour justify a Man without Rank and Fortune in clandestinely marrying a young Lady who is in Possession of both?'
Daily Advertiser April 30

1889. May 8, 1794 London Forum
'Is the following Assertion of that great moral Luminary, Dr. Johnson, the Result of vulgar and superstitious Fear, or the conviction of Truth supported by Evidence, "The Belief in Apparitions which prevails perhaps as far as human Nature is diffused could become universal only by its Truths, the Doubts of single Cavillers can very little weaken the general Evidence, since some who would deny it with their Tongues confess it by their Fears"?'
Daily Advertiser May 7

1890. May 15, 1794 London Forum
'Which has done the greater Injury to the real Interests of Religion, the superstitious Enthusiasm of the Fanatick, or the lukewarm Inattention of the regular Church Clergy?
That there has been of late Years an alarming Decay of vital Religion is a melancholy truth confirmed by general Experience, and yet never did the Annals of religious History present to the serious observer so

extensive a Variety of professing Sects as prevail at the present Day. This apparent Paradox can only be resolved by one of the two causes stated in the Question.'
Daily Advertiser May 14

1891. October 13, 1794 Morning Chronicle
'Several respectable Inhabitants of Westminster, having expressed their regret at the discontinuance of the WESTMINSTER FORUM, a Society of Gentlemen purpose tomorrow evening to open the GREAT ROOM, PANTON STREET in the Haymarket for FREE DEBATE, when the following classical and appropriate Question will be discussed, viz. Was Lucius Virginius justifiable or censurable for putting his Daughter to death, to prevent her Dishonour by the Tyrant Appius?'
The audience declared that Virginius was unjustifiable.

1892. October 21, 1794 Westminster Forum
'Are there more moral effects and less evils resulting from a Play-house, or a Methodist meeting?'
Morning Chronicle October 20

1893. October 28, 1794 Westminster Forum
GOD ALMIGHTY'S NEPHEW
'Ought RICHARD BROTHERS (who stiles himself GOD ALMIGHTY'S NEPHEW) to be received as a Prophet, or punished as an Imposter?
Richard Brothers, in two recent publications, has not only proclaimed himself a "Prophet of the Most High" but declared that he is next spring to proceed into Cheapside, turn his wand into a serpent, an earthquake is to ensue, and he is to be publicly acknowledged the Rod of the Stem of Jesse, the deliverer of the Jews, who is to lead that people in triumph to Jerusalem. To crown the whole, he assumes the title of "God Almighty's Nephew", and boasts with a most astonishing degree of assurance of "the divine communications of his uncle".
Impartiality compels the Managers to withhold their opinion of this blasphemous farrago. But they think it is a duty which they owe the peace of their country to undeceive many weak minds from groundless apprehension.'
Morning Chronicle October 27

1894. November 11, 1794 Westminster Forum
'To which of the following Causes mentioned by Mr. Hayley in his celebrated HISTORY OF OLD MAIDS, ought the Number of those Ladies to be imputed – The Perfidy of the Male Sex – Disappointment in the Tender Passion – or Peculiarity of Person and Temper?'
Morning Chronicle November 10

1895. November 18, 1794 Westminster Forum
SPIES, ROBBERS
'Which is the worst Character, the SPY, or the COMMON ROBBER?'

It was determined that 'The Spy is a more nefarious Character than the Common Robber.'
Morning Chronicle November 17

1896. November 25, 1794 Westminster Forum
'Which ought to be pronounced the most flagrant attack on British credulity, the Prophecies of Richard Brothers (who styles himself God Almighty's Nephew!), the Cock-lane Ghost, or the Bottle Conjuror? We have some considerable reason to expect Mr. Brothers will pay us a visit.'
Morning Chronicle

1897. December 2, 1794 Westminster Forum
'To bear which of the following situations demands the greatest exertion of fortitude: the Loss of Fortune; Ruin of Reputation; or a total Disappointment in the Tender Passion?'
Morning Herald

1898. December 4, 1794 London Forum
'Which of the following illustrious Characters has rendered the most essential services to his Country, the late immortal Earl of Chatham, the virtuous George Washington, or the patriotic Kosciusko?
The Managers have only to observe, that public debate is the best medium to illustrate such a resplendent class of characters, such a constellation of patriotic integrity, since, while we pay that tribute of respect which is due to the public virtues of others, we excite in ourselves a lively yet respectful, an animated yet loyal attachment to the constitutional liberties of our country.'
Morning Herald December 3

1899. December 9, 1794 Westminster Forum
'Which have proved themselves the truest Friends of their King and Country, those Persons who have endeavoured to procure a Reform of Parliament, or those who have resisted that Measure, as ill-timed and dangerous?
While doubt and uncertainty hung over the public mind, it became necessary to wave the right of debating political subjects. This was a sacrifice which the Managers offered to the quiet of their country. Stimulated by the same motive, a wish to promote order, they have yielded to the solicitation of several respectable and independent inhabitants of Westminster, and brought forward the above seasonable and appropriate subject. Gentlemen who intend to speak to the Question are strongly recommended to rest their arguments on Constitutional grounds.'
Morning Chronicle

1900. December 16, 1794 Westminster Forum
'Which have proved themselves the truest Friends of their King and Country, those Persons who have endeavoured to procure a Reform of

Parliament, or those who have resisted that Measure, as ill-timed and dangerous?'
Morning Chronicle

1901. December 18, 1794 London Forum
'Ought not every man who seduces a Female to be obliged by law to marry her?'
Morning Chronicle

1902. December 23, 1794 Westminster Forum
'Which have proved themselves the truest Friends of their King and Country, those Persons who have endeavoured to procure a Reform of Parliament, or those who have resisted that Measure, as ill-timed and dangerous?'
Morning Chronicle

1903. December 26, 1794 London Forum
'Are the Predictions of Richard Brothers, who stiles himself God Almighty's Nephew (relative to the present awful crisis of Europe, the eventual situation of this Kingdom, and his immediate appearance as the Prince and Prophet to conduct the Jews to Jerusalem) Missions of Divine Authenticity, Effects of Insanity, or artful Contrivances of am ambitious Imposter to aggrandize himself at the expence of public credulity?
Imposture, dangerous at all times, is never so truly destructive as when it allies itself to religious enthusiasm. . . [His] Principles, which, however apparently absurd, are rendered peculiarly interesting by the present disordered state of all civilized Governments, and the unprecedented convulsions which now agitate the whole of the European Continent.'
Morning Chronicle

1904. December 30, 1794 Westminster Forum
PARLIAMENTARY REFORM
'Which have proved themselves the TRUE FRIENDS OF THEIR KING AND COUNTRY – those Persons who have endeavoured to procure a CONSTITUTIONAL REFORM IN PARLIAMENT – or those who have opposed that Measure, as ill-timed and dangerous?'
Morning Chronicle

1905. January 1, 1795 London Forum
CONSTITUTIONAL LIBERTY
'Are Britons, for the blessings of a Free Constitution, principally indebted to King John, for signing Magna Carta, to Harry VIII, for freeing them from the dominion of the Pope, or to James II for abdicating the Throne?'
Morning Chronicle

1906. January 8, 1795 London Forum

'Do not the Decisions of the Juries on the late Trials for High Treason, effectually prove that the political Liberties of this Country exist at present in full vigour?'
Morning Herald

1907. January 13, 1795 Westminster Forum
'Which is the most predominant Principle – Love of Life, Love of the Fair Sex, or the Love of Liberty?'
Morning Herald January 12

1908. January 20, 1795 Westminster Forum
'Which is the most predominant Principle – Love of Life, Love of the Fair Sex, or the Love of Liberty?'
Morning Chronicle

1909. January 26, 1795 Ciceronian School of Eloquence, Globe Tavern, Fleet Street
'Ought the Father of a seduced Daughter totally to disclaim her, as an example to the rest of his Family, and Society at large, or humanely restore her to his former confidence, in the hope of reclaiming her?
A Society of literary Gentlemen, lamenting that there does not exist a respectable institution for the free discussion of liberal and animated subjects, where the Man who is ambitious of making a conspicuous figure in public life, or he who only wishes to attain the pleasing art of public speaking; might at the same time greatly improve and display his talents, have opened for that purpose the Ciceronian School of Eloquence. . . In the course of the season they will propose subjects which shall be found highly interesting to the Moralist, the Historian and the Politician.'
Morning Herald

1910. January 27, 1795 Westminster Forum
'Have the People of England just reason to believe that a Change of Administration would be productive of real benefit to the Country?'
Morning Herald

1911. February 2, 1795 Ciceronian School
'Ought the Assassination of Julius Caesar, by Brutus, to be execrated as a violation of the laws of humanity, or applauded as a meritorious and patriotic deed?'
Morning Chronicle

1912. February 3, 1795 Westminster Forum
'Have the People of England just reason to believe that a change of Administration would be productive of real benefit to the Country?
The Managers of the Westminster Forum can truly say, their Institution is respectable, because impartiality and moderation govern their public deliberations; the Gentlemen who honour them by the delivery of their sentiments, are persons of character and intelligence, their Auditors

are some of [the] most opulent and respectable Inhabitants of Westminster; and, not infrequently, persons of the first fashion and distinction.'
Decided 'that a change of Administration would operate for the good of the Nation'.
Morning Chronicle/Morning Herald February 10

1913. February 9, 1795 Ciceronian School
'It was decided (with the exception of two dissentient voices) that an immediate Peace is preferable to a continuance of the War.'
Morning Chronicle February 14

1914. February 10, 1795 Westminster Forum
'Have the Members of the Constitutional and Corresponding Societies, in their proceedings, proved themselves the deluded Followers of Faction, or the true Friends of their King and Country?
The Managers of this Institution, unconnected with any Party, will esteem themselves on this, as on all occasions, happy in being instrumental to confirm just and founded suspicion of public delinquency, or to weed from the actions of their countrymen any illiberal or unjust prejudice against individuals.'
Morning Herald

1915. February 16, 1795 Ciceronian School
'At the present moment of danger and difficulty, which best deserves the Public Confidence, Mr. PITT or Mr. FOX?'
Morning Chronicle February 14

1916. February 17, 1795 Westminster Forum
'Have the Members of the Constitutional and Corresponding Societies, in their proceedings, proved themselves the deluded Followers of Faction, or the true Friends of their King and Country?'
Morning Chronicle

1917. February 23, 1795 Ciceronian School
'At the present moment of danger and difficulty, which best deserves the Public Confidence, Mr. PITT or Mr. FOX?
Notwithstanding a large majority determined the above . . . in favour of MR. FOX, it having been suggested that the decision was unsatisfactory, as two Gentlemen of considerable abilities (Advocates of Mr. Pitt), were from interruption prevented from delivering their sentiments; and many others were disappointed of attending', the question will again be raised.
Morning Chronicle

1918. February 24, 1795 Westminster Forum
'Have the Members of the Constitutional and Corresponding Societies, in their proceedings, proved themselves the deluded Followers of Faction, or the true Friends of their King and Country?'
Morning Chronicle

1919. March 2, 1795 Ciceronian School
'At the present moment of danger and difficulty, which best deserves the Public Confidence, Mr. PITT or Mr. FOX?
Decided almost unanimously that Mr. Fox best deserves public confidence.'
Morning Chronicle February 28

1920. March 9, 1795 Ciceronian School
'Has the conduct of Earl Fitzwilliam been such as to justify the recent alterations made by Mr. Pitt in the Government of Ireland?'
Decided in favour of Earl Fitzwilliam.
Morning Chronicle March 7

1921. March 16, 1795 Ciceronian School
'Would an immediate Abolition of the African Slave Trade, be consistent with the real interests of Great Britain?'
Morning Chronicle

1922. March 17, 1795 Westminster Forum
'Ought Praise or Censure to be ascribed to the MINISTER, for his late BUDGET?
Reduced by a train of public misfortunes, to the necessity of heavy taxation, the objects of that taxation become matters of serious enquiry; the tax on Hair Powder (and its proposed substitute), Tea, British Spirits, &c. &c. will be most minutely examined throughout every effect, and traced to every dependency. A theme of this nature will, we should imagine, awaken general attention: since, however, we may differ with regard to political opinion, all feel the weight of enormous taxation, and the inconvenience of partial and oppressive Imposts.'
Morning Chronicle

1923. March 23, 1795 Ciceronian School
'Would an immediate Abolition of the African Slave Trade, be consistent with the real interests of Great Britain?
It was the unanimous opinion of a numerous and liberal Assembly that the African Slave Trade should be immediately abolished.'
Morning Chronicle March 21

1924. March 24, 1795 Westminster Forum
'Ought Praise or Censure to be ascribed to the MINISTER, for his late BUDGET?'
Morning Chronicle

1925. March 26, 1795 London Forum, Bartholomew lane near the Bank
'This Society will resolve itself into a Committee of the whole House, to consider of the Ways and Means for the current service of the year, for the kingdom of Utopia. The following, among many others equally

interesting, will be objects of Discussion: – Tax on Prophecies – Ladies' Lap Dogs, Sad Dogs, Surly Dogs, Snap Dogs, and Puppies of all descriptions – Poll Tax on Monkies – Passport to all Jews going to Jerusalem, their prophet having already appeared at Bethlehem – Tax on Scandal, by a duty on the beverage of Gossips – Limitation of Swine to their Hog-troughs – Annual License for Cuckold-makers, Political Apostates, Hungry Scotchmen, Irish Fortune-hunters, Crimps and Resurrection Men – Bill to restrain the Privilege of Rooks, Pigeons, Tom Tits, Owls and Birds of Passage, from conveying intelligence, free of all expence, from one place to another – Together with the Extraordinaries, Deficiencies, Estimates, &c. &c. &c. and State of the nation of Utopia.'
Morning Chronicle

1926. March 30, 1795 Ciceronian School
'Would Crimes be most effectually prevented by extreme severity or unbounded indulgence?
It was decided (with the exception of one dissentient voice) that Crimes would be most effectually prevented by a system of unbounded indulgence.'
Morning Chronicle

1927. March 31, 1795 Westminster Forum
'Does not sound Policy dictate an Union with Ireland, similar to that with Scotland, and the total Abolition of all Penal and Restrictive Statutes, against Dissenters and Roman Catholics, in both Kingdoms?
At this awful and momentous period, it becomes our interest as well as duty, to ascertain the most probable means of uniting this country, and all its dependencies, in the firmest bands of confidence.'
Morning Chronicle

1928. April 2, 1795 London Forum
'This Evening the House will open its third and last Sitting as a COMMITTEE OF WAYS AND MEANS for UTOPIA. Several Bills were committed in their last sitting; the Bill for the Limitation of Swine in their Hog Troughs was read a first time, with general satisfaction, and its further Consideration unanimously adjourned at a late hour to this evening, when it will open the Committee.
A Tax on Scandal, by a Duty on the Beverage of Gossips; Scolding Wives, and Sulky Husbands; Hungry Scotchmen, Irish Fortune-hunters, and City Toad-eaters; Bill to restrain the Privilege of Hawks, Rooks, Tomtits, Pigeons, Owls, and Birds of Passage, from conveying Intelligence, free of all expence, as heretofore, from one place to another; Reduction of National Spirits, by a Duty on opening the Mouth; with several others, equally interesting, will be brought before the house.'
Morning Chronicle

1929. April 6, 1795 Ciceronian School

'Is the motion recently made in both Houses of Parliament for a Committee to enquire into the State of the nation, justifiable on grounds of sound policy?

To prevent the inconvenience of too crowded an assembly, the tickets will be limited to a certain number. . .

It was almost unanimously decided, that an enquiry into the State of the nation was necessary and expedient.'
Morning Chronicle April 4

1930. April 7, 1795 Westminster Forum
MADNESS!!!
MR. HALHEAD AND THE MINISTER
'Does the Defence of Mr. Halhead, in support of Richard Brothers, or Mr. Pitt's zeal in the prosecution of the present War, evince the greater degree of insanity?

With regard to the latter part of the Question, if we may venture to predict, upon the Madness of War, and all its train of consequent evils, there must arise a discussion of the most animated nature, and replete with every thing that can interest our feelings as men and citizens.'
Morning Chronicle

1931. April 9, 1795 London Forum
'Which has deserved the best of his Country, William Pitt, Charles Fox, or Horne Tooke?

The friends of the Minister may assert his immaculate integrity. The supporters of Mr. Tooke may declaim on his intrepid perseverance in the service of the People; and the friends of Mr. Fox, may pourtray with admiration, that consistent attention to the interests of his country, and that indefatigable zeal for the rights of his fellow countrymen, which has ever marked his public conduct, and entitled him to the applause, gratitude, and veneration of every unprejudiced and disinterested Englishman.'
Morning Chronicle

1932. April 13, 1795 Ciceronian School
'To which of the following causes are we to attribute the present Fermentation in Ireland, the Imprudence of Earl Fitzwilliam, or the Duplicity of Mr. Pitt?

The Question . . . was unanimously decided in favour of Earl Fitzwilliam.'
Morning Chronicle

1933. April 16, 1795 London Forum
'Is the present disastrous situation of Great Britain, attributable to the intrigues of factious spirits at home, the malevolence of our antient inveterate enemies, or the blunders and obstinacy of Administration?'
Morning Chronicle

1934. April 20, 1795 Ciceronian School

FRANCE

'Would the re-establishment of absolute Monarchy, and the restoration of Louis the Seventeenth to the Throne of France, prove beneficial or injurious to the interests of Great Britain?'
Morning Chronicle

1935. April 20, 1795 London Forum

MR. PITT'S TRIAL BEFORE THE PUBLIC

'Has the Minister forfeited, or does he still retain the confidence of the people?
The Audience was uncommonly numerous; and the elegant assemblage of ladies who attended, evince how much even our fair countrywomen begin to feel for the alarming situation into which we have been plunged. – It is, however, but barely justice to observe, that the able and eloquent Defence of Mr. Pitt by two Gentlemen . . . highly merited those reiterated plaudits which they received.'
Morning Chronicle

1936. April 21, 1795 Westminster Forum
'Do not the Letters of Lord Fitzwilliam, Mr. Grattan's Answer to the late Address, and the State both of Ireland and this Country, prove the necessity of repealing the Test and Corporation Acts, and restoring Roman Catholics and Dissenters to those Privileges to which they conceive themselves entitled, as Men and Citizens?'
Morning Chronicle

1937. April 22, 1795 Ciceronian School

FRANCE

'Would the re-establishment of absolute Monarchy, and the restoration of Louis the Seventeenth to the Throne of France, prove beneficial or injurious to the interests of Great Britain?
It was decided with one dissentient voice, that the restoration of French Monarchy, would be injurious to the interests of Great Britain.'
Morning Chronicle

1938. April 23, 1795 London Forum
'Has the Minister forfeited, or does he still retain – the Confidence of the People?'
Morning Chronicle

1939. April 27, 1795 Ciceronian School

PRUSSIAN PERFIDY

'Has not the recent conduct of the King of Prussia fully proved the policy as well as the practicability of negotiating a Peace with the present Government of France?'
Morning Chronicle

1940. April 28, 1795 Westminster Forum

'Which have caused most mischief amongst mankind – Pettifogging Attorneys, Quack Doctors, or Methodist Preachers?'
Morning Chronicle

1941. April 30, 1795 London Forum
'Which ought to be considered the best friends of their Country, those who wear Hair Powder, or those who do not?
In a few days the tax will probably commence, every person will then be obliged, either to discontinue the use of Hair Powder, to mark their dislike to the War and the Minister; or else to continue it, as supporters of Administration; or, perhaps out of pity to the starving thousands it would otherwise rob of employment.'
Morning Chronicle

1942. May 5, 1795 Westminster Forum
'Does the present scarcity of Provision arise from any failure in our national produce, the monopoly of individuals, or the wickedness of Administration in obstinately prosecuting a system of Warfare?
This Society was the first which ventured to revive political discussion; public approval, unbounded patronage, and the most honourable support from many of the first Literary Characters have been the consequence.'
Morning Chronicle

1943. May 7, 1795 London Forum
'Is Connubial Happiness most frequently found in the Upper, Lower or Middle Walks of Life?'
Morning Chronicle

1944. May 12, 1795 Westminster Forum
'Does not the System of Moderation adopted by the French Convention, together with their suppression of the Jacobinic Faction, evince that the present rulers of France are persons with whom Great Britain may safely conclude a permanent and honourable Peace?'
Morning Chronicle

1945. May 14, 1795 London Forum
PRINCE OF WALES'S DEBTS
'Would the House of Commons derive greater honour from discharging the Prince of Wales' Debts, as a mark of national liberality – or from rejecting the measure, on account of the burthens already sustained by the People?
When the above subject was first proposed to the Managers, they felt extreme reluctance at its adoption, on account of its delicacy. Repeatedly urged by some of the first characters that support their Institution, they have complied with the request. . . In the course of the Debate, many opposite sentiments will, doubtless, meet with alternate support; but it is hoped all will unite in paying that tribute of respect due to the illustrious Personage to whom their arguments may allude.'
Morning Chronicle

1946. May 19, 1795 Westminster Forum
'Does Mr. Paine deserve Praise or Censure for his Age of Reason?'
Morning Chronicle

1947. May 21, 1795 London Forum
PARLIAMENTARY REFORM
PITT, HORNE TOOK, DUKE OF RICHMOND
'Which plan of Reform would most effectually promote the Happiness
and secure the Liberties of this Country, Mr. Pitt's, Horne Tooke's, or
the Duke of Richmond's?'
Morning Chronicle

1948. May 26, 1795 Westminster Forum
'Does Mr. Paine deserve Praise or Censure for his Age of Reason?'
Morning Chronicle

1949. June 2, 1795 Westminster Forum
'Does Mr. Paine deserve Praise or Censure for his Age of Reason?'
Morning Chronicle

1950. June 16, 1795 Westminster Forum
MR. PITT and the CONVENTION
'Which is the greater impediment to an immediate Peace, the
wickedness and obstinacy of the Minister, or the factions that prevail
in the French Republic?'
Morning Chronicle

1951. June 23, 1795 Westminster Forum
'Will those Members of the London Corresponding Society, who have
agreed to convene another Public Meeting, prove themselves, by that
measure, the Friends of Liberty – or the imprudent Disturbers of the
Public Peace?'
Morning Chronicle

1952. June 30, 1795 Westminster Forum
REVOLUTIONS IN ENGLAND, FRANCE, AND AMERICA
'Which was the most glorious event in the History of Man, the Revolution of England, the Independence of America, or the Emancipation
of France?
The Managers of this Institution think it a duty unequivocally to state
to the Public their independence of all party, and their determination
so to remain. On the present occasion they will most impartially attend
to the sentiments of the various Gentlemen who may address the Chair.'
Morning Chronicle

1953. July 7, 1795 Westminster Forum
'Do the Members of the London Corresponding Society deserve the
praise or censure of their Fellow-Citizens for holding the late Meeting
in St. George's Fields?

The gross calumnies inserted in the Ministerial Prints, relative to the above Meeting, have induced several Gentlemen to propose the subject for unbiassed discussion in the Westminster Forum. They thus publicly challenge the Prostituted Hirelings, who vent the venom of slanderous accusation, to meet them in an independent institution, and (if they can) substantiate their charges against the London Corresponding Society.'
Morning Chronicle

1954. July 14, 1795 Westminster Forum
'Do the Members of the London Corresponding Society deserve the praise or censure of their Fellow-Citizens for holding the late Meeting in St. George's Fields?'
Morning Chronicle

1955. July 21, 1795 Westminster Forum
'Which would be the most effectual method of reducing the high price of Provisions – the retrenchment of the luxuries of the rich, and the cessation of public dinners – the use of brown bread, as advised by his Majesty's Council – or by an immediate Peace to restore the Freedom of Commerce?
The situation of this Country demands the most serious attention of every well-wisher to its interests. It is by peaceable deliberations, and not by open acts of violence, that the British Government will be induced to redress the grievances of a suffering Nation. To ascertain the most effectual means is a Constitutional right and a Patriotic exertion.'
Morning Chronicle

1956. July 28, 1795 Westminster Forum
'Which would, to a Woman of sense and accomplishments, prove the most intolerable Companion in the Marriage State, a Spendthrift, a Miser, a Clown, or a Fop?'
Morning Herald

1957. August 4, 1795 Westminster Forum
'Which would be most advantageous to Great Britain – the Restoration of the Gallic Monarchy in the Person of Louis XVIII – or an immediate acknowledgment of the French Republic?
The failure of the late Emigrant Expedition, and the general situation of this Country, render it a subject of the utmost moment.'
Morning Chronicle

1958. August 11, 1795 Westminster Forum
'Would it not be advantageous to the liberty and happiness of the world, that Woman should equally partake all the Rights and Privileges of Man?
The above interesting and original enquiry is instituted at the particular request of two female citizens, distant relations of Mrs. Woolstonecroft.'
Morning Chronicle

1959. August 18, 1795 Westminster Forum
'Are Annual Parliaments and Universal Suffrage consistent with, or inimical to the true Spirit of the British Constitution?'
Morning Chronicle

1960. August 25, 1795 Westminster Forum
'In the present disastrous situation of this country, which would most effectually insure the blessings of Peace, and secure the happiness of the Empire, – continuing Mr. Pitt in Office – calling Mr. Fox to his Majesty's Councils – or forming a Third Party independent of either?'
Morning Chronicle

1961. August 27, 1795 London Forum
'Does not Mr. Paine's Age of Reason, particularly the assertion, that 'The Bible is an History of Wickedness, calculated to corrupt and brutalize Mankind' deserve the reprobation of every sincere Friend to Civil and Religious Liberty?'
Morning Herald

1962. September 1, 1795 Westminster Forum
'In the present disastrous situation of this country, which would most effectually insure the blessings of Peace, and secure the happiness of the Empire, – continuing Mr. Pitt in Office – calling Mr. Fox to his Majesty's Councils – or forming a Third Party independent of either? Any advocate for the Minister shall be heard with impartiality. That side of the question, we must confess, wanted supporters.'
Morning Chronicle

1963. September 3, 1795 London Forum
'Does not Mr. Paine's Age of Reason, particularly the assertion, that "The Bible is an History of Wickedness, calculated to corrupt and brutalize Mankind" deserve the reprobation of every sincere Friend to Civil and Religious Liberty?'
Morning Chronicle

1964. September 10, 1795 London Forum
'Which is the more culpable Character – the Man who lives unmarried a number of years with a trusting confidential female, and then forsakes her to marry another – or the wretched Woman, who, unable to endure the separation, desperately punishes his perfidy with death?
It must be sufficiently obvious, that the above interesting and affecting theme arose out of the late unfortunate circumstance of the death of Mr. Errington by Miss Broderick.'
Morning Herald

1965. September 15, 1795 Westminster Forum
THE POPE A JACOBIN
'Does the Letter of the Pope to Louis XVIII, advising him to relinquish his Claims to the Throne of France, "a Sacrifice to restore the Peace

of Europe", prove that even his Holiness is infected with Jacobin principles: or that he trembles for the safety of his Temporal Dominions?
The Jacobin principles of his Holiness the Pope must strike every person
as a most ludicrous idea; and, on the other hand, the victorious arms of
the French Republic, extorting Mildness from the source of Intolerance,
compelling the Papal Tripod to utter the voice of Peace, instead of
breathing the anathema of Slaughter and interdicting the Rights of
Human Nature, is a subject every way worthy those talents which the
Managers of the Westminster Forum can with certainty assure the
Public will be employed on the occasion.'
Morning Chronicle

1966. September 17, 1795 London Forum
'Is it most probable, that the measures now pursuing by the French
Convention will terminate in the Establishment of their present Consti-
tution; a Revolution in favour of the Jacobins; or the Restoration of
Gallic Royalty?'
Morning Herald

1967. September 22, 1795 Westminster Forum
SHAM PATRIOTS
'Which is hardest to be found – Honesty among Lawyers; Piety among
Divines; or Patriotism among the public Professors of Liberty?
We can only say, that we revere real Patriotism; but we esteem it a
Duty to hold Pretenders up to public animadversion.'
Morning Chronicle

1968. September 24, 1795 London Forum
'Is it not a duty which every well-wisher of his country owes to its
interests, immediately to enter into the London Corresponding Society,
while they pursue peaceable and constitutional measures; as the most
probable means of procuring a Reform in Parliament, and a termination
of the War?'
Morning Chronicle

1969. September 29, 1795 Westminster Forum
'In case of a general Peace, which conduct would a wise and prudent
man pursue – emigrate to America – to France – or to remain in
England?
We are now approaching the close of a war, the most disgraceful, as to
its principle and ruinous as to its tendency, of any in which this country
ever was unhappily engaged. The French Revolution must, in case of
a general pacification, materially alter the disposition of European politics: what then would be the conduct of any man who valued liberty and
safety? would he remain here? or would he emigrate? If he determine
on emigration, which must be most eligible to his purpose, and congen-
ial to his opinions, France or America?'
Morning Chronicle

1970. October 1, 1795 London Forum
'Is it not a duty which every well-wisher of his country owes to its interests, immediately to enter into the London Corresponding Society, while they pursue peaceable and constitutional measures; as the most probable means of procuring a Reform in Parliament, and a termination of the War?'
Morning Chronicle

1971. October 6, 1795 Westminster Forum
PITT UNDER PETTICOAT GOVERNMENT
'Which is most likely to subdue the Obstinacy and tame the untoward Disposition of the British Minister – a Peace – a Reform – or a Marriage?

Safe from the Bar, the Pulpit, and the Throne;
Yet touch'd and sham'd by Ridicule alone.

So sung Pope of one of the most distinguished characters of his days. How far the pointed ridicule of the above question may succeed with the Minister is not for us to determine.'
Morning Chronicle

1972. October 8, 1795 London Forum
'Which is the greater Trial of Female fortitude – the Loss of a Lover, or the Death of a Husband?'
Morning Herald

1973. October 13, 1795 Westminster Forum
'With all the acknowledged defects of the British Constitution, is it not a far more happy and secure Form of Government, than that now adopted by the French Nation?
In times like the present when the public mind is agitated on the one hand, by the dire effects of a wicked and inefficient Administration, and on the other, by the fine spun theories of visionary Politicians, it becomes every one who reveres the British Constitution, and among the most zealous of its votaries we would wish to rank ourselves, to point out its abuses, but to defend its glorious principle, its equal laws, its distributive justice.'
Morning Chronicle

1974. October 15, 1795 London Forum
'Is there any real Foundation for a belief in the Devil?
At the particular desire of several Persons, who were disappointed of admission when this question was discussed at the Westminster Forum, the Managers of this Society have consented to its adoption.'
Morning Herald

1975. October 20, 1795 Westminster Forum
343

'Do the avowed Principles and Political conduct of Mr. Fox entitle him to the Confidence and Support of the real Friends to the Rights and Liberties of Man?
We are authorised by Mr. Jones to announce, that his conduct at the late Meeting of Mr. Fox's Friends, which has been so much vilified, shall be vindicated by himself. Let the diurnal Retailers of Slander forsake their Garrets, meet that Gentleman before the Public, and either substantiate their assertions or apologise for their abuse.'
Morning Chronicle

1976. October 22, 1795 London Forum
A SHILLING FOR A QUARTERN LOAF!
'Ought the present high price of bread to be attributed to a scarcity of grain – a secret monopoly – or the unavoidable consequences of the war?
After the abundant harvest which report says we have experienced, what is the reason why bread is continued at one shill. per quartern loaf? – Does it rest with the earth – farmers and dealers in grain – or with the war and the minister?. . . While they most carefully avoid everything calculated to heat the public mind, they will not shrink back, with cowardly apprehension, from necessary investigation, like the present.'
Morning Chronicle

1977. October 27, 1795 Westminster Forum
'Is it more probable, that the Public Meeting of the London Corresponding Society, will accelerate or retard the Cause of Reform?
Several leading Members of the Corresponding Society, and many distinguished Gentlemen of opposite principles, will assuredly address the audience; and, if reliance can be placed on letters received, a strong opposition will be made to this meeting, as both ill-timed and dangerous. – The Managers recommend moderation, and an early attendance, to all parties.'
Morning Chronicle

1978. October 29, 1795 London Forum
'Which is most entitled to the Pity and Commiseration of Mankind – Mary Queen of Scots, or Antoinette of France?'
Morning Herald

1979. November 3, 1795 Westminster Forum
'Do the avowed Principles and Political conduct of Mr. Fox intitle him to the Confidence and Support of the real Friends to the Rights and Liberties of Man?'
Morning Chronicle

1980. November 5, 1795 London Forum
'Which of the three grand National Events has most contributed to the Happiness and Liberties of this Country, the discovery of the Powder

344

Plot, on the Fifth of November; the Landing of King William, on the Fifth of November; or the Acquital of Thomas Hardy on the Fifth of November?
Mr. Jones has promised to open the Question; and Mr. Bull will deliver an Ode suited to the occasion.'
Morning Chronicle

1981. November 10, 1795 Westminster Forum
'Do the avowed Principles and Political conduct of Mr. Fox entitle him to the Confidence and Support of the real Friends to the Rights and Liberties of Man?
The decision . . . was (by a considerable majority) that Mr. Fox is justly entitled to the confidence and support of the British Nation.'
Morning Chronicle

1982. November 12, 1795 London Forum
'Is it not contrary to Reason and Propriety; that Women should rule in Families?'
Morning Chronicle

1983. November 17, 1795 Westminster Forum
'Is not the prohibition of public discussion, a violation of the spirit of a free constitution?'
Morning Chronicle

1984. November 21, 1795 Westminster Forum
'Is it most probable that the atrocious Insults offered to his Majesty originated in the unredressed Calamities of the Poor – the meetings of the London Corresponding Society – or the vile Artifices of Administration to create a pretext for passing the Convention Bill?
It being very uncertain how many more nights this Society will be permitted to assemble on political subjects, all apology for deviating from the usual evening is unnecessary. With due gratitude for past favours, the Managers now offer the public opportunity to investigate the true source of the transaction.'
Morning Chronicle

1985. November 28, 1795 Westminster Forum
'Ought the Public Debating Societies and the late Meetings at Copenhagen House to be supported, as friendly to the Rights of the People; or suppressed, as the Causes of the Insult offered to His Majesty, and justifiable Reasons for introducing the Convention Bill?'
Morning Chronicle

1986. December 1, 1795 Westminster Forum
NO PITT! NO WAR!
'Is it not the duty of every Friend to the Constitution to petition his Majesty for the immediate Removal of the Minister, and the Discontinuance of the War?'
Morning Chronicle

1987. December 5, 1795 Westminster Forum
'Which ought to be deemed the most injurious Libel on the British Constitution – Mr. Paine's Rights of Man; or the late Pamphlet attributed to Mr. Reeves?'
Morning Chronicle

1988. December 8, 1795 Westminster Forum
'Are not the most probable Means left of saving the Country from the Despotism of the Minister – an immediate Junction of the Whig Interest and the Corresponding Society?'
Morning Chronicle

1989. December 12, 1795 Westminster Forum
'Are not the most probable Means left of saving the Country from the Despotism of the Minister – an immediate Junction of the Whig Interest and the Corresponding Society?
The above Question must be decided This Evening; after which the following important theme will be produced, viz. "Is not the present moment the proper time to conclude a permanent and honourable peace with the French Republic?" – We suppose this will be the Last Political Question that can be debated, before the two Bills now pending in Parliament pass into Law. The strict observance of order is enjoined. The numerous list of disputants that propose to address the Chair, are entreated to observe candour and moderation in their remarks. Thus will this Society have to publish in the face of the country, that to the very last it persevered in exercising a Constitutional Right, without giving one real ground of accusation on which its deliberation should be suspended.'
Morning Chronicle

1990. December 19, 1795 Westminster Forum
[LAST EVENING OF POLITICS]
MR. PITT'S IMPEACHMENT
'Is it not a duty which the House of Commons owe to the People – immediately to impeach the Minister?'
Morning Chronicle

1991. August 29, 1796 London Forum
'Which would most probably avert from the rising generation the untimely fate of the unhappy Weston – the vigilant activity of Magistrates; the earnest exhortation of Divines; or the salutary Restraints of Parents and Masters of Families?
The Managers of this Society with confidence assemble together, for the Season, that Public which has long patronised their Institution. The opinion of the most eminent Counsel has been taken with regard to the Legality of the Meeting, who have uniformly pronounced, that "The Convention Bills only affect Political Discussion". It is not the intention

of the Managers to oppose or evade Laws. It is their duty to submit to them. Political allusion is therefore, in any shape, inadmissible.
A numerous and polite audience decided almost unanimously in favour of the salutary restrictions of parents and masters of families.'
Morning Chronicle

1992. September 5, 1796 London Forum, Wych Street, opposite Lyons Inn
'Do not the unhappy Consequences which have resulted from Love unsanctioned by the holy tie of Wedlock, prove that Marriage is a Duty incumbent on Every Individual of the Human Race?
In framing the above Question, the Managers had not the most distant idea of anticipating the trial now pending, on the murder of Mr. Yates. It has been some months in their possession, and was sent by a Correspondent soon after the unfortunate affair of Miss Broderick and Mr. Errington.'
Morning Chronicle

1993. September 15, 1796 Westminster Forum, Brewer Street, Golden Square
'Are the late Suicides to be more imputed to avaricious Speculation; Disappointment in Love; or the modern Doctrines of Infidelity?
The Public may rest assured that every precaution has been taken on the part of the Managers to render this Meeting strictly Constitutional. All political remarks or allusions are utterly inadmissible. Any such attempt to disturb the Society and evade the Laws, will be immediately checked by the Chair. The Legislature has taken from the Society the right of Political Discussion; but its Members hope that (assisted by those Literary Characters, who start Volunteers in this popular and erudite Assembly) they may, on Subjects of Divinity, Morals, History and Science, continue to receive, as it shall be their united effort to deserve – the patronage of the Public.
The decision was against avaricious Speculation in Trade.'
Morning Herald/Morning Chronicle September 22

1994. September 22, 1796 Westminster Forum
'Has the Preaching of the Rev. Mr. Huntington, and the rest of the Methodists, been productive of more good or harm to Mankind in general?
The Managers observe, although they have not altered the question, yet a line ought to be drawn between the great body of Methodists and an individual. The violent temper of the Apostle of Titchfield street, they know too well to invite him; but should he attend, he shall receive that candour he has uniformly denied to others.'
Morning Chronicle

1995. September 26, 1796 London Forum
'Which is the more intolerable Yokefellow in Marriage, a Drunken Husband, or a Scolding Wife?

O, ye Scolding Wives, who annoy your neighbours with your daily, and disturb your Husbands with your nightly vociferations, come hither! – In the LONDON FORUM learn the virtue of silence, a virtue highly commendable in Woman; so shall we practice the duty of obedience, a duty indispensible to the peace of Wedlock! And you, ye Lovers of the Bottle, attend to the admonition of prudence! – The neglect of the Drunkard deserves the clamour of the Scold. This is therefore to give notice, that This Evening . . . a JURY OF SCOLDS will be impannelled, the oldest and most untamed Virago in the whole assembly will be elected Forewoman, and the punishment due to every Drunken Husband impartially ascertained.'
Morning Chronicle

1996. September 29 Westminster Forum
'Do the Talents, Virtues and Vices of Man depend on his Organization; or are they the result only of Education?'
Morning Chronicle

1997. October 3, 1796 London Forum
'Are the opinions of Dr. Gill, Mr. Toplady, Mr. Whitfield, Mr. Romaine, Mr. Winchester &c. founded in reason or revelation, that the Pope is Antichrist, and that his destruction is at hand?
The Society was . . . honoured with the sentiments of the Rev. Richard Clarke' and solicited for the attendance of the Rev. Arthur O'Leary.
Morning Chronicle

1998. October 6, 1796 Westminster Forum
'Has the Preaching of the Rev. Mr. Huntington, and the rest of the Methodists, been productive of more harm or good to Mankind in general?'
Morning Chronicle

1999. October 10, 1796 London Forum
FEMALE AGONY
'Which is the greatest Misfortune, to a Woman of Susceptibility, the Loss of a Lover by Banishment, Death or Marriage?'
Morning Chronicle

2000. October 17, 1796 London Forum
'Is the Answer of the Bishop of Landaff to Thomas Paine's Age of Reason, a satisfactory Refutation of the Principles of Infidelity?'
Morning Chronicle

2001. October 20, 1796 Westminster Forum
ASTROLOGY – FORTUNE TELLING
'Is it possible to foretell good or evil Fortune, Marriage, Death, the Elevation of Poverty, the Depression of Greatness, by the Science of Judicial Astrology?'
Morning Chronicle

2002. October 27, 1796 Westminster Forum
'Which are most consistent with Scripture and Reason, the Opinions of Dr. Priestley and Price, that the Wicked will be annihilated; the Calvinistic Decrees of Mr. Toplady; the Arminian Creed of Mr. J. Wesley; or the Universal Restoration of all Mankind, as preached by Mr. Winchester?'
Morning Chronicle

2003. November 3, 1796 Westminster Forum
'Is the Assertion of the Right Honourable C.J. FOX true, 'There are but two things superior to our Reason, the Love of Life, and the Association of the Sexes?'
The Westminster Forum being frequented by Ladies of the most respectable character, and in the higher situations of life, the utmost decorum is observed: the Managers have therefore taken the liberty of altering one word in Mr. Fox's assertion, and substituting another of the same meaning, but which will not admit perversion.'
Morning Chronicle

2004. November 7, 1796 London Forum
'Which is the greater Misfortune, a Man to be born without Sense, or a Woman without Beauty?
Political Allusion is utterly inadmissable.'
Morning Herald

2005. November 10, 1796 Westminster Forum
RAKES – TO THE LADIES
'Is the commonly received opinion true, "That Reformed Rakes make the best of Husbands"?'
Morning Chronicle

2006. November 12, 1796 Westminster Forum
'Has GENERAL WASHINGTON acted consistently with his own exalted Character, and the Welfare of his Country, in resigning the Presidency of the American Government?'
Morning Chronicle

2007. November 14, 1796 London Forum
'Ought the Church of Rome to be considered the object described by St. John as the "Whore of Babylon" whose destruction is at hand?
This long promised Question is now brought forward under particular advantages, the great Prophecies of Almighty Revelation seem now either fulfilling, or about to be fulfilled over the whole globe.'
Rev. Mr. Clarke to either open or close the debate.
Morning Chronicle

2008. November 17, 1796 Westminster Forum
'Which is the Production consistent with Truth – Mr. Paine's Age of Reason, or the Bishop of Landaff's Answer to that Work?'
Morning Chronicle

2009. November 21, 1796 London Forum
'Ought the Church of Rome to be considered the object described by
St. John as the "Whore of Babylon" whose Destruction is at hand?'
Morning Chronicle

2010. November 24, 1796 Westminster Forum
'Which is the Production consistent with Truth – Mr. Paine's Age of
Reason, or the Bishop of Landaff's Answer to that Work?'
Morning Chronicle

2011. November 28, 1796 London Forum
'Is the "Whore of Babylon" mentioned by St. John in the Revelations,
indicative of the Romish Church, the Mahometan Church, or the World
of Infidelity?
To this [question, the Managers] have been more inclined, not only to
evince their impartiality to both Catholics and Protestants; but on
account of a learned and ingenious Gentleman having signified his
intention of proving, that THOMAS PAINE is the WHORE OF
BABYLON mentioned by St. John.'
Morning Chronicle

2012. December 1, 1796 Westminster Forum
'Which is the Production consistent with Truth – Mr. Paine's Age of
Reason, or the Bishop of Landaff's Answer to that Work?'
Morning Chronicle

2013. December 5, 1796 London Forum
HOW TO MAKE ALL THE WORLD HAPPY
'Would it not be likely to prevent Conjugal Infidelity, and abolish quar-
rels between Man and Wife, if Married Persons had the Privilege of
Divorcement, as soon as they would declare upon oath, that they were
unhappy, and heartily tired of each other?
Among the Antients the Law of Divorce was carried to a considerable
extent. A neighbouring nation has revived the practice. How far such
a regulation would, in a well-organized Government, operate to the
cure of matrimonial infelicity, is a subject worthy the abilities which
are displayed in this institution.'
Morning Chronicle

2014. December 8, 1796 Westminster Forum
'Which is the Production consistent with Truth – Mr. Paine's Age of
Reason, or the Bishop of Landaff's Answer to that Work?
It may be departing from general practice, but we cannot avoid thus
publicly presenting our Thanks to the Rev. Mr. BENNET, for his elo-
quent and energetic defence of the Christian Religion.'
Morning Chronicle

2015. December 11, 1796 Westminster Forum
'The Bachelor's Apology "Are these times to marry"?'
Morning Chronicle December 8

2016. December 26, 1796 London Forum
'Is the Imprisonment of Mons. LA FAYETTE in the dungeons of Olmutz, the greater disgrace on France or America?'
Morning Chronicle

2017. December 28, 1796 Westminster Forum
'Was Marcus Brutus justifiable or censurable for the Assassination of Julius Caesar?'
Morning Chronicle

2018. January 3, 1797 Westminster Forum
DEVIL OR NO DEVIL
'Is there any real Foundation for a Belief in the Devil?'
Several gentlemen have promised to support 'the opinion of the great and pious Dr. Fleming, in his "Discourse on the non-entity of Satan" – To these we must subjoin a communication indeed of an extraordinary measure: An elderly Lady, in an Epistle dated from "Walnut-tree Walk" declares she has frequently seen, conversed with, and been tempted by the Devil.
Nothing impious, nothing prophane, a reverence to Deity, and a proper regard to his constituted authorities pervaded the whole discussion.'
Morning Chronicle

2019. January 5, 1797 Westminster Forum
THE DEVIL ADJOINED
'Is there a real foundation for a belief in the Devil?'
Question went in the affirmative.
Morning Herald January 12

2020. January 9, 1797 Westminster Forum
VORTIGERN AND ROWENA
'Do the Shakespearean Manuscripts, the Play of Vortigern and Rowena, and the Apology of Mr. Ireland, Jun., exhibit stronger Proofs of Authenticity, flagrant Imposition, or the Credulity of Persons of Genius?'
Morning Chronicle

2021. January 12, 1797 Westminster Forum
RUSSIA, KOSCIUSKO AND LA FAYETTE
'Ought not the generous conduct of the Emperor of Russia towards the Polish General Kosciusko to serve as an incitement to the Emperor of Germany to liberate the unfortunate LA FAYETTE?
Impressed with the vast importance of this Question, the Managers commit it to the public discretion and the abilities of the Gentlemen who support the Westminster Forum, with the following simple remark:

This being one of the few public themes which the Society can with safety discuss, it is hoped no Gentlemen will attempt to advert to the Government of this country, but argue the subject on the broad base of universal benevolence and individual justice.'
Morning Herald

2022. January 16, 1797 Westminster Forum
DEPARTED SPIRITS
'Is it probable that any departed Spirit ever visited, or conversed with a Mortal?
The above Question arises out of a subject on which the Religious and Philosophical World have long been alike divided. In this Society it must receive the most ample investigation, from the number of Clerical and Literary Gentlemen by whom the institution is patronized. Many strange stories have been propagated concerning Apparitions, the Managers thus publicly declare, that they shall feel themselves gratified by the attendance of any person who can positively declare to the Audience, that they have either seen or conversed with a departed Spirit. – Indeed this theme, of all others, comes nearest to the human feelings; the state of Man, after death, opens the most rational and important enquiry to which we can devote our time and attention.'
Morning Chronicle

2023. January 19, 1797 Westminster Forum
THE DEVIL CONTINUED
'Is there any real foundation for a belief in the Devil?
The Managers of this Society thought, after the Debate which ensued on the above subject, they had dismissed it with credit to themselves, and honour to the various Reverend, Literary, and respectable characters who took part in the contest: But the decision having been much arraigned, they have (to evince their impartiality) once more appointed it for Public Debate. . . No Political Remarks permitted.'
Morning Herald

2024. January 23, 1797 Westminster Forum
A FATHER'S REMEDY FOR FEMALE RUIN
'Ought not every Seducer of Virgin Innocence to be compelled to marry the unfortunate victim of his Treachery?
The Debate will, doubtless, be an affecting lesson of moral instruction; we were forcibly struck with the Gentleman's melancholy Epistle in which the Question was enclosed: Three Daughters, and each the unfortunate Victim of Seduction! – Well might the Gentleman conceive the remedy offered in the above enquiry; parental anguish is visible in every line of the letter; of the efficacy, however, of the remedy, the Debate must be the Criterion.'
Morning Chronicle

2025. January 26, 1797 Westminster Forum

'Ought not every Seducer of Virgin Innocence to be compelled to marry the unfortunate victim of his Treachery?'
Morning Chronicle

2026. January 30, 1797 Westminster Forum
PAINE'S LETTER TO GENERAL WASHINGTON
'Does not Mr. Paine deserve the reprobation of every Friend of Liberty and Humanity, for his recent attack on the Character of General Washington?
The Adjournment of this most important Question was moved . . . by Mr. J. Gale Jones. . . It was carried with universal approbation, by an audience consisting of upwards of five hundred persons, among whom the Managers had the honour of perceiving several Noblemen, Magistrates, and Gentlemen of the first respectability in the Country. . . No political remarks pertaining to this Country permitted.'
Morning Herald February 2

2027. January 30, 1797 London Forum, Fleet Street, near Fetter lane
A Lady's Question concerning Love and Apparitions.
'Is the assertion of a celebrated author true, – That mutual love between man and wife is like apparitions, talked of by all, but perceived and felt by none?'
Morning Chronicle

2028. February 2, 1797 Westminster Forum
'Does not Mr. Paine deserve the Reprobation of every Friend of Liberty and Humanity, for his recent attack on the Character of General Washington?'
Morning Herald

2029. February 6, 1797 Westminster Forum
'Does not Mr. Paine deserve the Censure of every Friend of Liberty and Humanity, for his recent Attack on the Character of General Washington?
At the particular request of Mr. J. Jones (whose splendid exertions last Thursday Evening in the defence of General Washington will be remembered as long as the Westminster Forum shall remain a Literary Institution) an Amendment was moved on the terms of the question. That Gentleman submitted the word "Censure" for "Reprobation". It was decided that Mr. Paine deserves censure for his attacks on General Washington.'
Morning Chronicle

2030. February 9, 1797 Westminster Forum
ANOTHER OF ROBESPIERRE'S MURDERS
'Supposing a Mariner ship-wrecked, with his Mother, Wife, and Child; having Time and Power to save only one of the three, which ought to be the object of his protection?

A French Emigrant of distinction was lately in the company of several Ladies, relating the circumstance of one of his countrymen (whose father was guillotined under the Tyranny of Robespierre) escaping to sea in an open boat, with his Mother, Wife and Child; the melancholy result of which was, that he saved only the Child, and lost the Mother and Wife in the devouring element. – The conversation turned on which of these tender ties ought the unhappy man to have bestowed his Protection? – The dispute was ultimately submitted by the Ladies to the Managers of the Westminster Forum. – Proud to oblige . . . in reviving an enquiry penned by so great a man as Mr. Toplady.'
Morning Chronicle

2031. February 13, 1797 Westminster Forum
'On an Impartial Review of the Public Conduct and Writings of Thomas Paine, ought he to be considered the Friend and Reformer of Mankind – or the artful Incendiary, bent on disturbing the Peace of Nations?
For further particulars the Public are referred to the Bills of the Society, posted about various parts in this Metropolis.'
Morning Chronicle

2032. February 13, 1797 London Forum
'Which is the greatest Nuisance to Society – Knavish Attornies, Quack Doctors, or Insurance Lottery-Office-Keepers?'
Morning Chronicle

2033. February 16, 1797 Westminster Forum
A TRIAL, T. PAINE A PATRIOT OR AN INCENDIARY
'On an Impartial Review of the Public Conduct and Writings of Thomas Paine, ought he to be considered the Friend and Reformer of Mankind – or the artful Incendiary, bent on disturbing the Peace of Nations?'
Morning Chronicle

2034. February 20, 1797 London Forum
WHAT IS HELL?
'Is Hell to be considered as a Place of Eternal Corporal Punishment – a Purgatory to Expiate Sin – or the Remorse of a Guilty Conscience? N.B. In this Society may be had a new Publication, called A Defence of Itinerant Preachers.'
Morning Chronicle February 18

2035. February 20, 1797 Westminster Forum
A MAN FOR THE LADIES
'Which Qualification most effectually secures to a man the approbation and love of the Fair Sex, Wit, Courage, or Politeness?'
Morning Chronicle

2036. February 23, 1797 Westminster Forum
FATE AND FREE WILL
'The Publication announced this Day, under the title of "A General

and Introductory View of Professor KANT'S Principles concerning Man, the World, and the Deity" has occasioned the following Question. . .
"Was Man originally created a free and accountable Agent; or the Child of an inevitable Necessity?"
Mr. Nitsch, the Author of the above Work, who has lectured on Kant's principles several times in London, and whose party maintains the Freedom of Human Volition, is expected to be present.'
Morning Herald February 21

2037. February 27, 1797 London Forum
MESSRS. FOX, BURKE AND ERSKINE
'Which of the following Characters is likely to be most admired by posterity for genius, talents, and virtue, Mr. Fox, Mr. Burke, or Mr. Erskine, the English Barrister?'
Morning Chronicle February 25

2038. February 27, 1797 Westminster Forum
THE RASH VOW OF JEPTHA
'Was Jephta a justifiable or condemnable character, for sacrificing his Daughter according to his rash vow?'
Morning Chronicle

2039. March 2, 1797 Westminster Forum
DISSERTATION ON FOOLS
'Which of the three prevailing Follies of the Human Mind is most deserving Censure, the Pride of Ancestry; the Arrogance of Wealth; or the Ostentation of Learning?'
Morning Chronicle

2040. March 6, 1797 Westminster Forum
His Holiness the POPE
'Does not the present situation of affairs in Italy confirm the opinions of the late Rev. Mr. Romaine, Archbishop Tillotson, Messrs. Whitfield, Wesley, and the numerous Protestant Divines, who have asserted that the Pope is Anti-Christ, and that the destruction of his power would be accomplished in the 18th Century?
Perhaps at this very moment, the Republican General is thundering at the gates of Rome. – Perhaps the mortal, whose long train of predecessors have impiously assumed the attributes of the most high – cantoned out the Kingdoms of the Globe – formally pronounced the curse of God on every Protestant Prince in Europe, and laid every inch of ground in this our Island, under the malediction of Heaven – may (with all his infallibility) be reduced to seek an asylum, even in this "Land of Heretics!!!" '
Morning Chronicle

2041. March 9, 1797 School of Eloquence, Old Change, Cheapside

'Which is most commendable, Industry in the Poor, or Benevolence in the Rich?'
Produce of the sale of tickets, one shilling each, to be applied to the Society for the Relief and Discharge of Persons imprisoned for Small Debts.
T.C. Andrews, secretary.
Morning Chronicle March 3

2042. March 9, 1797 Westminster Forum
CRIME OF SEDUCING A MARRIED LADY'S AFFECTIONS
'Is not the Seducer of a Married Lady's Affections from her Husband as great a Criminal as the Common Robber; and were not those States justifiable which punished the crime with Death?'
Morning Chronicle

2043. March 13, 1797 Westminster Forum
'Mr. PAINE'S NEW PAMPHLET – How to make all the POOR happy without injuring the RICH'
'Would not the plan proposed by Mr. Paine to the French Nation in his last new pamphlet called "Agrarian Justice" effectually eradicate the evils of Poverty – prevent, in a great measure, the Commission of Crimes – and alleviate the Distress of Old Age and Infirmity?
The following is the general outline of Mr. Paine's Plan: – To create a National Fund, by a levy of 10 per cent, on all property, at the death of its possessor. – To pay every person now living of the age of 21 years the sum of 15*l.* sterling, to enable him or her to begin the world – And also 10*l.* sterling per annum, during life, to every person now living, of the age of 50 years, and to all others when they shall arrive at that age, to enable them to live in Old Age without Wretchedness and to go decently out of the world.'
Morning Chronicle

2044. March 15, 1797 Westminster Forum
'Is virtue (in this World) its own reward, and vice its own punishment? The Managers have deviated from their usual evening, to accommodate Mr. Jones with the Room for his Oration on Thursday.'
Morning Chronicle

2045. March 20, 1797 Westminster Forum
REAPPEARANCE OF THE DEAD
'Is it probable, that any departed Spirit ever appeared to, or conversed with, a Mortal?'
Morning Chronicle

2046. March 23, 1797 Westminster Forum
ADAM'S FALL
'Is the Argument on which the Deists deny the Christian Religion founded on rational and solid grounds, because, for the Transgression of Adam, they cannot, by the principles of common justice, account

for the propriety of the atonement of an innocent being, whose whole life was one continued exercise of piety, humility, and universal benevolence?'
Morning Chronicle

2047. March 27, 1797 Westminster Forum
FARO LADIES – St. James's and St. Giles's
'Which is the greater plague to her Husband, and disgrace of her Sex, the untamed Scold of St. Giles, or the fashionable Female Gamester of St. James's?'
Morning Chronicle

2048. March 30, 1797 Westminster Forum
'Is it probable, that any departed Spirit ever appeared to, or conversed with, a Mortal?'
Morning Herald

2049. April 3, 1797 Westminster Forum
THE SURE WAY TO GET AN HUSBAND
'Which will, in the present times, most effectually secure an Husband to the Lady who wants one, the Possession of Beauty, Riches, or Understanding?'
Morning Chronicle

2050. April 6, 1797 Westminster Forum
BEHEADING OF THE QUEENS OF FRANCE AND SCOTLAND
'Which of the following Royal Sufferers is more entitled to the Pity of Mankind, Mary of Scotland, or Antoinette Queen of France?
An attempt has been made by certain individuals of this parish to stop the meetings of the Westminster Forum, by sueing for penalties under the Sedition Acts. For this purpose (and that in more than one instance!) no less than FOUR actions have been served on the same person. We suppose the number of Writs issued and intended to be issued will amount to upwards of FORTY!!! Under these circumstances (so VERY HONOURABLE to those who have produced them!) the Managers are not deterred by the contrived weight of expence from asserting their legal and constitutional Rights: – they will appeal to the Laws of their Country for protection; and they trust to the magnanimity of Englishmen to support them in that application. Obedience to laws, but a steady, a determined assertion of Rights has been the uniform course of Direction which they have pursued, and by which they intend to abide.'
Morning Chronicle

2051. April 10, 1797 London Forum
WHAT IS WOMAN?
'Which is more Repugnant to Truth and Experience, the Doctrine of Mahomet, that Women have no Souls, or the Opinion of Mrs. Wool-

stonecraft, that they possess Mental Endowments equal, if not superior, to Men?
A Young Lady, who declares she will give her hand to no man who will not declare he believes the Understandings of Women to be equal to those of Men, sent the above Question to the Managers.'
Morning Chronicle April 8

2052. April 10, 1797 Westminster Forum
SELECT VESTRIES – ATTEMPT TO CRUSH THE DEBATING SOCIETIES
'Ought not the Interference of the Select Vestry of St. James Parish with the Moral, Literary, and Philosophical Discussions of the Westminster Forum (which are in no case restricted by the late Acts of Parliament) together with the general Conduct of Select Vestries, to operate as a warning to all open Parishes how they permit Select Vestries to be established among them?
With a thorough Conviction of the legality of their Institution, and firm reliance on the support of their Countrymen, the Managers of the Westminster Forum make a most solemn Appeal to the Public. – Their reverence of the British Constitution has been evinced by their uniform obedience to all its Laws. – Venerating, as they do the person of the Sovereign, there is no sedition in publicly expressing their abhorrence and contempt of the Petty Tyrants of a Parish. They will expose them to the utmost of their power. – To preserve the Peace, and protect the Constitution, they would hazard their lives; but there certainly can be no crime in "stirring up hatred and contempt" of gluttony, gormandizing, and oppression. – The Independent Inhabitants of every Parish (and St. James's in particular) are requested to attend.'
Morning Herald

2053. April 13, 1797 Westminster Forum
SAVE-ALL and SPEND-ALL
'Which Character is more injurious to Society, the Spendthrift or the Miser?
An "History of the enormities of Select Vestries" is preparing for the Press, and will shortly be published.'
Morning Chronicle

2054. April 15, 1797 London Forum
WOMAN – What is she?
'Which is more repugnant to truth and experience, the doctrine of Mahomet, that Women have no Souls – or the Opinion of Mrs. Woolstonecraft, That they possess mental endowments equal, if not superior, to men?'
Morning Chronicle

2055. April 17, 1797 London Forum
'Can Jealousy exist without true Love?'
Morning Chronicle April 15

2056. April 17, 1797 Westminster Forum
LIBERTY OF SPEECH – ENORMITIES AND OPPRESSION OF SELECT VESTRIES
'Ought not the interference of the Select Vestry of St. James's Parish with the Moral, Literary, and Philosophical Discussions of the Westminster Forum (which are in no case restricted by the late Acts of Parliament) together with the general Conduct of Select Vestries, to operate as a warning to all open Parishes how they permit Select Vestries to be established among them?
At the conclusion of the . . . debate, not one hand, out of a numerous audience, was held up in favour of Select Vestries.'
Morning Chronicle

2057. April 24, 1797 London Forum
GHOSTS AND ASTROLOGERS
'Is it true that a departed spirit ever appeared to any person in this world, and can future events be foretold by the science of astrology?
A Gentleman of unquestionable veracity will, in the course of the evening's debate, relate a remarkable discovery he made in his own family, in consequence of having consulted an astrologer. Any professor of astrology, who may wish to speak in defence of the science, will be heard with candid attention.'
Morning Chronicle

2058. April 24, 1797 Westminster Forum
TRUE CHARACTER OF A METHODIST
'Ought the People called Methodists to be considered as artful Hypocrites, gloomy Enthusiasts, and contracted Bigots; or Men of genuine Piety, who have revived the great Work of Religion among Mankind?'
Morning Chronicle

2059. April 27, 1797 Westminster Forum
'Ought the People called Methodists to be considered as artful Hypocrites, gloomy Enthusiasts, and contracted Bigots; or Men of genuine Piety, who have revived the great Work of Religion among Mankind?'
Morning Chronicle

2060. May 4, 1797 Westminster Forum
WHAT IS WOMAN?
'What is the true Condition of Woman, the Equal, the Inferior, or the Superior of Man?'
Morning Chronicle

2061. May 8, 1797 London Forum
DEPARTED SPIRITS AND ASTROLOGERS
'Did a departed Spirit ever appear to any Person, and can future Events be foretold by the Science of Astrology?
An Astrologer last Monday evening pledged himself to cast the nativity of a Gentleman who spoke against the Science, and to announce his destiny this evening.

W. Adam's Defence of Methodist Preachers may be had in this Society.'
Morning Chronicle

2062. May 8, 1797 Westminster Forum
A WIFE WITH LOVE OR MONEY
'Which ought a prudent Man to choose for a Wife (supposing he could
have either) a Woman with a Fortune, who does not love him, and for
whom he entertains no Affection; or a Woman with no Fortune, that
loves him, and whom he tenderly regards, admitting their mental, personal, and acquired accomplishments to be nearly alike?
This Question was transmitted to the Managers by a Gentleman . . .
from a party of Ladies and Gentlemen who will sail in the next Packet
to India.'
Morning Chronicle

2063. May 11, 1797 Westminster Forum
'Do the Powers, Capabilities, and Mental Perfections of Woman prove
her the Equal, the Inferior, or the Superior of Man?'
Morning Chronicle

2064. May 15, 1797 Westminster Forum
WHAT IS THE DEVIL?
'Is the Devil a mere Phantom of the Imagination; a Scriptural Figure,
typical of the Principle of Evil; or a fallen infernal Spirit, the personal
Agent of the Almighty to punish the Wicked?'
Morning Chronicle

2065. May 18, 1797 Westminster Forum
MISS FARREN – LESSON FOR THE LADIES. LOVE, HONOUR AND FORTUNE
'Does not the late elevation of Miss Farren to the rank of a Countess
(when contrasted with the many Examples of Female Frailty on the
Stage) demonstrate this striking Truth to the British Fair – "That
Female Virtue is the only certain Road to Honour and Happiness"?'
Morning Chronicle

2066. May 22, 1797 Westminster Forum
'Is there any Truth in Dreams?'
Morning Chronicle May 18

2067. June 1, 1797 Westminster Forum
ROMAN PATRIOTS RETIRING FROM CORRUPTION
'Does the following observation of CATO to his Son (taken from Addis-
on's celebrated Tragedy) exhibit stronger Proofs of stoical Pride – a
cowardly Desertion of Public Duty – or the indignant Emotions of genu-
ine Patriotism?
  When Vice prevails, and impious Men bear Sway,
  The Post of Honour is a private Station?'
Morning Chronicle

2068. June 5, 1797 Westminster Forum
'Which is the more inhuman Character – the Man who artfully and deliberately seduces the Daughter of his Friend – or the wretched and rigorous Father who abandons his Child to Infamy in Consequence of that Seduction?'
Morning Chronicle June 1

2069. June 15, 1797 Westminster Forum
ADAM, EVE AND THE SERPENT
'Which was more criminal in eating the forbidden Fruit, Adam or Eve? There are many original ideas which emanate from the enquiry – the powers of Man prior to the Fall – how far the tender passion prevailed, even in the days of innocence – what would have been the state of Nature, if Adam had resisted the Apple after Eve had eaten, &c &c.'
Morning Chronicle

2070. June 19, 1797 Westminster Forum
'Can any circumstances justify a Man for selling his Wife?'
Morning Chronicle June 15

2071. June 29, 1797 Westminster Forum
DANGER of Admitting DEISTS to PUBLIC TRUSTS
'Is it probable the Man can be a worthy Member of Society, or safely admitted to public Trusts, whose Principles lead him to a Disbelief in a Providence in this Life and a Denial of his own Immortality in the next?'
Morning Chronicle

2072. July 3, 1797 Westminster Forum
'Is it probable that man can be a worthy member of society, or safely admitted to public trusts, whose principles lead him to a disbelief in a Providence in this life and a denial of his own immortality in the next?'
Morning Chronicle

2073. July 6, 1797 Westminster Forum
MAN, IMMORTALITY, PROVIDENCE
'Is it probable the Man can be a worthy Member of Society, or safely admitted to public Trusts, whose Principles lead him to a Disbelief of a Providence in this Life and a Denial of his own Immortality in the next?'
Decided that such a man cannot be a worthy Member of Society 'by a decided majority'.
Morning Chronicle

2074. July 10, 1797 Westminster Forum
LAW OF LOVE – TRIAL OF COQUETTES
'Can any possible circumstances justify the conduct of the Lady who encourages the serious addresses of more than one man at the same time?'
Morning Chronicle

2075. July 13, 1797 Westminster Forum
MR. ERSKINE
'Have the Enemies of Religion any rational grounds in arraigning the consistency of Mr. Erskine for his late energetic defence of Christianity against Paine's Age of Reason?'
Morning Chronicle

2076. July 17, 1797 Westminster Forum
'Ought not the death of that distinguished literary and political genius Mr. Edmund Burke to be universally lamented as a national calamity?'
Morning Chronicle July 13

2077. August 21, 1797 Westminster Forum
SALE OF WIVES
'Which practice is more disgraceful to a civilized State, a Man selling his Wife at Smithfield; or Fathers sending out their Daughters Adventurers for Husbands to an Indian Market?
If Satire is the proper last of Vice – if those Practices which disgrace a Nation demand public reprobation, the above Question must be interesting – we had almost said important . . . has lately occurred (to the disgrace of our Police, and the dishonour of the Sex) of Husbands publicly selling their Wives at Smithfield – The practice of sending the most beautiful young Females as Matrimonial Adventurers to a Foreign Land, unprotected and exposed to every danger, appears to us at least as criminal.
Mr. Erskine's Speech on the Age of Reason may be had as above, price 2d.'
Morning Chronicle

2078. August 24, 1797 Westminster Forum
'Is it possible for a Lawyer to be an honest Man?'
Morning Chronicle August 21

2079. August 28, 1797 Westminster Forum
HONESTY AMONG LAWYERS
'Is it possible for a Lawyer to be an honest Man?'
Question 'carried in the affirmative'.
Morning Chronicle

2080. August 31, 1797 Westminster Forum
WHERE IS HAPPINESS?
'In which Situation of Life is most Happiness to be found: the elevated Walks of Wealth and Grandeur, the busy Scenes of Trade and Commerce, or the humble Shades of Domestic Ease and Retirement?'
Morning Chronicle

2081. September 4, 1797 Westminster Forum

THE SOUL'S IMMORTALITY

'Has a Man, possessed of rational Faculties, any just grounds for a denial of the Soul's Immortality?

As the usual time of the year for the commencement of Debating Societies, the Managers of the Westminster Forum behold their institution patronised by the learned, the noble, and the respectable among mankind, their doors still open from the last season, their popularity undiminished, and the late iniquitous attempt to wrest the Laws to the destruction of Free Debate, (not political) thereby rendered publicly ridiculous. – Under these highly flattering circumstances a public avowal of principles becomes indispensible. – Order and impartiality shall be invariably observed. – The Managers of this Society disclaim all party influence. A regular obedience to existing laws, devoid of any fulsome or servile adulation of their dispensers, is the line of public rectitude which they intend to pursue; and by which they wish their reverence to the British Constitution to be estimated. On the glorious independent principles of the WHIG CLUB OF ENGLAND they erect their claim for public approbation – those principles maintained by Mr. Fox and his illustrious coadjutors, which form at once the barrier of the People's Liberties, the sacred guards of the Protestant Faith, and the Sovereign's most effectual security.'
Morning Chronicle

2082. September 7, 1797 Westminster Forum

THE COMET

'Is it probable that Comets are, as maintained by Astrologers, and many eminent religious characters, awful presages of the fate of Nations, and the probable means of the last grand conflagration; or a part of the system of nature, yet unexplored by the discoveries of science?

Burnet ascribes the deluge to the approach of a Comet; Sir Isaac Newton was of opinion, that the burning of the world, and the final dissolution of all things would be caused by the fiery contact of a Comet with the earth.

Mr. Erskine's Speech on the Age of Reason may be had as above; price two pence.'
Morning Chronicle

2083. September 11, 1797 London Forum

MAN OR WOMAN

'On a fair comparison of the privileges and enjoyments of both Sexes, is it better to be a Man or Woman?

Wit and ingenuity, countenanced by delicacy, will lend their aid to enliven the enquiry, expand the reflective powers, and invigorate the imagination. Morality and decorum must always retain the ascendancy in this Institution, and any infringement upon their prerogative will meet with merited rebuke.'
Morning Chronicle

2084. September 11, 1797 Westminster Forum

IS MAN IMMORTAL?
'Has a Man, possessed of rational Faculties, any just grounds for a denial of the Soul's Immortality?
The Immortality of the Human Soul was . . . voted by a decided majority.'
Morning Chronicle

2085. September 14, 1797 Westminster Forum
'Is not that Man guilty of a Breach of the Laws of Nature, and Moral Virtue, who during Life makes any distinction between, and does not at his death as effectually provide for his Illegitimate as his Legitimate Offspring?'
Morning Chronicle September 11

2086. September 18, 1797 Westminster Forum
TRANSPORTATION OF PICHEGRU AND THE FRENCH DEPUTIES
'Does not the Transportation of the celebrated General Pichegru and his Colleagues (without any form of trial) prove the French Government to be actuated by that very Spirit of Despotism which they have so long and loudly condemned in other Nations?'
Morning Chronicle

2087. September 18, 1797 London Forum
'Does not the fate of General Pichegru and the 64 Representatives of the People of France, prove that independence of opinion does not exist in the Legislature, and that virtue and integrity are no securities against the jealousy and tyranny of the French Directory?
The late conduct of the Directory has exhibited to the World an act of unparalleled tyranny, which they justify by the state pretext of the public weal; if Democracy justifies such proceedings, and can reconcile them with liberty, Mankind are indebted to those who collectively or individually endeavour to protect them from a system fascinating only to theory, but in the practice, hostile to every principle of justice, morals and law.'
Morning Chronicle

2088. September 21, 1797 Westminster Forum
REASON of General PICHEGRU; or TYRANNY of the FRENCH DIRECTORY
'Ought the Transportation of General Pichegru and the Sixty-four Members of the Two Councils to be considered as an Act essential to the Safety and Preservation of the French Republic; or an arbitrary and unjustifiable Exertion of Lawless and Despotic Power?
The Question, as it now stands, was suggested to the Managers by a distinguished Gentlemen of the Irish Bar.
Mr. J. Gale Jones and several other Speakers of eminence delivered their sentiments most pointedly against the Tyranny of the Directory. Mr. Jones in a most animated Oration, drew a line of distinction between the Proof of Guilt and the Tyranny of condemning Men with-

out a public Trial; and the Audience sanctioned his opinion by their decision.'
Morning Chronicle

2089. September 25, 1797 London Forum
TO CHRISTIANS OF ALL DENOMINATIONS, and OTHERS
MR. COOPER'S RELIGIOUS DOUBTS
'Does not the Confession made by Mr. Cooper, at Sion Chapel – that his Faith was staggered by reading Mr. Winchester's Book, afford reason to believe that the Doctrine of Universal Restoration is founded on Scripture, and harmonizes with the Attributes of the Supreme Being?'
Morning Chronicle

2090. September 25, 1797 Westminster Forum
GUILT or INNOCENCE of PICHEGRU and the SIXTY-FOUR MINISTERS
'Does the Evidence laid before the Legislative Assembly, together with the recent Events which have agitated the French Republic, more strongly establish the Guilt or Innocence of PICHEGRU and the Sixty-four Deputies?
The present Question will be most impartially discussed, and that fair Trial instituted at the Westminster Forum, which was denied Pichegru and his Associates at Paris. . .
The probability of Pichgru's Innocence, was . . . voted by a decided majority.'
Morning Chronicle

2091. September 28, 1797 Westminster Forum
CONJUGAL INFIDELITY
'Are the numerous and recent instances of Conjugal infidelity more ascribeable to the inattention of Husbands, the levity of Wives, the villainous artifice of Seducers, or the flattery and adulation bestowed on the British Fair, anterior to Marriage?'
The above Question 'was presented to this Society by a respectable Clergyman of the Church of England. . . The concluding sentence of that Gentleman's letter places the moral tendency of such subjects in a striking point of view: "To you, Gentlemen, it belongs, in no inconsiderable degree, to influence the public taste, and to improve or vitiate public morals; how many of our enjoyments depend on the softer Sex! and what lamentable instances of female degeneracy have lately appeared! Sirs, in exploring the sources of this evil, you perform a duty which you owe Society, and by thus seconding the moral effort of the Pulpit, you will render your institution a school of virtue".'
Morning Chronicle

2092. October 2, 1797 Westminster Forum
LA FAYETTE – DUNGEONS OF OLMUTZ
'Upon an impartial Review of the Life and Actions of the celebrated French General LA FAYETTE, ought he to be considered as the firm

and intrepid Patriot; or the artful and temporising Supporter of privileged Despotism?
This question was presented to the Society by Mr. John Gale Jones. . .
It is true, Tories and Republicans have alike assailed [Lafayette's] character. Burke, and a French Writer of eminence, have both meanly calumniated him during his captivity! but, like our own Fox, he appears to have been actuated by the love of social order, erected on the unalienable rights of human nature.'
Morning Chronicle

2093. October 5, 1797 Westminster Forum
DEATH for a SISTER'S SEDUCTION!
'Can any circumstances justify that Brother who punishes with Death the Seducer of his Sister?
Appeals to the sword are dreadful; but if any circumstances can justify duelling (that point on which honour and morals have, through every age, been at variance) it must, in the bosom of a man of honour, be the attempt to violate a Sister's Virtue.'
Morning Chronicle

2094. October 9, 1797 Westminster Forum
DUELS!
SEDUCTION – A BROTHER'S DUTY to a RUINED SISTER
'Can any circumstances justify that Brother who punishes with Death the Seducer of his Sister?
How nearly allied, we had almost said incorporated, the Honour of a Sister with a Brother's happiness! How necessary, even to our existence as a State, is the preservation of Female Virtue!
The decision of a numerous and polite Audience . . . was against Duelling in any case whatever.'
Morning Chronicle

2095. October 12, 1797 School of Eloquence, Coachmakers Hall
'Is Knowledge necessary to Happiness?'
Tickets, one shilling each; T. C. Andrews, Sec. 'for the benefit of the Literary Fund'.
Morning Herald

2096. October 12, 1797 Westminster Forum
SEDUCTION PERPETRATED BY A SOLDIER AND A PRIEST
'Which of the following Characters most deserves the Reprobation of Mankind – the Military Man, who under the Tie of Consanguinity, and in defiance of the Laws of Hospitality, seduces the Innocent entrusted to his honour; or the artful Ecclesiastic, who, under the pretence of preserving Female Chastity, betrays the helpless Orphan committed to his care?'
Morning Chronicle

2097. October 16, 1797 Westminster Forum

'Which of the following Characters most deserves the Reprobation of Mankind – the Military Man, who under the Tie of Consanguinity, and in defiance of the Laws of Hospitality, seduces the Innocent entrusted to his honour; or the artful Ecclesiastic, who, under the pretence of preserving Female Chastity, betrays the helpless Orphan committed to his care?'
Morning Chronicle

2098. October 19, 1797 Westminster Forum
'Which of the following distinguished men has been the greatest sufferer in the cause of Freedom: La Fayette – Dumourier – or Pichegru?'
Morning Chronicle October 16

2099. October 25, 1797 School of Genius, Haymarket
BACHELORS BROUGHT TO TRIAL
'Can the Man who lives Unmarried till the Age of Thirty be considered as a good Member of Society?
A young unmarried Lady favoured the Managers with this singular Question. It involves the important consideration of the propriety of early Marriage, and calls upon every old Batchelor to defend himself. In the course of the Debate, several curious Anecdotes are expected to be related concerning some old Bachelors in High Life.
A new and interesting Pamphlet, called 'The Republican Minister' is sold at Symond's, Paternoster-row.'
Admittance 6d.
Morning Chronicle

2100. October 26, 1797 Westminster Forum
BEST SECURITY of a NATION
'In what does the chief Security of a State consist, the vigour of its Laws; the strength of its Fortifications; or the love and confidence of its People?'
Morning Chronicle

2101. October 30, 1797 Westminster Forum
T. HARDY
ILLUMINATION – THEIR UTILITY; or DANGER and EXTRAVAGANCE
'Ought the conduct of THOMAS HARDY, in refusing to illuminate his house on account of the late Naval Victory, to be considered as a mark of obstinate singularity: or as a public example well worthy of imitation of every friend to Order and Humanity?
The . . . Question concerning Illuminations (after being ably argued on both sides) was decided against the Practice.'
Morning Chronicle

2102. November 2, 1797 Westminster Forum
A WORD TO THE WISE
WEDLOCK or a SINGLE LIFE
'Which is the wiser man – he who marries, or he who remains single?'
Morning Chronicle

367

2103. November 6, 1797 Westminster Forum
EMPEROR OF GERMANY — PEACE WITH FRANCE
'Has the Emperor of Germany acted consistently with the dignity and safety of his Crown, and the general welfare of Europe, in concluding a separate Peace with the French Republic?'
Morning Chronicle

2104. November 9, 1797 Westminster Forum
'Has the Emperor of Germany acted consistently with the dignity and safety of his Crown, and the general welfare of Europe, in concluding a separate Peace with the French Republic?
The Managers have the honour of announcing . . . the total overthrow yesterday, in the Court of King's Bench, of the SIXTEEN Actions brought by the junto of St. James's Parish, against four Gentlemen for Speaking in this Society; an event at which every lover of Liberty must rejoice, and in which every advocate for Liberty feel himself deeply interested.'
Morning Chronicle

2105. November 13, 1797 Westminster Forum
SELECT VESTRIES
'Does not the recent wasteful expenditures of Parish Money, squandered in Sixteen groundless Actions against the Westminster Forum, together with similar instances of unprincipled profusion, call loudly for the Abolition of the Select Vestry?
The remainder of the Sixteen Actions, (brought in the name of one Chadwell, a beadle of St. James's Parish) . . . were – on an humiliating motion of the Plaintiffs – ordered by the Court of King's Bench to be discontinued!!! On a moderate computation, upwards of two hundred pounds must have been expended in this quixotic scheme of folly and wickedness! – An enormous sum to be discharged by a Parish Beadle! – To the good sense of the parishioners of St. James's Parish the above question is therefore addressed: It concerns likewise every man who has felt the lash of petty tyrants in other parishes. . .
In thus publicly presenting their acknowledgements to the great and independent characters, who have generously given their assistance on this trying occasion, the Managers but discharge a debt of public gratitude.'
Morning Chronicle

2106. November 16, 1797 Westminster Forum
WHICH to FOLLOW, PRUDENCE OR LOVE!
'Ought two Persons, possessed of mutual Attachment, but devoid of Fortune, to separate from Motives of Prudence; or to Marry, trusting to Providence and Industry for Support?'
Morning Chronicle

2107. November 20, 1797 Westminster Forum
GENERAL REVIEW of the WRITINGS OF BURKE against FRANCE
'Has the Progress of the French Revolution justified the Opinions of the late Mr. Burke?'
Morning Chronicle

2108. November 23, 1797 Westminster Forum
'Is the Love of Liberty – the Love of Life – or the Love of the Fair Sex, the most predominant principle in human nature?'
Morning Chronicle November 20

2109. November 30, 1797 Ciceronian School, Haymarket
'Ought Eloquence to be encouraged in an enlightened and civilized state?
If in this Address we profess but little, it is not because we are destitute of resources, but that we are unwilling to imitate the conduct of those, who have too frequently roused the public curiosity to an improper height of expectation, only to render them the more sensible of a severe disappointment. Admission 6d.
It was decided by a large majority, that Eloquence ought to be encouraged.'
Morning Chronicle

2110. November 30, 1797 Westminster Forum
QUESTION from a LADY – LOVE and SEDUCTION
'Can the man, who really Loves a Woman, deliberately Seduce her?
No circumstance can be more grateful to the Managers of this Institution than its present celebrity – a celebrity they conceive to have arisen from their establishing, in a legal contest, the Right of Free Debate, and from never publishing in their advertisements any circumstance that was not literally fulfilled. From this line of conduct no consideration shall ever tempt them to depart; they will to the utmost of their power, defend the one, and studiously avoid deceiving the other.'
Morning Chronicle

2111. December 4, 1797 Ciceronian School
MIRACLES
'Is the Belief of Miracles, an essential part of the Christian Religion?
While the Christian Religion is universally acknowledged to be in itself a pure and amiable system of Morality, many even of its most strenuous supporters have been of opinion, that the adoption of mysterious Tenets, tended rather to weaken its influence, than to strengthen the conviction, or encrease the number of its Proselytes.'
Morning Chronicle

2112. December 4, 1797 Westminster Forum
MAN'S EVERLASTING MISERY: OR ETERNAL REDEMPTION!
'Is the Doctrine of the Calvinist Methodists – or the Doctrine preached

369

by the Followers of Mr. Winchester – the Doctrine contained in the Bible?'
Morning Chronicle

2113. December 7, 1797 Westminster Forum
WISE MEN and FOOLS!
'Is the following assertion of Mons. Necker true or false, Fools are the happiest of Mankind; since it is impossible to be at once happy and wise?'
Morning Chronicle

2114. December 7, 1797 Ciceronian School
'Is the violation of a Promise, a breach of Morality?'
Morning Chronicle December 4

2115. December 11, 1797 Westminster Forum
'Has not the French Government, in ceding Venice to the German Despot, violated the Faith of Nations, and departed from their avowed principle of restoring the Liberty of Mankind?'
Morning Chronicle December 7

2116. December 11, 1797 Ciceronian School
PROMISES
'Is the Violation of a Promise a Breach of Morality?'
A Speaker asserted that 'all Promises, Obligations, Appointments, &c. which tend to restrict the future opinions of men, or bind them to any particular plan of conduct, are inimical to the welfare and happiness of society, and repugnant to the principles of morality and justice.' He will defend this position.
Morning Chronicle

2117. December 11, 1797 London Forum
A new BUDGET of TAXES will be opened THIS EVENING
'Would it be proper to adopt the following taxes as some relief to the middle class of Housekeepers from double and treble rates, viz. A tax of 50*l.* per annum on every old maid and batchelor (not being housekeepers) whose incomes amount to 200*l.* a year each. A License of 50*l.* for every Player, Opera Dancer, and Singer, engaged at a salary of 16*l.* per week. A Stamp duty of sixpence on every Admission to places of public entertainment. A duty of one shilling on every sheet of a Counsel's Brief, with which a fee of ten guineas is given; and a duty of one pound upon the registry of every marriage that is not by public banns.'
Morning Chronicle

2118. December 18, 1797 London Forum
ATTEND, O MAN, tO SCRIPTURE PROPHESIES
'Does not Divine Revelation prove that the Pope is Antichrist; that his total destruction is at hand, and that the present extraordinary events

that agitate all Europe, are signs of the speedy fulfillment of the Prophesies?
Let not the People murmur, but direct their attention to the fulfillment of the Prophesies. The arm of the Almighty (according to the opinion of the most learned divines) is visible in the grand movements that now agitate Europe.'
Morning Chronicle

2119. December 21, 1797 Westminster Forum
DEATH OF COLONEL FITZGERALD
'Ought the Death of Col. Fitzgerald to be approved, as a just punishment for Seduction, and prevention of mediated Violence; or reprobated as an act of merciless Revenge?'
Morning Chronicle

2120. December 26, 1797 Westminster Forum
'Are the Methodists, as asserted by Deists, artful Hypocrites – are they gloomy Enthusiasts and contracted Bigots, as maintained by many Divines, both of the establishment and among the Dissenters – or Men of genuine Piety, who have revived the great work of Religion among Mankind?'
Morning Chronicle December 21

2121. December 28, 1797 Westminster Forum
MAN, a TYRANT; WOMAN, a SLAVE
'In the present Association of the Sexes, is not Man a Tyrant and Woman a Slave?'
Morning Chronicle

2122. January 1, 1798 Westminster Forum
'Was the following Assertion of that illustrious Statesman Mr. Fox founded on Truth – It is not the particular Form of Government, but the integrity of its Rulers, that constitutes the Happiness of a People?'
Morning Chronicle December 28, 1797

2123. January 4, 1798 Westminster Forum
'Was the following Assertion of that illustrious Statesman Mr. Fox founded on Truth – It is not the particular Form of Government, but the integrity of its Rulers, that constitutes the Happiness of a People?'
Morning Chronicle

2124. January 8, 1798 Westminster Forum
'Was the following Assertion of that illustrious Statesman Mr. Fox founded on Truth – It is not the particular Form of Government, but the integrity of its Rulers, that constitutes the Happiness of a People? A polite and numerous Audience decided that the particular Form of Government, and not the integrity of its Rulers, constitutes the Happiness of a People.'
Morning Chronicle

2125. January 11, 1798 Westminster Forum
'Have Parents any justifiable right to controul the Affections of their Children?
The audience decided, almost unanimously, that parents are not justifiable.'
Morning Chronicle

2126. January 15, 1798 Westminster Forum
POWER of RELIGION on SOCIETY
'Can good Morals generally exist without Religious Motives?
The power of Religion, as it affects the morals of mankind, becomes doubly interesting in an age like this, when an infidel philosophy, under the specious mask of refinement, is attempting the annihilation of that divine system of morals, which has held mankind together in the bonds of amity for ages.'
Morning Chronicle

2127. January 18, 1798 Westminster Forum
'Does the personal existence of the Devil – the agency of Witchcraft and Infernal Spirits – together with the belief in Apparitions, form any part of the Christian System, or can they be supported by human reason and probability?'
Morning Chronicle

2128. January 22, 1798 Westminster Forum
HYPOCRISY and INFIDELITY
PAINE versus HUNTINGTON
'Which has been more injurious to the Christian Religion, the Publications and Preaching of William Huntington, or the Writings of Thomas Paine?
The Rev. Mr. Huntington, alias Hunt; alias Parson Sack, alias the Archbishop of Titchfield-street, alias the Coal-heaver, alias the Viper, alias the Spiritual Blackguard, &c. &c. having preached and published what he calls a Sermon on his Majesty going to St. Paul's (wherein he consigns the whole political world, who oppose Mr. Pitt, to eternal perdition, and abuses, without distinction or remorse, most of the great religious characters of this Metropolis) gave rise to the above question. It is not a little extraordinary that a man without learning, and who instead of possessing that piety and meekness, which should adorn the evangelical character, exhibits nought but the bitterness of a daemon – the abuse of a Billingsgate – the effrontery of a Bartholomew Fair Conjuror, should dare to prophane the ministerial character, by pronouncing Mr. Fox in a state of damnation, the Rev. Mr. Cooper one of the Devil's Drummers, and Rev. Mr. J. Wesley now in hell, and himself almost the only Evangelical Minister in the island. We think it a duty to expose such a man – we thus publicly dare him to attend the debate, where he can be answered, and not to issue his venom alone from the pulpit, where he is protected from replication.'
Morning Chronicle

2129. January 25, 1798 Westminster Forum
DESTRUCTION OF THE POPE
'Are there not abundant reasons to support the Belief, that the Pope is Antichrist, or the Man of Sin; and the French are the Instruments appointed by Providence for his Destruction?
The recent events transacted at Rome, must powerfully impress on the public mind the importance of the above question. Perhaps, at this moment the power of the Pope is overthrown; and "Babylon, the mother of Harlots, and the abomination of the earth, drunk with the blood of the Martyrs" is herself enduring the long predicted vengeance of the Almighty. Such would be the language of a Protestant on the occasion. We have, however, no objection to hear any Catholic defend his Church – we expect it from some Gentlemen who may attend. And only observe, that on a question of this nature, impartiality shall be our governing principle, we wish not to close our ears against conviction; but we think it a duty to ascertain the evidence of prophetic fulfillment.'
Morning Chronicle

2130. January 29, 1798 Westminster Forum
WHAT IS MARRIAGE
'Is not Marriage (notwithstanding all its Cares and Difficulties) the happiest State in which Man or Woman can be placed?
The above Question is presented under considerable expectations. It was enclosed in a letter from a respectable Tradesman of this City and his wife, who are now retiring on the honest savings of a life of industry. It states, that they have been married twenty-seven years, and never for one quarter of an hour repented their engagement.'
Morning Chronicle

2131. January 30, 1798 Westminster Forum
'Which is the most striking characteristic of a Ladies' Man – Wit, Courage or Politeness?'
Morning Chronicle

2132. February 1, 1798 Westminster Forum
Rev. MR. TOPLADY'S SPEECH – SOULS OF BRUTES
'Is the Opinion of the Rev. Mr. Matthew Henry, Mr. Toplady, and many eminent Divines and Philosophers, true or false, viz. It is highly probable that Brutes have Souls, and are equally entitled to Immortality with the Human Race?
In the course of the Evening, a speech delivered on this subject in the year 1773, by the Rev. Mr. Toplady, and which was found among his Manuscripts, will be read by a Gentleman. That great and good man there decidedly proves, by a variety of arguments, which we had almost pronounced unanswerable, that the Brute Creation is immortal.'
Morning Chronicle

2133. February 8, 1798 Westminster Forum

MARRIAGE IMPARTIALLY CONSIDERED

'Is not Marriage (notwithstanding all its cares and difficulties) the happiest State in which Man or Woman can be placed?'
Morning Chronicle

2134. February 12, 1798 Westminster Forum
'Which is the greater outrage on Reason and Religion, and more destructive of the hopes and happiness of the human race, Mr. Paine's pronouncing "the Bible an History of Wickedness calculated to corrupt and brutalize Mankind"; or the assertion of the Rev. Mr. Huntington, "That every Jacobin will be damned"?'
Morning Chronicle February 8

2135. February 19, 1798 Westminster Forum
HELVETIUS, GODWIN, HOLCROFT, &C.
NEW SCHOOL PHILOSOPHY
'Are not the writings of Helvetius, Godwin, Holcroft, and other Philosophers of the New School, calculated to destroy the Happiness of Mankind; and shake the foundation of all Civil Society?
In an age of scepticism, like the present, which the Bishop of Landaff, with great propriety, terms 'The Age of Infidelity', the above must present itself to public view, as a question of the first importance. Through the medium of the Press, the writings of Godwin fall into almost every hand; it is therefore a public duty to examine their tendency.'
Morning Chronicle

2136. February 22, 1798 Westminster Forum
'Are not the writings of Helvetius, Godwin, Holcroft, and other Philosophers of the New School, calculated to destroy the Happiness of Mankind; and shake the foundation of all Civil Society?'
Morning Chronicle

2137. February 26, 1798 Westminster Forum
'Do public and private Theatrical Representations tend more to vitiate or improve the Morals of Mankind?'
Morning Herald

2138. March 5, 1798 Westminster Forum
'In this age of conjugal depravity, ought the singular conduct of Crook the Taylor, as displayed in a recent Crim. Con. Trial, to be shunned as a mean and mercenary exposure of Female Frailty; or imitated, as a virtuous and laudable communication to an injured Husband?'
Morning Chronicle

2139. March 8, 1798 Westminster Forum
'Which are more frequently the Seducers – the Men or the Women?'
Morning Chronicle March 5

2140. March 12, 1798 Westminster Forum
'Which of the following Qualifications will most effectually ensure to a Lady a good Husband – Beauty, Riches, or Understanding?'
Morning Herald

2141. March 14, 1798 Westminster Forum
'Do the Talents, Virtues, and Vices of Man depend upon his Organization, or are they the Result of his Education?'
Debate opened by Mr. J. Gale Jones.
Morning Herald March 12/Morning Chronicle

2142. March 15, 1798 Westminster Forum
'Can any real or supposed advantages, resulting to Mankind from the study of Anatomy, form an excuse for the present practice of disturbing the remains of the dead, and agonizing the feelings of the living, by robbing Church yards and Burial Grounds?'
Morning Herald March 22

2143. March 19, 1798 Westminster Forum, Brewer Street, Golden Square
'Do public and private Theatrical Entertainments tend more to vitiate or improve the Morals of Mankind?'
Morning Herald

2144. March 21, 1798 Westminster Forum
'Do the Talents, Virtues, and Vices of Man depend upon his Organization, or are they the Result of his Education?'
Morning Herald March 19

2145. March 22, 1798 Westminster Forum
'Can any real or supposed advantages, resulting to Mankind from the study of Anatomy, form an excuse for the present practice of disturbing the remains of the dead, and agonizing the feelings of the living, by robbing Church yards and Burial Grounds?'
Morning Herald March 19

2146. March 26, 1798 Westminster Forum
PREVENTION of STEALING DEAD BODIES
'Would it not be consistent with the justice of any Civilized State – become an adequate Remedy for the Robbery of Burial Grounds – and tend to the prevention of Duelling and Suicide – if the Bodies of all Persons guilty of those Crimes, were delivered to the Surgeons for Dissection?
On the present occasion we again respectfully solicit the attendance of those Medical Gentlemen who so ably defended their profession. Will they pardon one solicitation – That they would recommend their Pupils to refrain from those clamorous – we might say rude, interruptions of Gentlemen who opposed them? It is the triumph of reason, and not

that of unmanly interruption, which should adorn the victorious com-
battants of a rational literary Assembly.'
Morning Chronicle

2147. March 29, 1798 Westminster Forum
'Do public and private Theatrical Entertainments tend more to vitiate
or improve the Morals of Mankind?
The Decision . . . was (almost unanimously) in favour of the Morality
of the Stage.'
Morning Herald/Morning Chronicle April 4

2148. April 2, 1798 Westminster Forum
'Which is more likely to terminate in an happy Marriage (or in any
Marriage at all) a long or a short Courtship?'
Morning Herald

2149. April 3, 1798 Westminster Forum
'Which is more desirable – to be alive to all the keen feelings of sensibility, or, wrapt in Stoical apathy, to remain indifferent to the miseries of
mankind?'
Morning Herald April 2

2150. April 4, 1798 Westminster Forum
'Which is the primary cause of the immorality of the age – the Licentiousness of Female Opera Dancers – the Infidel Notions disseminated
in the Lower Classes – or the Sunday Routs, Concerts, and Card Parties
held among the Persons of Fashion?
It will remain with the higher orders of the fashionable world, or those
who advocate them, to prove that the example of the Nobleman who
violates the Sabbath hath not a tendency to vitiate the morals of the
poorest peasant.'
Morning Herald April 3

2151. April 5, 1798 Westminster Forum
'Which forms the surer basis of Human Happiness, the lasting Comforts
of Friendship, or the captivating Joys of Love?'
Morning Herald April 4

2152. April 7, 1798 Westminster Forum
'Which, to a Lady of Prudence and Virtue would prove the least Mar-
riageable Evil, a Spendthrift, a Miser, a Clown or a Fop?'
The audience voted almost unanimously in favour of the Clown.
Morning Herald April 5/Morning Chronicle April 9

2153. April 9, 1798 Westminster Forum
THE REV. MR. HUNTINGTON A MAN OF GOD; or, a WOLF in SHEEP'S CLOTHING
'Is Mr. Huntington a Credit, or a Disgrace, to the venerable name of
Methodist?

What man that feels the importance of revealed truth, but must be roused to indignation at declaring that eminent Servant of the Most High, Mr. John Wesley, "an agent of the Devil, while on Earth – and now suffering with the damned in Hell", asserting "that Infants (nay even those unborn) may be in a state of perdition", and finally damning, without distinction, the men who adore the British Constitution, but who dislike the present Ministry, with those who would promote its ruin. We think it a duty to mention, that Mr. Huntington (notwithstanding his present sentiments) was, not many months since, one of the most virulent, impudent abusers of the Bishops, and the whole discipline of the Church of England, that ever mounted a pulpit. What has wrought this wonderful change? He surely does not imagine that a pair of lawn sleeves can be an appropriate covering for a Coal Sack! Be that as it may, it is not our business to arraign his vanity in this advertisement.'
Decided by a considerable majority that the doctrines of Mr. Huntington are a disgrace on the name of Methodist.
Morning Chronicle April 9/12

2154. April 12, 1798 Westminster Forum
'Is it probable that the Moon is inhabited by Beings like the Earth?
Whether the Planetary World is, or is not inhabited, is a subject that has employed the talents of the Wise and Scientific from Newton down to Walker – We respectfully solicit the presence and opinion of those Gentlemen who have made the motions and laws of the Heavenly Bodies their peculiar study: and hope, at least, to produce a discussion not altogether unworthy of the Public ear.'
Morning Herald

2155. April 16, 1798 Westminster Forum
'Which is the more grievous calamity, a bad Husband, or a bad Wife?
A Court Leet of Hymen, to determine all Matrimonial Disputes, when a Jury (half Males and half Females) will be duly impannelled. Thither are Men and their Wives (having any complaints against each other) are desired forthwith to repair, and state their several Grievances, in order that they may be duly redressed. N.B. Old Maids and Bachelors admitted below the Bar and Widows into the Gallery.'
Morning Herald

2156. April 16, 1798 London Forum
'Are the Opinions of Mrs. Wolstencroft Godwin true – that Women are equal in Intellect to Men; and that an equal Participation of Rights and Privileges would tend to promote Female Happiness, and ameliorate Society?
The Managers of this Institution feel it a duty they owe Society, and more particulary the Fair Sex, to submit to Public Discussion, a Question, which includes the leading Propositions of a Work every day rising in Public Estimation; they also beg leave to inform the Public, that a Pupil of the late Mrs. Wolstencroft Godwin will most assuredly defend

her tenets. This Lady would have delivered her Sentiments on the discussion of a similar Subject, which took place lately in the City, had it not been for the seclusive rules of the Institution; and we have also been desired to add, that our Fair Correspondent is entirely unacquainted with any other Female Speaker. We have also been promised by the leading Members of the School of Eloquence, and other Gentlemen of the first literary eminence, their support on this evening.'
Morning Herald

2157. April 19, 1798 Westminster Forum
'Which displayed the greater Despotism, the Crowned Heads, who combined in the Plunder of Poland, or the French Directory in their recent Barbarous and Perfidious Treatment of the Swiss and Cisalpine Republics?'
Morning Herald April 16

2158. April 23, 1798 Westminster Forum
'In which situation do the Fair Sex appear more lovely in the eyes of Man, and act more consistently with the design of their Creator – when confining themselves to the domestic duties of the Wife and the Mother – or when writing Histories, Plays, Romances &c. and pursuing the attainment of those masculine functions, for which the adherents of the late Mrs. Woolstonecroft contend they are by nature qualified?'
Morning Herald

2159. April 26, 1798 Westminster Forum
'In which situation do the Fair Sex appear more lovely in the eyes of Man, and act more consistently with the design of their Creator – when confining themselves to the domestic duties of the Wife and the Mother – or when writing Histories, Plays, Romances &c and pursuing the attainment of those masculine functions, for which the adherents of the late Mrs. Woolstonecroft contend they are by nature qualified?'
Morning Herald

2160. April 30, 1798 Westminster Forum
FEMALE VOLUNTEERS – JUDGES – MEMBERS OF PARLIAMENT – JURORS
'Would it increase the happiness of the Fair Sex, and promote the general advantage of Society, if Ladies were actually invested with all those privileges and offices for which the late Mrs. Woolstonecraft contended they are by nature and propriety qualified?'
Morning Chronicle

2161. May 2, 1798 Westminster Forum
'Would not the Fair Sex be justifiable in pronouncing a public vote of censure on every Man who voluntarily continues unmarried till after the age of 30?'
Morning Chronicle April 30

2162. May 3, 1798 Westminster Forum
ASTROLOGY, commonly called FORTUNE TELLING
'Is it possible to foretell the good or evil Fortunes of mankind by the Stars which rule at the hour of Birth?
A Gentleman who has had some of the most extraordinary occurrences possible in his life, thus throws down the gauntlet to any Astrologer, publicly to cast his Nativity – and inform the Audience (if he can) of the circumstances.'
Morning Chronicle

2163. May 7, 1798 Westminster Forum
'Ought Baron Swedenburgh to be considered an artful and blasphemous Imposter – or a Prophet divinely inspired by the Almighty?'
Question sent by 'a Divine who has attended Mr. Proud's Lectures at the New Jerusalem Temple'.
Morning Chronicle May 3

2164. May 9, 1798 Westminster Forum
'Are the boasted Liberties of the French Republic real or imaginary?
In a season like this, of acknowledged darkness and dismay, of impending peril and calamity, the Managers of the Westminster Forum would in their own opinion, be as far from discharging their duty to the Public, as from gratifying their feelings as Englishmen, did they not, on this occasion, particularly remind the Disputants of that fixed and invariable law of the Society, which prohibits any Remarks on the Government and Constitution of this country.'
Morning Herald

2165. May 10, 1798 Westminster Forum
'Is it possible to foretell the good or evil Fortune of Mankind by the Stars which rule at the Hour of Birth?'
Morning Herald May 9

2166. May 14, 1798 Westminster Forum
'Are the boasted Liberties of the French Republic real or imaginary?'
Audience decided that those Liberties were imaginary.
Morning Herald

2167. May 16, 1798 Westminster Forum
'Which enjoys the happiest situation, the blooming Virgin, surrounded by admirers; the amiable Wife, employed in the instruction of her offspring; or the sprightly Widow, exulting in her deliverance from a tyrant?'
Morning Herald May 14

2168. May 17, 1798 Westminster Forum
'Is the following remark true or erroneous – Rakes when they marry and reform, make the best of Husbands?'
Morning Herald May 14

2169. May 21, 1798 Westminster Forum
'Which have acted more consistently with the Christian Character – the Rev. Mr. Rowland Hill, Mr. Wilks and the great Body of Methodists, in supporting the Missionary Society – or the Rev. Mr. Huntington, and others, in their virulent Opposition to the Measure?
The attempt to civilize the heathen world, by conveying to them the blessings of christianity, is now generally known, and as generally approved. Mr. Huntington, has however, thought proper on this, as on many other occasions, to evince that bitter acrimonious Spirit for which he is so eminently distinguished. – He has pronounced the Missionary Society – "One of the Devil's Rattles"! We think Mr. Rowland Hill, with much propriety observed, "That such a mind must be equally lost to the glory of God and the good of man". However, we do not wish to prejudge Mr. Huntington.'
Morning Chronicle

2170. May 24, 1798 Westminster Forum
'Is it possible for human Ingenuity to vindicate the Conduct of France toward America?'
Morning Chronicle May 21

2171. May 26, 1798 Westminster Forum
'Is it possible for Persons who have lost the object of their first Love, either by death, marriage, or accident, ever to regard another with equal affection?'
Morning Herald

2172. May 28, 1798 Westminster Forum
'Is it probable a Lawyer can be an Honest Man?'
Morning Herald

2173. May 31, 1798 Westminster Forum
PUBLIC MEN FIGHTING DUELS
'Can any possible provocation, on public or private occasions justify Men, whose Lives are valuable to the Community, in fighting Duels?'
Morning Chronicle

2174. June 4, 1798 Westminster Forum
'Which is the greater crime, deliberately to seduce and abandon female virgin innocence, or to artfully alienate a wife's affections from her husband; and violate the Marriage Covenant?'
Morning Herald

2175. June 7, 1798 Westminster Forum
'Is the following generally received opinion, a truth or a vulgar error; women when completely depraved, are capable of greater wickedness than men?
This being one of those Occasions in which the Powers of Female Intellect are loudly demanded in Favour of the Sex, it is hoped that one if

not both of the Ladies who have addressed the polite Audience who support this Society, will again advocate Female Virtue with the captivating Exertions of Female Eloquence.'
Morning Herald

2176. June 11, 1798 Westminster Forum
'Who approach nearest to the Purity of Primitive Christianity – the Quakers, the Methodists, the Dissenters, the Church of Rome, or the Church of England?'
Morning Herald June 7

2177. July 16, 1798 Westminster Forum
'In a comparative Review of the Pleasures and Pains of Existence, which enjoys more happiness, Man or Woman?
The above Question was transmitted to the Managers from a celebrated public Female Character: conceiving it one of those themes which amuse while they instruct, and possess the power to captivate for the moment, and yet strike some moral truths home to the heart, they have produced it thus early. . . Indeed, this Question appears peculiarly adapted to that [female] eloquence, which, if it yield the palm, on some occasions, to masculine energy, on others, rises superior in brilliancy of thought, and all the captivating powers of original fancy.'
Subscriptions for Admission the whole Season 1. 11s. 6d.
Morning Herald

2178. July 23, 1798 Westminster Forum
'Do not the French appear to be the blind instruments in the hands of Almighty Providence for the Destruction of Popery, the Calling of the Jews, and the Fulfillment of those great Events recorded in Scripture Prophecy?'
Morning Herald

2179. July 30, 1798 Westminster Forum
'Is the Idea of First Love a delusion of warm imaginations, or a permanent Prepossession of the Mind, of which Persons seldom or ever divest themselves through Life?
It has long been held in doubt by those who have made the theory of the human mind their study, whether those persons who assert "That a First Impression of Love can never be totally erased from the Heart", are not romantic characters who deceive themselves. This Question fairly meets that doubt – And, without attempting to prejudice the subject, we think we are warranted in asserting that some of the most deplorable evils in existence may be ascribed to this idea, whether real or imaginary. Of this the unfortunate Hammond, the still more unfortunate Hackman, and many other examples, both ancient and modern, might be adduced as most lamentable instances.'
Morning Herald

2180. August 9, 1798 Westminster Forum

'Do the Vices of Society arise more from the Pride and Profligacy of the Rich, or from the Ignorance and Depravity of the Poor?
From the present question much is expected. How freely do some writers arraign the Vices and Follies of the Great! with what severity do others condemn the Conduct of the Poor!'
Morning Herald

2181. August 13, 1798 Westminster Forum
'Which have proved themselves the greatest Ornaments of the Stage, and the genuine Representatives of human nature – Messr. Garrick, Palmer, Mossop, Barry, Sheridan, Mrs. Crawford, Mrs. Yates, Mrs. Pope, and the Actors and Actresses of the Old School; or Messr. Kemble, Pope, Holman, Lewis, Mrs. Jordan, Mrs. Powell, Mrs. Siddons, and those of the New?'
Morning Herald August 9

2182. August 16, 1798 Westminster Forum
'Can any possible Circumstances justify a Woman in marrying one Man while she loves another?
After the example of Mrs. Farmer (the present Mrs. Powell), Miss Smith, and other eminent Literary and Dramatic Ladies who have honoured this Institution by a display of Female Excellence, our fair Correspondent, has nothing to fear either from the charge of impropriety in herself, or want of candour in the public. And, with every respect due to her merit and her sex, we wait the event of her choice.'
Morning Herald

2183. August 20, 1798 Westminster Forum
'Which enjoys the greater Portion of Happiness, the blooming Virgin, surrounded by Admirers – the amiable Wife, employed in the care of her Offspring – or the sprightly Widow, exulting in her deliverance from a Tyrant?'
Morning Herald August 16

2184. October 10, 1798 London Forum, Capel Court
'Is the Doctrine maintained by the late celebrated Soame Jenyns, in his View of the Internal Evidence of the Christian Religion, founded on Scripture, and countenanced by Reason, viz. That those who are actuated by the boasted Principles of Valour, Patriotism, and Friendship, may be virtuous and honest men, but cannot be Christians?'
Morning Herald

2185. October 22, 1798 Westminster Forum
'Is Learning a desirable Qualification in a Wife?'
Morning Herald

2186. October 25, 1798 Westminster Forum

'Do not the last dying words of the late Mr. J. Palmer, "O God! there is another and a better world!" contain the only sentiment which can enable us to bear the evils of this life with fortitude?'
Subscriptions for the whole Season (price one Guinea).
Morning Herald October 22

2187. November 1, 1798 Westminster Forum
'Will the sum of human happiness be increased or diminished, if Buonaparte should wrest Egypt from the Porte, and restore the ancient Liberties of the Grecian Republics?'
Morning Herald

2188. November 5, 1798 Westminster Forum
'Is the opinion of the celebrated Mr. Addison true, "A bad Husband may be reformed by an amiable Wife, but bad Wives are incorrigible"?'
Morning Herald November 1

2189. November 8, 1798 Westminster Forum
'Is the assertion of Mr. Addison true, "that a bad Husband may be reformed by an amiable Wife, but bad wives are incorrigible"?
Mr. Addison is an Author who ranks high among the Literati of this country. To a mind rich in all the stores of knowledge, he united a genius, equalled by few, excelled by none. His Moral Essays, in the Spectator, must endear him to every lover of virtue; and his unaffected exemplary piety transmits a reverence, inseparable from his name, to succeeding generations.'
Morning Herald

2190. November 12, 1798 Westminster Forum
'Does the clause of Obedience, in the Marriage Ceremony, bind a Wife to obey her Husband at all times?'
Morning Herald

2191. November 15, 1798 Westminster Forum
'Ought the Truth to be spoken at all Times?'
Morning Herald November 12

2192. November 29, 1798 Westminster Forum
'Is it true that any Ghosts or Departed spirits ever did appear to a Mortal in this World?'
Morning Herald

2193. December 3, 1798 Westminster Forum
'Ought not the Violation of a solemn Promise of Love given to one virtuous woman, to render a man ineligible to marry any other?
The Public are respectfully apprised, that to accommodate the Gentlemen belonging to the School of Garrick (a private Theatrical Society held in this place) the Westminster Forum will in future be held on Mondays and Fridays.
Morning Herald

2194. December 7, 1798 Westminster Forum
'Would General Pichegru (under all the circumstances of his banishment) be justifiable in turning his arms against the French Republic?'
Morning Herald December 3

2195. December 10, 1798 Westminster Forum
'Do not the circumstances of Mr. Tone's suicide confirm the celebrated axiom of Dr. Johnson, "That in no case is any human being justifiable in committing the dreadful act of Self-Slaughter"?'
Morning Herald

2196. December 14, 1798 Westminster Forum
'Does that exclusion from society, and forfeiture of character, which women of reputation stick to the first act of female frailty, operate more powerfully to keep the sex virtuous, or render them desperate in vice?'
Morning Herald December 10

2197. December 29, 1798 Westminster Forum
'Is it true that any ghosts or departed spirits ever appear to a mortal in this world?'
Morning Herald

2198. January 11, 1799 Westminster Forum
'Is Mr. Pope's dictum, inculcated throughout his Essay on Man, founded on truth or ascribable to an erroneous judgment, Whatever is, is right?'
Morning Chronicle

2199. January 14, 1799 Westminster Forum
'In times of public difficulty, would it not be wise in any Nation to oblige the unmarried of both sexes, above the age of twenty five and under fifty, who should refuse an offer of marriage from a person of fair character, to forfeit a third of their income toward the exigencies of the state under which they live?'
Morning Herald

2200. January 18, 1799 Westminster Forum
'Which is the greater crime, to seduce a Married or an Unmarried Woman?
The moral effect of those Societies has long been acknowledged by the great, the good and the enlightened. We hope by the present debate to add one more trophy to those which virtue has already acquired in this Institution.'
Morning Chronicle

2201. January 21, 1799 Westminster Forum

'Have not the Doctrines of a new School [of] Philosophy as taught by Mirabeau, Anacharsis Cloots, &c. in France and Godwin, Holcroft &c. in England, impeded the course of European liberty, and contributed to blast the Hope of Immortality in the human Race?'
Morning Chronicle

2202. January 28, 1799 Westminster Forum
'Have not the doctrines of a new School Philosophy as taught by Messrs. Godwin and Holcroft &c. impeded the course of European liberty and contributed to blast the Hope of Immortality in the human Race?'
Morning Chronicle

2203. January 30, 1799 Westminster Forum
'Have not the doctrines of a new School Philosophy as taught by Messrs. Godwin and Holcroft &c. impeded the course of European liberty and contributed to blast the Hope of Immortality in the human Race?'
Morning Chronicle

2204. February 1, 1799 Westminster Forum
'In the Marriage State, which constitutes the greater Evil, Love without Money, or Money without Love?'
Morning Chronicle January 30

2205. February 4, 1799 Westminster Forum
'Ought these persons to be accounted sincere and rational Christians who deny the personal existence of the Devil, and the Eternity of future punishment?'
Morning Chronicle

2206. February 6, 1799 Westminster Forum
'Ought Masquerades to be permitted as fashionable Amusements – or suppressed as scenes of Riot, Vice and Dissipation?'
Morning Chronicle

2207. February 8, 1799 Westminster Forum
'Which constitutes the greater matrimonial evil, Love without Money, or Money without Love?'
Morning Chronicle February 6

2208. February 11, 1799 Westminster Forum
'Which constitutes the greater matrimonial evil, Love without Money, or Money without Love?'
Morning Chronicle

2209. February 13, 1799 Westminster Forum
'Ought these persons to be accounted sincere and rational Christians who deny the personal existence of the Devil, and the Eternity of future punishment?'
Morning Chronicle February 11

2210. February 13, 1799 School of Eloquence, Coachmakers hall
'The Friends of this Institution and the Public in general, are respectfully informed, that a Society, lately established under the same name, is not supported by, or connected with the Members of this Institution – the plan and object of the Societies differing very materially, the Members of the Original School of Eloquence feel it a duty to themselves to disclaim all connection with any body of men assuming their name. Due notice will be given of the recommendation of the Debates of this Institution.'
Morning Chronicle

2211. February 18, 1799 Westminster Forum
'Has more Mischief arisen among Mankind from the fatal controul of Parents over their Children respecting Marriage; or from the hasty and injudicious choice which young Persons but too frequently make in opposition to the mature Judgment of their parents?
The audience decided against parental rigour.'
Morning Chronicle

2212. February 22, 1799 Westminster Forum
'Is it consistent with Scripture and Reason to believe that the Devil has a personal Existence, and that those who die without repentance will be under his dominion to all Eternity?
We beg the public to understand, that with that ancient and respectable Institution, the London Forum (although we have no blended concern as to laws, or other interior arrangements) yet we hold an union of principles, which, for our safety, as well as character, we wish to keep separate from the Mushroom Atheistical Combinations, which Party Venom raises on the hot-bed of Indigence.'
Morning Chronicle

2213. February 25, 1799 Westminster Forum
'Can any consideration whatever apologize for, or justify the practice of robbing Church yards of the Remains of the Dead?'
This question brought forward because 'of the recent robbery in St. Giles' Church yard'.
The question was decided in the affirmative.
Morning Chronicle

2214. March 1, 1799 Westminster Forum
'Is the assertion of Socrates true, that Women in Mischief are Wiser than Men?'
Morning Chronicle

2215. March 4, 1799 Westminster Forum
'Would not the following regulations prevent, in a great measure, the robbing of Church-yards, and the consequent agony suffered by friends and relatives, viz. to give for dissection all suicides, paupers, mal-

efactors, and every person dying in prison, and each Surgeon to enter into a bond to bequeath his own body for that purpose?

It was the strong ground of objection with many of the Students, who delivered their opinions last Monday evening, "If the practice is stopped, what shall we do for subjects?" The Managers conceive that the ingenious Author of the above Question has fairly met the objection. We think this Question of the highest national utility, inasmuch as it affects the feelings of thousands, and the progress of the most useful as well as noble Science in which man can be engaged, namely the Knowledge of the Human Frame, and all its wonderful Dependencies. . . Happy will the Managers feel themselves, should any hint be dropped in the course of the Debate that may be the means, should this subject ever occupy the wisdom of Parliament, of permitting the Dead to rest quiet in their graves, and yet affording Professional Gentlemen the means of prosecuting their researches, to the advancement of their science, and the good of mankind.'
Morning Herald

2216. March 8, 1799 Westminster Forum
'Ought Masquerades to be patronized as fashionable amusements, or discounted as scenes of vice, riot and dissipation?'
Morning Herald March 4

2217. March 18, 1799 Westminster Forum
'Is it not possible, by thorough Scientific Knowledge, both of Astronomy and Astrology, to foretell Marriage, Death, Good or Evil Fortune, and other Events in the Life of Mankind?
The various systems of Astrology, from Ptolemy down to Ranger and Sybley, will be open to the animadversions of the curious and learned Professor. Several Gentlemen of Astrological celebrity are expected to attend.'
Morning Herald

2218. March 18, 1799 School of Eloquence, opposite Villiers Street, Strand
'Are Prosecutions for Opinion beneficial or injurious to the State?'
Morning Chronicle

2219. March 19, 1799 Westminster Forum
'Which stands the best chance of getting happy through life, a woman without a husband, or a man without a wife?'
Morning Herald

2220. March 20, 1799 School of Eloquence
'Are the Observance of Public Fasts or Thanksgiving Days on any particular occasion consistent either with reason or the moral and divine precepts of the Christian Religion?
A Society is forming [as an adjunct to the School] for Religious Enquiry.'
Morning Chronicle March 18

2221. March 20, 1799 Westminster Forum
'To which is Great Britain most indebted for her National Grandeur, the Integrity of her Mercantile Connections, the Bravery of her Naval Commanders, or the Abilities of her Historians, Philosophers, Divines, Poets and Men of Genius?'
Morning Herald

2222. March 21, 1799 Westminster Forum
'Which is the most reasonable opinion, that maintained by Lord Shaftesbury, "that man is naturally virtuous", that believed by many religious persons, "that he is naturally wicked" or that supported by Helvetius, Locke, &c. "that he is naturally neither the one nor the other; but that all his virtues and his vices arise out of his education, his mind being in infancy like a sheet of blank paper"?'
Morning Herald

2223. March 23, 1799 Westminster Forum
A WOMAN'S APPEAL on the RUIN of the SEX
'Which conduct ought most to be applauded, for pardoning the Errors of Human Nature, in Opposition to the Prejudices of Mankind – that of the Man who marries an accomplished Female after one Deviation from Virtue – that of the Husband who receives to his Arms the repentant Wife who has violated her Marriage Covenant – or that of the Father who affords an Asylum in the Bosom of his Family to his Seduced Daughter?
We received the above Question (found among the papers of a celebrated female literary character lately deceased) from a Gentleman whose repeated favours bestowed on this Society are recognized with grateful pleasure. – It is new – it is important – it is interesting. Too long has the restoration of female happiness, forfeited from accident, fatal partialities, or subtle snares, been neglected by mankind. Woman, for one error, is consigned to deathless infamy; the door of reformation is fast barred against her by the hand of cruel prejudice, and she is compelled to purchase every hour's existence by a further prosecution of crime.'
Morning Chronicle

2224. March 23, 1799 School of Eloquence
RESTORATION OF THE JEWS
'Does either reason or Scripture afford any convincing arguments for a belief in the final restoration of the Jews?'
Morning Chronicle

2225. March 25, 1799 Westminster Forum
'Is Man, as contended by Lord Shaftesbury, naturally virtuous, – is he, according to some Religionists, naturally wicked – or is he, as main-

tained by Locke, Helvetius, &c. naturally neither the one nor the other, his mind being in infancy like a sheet of blank paper?'
Morning Chronicle March 23

2226. March 29, 1799 Westminster Forum
'To which is Great Britain most indebted for her National Grandeur, the Integrity of her Mercantile Connections, the Bravery of her Naval Commanders, or the Abilities of her Historians, Philosophers, Divines, Poets and Men of Genius?
It was decided that the national greatness of Great Britain is owing to the integrity of her mercantile connection.'
Morning Herald/Morning Chronicle April 1

2227. April 1, 1799 Westminster Forum
'Which is the most reasonable opinion – that maintained by Lord Shaftesbury, "That man is naturally virtuous"; – that believed by many religious persons, "That he is naturally wicked"; – or that supported by Helvetius, Locke, &c. "That he is naturally neither the one nor the other; but that all his virtues and his vices arise out of his education, his mind being in infancy like a sheet of blank paper"?'
Morning Herald

2228. April 3, 1799 Westminster Forum
'Are the miseries and distress of persons of genius more ascribable to their own imprudence, or a want of patronage in the Public?
The Public must recollect an elderly Lady who spoke in this Society with much ability in defence of Mr. Garrick, Mrs. Yates, Craufurd, and for the Old School of Actors. It proves to have been a Mrs. Hart, formerly Mrs. Reddish, of Drury Lane Theatre. This unfortunate, though wonderfully accomplished Woman, died last Sunday week, amidst that misery and distress which "has not left her even a Grave". The Managers purpose opening this Society to defray the Expences of her Funeral. It is hoped that those feeling minds that revere departed merit will patronize the undertaking. . . In thus appealing to the benevolence of the Public, to furnish the means of paving the last tribute of respect to a Woman of Genius, the Managers are confident they shall not want support. They have only to lament that the Miseries of this accomplished woman were, by her own delicacy, kept concealed, till death prevented any possible relief.
The Audience were nearly divided; we believe the majority was on the side that "The Misfortunes of Persons of Genius are ascribable to their own Imprudence".'
Morning Herald

2229. April 5, 1799 Westminster Forum
'From which of the following Characters has Society most Mischief to dread – the finished Libertine – the Religious Hypocrite – or the Speculative Infidel?'
Morning Herald

2230. April 7, 1799 School of Eloquence
'The important subject of Free Will or Necessity' was discussed.
Morning Chronicle April 11

2231. April 8, 1799 Westminster Forum
'Can either of the following Assertions be justified – Baron Swedenburgh's – He was taken into Hell, where he saw John Calvin; and up to Heaven, where the Apostle Paul told him – "He repented writing the Epistle to the Hebrews?" the Rev. Mr. Huntington's – "Arminianism (and not the Pope) is Antichrist; and the Rev. Mr.Westley (as head of that Sect) is now in Hell!" If neither can be justified – which deserves greater condemnation from a Christian and a man of candour?'
Morning Chronicle April 5

2232. April 11, 1799 School of Eloquence
'Does the Assertion of Mr. Pope appear to be true: "Whatever is, is right"?'
Morning Chronicle

2233. April 15, 1799 School of Eloquence
'Which is more favorable to happiness, a Natural or a Civilized State?'
Morning Chronicle

2234. April 18, 1799 School of Eloquence
'Pope's assertion "That every Woman is at Heart a Rake" to be discussed.'
Morning Chronicle

2235. April 19, 1799 Westminster Forum
'From which of the following Characters has Society most Mischief to dread – the finished Libertine – the Religious Hypocrite – or the Speculative Infidel?'
Morning Herald

2236. April 22, 1799 School of Eloquence
'Does Mr. Godwin deserve praise or censure for his Essay on Political Justice?'
Morning Chronicle

2237. April 22, 1799 Westminster Forum
'Did Pope publish the greater Libel on the Female, or Otway on the Male Character, when the latter asserted, that, "Men, in their dealings with the Fair Sex, are by Nature treacherous, cruel, false and inconstant" – or when the former, in his celebrated Essay on Man, pronounced "Every Woman at heart a Rake"?'
Morning Herald April 19

2238. April 25, 1799 School of Eloquence

'Which is the most useful Member of Society, the active or speculative Man?'
Morning Chronicle

2239. April 29, 1799 School of Eloquence
'Which is the more frequent cause of Divorce, the lenity of the female or the tyranny of the male?'
Morning Chronicle

2240. May 2, 1799 School of Eloquence
'Do Theatrical Entertainments tend more to corrupt or improve the morals of society?'
Morning Chronicle April 29

2241. May 3, 1799 Westminster Forum
'Are Divorces more ascribable to the neglect and inattention of Husbands [or to the behavior of Wives]?'
Husbands are more often at fault.
Morning Chronicle May 6

2242. May 6, 1799 Westminster Forum
'Can true Love (from neglect, disappointment, ill-usage, or any other cause) ever degenerate into Hatred?'
It was decided that real love could not.
Morning Herald/Morning Chronicle May 10

2243. May 10, 1799 Westminster Forum
'Which is the happiest term of human existence, the Single State, the Married State, or that period, when by death a Husband is delivered from a Termagant, or a Wife from a Tyrant?'
Decided that the married life was the most happy.
Morning Herald/Morning Chronicle May 13

2244. May 11, 1799 Westminster Forum
'Which is the most miserable condition, the seduced Female, the Wife married to an abandoned character, or the Old Maid, hopeless and despairing, withering on the Thorn of Virginity?
There being no plays this Evening, the Westminster Forum . . . will be open.'
Morning Herald

2245. May 13, 1799 Westminster Forum
'Which of the following characters is more condemnable; the single man, who artfully and deliberately seduces a married woman; or the married man, who neglects his wife and beggars his family, by keeping a mistress?'
Morning Chronicle

2246. May 15, 1799 Westminster Forum

'Did Mr. Pope publish the greater Libel on the Female – or Otway on the Male Character in the following assertions: Otway – "Men (in love matters) are by nature treacherous, cruel, false and inconstant". Pope – "Every Woman is at heart a Rake"?'
Morning Chronicle May 13

2247. May 24, 1799 Westminster Forum
'Which ought to be a Man's chief object in his Choice of a Wife – her personal Accomplishments – her fortune – or her temper and disposition?'
Morning Chronicle

2248. May 27, 1799 Westminster Forum
'Does the possession of great talents and exalted genius in the Male Character, and beauty and accomplishments in the Female, aggravate or palliate error and indiscretion?'
Morning Chronicle

2249. May 31, 1799 Westminster Forum
'Which exhibits the strongest motive to avoid Vice and pursue Virtue – the Life of Georgina Anne Bellamy, or of Mary Woolstonecroft Godwin?'
Morning Chronicle May 27

INDEX TO DEBATES

LONDON RECORD SOCIETY

The London Record Society was founded in December 1964 to publish transcripts, abstracts and lists of the primary sources for the history of London, and generally to stimulate interest in archives relating to London. Membership is open to any individual or institution; the annual subscription is £12 ($22) for individuals and £18 ($35) for institutions. Prospective members should apply to the Hon. Secretary, Miss Heather Creaton, c/o Institute of Historical Research, Senate House, London WC1E 7HU.

The following volumes have already been published:

1. *London Possessory Assizes: a calendar,* edited by Helena M. Chew (1965)
2. *London Inhabitants within the Walls, 1695,* with an introduction by D.V.Glass (1966)
3. *London Consistory Court Wills, 1492–1547,* edited by Ida Darlington (1967)
4. *Scriveners' Company Common Paper, 1357–1628, with a continuation to 1678,* edited by Francis W. Steer (1968)
5. *London Radicalism, 1830–1843: a selection from the papers of Francis Place,* edited by D. J. Rowe (1970)
6. *The London Eyre of 1244,* edited by Helena M. Chew and Martin Weinbaum (1970)
7. *The Cartulary of Holy Trinity Aldgate,* edited by Gerald A. J. Hodgett (1971)
8. *The Port and Trade of early Elizabethan London: Documents,* edited by Brian Dietz (1972)
9. *The Spanish Company,* edited by Pauline Croft (1973)
10. *London Assize of Nuisance, 1301–1431: a calendar,* edited by Helena M. Chew and William Kellaway (1973)
11. *Two Calvinistic Methodist Chapels, 1748–1811: the London Tabernacle and Spa Fields Chapel,* edited by Edwin Welch (1975)
12. *The London Eyre of 1276,* edited by Martin Weinbaum (1976)
13. *The Church in London, 1375–1392,* edited by A. K. McHardy (1977)
14. *Committees for the Repeal of the Test and Corporation Acts: Minutes, 1786–90 and 1827–8,* edited by Thomas W. Davis (1978)
15. *Joshua Johnson's Letterbook, 1771–4: letters from a merchant in London to his partners in Maryland,* edited by Jacob M. Price (1979)

16. *London and Middlesex Chantry Certificate, 1548,* edited by C. J. Kitching (1980)
17. *London Politics, 1713–1717: Minutes of a Whig Club, 1714–17,* edited by H.Horwitz; *London Pollbooks, 1713,* edited by W.A. Speck and W.A. Gray (1981)
18. *Parish Fraternity Register: Fraternity of the Holy Trinity and SS.Fabian and Sebastian in the parish of St. Botolph without Aldersgate,* edited by Patricia Basing (1982)
19. *Trinity House of Deptford: Transactions, 1609–35,* edited by G.G.Harris (1983)
20. *Chamber Accounts of the sixteenth century,* edited by Betty R. Masters (1984)
21. *The Letters of John Paige, London Merchant, 1648–58,* edited by George F. Steckley (1984)
22. *A Survey of Documentary Sources for Property Holding in London before the Great Fire,* by Derek Keene and Vanessa Harding (1985)
23. *The Commissions for Building Fifty New Churches,* edited by M.H.Port (1986)
24. *Richard Hutton's Complaints Book,* edited by Timothy V. Hitchcock (1987)
25. *Westminster Abbey Charters, 1066-c. 1214,* edited by Emma Mason (1988)
26. *London Viewers and their Certificates, 1508–1558,* edited by Janet S. Loengard (1989)
27. *The Overseas Trade of London: Exchequer Customs Accounts, 1480–1,* edited by H.S.Cobb (1990)
28. *Justice in Eighteenth-century Hackney: the Justicing Notebook of Henry Norris and the Hackney Petty Sessions Book,* edited by Ruth Paley (1991)
29. *Two Tudor Subsidy Assessment Rolls for the City of London: 1541 and 1582,* edited by R.G.Lang (1993 for 1992)
30. *London Debating Societies, 1776–1799,* compiled and introduced by Donna T. Andrew (1994 for 1993)

Most volumes are still in print; apply to Clifton Books, 34 Hamlet Court, Westcliff on Sea, Essex SS0 7LX. Price to individual members £12 ($22) each, to non-members £20 ($38) each.